Coral and Concrete

SERIES EDITORS
Patricio Abinales
Terence Wesley-Smith

ADVISORY BOARD
R. Anderson Sutton
Cathryn Clayton
Lonny Carlile
Alex Mawyer
David Hanlon
Young-a Park

Asia Pacific Flows seeks to critically engage with the well-established notion of "flows," highlighting the dynamism behind their physical, cultural, economic, and political connections and the entangled relationships and disruptions that characterize them. Its approach is multidisciplinary and its area of research is multisited across the Asia Pacific, within Asia, and within the Pacific, now and in the past. The series encourages works that craft a space for new paradigms that examine and problematize concepts like regionality and boundary.

Coral and Concrete

Remembering Kwajalein Atoll
between Japan, America, and
the Marshall Islands

GREG DVORAK

University of Hawai'i Press
Honolulu

School of Pacific and Asian Studies
University of Hawai'i, Mānoa

© 2018 University of Hawai'i Press
All rights reserved
Paperback edition 2020

Printed in the United States of America

25 24 23 22 21 20   6 5 4 3 2 1

Library of Congress Cataloging-in-Publication Data
Names: Dvorak, Greg, author.
Title: Coral and concrete : remembering Kwajalein Atoll between Japan, America, and the Marshall Islands / Greg Dvorak.
Other titles: Asia Pacific flows.
Description: Honolulu : School of Pacific and Asian Studies, University of Hawai'i, Manoa : University of Hawai'i Press, [2018] | Series: Asia Pacific flows | Includes bibliographical references and index.
Identifiers: LCCN 2018008647 | ISBN 9780824855215 (cloth ; alk. paper)
Subjects: LCSH: Kwajalein Atoll (Marshall Islands)—History. | Kwajalein Atoll (Marshall Islands)—Relations—Japan. | Japan—Relations—Marshall Islands—Kwajalein Atoll. | Kwajalein Atoll (Marshall Islands)—Relations—United States. | United States—Relations—Marshall Islands—Kwajalein Atoll.
Classification: LCC DU710 .D86 2018 | DDC 996.8/3—dc23
LC record available at https://lccn.loc.gov/2018008647

ISBN 978-0-8248-8429-1 (pbk.)

Cover art: Coral at Pikeej, west reef, Kwajalein Atoll, 2016. Photo by author.

University of Hawai'i Press books are printed on acid-free paper and meet the guidelines for permanence and durability of the Council on Library Resources.

Dedicated to my father
Walter Lee Dvorak
whose curiosity and bravery navigated us across the horizon,

my mother
Christine Grace Dvorak
who inspired me to chase my dreams,

and

Kwajalein Atoll
about whom I dreamt.

Contents

Acknowledgments	ix
Notes on Style	xiii
Maps	xix
Glossary	xxiii
Prelude: The Middle of Now-here	1

CHAPTER 1
Coral and Concrete: Paradigm for Pacific Pasts — 18

CHAPTER 2
Mapping "the Martial Islands": Imagi-Nations and Mythologies of Kwajalein — 33

CHAPTER 3
Chasing the Chieftain's Daughter: Dancing Japan's Pacific Desires — 61

CHAPTER 4
Bones: Confronting the Atollscapes of War — 92

CHAPTER 5
Capturing Liberation: American Imag(in)ings of the Battle of Kwajalein — 112

CHAPTER 6
The Haunted Bathtub: Encountering the Spirits of the Atoll — 157

CHAPTER 7
Dislocations: Moving Land, Moving People — 167

CHAPTER 8
	Homecoming, 2016: The Ri-Kuwajleen Revolution	193

CHAPTER 9
	Atollism: Reconnecting Kwajalein's Past into the Present	233

Notes	249
Works Cited	279
Image Notes	295
Index	299

Acknowledgments

This cultural history of Kwajalein and intersections of empire in the Marshall Islands has, in some ways, taken my whole life to write. My observations as a small child walking along the reefs of this immense atoll, and the many learnings I experienced living between Oceania, the United States, and Japan, were all made possible through the generosity of countless people and organizations. Unfortunately, I cannot acknowledge everyone in this limited space, but I want to thank the many people who made this book possible.

I first thank the institutions that sponsored my archival and ethnographic research, and this book publication, throughout its different stages of development. This project was first supported by an East-West Center Degree Fellowship at the University of Hawai'i, and later by an International Postgraduate Research Scholarship at the Australian National University. I also benefited from an Australian Research Council Discovery Project Grant titled "Oceanic Encounters: Colonial and Contemporary Transformations of Gender and Sexuality in the Pacific" (DP0451620), led by Margaret Jolly. Follow-up work in the Marshall Islands in 2009–2010 was supported by a fieldwork grant from the Wenner-Gren Foundation (Grant 7711). Research in Japan was supported by grants from the Japan Foundation and the Japan Society for the Promotion of Science. Further projects were undertaken as part of the joint research I conducted under a grant from the Toyota Foundation which I titled "Transoceania: Pacific Approaches to Empire, War, and Globalization between the Islands of Japan and Micronesia" (D10-R-0322). Toward the publication of this book, I am grateful for a generous donation from the University of Hawai'i History Department. I thank Hitotsubashi University, the University of

Tokyo, and Osaka University also for the several opportunities they gave me to travel to the Pacific to continue my work. This book was also made possible by funding from the Waseda University Humanities and Social Sciences English Publishing Grant.

I also thank the wise scholars, teachers, and colleagues who have nurtured my journey. During my work at the Australian National University and afterwards, I was empowered by the compassion and vision of Margaret Jolly, Tessa Morris-Suzuki, Greg Dening, Paul D'Arcy, and Gary Kildea, all five of whom urged me, from very different vantage points, to focus on the details and the emotionality of the complex subjects with which I worked. I am particularly indebted to the bottomless kindness of Margaret for her patience, friendship, and faith in my ability to complete this journey; to the playfulness of Greg and his partner Donna for their keen guidance in instilling a sense of performance and vulnerability in my approach; and for the integrity and commitment to justice that Tessa embodied as she helped me to research the Japanese empire. At the University of Hawai'i Center for Pacific Islands Studies, I was also blessed by the passionate mentorship of David Hanlon, Vilsoni Hereniko, Katerina Teaiwa, and Terence Wesley-Smith.

From the inception of my graduate project and through the decade since receiving my doctorate and writing this book, I have also been appreciative of the mentors, colleagues, and friends who have provided significant insight, support, and feedback or who have invited me to be a part of conferences and publications where I could explore my ideas further. Yaguchi Yujin, Vince Diaz, and Geoffrey White have all been huge influences on my work, and I am greatly indebted to them. Additionally, for their help and thoughts at various stages of this project, I thank Kalissa Alexeyeff, Robert Barclay, Niko Besnier, Elden Buck, Keith Camacho, John Carty, Simon Choo, Romit DasGupta, Jon Goss, Hanako Heine, Francis X. Hezel, Higuchi Wakako, Lauren Hirshberg, Humiko Kingzio, Iitaka Shingo, Kathy Jetñil-Kijiner, Jessica Jordan, Kawabata Kohei, Kurata Yōji, Kurosaki Takehiro, Monica LaBriola, Daniel Long, Joel Matthews, Phillip McArthur, Anne Perez-Hattori, Mita Takashi, Selina Tusitala Marsh, Nakamura Fuyubi, Nishimura Akira, Nishino Ryōta, Ōta Kazutaka, Ashwin Raj, Satō Tatsuya, Bill Savage, Jyotirmaya Sharma, Frances Steel, Carolyn Strange, Suganuma Katsuhiko, Skip Swanson, Tada Osamu, Ty Kāwika Tengan, Ranson Tilfas, James Viernes, Julie Walsh, and Yoshimi Shunya.

Acknowledgments

Out of the many people who collaborated with me from the Marshall Islands, I wish to extend a special *koṃṃoltata* to thank Iroojlaplap Imata Kabua, Irooj and Senator Michael Mañini Kabua, First Lady Emlain Kabua, Irooj and President Christopher Loeak, President Kessai Note, Ambassador Amatlain Kabua, and Ambassador Tom Kijiner. I also thank my Marshallese family members from Ebeye who helped with translation: Laan Emos, Hancelly Pound, Billy Pound, and Kattli Heine. I wish also to extend my thanks to Carmen Bigler, Chuji Chutaro, Maryia deBrum, Tony deBrum, Harrington Dribo, Neijon Edwards, Giff Johnson, Anjojo Kabua, Kili Kabua, Deo Keju, Jack Niedenthal, Annette Note, Fumiko and Yoshi Kemem, Lynn Lanej, Arkila Langrus, Ato and Neilon Ḷañkio, Julius Lejjena, Noda Lojkar, Hideo Milne-Suzuki, Senator Dennis Momotaro, Jorion Ninjine, Fred Pedro, Ramsey Reimers, Julian Riklon, and Mark Stege.

This book would not have been possible without the support of many other people and organizations within the American community of Kwajalein, such as the Marshallese Cultural Center and its founders Eric and Cris Lindborg, as well as countless other individuals, including Shigeko Jackson, Paul McGrew, Masina McCollum, Simone Smead, Alan Taylor, and many others. I want to emphasize that this book does not necessarily reflect any of their views, nor are any of these parties responsible for the content I have published. Also on Kwajalein, my conversations with Leslie Mead, Jimmy Matsunaga, Ray Wolff, and Bill Remick were especially helpful.

Aside from the people listed above, in Japan and Korea, I have been fortunate to have the support of fellow researchers, students, families with ties to the Japan's colonial history or present-day Pacific ties, and bereaved families of war dead. I thank the Marshall Islands Bereaved Families Association, its president Takabayashi Yoshio, former president Kurokawa Makoto, Kusaba Hiroshi, Inoue Yoshio, and Satō Ryūichi for their generous openness and invitation to join them on pilgrimages to Kwajalein. I also thank Kobayashi Izumi of the Japan Pacific Islands Area Research Center for inviting me to help establish the Japan Association for Pacific Islands Studies. Fukudome Noriaki helped connect me to the Korean Truth Commission on Forced Labor under Japanese Imperialism in Seoul, where I was assisted by Kim Myung Hwan and invited to the home of Lee Inshin. Tochigi Akira at the Japan Film Center also helped me to discover an entirely fresh cinematic dimension on Japanese colonialism in Micronesia. I am also grateful to my students Arai Ryu, Ishii Shimpei, and Jae-Young Park, who deserve special mention for helping to translate Japanese and Korean materials related to Japanese colonialism. In Miyazaki-ken, my friends Sakamoto Masafumi, Saitō Kenichi, Iwakura Naoya, and Arima Harunari were also of enormous assistance in the early stages of this research.

Sadly, many of the people who selflessly gave of themselves to help me make this project a reality are no longer living. In particular, I am constantly inspired by my memories of Greg Dening and his invitation to "dance on the beaches of the mind" with him. I was also nurtured on my journey and inspired by my late friend Teresia Teaiwa, whose critical and creative feminist interventions in Oceania led me to so many meaningful ways of seeing power and inequality in Marshallese history. Meanwhile, Kaname Yamamura, with his vivid recollections of prewar days in the Marshall Islands, spoken in fluent Japanese, helped me to imagine a long-gone past that bridged Japan with the Pacific Islands. I also thank my kind Ri-Kuwajleen friend Anjain Rowa, a former Kwajalein employee who passed away long before this project was complete but who provided many insights and brave perspectives that I took to heart. And I am especially thankful to my late Bubu, Neitari Pound, for all the gifts of knowledge and the warm welcome she extended to me throughout my life.

Finally, a project of this magnitude could not be completed without the unwavering support of my family. From the bottom of my heart, I wish to thank my late father, Walter, who brought Kwajalein into my family's life and compassionately engaged with the Marshall Islands, while believing in peace despite the hostility of the Cold War. I also thank my mother, Christine, and my brother, Tim, for their endless belief in me and their reminding me to laugh at myself always. And to Ono Kenji, *arigatō* for being the most supportive partner anyone could ever wish for.

Notes on Style

Text and Image

As Greg Dening reminds us, history is a "performance" (2004, 326), and I accept his invitation to perform my storytelling rather than present my images and words as mere data or evidence. My use of visuals is inspired partly by the work of W. G. Sebald, who placed evocative photographs and other ephemera directly into his fictional and autobiographical work, as a meditation on the relationship between image and narrative (see, for example, Sebald 2000). I also pay homage to the cultural studies/art-history-inspired work of Andrea Feeser and Gaye Chan, whose photographic and historical study *Waikiki: A History of Forgetting and Remembering* (2006) pays just as much attention to its own semiotics as it does to the semiotic texts it critiques. Not only do these books value the visual in their mode of communication; they also demand that the reader pause and engage seriously with these images of landscapes and ephemera at a particular junction in the written narrative, instead of as an afterthought or a decorative device.

Instead of captioning, commentary on each image appears in the main text, and source or background information appears in the image notes at the end of the book. My use of maps also needs some prefatory remarks. Chapter 2 is a critique of the ways in which power and discourses of nationalism are projected onto physical space, and so I treat each of the maps in that section critically, less as literal representations of place than as texts to be decoded. From a Pacific navigational view, the very notion of a map as a view of earth as seen from above is something that demands critique. But these semiotic approaches simultaneously create challenges; for as much as I critique the imperial optics that have shaped Oceanian histories, my project also introduces Kwajalein and Marshall Islands geography to those who are not familiar with this part of the world. For this purpose of orientation, I have included several descriptive maps in the preliminaries.

Language and Orthography

MARSHALLESE

I have aimed to be as consistent as possible in my spellings of the three main languages that appear throughout the text, but I have been faced with a number of orthographic considerations that are almost as important to my argument as the myriad perspectives and "atoll-scapes" I introduce herein.

The Marshallese language (*kajin ṃajel*) is an intricate Austronesian language that includes many pronunciations that do not exist in English. Many attempts have been made to transcribe Marshallese since the beginning of colonial contact, and dictionaries were compiled not only by Europeans but by Japanese explorers as well. Up until recent decades, most spelling was based on the way it appeared in the Marshallese translation of the Bible, but this was changed by the publication in 1976 of the *Marshallese-English Dictionary,* in which Abo, Bender, Capelle, and deBrum created a new system (including new diacritics) that was more representative of the distinctive pronunciations of the Marshallese language. This system has become the standard by which Marshallese is written in many contexts, but the "old" (or "ecumenical") spellings are still in widespread use, and many Marshall Islanders (and many long-time residents of the Marshall Islands) do not consistently use the "new" orthography.

Marshallese personal and place names often become unrecognizable when placed in the new spelling, which has led many scholars and writers to adopt a compromise between the two systems in order to avoid confusion. I have chosen to use the older spellings of most major place names and personal names throughout the book for the reader's ease of recognition. For example, I write "Kwajalein"—the way the name of the atoll has been spelled for most of the twentieth century on English-language maps—in most of the book, rather than the new spelling, "Kuwajleen," which I use in the context of a specifically Marshallese reading of place and identity. My purpose in doing so is not to marginalize Marshallese views but rather to make those views accessible to readers who have only been familiar with the more hegemonic, imperial histories of war and colonialism.

There are other problems with Marshallese place names, however, that stem from the fact that many islands and atolls have been given numerous names and extremely variant spellings over the years. For these places in Kwajalein that are not widely known, I have attempted to use the newer orthography—such as in the case of Āne-Ellap-Kan, known to Americans as "Carlos" or "Ennylabagen" or to Japanese as "Enīerāpukan"—but I have indicated the variant spellings or names in parentheses at least the first time any of these names appear in the text. The University of Hawai'i Center for Pacific Islands Studies has generously allowed me to reproduce a map (see map 2) that uses the "old" more recognizable orthographies for Marshallese atolls.

The *Marshallese-English Dictionary* by Abo, Bender, Capelle, and deBrum (1976) offers a comprehensive guide for how Marshallese spellings should be read, and it is now conveniently available in an online electronic version: http://www.trussel2.com/MOD/index.htm.

Rudiak-Gould (2004) has also done a thorough job of illustrating proper Marshallese spelling and grammar for learners.

JAPANESE AND KOREAN

Many of the sources I consulted for this project were written entirely in Japanese. I have romanized all words or proper names according to the Hepburn system, the standard orthography prescribed by the Japanese Ministry of Education (Monbukagakushō). There are a few exceptions to this, however, when for example I quote a particular source that has already used a variant romanization, or when a personal or corporate name has typically been spelled in a particular way, such as a brand name.

Japanese is written in a combination of phonetics and characters adapted from Chinese (*kanji*), but its pronunciation is standardized and can be represented entirely by the phonetic syllabaries *hiragana* and *katakana*. In transliterating these syllables into English, long (extended) vowels are represented by macrons (for example "ō"), except in the case of some of the most commonplace names (such as Tokyo or Osaka, which both actually have long vowels in their names). I have also followed contemporary romanization practice by omitting the apostrophe that was once often used in some systems of romanization to separate the consonant "n" sound and a subsequent vowel (such as in *renai,* "love," spelled in some systems as *ren'ai*). This is the case with the place name Nanyō, a term that has at times been spelled "Nan'yō," as in Peattie's seminal work about Japanese colonialism in Micronesia of the same title (Peattie 1988). Though a correct variant spelling, this was not how Nanyō was usually written in roman letters during the colonial period.

Finally, I should note that Japanese (and Korean) names are written in the order of family name followed by given name. I have followed this standard throughout the book, except in the case of individuals who have Japanese ancestry but are not actually Japanese nationals. For example, I mention many Marshall Islanders and some Americans who possess Japanese names, and I have preserved the usual order in which they write their own names. I have also done this with quotations from other sources and in bibliographic citations for Japanese authors who have published in English.

Personal Narratives and Personal Names

As I explain in the introduction to this book, this project represents a complex journey between very different cultural and political contexts in the present and the past. Because of this, I have had to be creative and sensitive in my approach, both in researching these histories and in communicating them. Although my research was historical in nature, some of the issues I dealt with were controversial in the present-day, and I also worked in very special environments that required me to exercise special caution in protecting the identities of my interlocutors. I thus conducted my work according to the protocol that I devised in advance of my research, with approval from the Marshall Islands Historical Preservation Office, the traditional leadership of Kwajalein Atoll, and in collaboration with the Marshallese Cultural Center, with permission from the military installation of Kwajalein islet itself.

Although I have identified in this book some of the political figures that made their positions clearly known, there were many others with whom I spoke that could have been compromised by having their identities revealed. I chose thus to protect the identities of many Marshallese whose candid opinions (or descriptions of their actions) might have created problems for them with the traditional leadership. Many American and Marshallese employees of the military installation also

Notes on Style xvii

happily and frankly conversed with me about their experiences and personal histories at Kwajalein, and most of them were willing to be identified in my project; however, I chose to make many of these conversations anonymous as well. Aside from these communities in the Marshalls, the Japanese groups with whom I worked were, for the most part, eager to relate the stories of their loved ones who died in the Pacific War, and they were extremely forthcoming and willing to be identified in this work. There were others in Japan, however, who for political reasons chose to share their opinions on the condition that I did not use their names.

My strategy for dealing with these ethical issues has been to obscure the identities of many of my interlocutors and/or to obscure identifying details about their narratives. I follow Tessa Morris-Suzuki's (2007) protocol whenever I am citing an anonymous source with a pseudonym by enclosing that name in quotations the first time it appears in the text.

Violent Language

An important objective of this project is to expose structural violence and systematized racism. As with my choice to include war photographs, propaganda, and other graphic ephemera from the visual archive, my intention is to confront and critique the violent but normalized semiotics of racialized dehumanization that saturated public narratives. I chose to sparingly cite examples of pejorative and offensive words used in their original contexts, such as the Japanese racist terms for indigenous people or American terms for Japanese or Koreans, to call attention to the way violence and hate were naturalized into everyday speech, which resulted in the erasure or demonization of vast populations of people. Chapter 5, in which I do a forensic reading of the semiotics of war photography in the invasion of Kwajalein Atoll, is a study of war photographs and the original captions that were attached to them. In reproducing those original captions, to avoid any confusion on the part of readers who may misconstrue such captions as my own personal word choice, I have altered "Jap" to "Jap[anese]" wherever possible or omitted the word entirely.

Maps

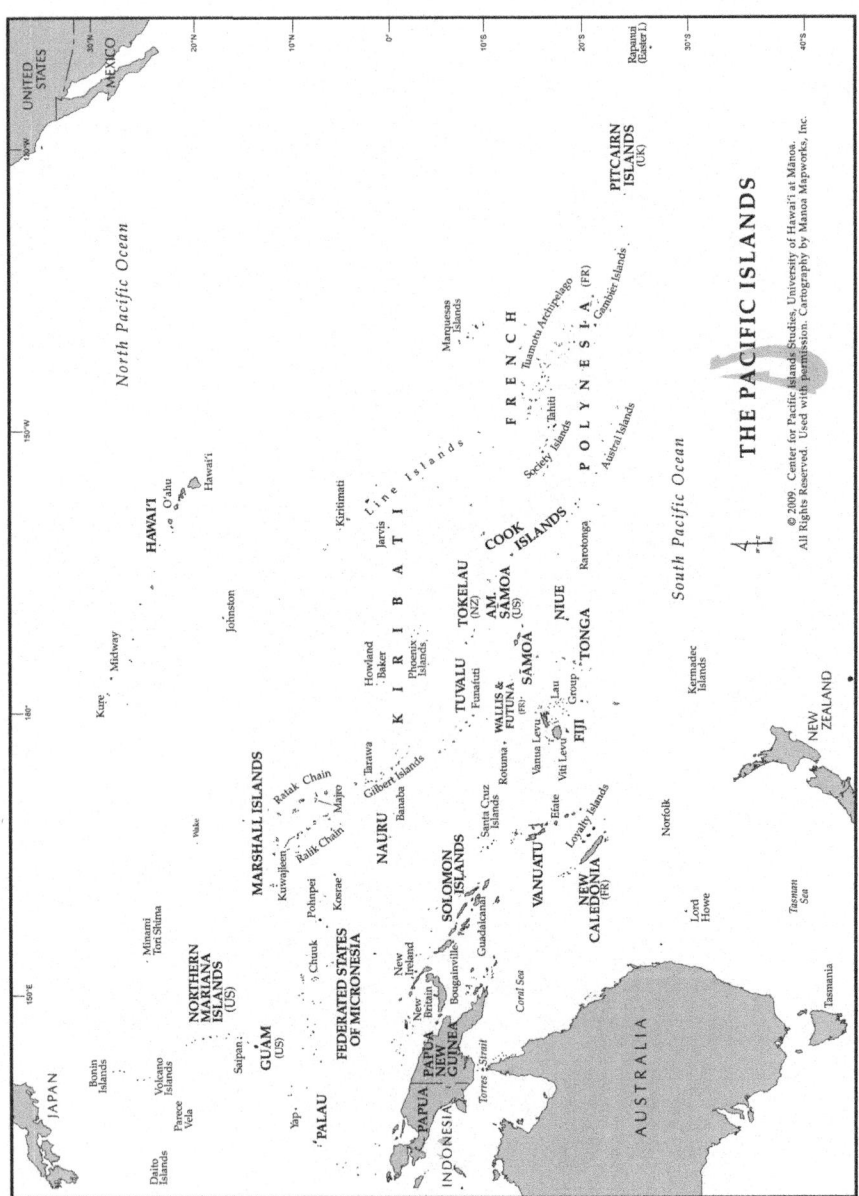

Map 1. The Pacific Islands (courtesy of University of Hawai'i Center for Pacific Islands Studies, 2006)

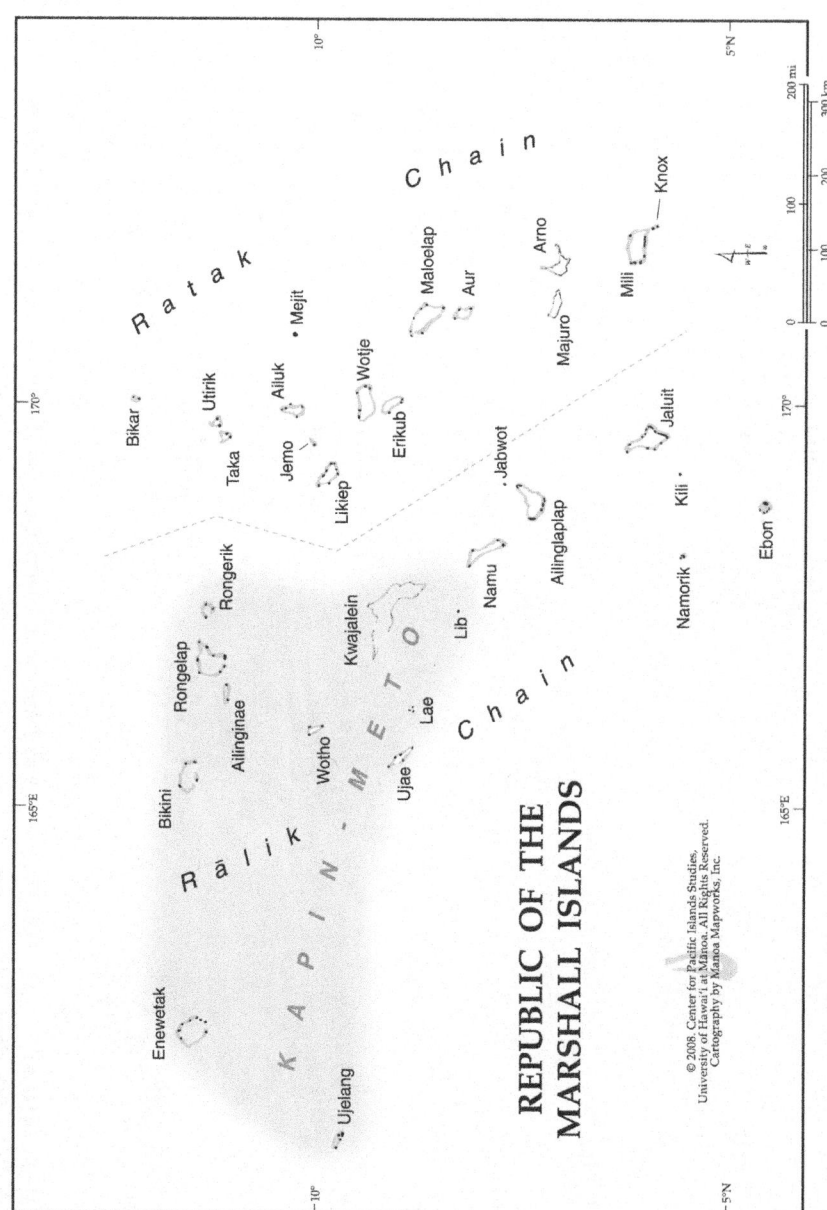

Map 2. The Republic of the Marshall Islands, showing the Kapin-Meto region (courtesy of University of Hawai'i Center for Pacific Islands Studies, 2008)

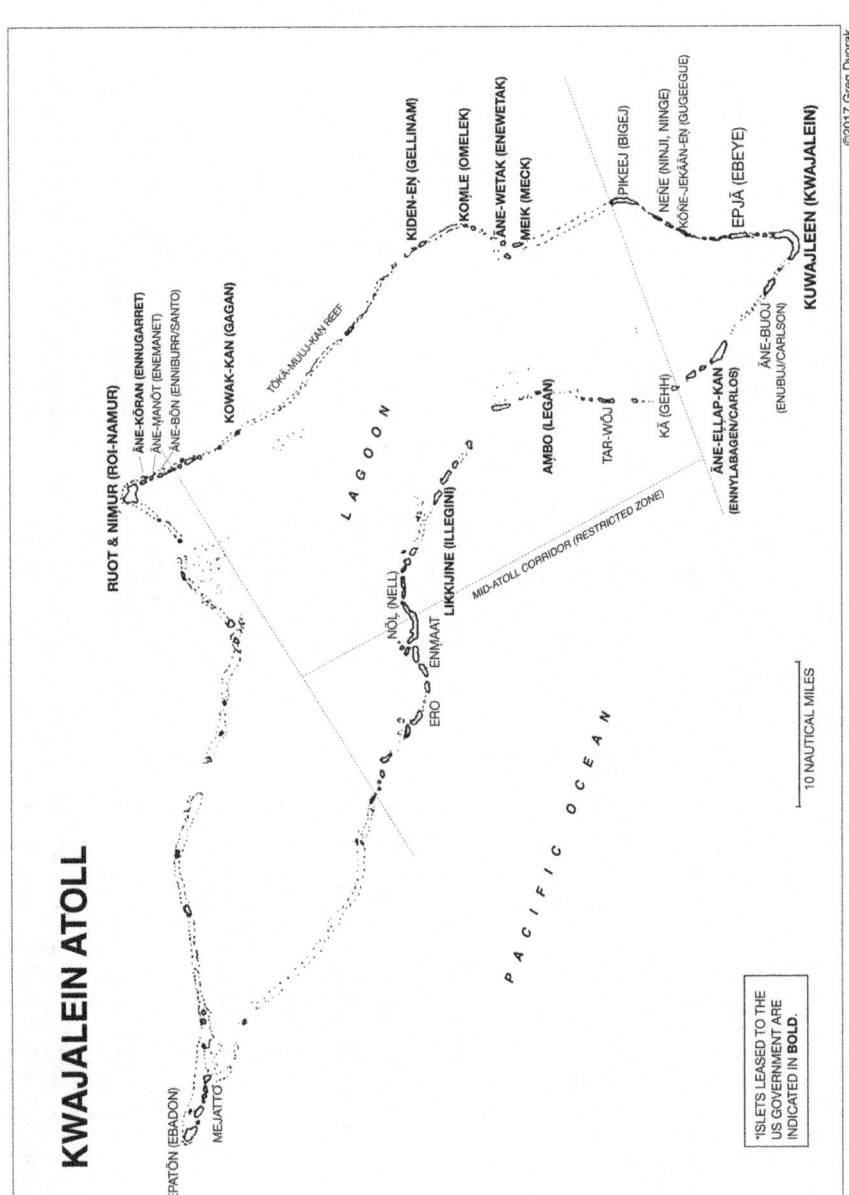

Map 3. Kwajalein Atoll with Marshallese and American islet names (by Greg Dvorak 2017, compiled from Marshallese, American, and Japanese maps)

Glossary

Because of my frequent use of unfamiliar non-English words and expressions in this book, as well as a number of place names and several acronyms, here I am providing as a reference a compilation of most of the terms that are repeated throughout the text. Each term is listed alphabetically and demarcated by a code corresponding to the context from which it originates: [M] for Marshallese, [J] for Japanese, [E] for American (or general English use). For reference, for Japanese terms, I am also providing the original Japanese characters as a gloss.

aeloñ [M] an atoll, island, land.

aḷap [M] a clan head assigned to manage land on behalf of the *irooj*. Like the *rijerbal* and *irooj*, this group forms a social class that functions in the land tenure process.

anshō [J] 暗礁 a reef, sunken rock, obstacle, impasse.

arigatō [J] 有り難う thank you.

bai [Palau] a meeting house.

baijin [M] lit. "poison," a term often used to refer to harmful nuclear radiation.

banzai [J] 万歳 an exclamation of celebratory enthusiasm, rather like the English "hurrah," but also with the literal meaning of "long life," and used in expressions like "Tennō-heika banzai!" ("Long live the emperor!")

baal [M] the reef edge, drop-off, open pool, fissures in the reef, opening out to sea (also the name of a species of coral).

bar [M] hard, sharp, rocky reef coral close to islets, between the flat reef foundation coral and the beach, sometimes forming between islets but right at the shore.

bok [M] granular, soft coral sand.

bijin [J] 美人 lit. "beautiful person," a beautiful woman.

Bravo [E] the code name given to a major nuclear test conducted on March 1, 1954, at Bikini Atoll, involving the largest nuclear detonation by the United States, the first test of the Castle series of nuclear tests in the Marshall Islands.

bubu [M] grandmother.

bwebwenato [M] telling stories or history, "talking story," oral traditions.

bwij [M] one's (matri)lineage.

bwiro [M] a Marshallese food made from fermented, preserved breadfruit.

Chamoro [J] チャモロ a prewar Japanese racial classification for Islanders all across the Nanyō Guntō district that describes people of mixed (usu. European and Islander) heritage, as distinct from indigenous Chamorro (or Chamoru) Mariana Islanders, from which the term was derived.

COM [E] acronym for Congress of Micronesia, a forum of elected leaders throughout the different island districts of the former US Trust Territory of the Pacific Islands in Micronesia.

Compact (of Free Association) [E] an agreement between the United States and three former Nanyō Guntō/Trust Territory of the Pacific island entities: the Republic of the Marshall Islands, the Federated States of Micronesia, and Palau.

coralhead [E] a large colony of thousands of coral polyps of the same genetic makeup, or a number of different colonies that are all clustered together to form a large mass. Coralheads can join together in shallow areas to form reefs and islands.

Dai Tōa Kyōei Ken [J] 大東亜共栄圏 The Greater East Asia Co-Prosperity Sphere, one of the regional imaginaries of Imperial Japan through which Japan claimed to protect and advance the interests of Asia and Oceania.

dojin [J] 土人 a derogatory obsolete term meaning "native" (literally "dirt person").

Ebeye [M] also Epjā (new spelling), Ebize エビゼ (Japanese). A small islet of Kwajalein Atoll, located roughly seven kilometers to the north of

Glossary

the main islet of Kwajalein, on which thirteen thousand Marshall Islanders live, most of whom have migrated there either because of American relocations due to weapon testing or because of the job opportunities and convenience of the military installation nearby.

Ebon [M] also Epoon (new spelling) the farthest southerly atoll of the Marshall Islands, close to the equator, site of the first Protestant mission in 1857, several trading companies, and a small phosphate-mining operation of Nanyō Takushoku Kaisha (Nantaku) in the 1930s.

emman [M] good.

enka [J] 演歌 modern Japanese-style popular ballad music.

fa'afāfine [Samoa] a "third-gender" (transgender or bigender) person, born biologically male, who lives "in the manner of a woman" and takes on social roles usually attributed to women.

fundoshi [J] 褌 a Japanese-style loincloth.

furusato [J] 故郷 one's home province or hometown, near and dear to one's heart.

gakkō [J] 学校 school (in the Marshall Islands, Marshallese used this term to describe what were officially referred to by Nanyō Guntō authorities as *kōgakkō*, public schools for Islanders, as distinct from *nihonjin-gakkō*, schools for Japanese children).

geta [J] 下駄 Japanese-style wooden clogs.

gunka [J] 軍歌 patriotic military songs.

gunzoku [J] 軍属 a civilian in the employ of the military.

gyokusai [J] 玉砕 a term referring to the act of suicidal self-sacrifice (usually en masse) during the Asia Pacific War for the emperor.

hakama [J] 袴 formal Japanese-style attire for men consisting of a divided skirt.

heitai [J] 兵隊 a soldier or sailor.

hinomaru [J] 日の丸 the emblem of the rising sun, or the Japanese flag.

hiragana [J] 平仮名 the forty-seven cursive symbols of the Japanese phonetic syllabary.

Hoppō [J] 北方 the "North," or northerly territories as seen geographically from Japan.

inaka [J] 田舎 the countryside, rural areas.

iokwe [M] a greeting that is typically used to say "hello," but also means "love," in much the same way as the Hawaiian greeting "aloha" is used. Literally the expression is said to mean, "I love you," but some people interpret the roots of the word to mean "you are a rainbow," though this translation is disputed.

ireisai [J] 慰霊祭 a memorial service.

irooj [M] a chief, the highest social class in the Marshall Islands.

iroojlaplap [M] a paramount chief.

izoku [J] 遺族 bereaved families.

jā [M] navigational seafaring term meaning "to jibe" (change course by swinging a sail across the wind).

Jaluit [M] also Jālooj or Jālwōj in new spelling of Marshallese, Yarūto (ヤルート) in Japanese. An atoll located in the southern Marshall Islands, in the Rālik chain, that became a major hub and administrative capital during both the German and Japanese colonial projects in Micronesia. Its main islet of Jebwad (Jabor) was the site of a small but bustling trading port town. Other islets in the atoll were also the homes of prominent chiefs, and during the war years, the large islet of Jaluit-Jaluit (Jālooj-Jālooj) and the islet of Iṃwej (Imiej) became Japanese military facilities.

jambo [M] (to take) a stroll or a random excursion/trip (by any means of transportation), derived from the Japanese word *sanpo*, which is more limited in meaning to the meaning of "taking a walk."

jebwa [M] a proprietary stick dance originating in Rālik that is only performed on special occasions and with the blessing of the *irooj*.

JICPOA [E] acronym for Joint Intelligence Center Pacific Ocean Areas, a division of the US armed forces formed in 1943 to gather intelligence on Japanese military activities during the Pacific War.

jodik [M] an invasion, from the Japanese word *jōriku* (上陸).

jowi [M] one's (matri)clan.

kaitaku [J] 開拓 resettlement and "pioneering" cultivation projects of wasteland, such as the policies initiated by Japan for out-migration in the early twentieth century and in the immediate postwar era to generate jobs and homes for displaced populations in rural areas.

kajoor [M] commoners, as distinct from chiefs (*irooj*); power.

Glossary

Kanaka [J] カナカ in the Japanese prewar usage, a (dark-skinned) Islander.

kanji [J] 漢字 Chinese ideographs stylized and standardized for use in the Japanese language.

kanshō [J] 環礁 atoll.

kapijukenen [M] one's ancestral home, "land of inheritance," firm and stable, rooted (also *kapijubar,* a plant that roots all the way down into the bar layer of rocky coral).

Kapin-Meto [M] lit. "the bottom of the sea," the northwestern region of the Marshall Islands; alternatively, the northwestern corner of Kwajalein Atoll.

katakana [J] 片仮名 one of the phonetic syllabaries for writing Japanese, used in the prewar period in place of hiragana in most printed material. In premodern times, it was a script that was used mainly by men. In contemporary times, it is used to write non-Japanese words or to add emphasis.

katsuo bushi [J] 鰹節 dried bonito (skipjack), often shaved into thin slices and used as a condiment and flavoring for dashi soup stock.

KMR [E] acronym for Kwajalein Missile Range, former name for Reagan Test Site.

(tanki) kōin [J] 短期工員 a (short-term) conscripted laborer working for the Japanese Imperial Military during the war.

kommool [M] thank you.

KRS [E] acronym for Kwajalein Range Services, the corporate consortium of defense and logistics companies that manages American operations at Kwajalein Atoll for the United States Army.

Kuezerin [J] クエゼリン Kwajalein (also Kezerin ケゼリン, Kuwajerin クワジェリン, Kōjaren コージャレン, Kowajiren コワジレン in various texts dating back to 1884).

kusentei [J] 駆潜艇 a submarine chaser.

Kuwajleen [M] Kwajalein.

lale [M] to look.

lerooj [M] a female chief.

lejman jūri [M] the principle by which women have the authority to arbitrate conflicts in Marshallese society.

mā [M] breadfruit (a Pacific staple food that grows on trees, rich in starch, usually roasted, baked, boiled, or fried before eating; with a taste similar to potatoes).

Majuro [M] also Mājro in the new Marshallese spelling; the capital atoll and main population center of the Republic of the Marshall Islands, located in the Ratak chain.

Ṃajel [M] the Marshall Islands.

-Maru [J] ～丸 a suffix that is placed at the end of Japanese ship names.

MILGOV [E] acronym for the US military government that administered Micronesia after Japan's defeat.

Mili [M] Mile in the new Marshallese spelling; the second largest atoll in the Marshall Islands after Kwajalein in terms of land area, the farthest eastern edge of the Republic of the Marshall Islands (and the former Japanese empire).

minyō [J] 民謡 Japanese regional folk song.

minzoku [J] 民族 an ethnic group or racial category.

Naichi [J] 内地 "mainland" Japan in relation to its outlying occupied territories and colonies, still used today to differentiate Okinawa from the rest of Japan.

nanshin [J] 南進 the principle of "southward advance" championed by Japanese expansionists in the early twentieth century.

Nanyō [J] 南洋 the South; also the general "South Seas," not the formal colonial government but the economic sphere that stretched all the way to Melanesia and into parts of Southeast Asia, most of which was centered around Taipei.

Nanyō-chō [J] 南洋庁 the civil government, headquartered in Palau, that administered the Japanese mandated territories of Micronesia (the Nanyō Guntō).

Nanyō Guntō [J] 南洋群島 the "South Seas Islands," the islands of Micronesia lying north of the equator, which were ceded to Japan by Germany and mandated by the League of Nations to Japan in 1922.

NBK (also BK) [J] 南洋貿易会社 acronym for Nanyō Bōeki Kaisha (the South Seas Trading Company), a Japanese enterprise that developed much of Micronesia in the prewar period.

ninpu [J] 人夫 an obsolete, pejorative term for a manual laborer or con-

Glossary xxix

struction worker, many of whom were conscripted from Korea (*neiṃbu* in Marshallese).

nisshōki [J] 日章旗 the proper name for the Japanese (rising sun) flag.

Nitijela [M] the democratically elected lower house of the Republic of the Marshall Islands' hybrid parliamentary and presidential system of government, which is complemented by the Council of Irooj, consisting of twelve chiefs who advise the legislature.

odoru [J] 踊る to dance.

ofuro [J] お風呂 a Japanese-style hot bath for soaking.

Operation Crossroads [E] the first series of nuclear tests conducted by the United States at Bikini Atoll, Marshall Islands, in the summer of 1946. It consisted of two twenty-one-kiloton detonations, Able and Baker.

Operation Flintlock [E] the United States' campaign against Imperial Japan in the Marshall Islands between January and February 1944 at Kwajalein and Enewetak Atolls, which paved the way for onward "steppingstone" bombardments to Chuuk and farther west across the Pacific (also the name of a nuclear testing program conducted in Nevada in the 1960s).

Operation Homecoming [M] the largest protest of the Marshallese landowners of Kwajalein Atoll that began in June of 1982 and involved over a thousand protestors who reoccupied their land to push the Marshall Islands and the United States government to produce a favorable lease agreement.

pedkat [M] coral mud.

pedped [M] flat open reef coral, foundation coral, reef, the floor of a house.

Rālik [M] The western chain of the Marshall Islands, the "sunset" archipelago.

Ratak [M] The eastern, "sunrise," chain of the Marshall Islands.

Roi-Namur [M] also Ruotto-Nimuru ルオット・ニムル (Japanese). Two islets (Roi and Namur) that were linked by a causeway during the Japanese fortification of Kwajalein Atoll and later served as a major military air base for the Japanese Imperial Navy. The conjoined islets were heavily bombarded during the American invasion, but several Japanese emplacements remain. Currently these islets are used mainly as a radar-tracking and space-surveillance site.

reisha [J] 霊砂 lit. "spirit sand"—sand, rocks, objects, and other materials gathered at a loved one's place of death and treated as sacred relics in lieu of human remains that cannot be located or properly exhumed.

rijerbal [M] a worker, the commoner class of people who hold land rights and take care of land on behalf of *irooj* and *aḷap*.

Ri-Kuwajleen [M] The "Kwajalein People," either the original inhabitants of Kwajalein Atoll or the clan of the same name.

ripālle [M] a Westerner, a (white) foreigner.

RMI [M] acronym for the Republic of the Marshall Islands.

RTS [E] acronym for Reagan Test Site at United States Army Kwajalein Atoll.

rukjanleen [M] literally, "gathering up the flowers to give to you," the origin of the name Kwajalein.

sakura [J] 桜 cherry (blossoms).

sango [J] 珊瑚 coral.

sashimi [J] 刺し身 sliced raw fish (*jajimi* in Marshallese).

seinendan [J] 青年団 a young men's organization or battalion.

Seiyō [J] 西洋 the West.

setsueibutai [J] 設営部隊 a construction battalion.

shamisen [J] 三味線 a three-stringed Japanese guitar or banjo.

shima [J] 島 island.

shōchū [J] 焼酎 distilled spirits, usually made from sweet potatoes and popular in Kyūshū.

shūchō [J] 酋長 orientalist prewar word meaning a chief, chieftain (Marshallese, *irooj*).

shūchō no musume [J] 酋長の娘 a "chieftain's daughter."

tabi [J] 足袋 Japanese socks (or special footwear for workers) designed with a split toe, usually for use with *geta* or other sandal-like shoes.

takuan [J] 沢庵 pickled daikon radish made with fermented rice bran.

Tarḷañ [M] archaic name for Kwajalein and name of a large coralhead from which the atoll is legendarily said to have formed in the deep-time past.

tatami [J] 畳 Japanese straw floor coverings.

tokkōtai [J] 特攻隊 short for *tokubetsu kōgekitai*, "special attack forces"

Glossary xxxi

that were mobilized late in Japan's Pacific War campaigns and were made up of specially trained young pilots who were sent on suicide missions to guide attacks on enemy targets; commonly called kamikaze outside Japan.

tōmin [J] 島民 the formal term used for "islanders" in the Nanyō Guntō.

torii [J] 鳥居 a Shintō shrine gate or archway.

Toyō [J] 東洋 the East.

TTPI [E] acronym for the United States Trust Territory of the Pacific Islands, established in 1947 when the United States took over administration of Micronesia from Japan after the war.

umi no seimeisen [J] 海の生命線 lit. "lifeline of the sea," an expression used to describe the Nanyō Guntō islands of Micronesia as a strategic buffer of naval power against the potential aggression of enemies, such as the United States.

undōkai [J] 運動会 a sports day or athletic meet.

USAG-KA [E] acronym for United States Army Garrison Kwajalein Atoll, formerly USAKA (United States Army Kwajalein Atoll).

USASMDC [E] acronym for United States Army Space and Missile Defense Command, the branch of the armed forces that is in charge of Kwajalein Atoll.

USMC [E] acronym for United States Marine Corps, the division of the US armed forces that invaded Kwajalein Atoll.

utilomar [M] a delicate white night-blooming flower with a sweet fragrance akin to heliotrope, jasmine, and honeysuckle, considered valuable in making chiefly adornments; the official flower for Kwajalein Atoll and the variety of special blossoms thought to have attracted people from all corners of the earth to "harvest" Kwajalein's many fruits.

wāto [M] a land parcel; the Marshallese unit for measuring ancestral tracts of land.

wōd [M] coral, a coralhead.

yakyū [J] 野球 the Japanese word for baseball (literally "field ball"), a term that is used nowadays in Marshallese as well, despite the American influence.

yashi [J] 椰子 coconut palm trees.

PRELUDE

The Middle of Now-here

Introducing Kwajalein

ISLANDS OF ABUNDANCE, islands of starvation, islands of connectedness, nearly one hundred flat coral islets of various sizes make up Kwajalein (Kuwajleen) in the Marshall Islands, the largest inhabited atoll on earth. Seen from the heavens, they form a gigantic crescent-shaped necklace of bright turquoise, cobalt, green, and white that seems to float upon the water, strung together by a dynamic, living, ancient reef. Built over thousands of years by coral that has migrated on ocean currents from far away, the atoll teaches of both past and present to all who will listen. It is a symbol for the interconnected, multilayered histories of our contemporary world.

For many people in the world, little places like Kwajalein are too small to be important—"the middle of nowhere," they say. Even "Micronesia," the regional name chosen by geographer Domeny de Rienzi in 1831 to map the islands described by explorer Jules Dumont D'Urville, means nothing but "tiny islands," as if that were their only defining feature (Hanlon 1998, 1–2). From continental worldviews, where the land is mapped and the sea is boundless blank space, places like the Marshall Islands, where there is more water than land, are often described by what they lack rather than by what they possess. Veteran Bruce Muench describes a sign that was displayed at the US naval base air terminal lodge after the American invasion in the 1940s. It read:

> WELCOME TO KWAJALEIN
> NO WHISKEY ATOLL
> NO WOMEN ATOLL
> NO NOTHING ATOLL
> (Muench 2002, 54).

For the Ri-Kuwajleen, the original Marshallese inhabitants of Kwajalein, of course this has never been the case. The whole atoll is rich in meaning: not only is land precious and imbued with significance but the lagoon and outer ocean are valuable as well. Coral-heads and reefs have names; seemingly invisible sea routes crisscross the surface of the water and are memorized in navigation chants.[1] Individuals chart their genealogies between islands and across great distances, and history is told and learned not just in landscapes but in atollscapes.[2]

For the generations of Marshallese, Americans, Japanese, and others who have lived here, and for the military and colonial superpowers that have used the atoll for their own purposes, Kwajalein is anything *but* the middle of nowhere. Though it may sit amidst the vastest ocean on Earth, this is an atoll that has been a major intersection—if not an epicenter—of Oceania and indeed the whole world, at least throughout the past century. Its many layers of deep-time sediment represent ages and ages of knowledge that is available to us in the present day. It is neither timeless nor placeless; it is relevant and important in understanding the workings of both island societies and superpowers, local and global.

Kwajalein is, rather, the middle of *both* now and here, not nowhere but now-here. In this book, I explore this place in the middle of its now-ness and here-ness, as an example of how history can be told through the metaphor of coral, an analogy that is by its very nature Oceanic and multilayered. Departing in the middle of now-here and visiting many of the pasts that are sedimented into the present, we will voyage through the atollscapes of Kwajalein.

Setting and Background

Kwajalein is a place that has been called multiple names throughout its past, and even in its present. It is called Kuwajleen in the Marshallese language, Kuezerin in Japanese, and often the main islet is called "Kwaj" by the Americans who live there today.[3] It is one of the twenty-nine atolls and five islands that make up Aeloñ in Ṃajel—the Republic of the Marshall Islands (RMI)—a sovereign democratic country with a population of seventy-three thousand Ri-Ṃajel, Marshall Islanders.[4] These islands and atolls are spread across a vast stretch of the Central Pacific, encompassing more than two million square kilometers of ocean, most of the distance above the equator and west of the International Date Line between the Hawaiian Islands and the Federated States of Micronesia. Kwajalein Atoll is located 440 kilometers northwest of the RMI capital of Majuro Atoll (almost an hour's flight along the airline route that island-hops across Micronesia), at about nine degrees above the equator. It is 3,936 kilometers from Honolulu, 4,124 kilometers from Tokyo, and 5,260 kilometers from Canberra, Australia.

Were we able to view Kwajalein Atoll underwater clearly at a distance, from the side we would see a massive collapsed volcanic ridge towering 2,134 meters above the dark sea floor, with a crest of coral piled up high upon its upper altitudes, forming a crest of islets that break through the water. The atoll's comparatively shallow and calm lagoon (roughly 60–80 meters deep) is tremendously large, with a surface area of 2,848 square kilometers, and it can take more than a day to navigate the distance of 130 kilometers from one tip to another by small boat. In contrast, the total land area of Kwajalein's ninety-three islets amounts to roughly 16.4 square kilometers in total, ranging from barren sandy islets that are sometimes submerged by the tides to broad, lush islets covered in jungle. Kwajalein Islet, at the southernmost tip, is the largest in the atoll, and Roi-Namur and Epatōn (Ebadon) are the next largest islets, located at the northernmost and easternmost tips, respectively. Narrow and slender Ebeye, the most populated islet in the atoll and home to an estimated thirteen thousand Marshall Islanders, is located only three kilometers north of Kwajalein.[5]

Marshallese have lived for centuries on their small atolls and have a proud legacy of surviving and making the most of their circumstances despite harsh conditions and tide after tide of colonial influence. Contemporary theories of migration, based on linguistic and archaeological evidence, generally agree that Oceania was settled in a number of different waves over the course of thousands of years, as part of the great Austronesian migration. According to Kirch, the islands of the Pacific Ocean were settled at least 3,500 years ago, when early migrants moved from parts of what is now Southeast Asia (including Taiwan and the Philippines) into Near Oceania and mixed with the local Papuan populations that had already inhabited Melanesia for more than thirty-five thousand years (Kirch 2000, 86).[6] Later generations of voyagers are then believed to have honed their navigational skills before journeying eastward from Vanuatu and the Solomons to colonize the islands of Tonga, Samoa, and Fiji, and also northwards via Kiribati across the equator into the northern Marshall Islands (Kirch 2000, 167). Archaeological studies suggest that Bikini Atoll was settled as early as 2,800 years ago (Rainbird 2004, 86), and Kwajalein was settled at least 2,000 years ago (Beardsley 1994).[7]

Marshallese cosmologies passed through generations tell a different origin story from these scientific migration studies, in the form of intricate chants that educated youth in how to behave and how to understand their own identities and genealogies in relation to their environment, as well as how to make sense of the world through navigational knowledge. In 1975, Jelibōr Jam related to anthropologist Jack Tobin a story about the beginning of the world, explaining that four skies of the east, west, north, and south were formed from four posts, after which two men—Ḷowa and Ḷōm̧tal—appeared. Ḷowa created the rocks and the reefs and the islands. Ḷōm̧tal made the sea, making it flow in all directions and bringing the first fish, as well as the sky and the birds that flew through it. This was followed by the arrival of two men named Ḷewōj and Ḷaneej, who were skilled in tattooing. They named the fish and gave them colors, proceeding to color and design the creatures of the land and the air as well, and finally humans, giving them unique faces. From this, the world expanded as a powerful woman creator generated Marshallese culture step by step. She gave birth to the first coconut, which led to sustenance and sennit rope and the building of the first canoe. Different communities of men and women separated into clans with different skills, and they spread out into different parts of the islands, but the woman—much like a mother of the people—warned them not to fight, but to pool their skills to work together and love one another (Tobin 2002, 11–26). This precious and elaborate story goes on to talk of important spirits and cultural codes that set the standards for Marshallese culture and identity. It is but one of many histories encoded in chants, songs, dances, proverbs (*jabōnkōnnaan*), and other oral traditions of (hi)storytelling (*bwebwenato*) that have transmitted Marshall Islander knowledge over thousands of years.

In contrast to this deep-time history, the history of colonial contact at Kwajalein and other atolls of the Rālik and Ratak is relatively short and recent. Hezel writes that it was not until 1521 that Europeans made contact with Islanders, when Magellan arrived at Guam after sailing in such calm conditions across the ocean without encountering people or islands that he named it "Mar Pacifico," the Pacific (Hezel 1983, 1). The first contacts between Marshall Islanders and Spaniards did not take place until 1529, after which encounters were relatively minimal. Spanish trading ships had to pass through these islands between the "Spice Islands" in Southeast Asia and "New Spain" in Central America, and it was on one of these voyages that Aloyso de Arellano "discovered" Kwajalein for Spain in 1565 when he accidentally went off course (Spennemann 2004, 4). This was all in sharp contrast to western Micronesia, where the aggressiveness of ongoing European colonialism deeply impacted and transformed the lives of the Mariana Islanders through the next two centuries (Hezel 1983, 47).

Over the decades, different European powers made their mark on Oceania as they dominated trading routes and pursued strategic initiatives. Dutch and Portuguese traders eventually rose to power in the seventeenth century over the control of the spice trade, followed by the British in the late 1700s. British captain John Marshall passed Kwajalein and the island group it belonged to (then called the Mulgraves) in 1788 aboard the *Scarborough,* commanding a fleet of convict ships from London to Port Jackson, Sydney (Spennemann 2004, 22). It was this passage that eventually led to the "discovery" of the atolls that came to be known on European maps, after Marshall, as the Marshall Islands. Marshall's colleague, Thomas Gilbert, likewise had another group named after himself, the Gilbert Islands (Kiribati).

Missionary activity in the Marshalls followed these first contacts when a powerful *irooj* (chief) named Kaibuke granted access to the Protestant missionaries of the American Board of Commissioners for Foreign Missions (ABCFM) and a mission was established at Ebon in 1857 (Hezel 1983, 201). These missionaries radically influenced Marshallese ways of living by building mission schools, discouraging indigenous practices, and promoting most European customs except for the use of firearms and alcohol (Hezel 1983, 205).

Copra trading, centered largely around Jaluit (Jālooj) Atoll, was the industry by which German and Portuguese businessmen began to establish a stronghold in the Marshalls in the 1860s, leading eventually to Germany's establishment of a Marshall Islands Protectorate in 1885. During this period, a small German settlement was built at Jaluit Atoll, and Kwajalein became one of the trading centers for copra as well (Hezel 1983, 210–226). The capitalist ventures of the copra trade consolidated chiefly power in the main islands of the more populated atolls, as traditional leaders forged close alliances with European settlers and administrators.[8]

Meanwhile, Japanese economic interests in Oceania had been

expanding since the late 1800s, and by World War I Japan had also accumulated enough maritime prowess to easily seize these Micronesian territories in 1914 at a time when Germany was at its most vulnerable (Peattie 1988, 38–40). In a relatively peaceful confrontation, Japanese forces took over the former German territories and, in 1922, established the Nanyō Guntō (South Seas Islands) territories of Japan under a League of Nations international mandate (*inin tōchi ryō*). This "guardianship" was a compromise, as there was a considerable debate between Japanese opinion leaders over the virtues of annexation; yet "the structure, style, and substance of Japan's mandatory rule were, inevitably, those of a colonial power" (Peattie 1988, 61).

Japan was much more vigorous in its colonial administration of Micronesia than its European predecessors had been, and even though the Marshall Islands was on the far fringes of the Nanyō Guntō, it still experienced an intense transformation. Whereas Germans had seen the Marshalls and other island groups as "remote trading stations," Japanese were intent on developing education, the economy, and other aspects of the infrastructure in ways that were "unrivaled elsewhere in the Pacific" (Peattie 1988, 68). At first this Japanization of Micronesia only slightly influenced Kwajalein Atoll, which remained a rural trading post throughout much of the Japanese colonial period, but the port of Jabor (Jebwad) in Jaluit Atoll continued to thrive as a hub of economic activity, and a small Japanese town gradually developed—complete with noodle restaurants, a department store that sold *kimono* (Japanese traditional clothing) and various supplies, a photo studio, and frequent *sumō* wrestling matches.[9]

Later, Kwajalein was selected by the Imperial Navy to serve as a major command center on the front lines in the Pacific campaigns of World War II, and it was rapidly fortified and transformed. This process was not complete in 1944, when American forces stormed the atoll on their way across Oceania to Tokyo. The war left a devastating wake of death and destruction, not only for the Marshall Islanders whose lives were severely altered by their experiences of loss, but also for the thousands of Japanese soldiers and Korean laborers who perished in the confrontation.

Ever since US Marines seized the atoll from Imperial Japan, Kwajalein has served as a base for American military operations, including the nuclear tests conducted by the US Department of Energy. Along with the rest of the Marshall Islands, in the postwar period the atoll was subsumed into the US Trust Territory of the Pacific Islands beginning in 1947, and it was administered under what many have argued was a "strategic colony" (Lutz 1984). This lasted through 1979, when the Republic of the Marshall Islands was established as a self-governing independent nation, and ever since 1986 it has been in "free association" with the United States.

Nowadays, at least from the perspective of the United States government, Kwajalein is known officially as "USAG-KA," or US Army Garrison, Kwajalein Atoll, yet another one of the atolls changing names (most likely it will assume another military name as the years pass). Technically, it is a military installation, a grouping of facilities on eleven islets leased from Marshallese landowners through an agreement with the Republic of the Marshall Islands. It forms a vital hub of the United States Army Space and Missile Defense Command (USASMDC), headquartered in Huntsville, Alabama. As can be inferred from its name, the Ronald Reagan Ballistic Missile Defense Test Site (RTS) serves mainly as a place to host long-range intercontinental ballistic missile interception tests, as well as various other space-surveillance and launch projects for government agencies and private corporations.[10] Though there are few fences or reinforced borders, all these installation islets are highly secured and completely off-limits to anyone not authorized to be there.

USAG-KA is based primarily on Kwajalein islet, where almost all the installation's roughly 1,200 employees and family members live. Another small percentage of its personnel lives at the other end of the atoll on Roi-Namur.[11] Some of these employees also commute daily by airplane, helicopter, or boat to any of the other islets where facilities are sited in the atoll. The installation is unique, however, because although it is run by the military and managed by a consortium of defense contractors, almost all its residents and staff members are civilians (only a handful of people are active military personnel). Most of these employees are American citizens who work for the contractors and do jobs that range from "pools and beaches" supervisors and high school teachers to mission launch specialists, and many have contracts that allow them to bring their families with them (although this number has been decreasing steadily). A small number of Marshallese employees also have night jobs that provide lodging in the installation, or supervisory positions that allow them to live there with their families, but for the most part Marshallese who work on the base are required to commute from the islet of Ebeye every day.

In order to support a predominantly civilian, educated middle-class population, the US Army has, ever since the 1960s, paid special attention to the standard of living available on Kwajalein islet. Developing the islet through trial and error with comfortable living quarters, recreation facilities, a fully functional school system, a hospital, shops, and many other amenities, the US Army hoped to create a "quality of life" on par with a small American town (Linka 1977). Basing their designs roughly on their hometowns in suburban New Jersey, engineers from the defense contractor Bell Laboratories created a small and cozy environment that, in its heyday in the 1960s, reached a population of four thousand people (Wypijewski 2000, 13). This main islet of Kwajalein (below), despite its various military acronyms and official names, gradually came to be known affectionately by Americans and many Marshallese as "Kwaj."

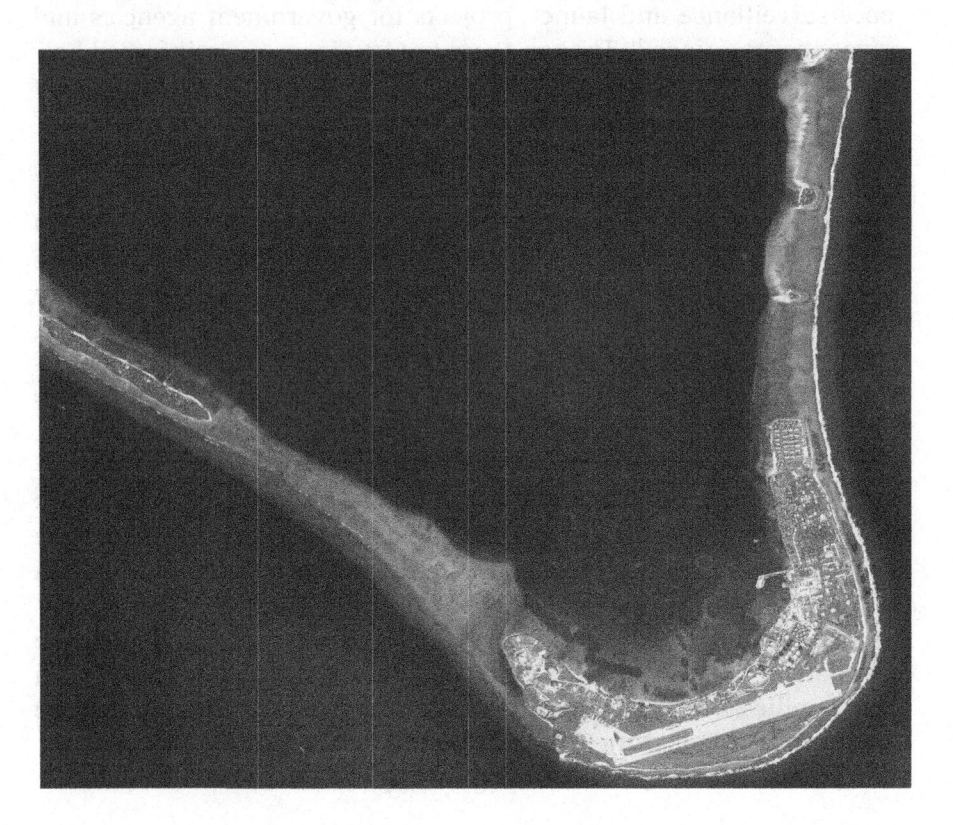

Seen from above, boomerang-shaped and poised between the other southernmost islets of the atoll that sit upon the reef, contemporary Kwaj is neat, orderly, and green—covered with fresh green lawns and concrete. Its large military airstrip dominates nearly half of the islet's four kilometers of length and one kilometer of width. The tight grid of houses at the northern end of the islet is shaded by a dense canopy of palm trees and divided by smoothly paved streets. At the other end of the islet are water tanks and sewage treatment plants, warehouses, and various missile-tracking facilities. The lagoon-side edge of Kwaj is lined with three beaches, and a marina in the center of the islet is filled with sailboats. Next to the airstrip on the ocean side is the golf course. Around its perimeter is the fringe of coral reef, the tremendously deep outer ocean and the relatively shallow inner lagoon.

Now, of course, this is only the surface layer of Kwajalein. In this photograph, it is almost possible to make out the dark shadows in the shallows of the lagoon where craters were blasted in the reef by wartime bombings and postwar landfill dredging projects, or where Japanese warships still sleep on the sea floor. But nothing about this image reveals how the golf course was once a Marshallese labor camp, and before that a bloody battlefield where Japanese, Koreans, Islanders, and Americans lost their lives. Nothing about this image of transplanted American suburbia suggests that the site of the current runway is where there was once a small Japanese public school for Islanders, or that there were impressive homes for the high-ranking chiefs of this atoll who gathered here regularly to make important decisions. No one can see where the bones of Japanese soldiers and Korean laborers are buried or where the sacred Marshallese gravesites used to be.

Like the pristine landscape of the military installation at USAG-KA today, American hegemony has neatly buried the histories of many Others in the Pacific. Now and here at Kwajalein, there are many histories that exist in the multiple layers of the atoll. This book aims to dig beneath this top American layer to reveal what stories lie hidden beneath the surface.

Kwaj Kid: My Background

Before I begin to dig into the many layers of the atoll, allow me to relate how my own life history intersects with Kwajalein Atoll. In the early 1970s, my father's job as an engineer for a major defense firm gave him the opportunity to relocate our family from the United States to Kwajalein Missile Range, and because my parents were almost thirty years old, adventurous, and fascinated by the world, they decided to leave their families in Philadelphia and New Jersey to experience life in the Pacific.

What they thought would be a challenging sojourn on a remote chunk of coral ended up being a pleasant way of life in a friendly, laid-back American community on an island where the only modes of transportation were rusty old bicycles. Far from the United States and not the strict military lifestyle they imagined, it was an older way of life, a throwback to the "good old days" when there was no television and people all said hello to each other on the street. It was a time of beach barbecues with Bee-Gees and John Denver records playing as everyone gathered to watch yet another breathtaking sunset.

As a child growing up in the American community of Kwaj, I was not aware of the other histories that had preceded my safe and carefree life, even though my playground was literally on top of the site of one of the bloodiest battlefields of the Pacific War, on Marshallese ancestral land. I did not quite understand why there were old, decaying Japanese buildings all over the atoll, even though we were all Americans. In my first-grade class, we celebrated Columbus Day and gave thanks for the "friendship" between the "pilgrims" and the "Indians" who founded America, while never learning anything about the Marshall Islanders who allowed us to use their land to test missiles and live our comfortable lifestyle.[12]

Life on Kwaj was indeed comfortable. That the atoll was a place to test missiles was really an afterthought for many American civilians, especially little children like me. My father would fly up to Roi-Namur each day in a small Caribou aircraft, a small cargo plane that shuttled the engineers—dressed in collared aloha shirts, shorts, and sneakers—up to their work stations at the ALTAIR and TRADEX radars. Sometimes he would stay late at night and call to tell us to look up in the sky, where we would see bright streaks of light as the re-entry vehicles pierced the atmosphere and soared down into the darkness of the open ocean or the center of the lagoon. But most evenings, just before the siren that went off each night at six o'clock, I would sit outside on the curb and wait for my father to cycle back home from the air terminal. We would all change into our bathing suits, and with my mother we would go down to Emon Beach[13] to have a quick swim before dinner.

My mother worked part-time at a range of different jobs, and she was quite active in the community. She was involved also in the Kwajalein Women's Club, which did various activities with Marshallese women on different islets in the atoll. She also spent much time with me, and we used to ride our bicycles down to one of the two ponds of sea turtles, where we fed the gigantic creatures together and reached our hands into the water to pet their smooth shells. After my little brother was born on the island in 1978, she continued her active lifestyle, scuba diving on weekends and even running part of a marathon with my father in Majuro with my brother strapped to her back.

Meanwhile I was like most little Kwaj Kids, wandering around the island and exploring its every corner with my friends. The safety of a small island with no traffic and virtually no crime made it easy for even six- and seven-year-olds to be as adventurous as they liked, even though the teenagers on the island frequently got into trouble, drinking beer after dark in secret hideaways or sneaking into dangerous off-limits parts of the base.[14] I was more interested in chasing my cat down in between the big coral rocks that acted as a breakwater for the gently lapping lagoon in front of the trailer where we lived. Climbing up into the high reaches of pandanus trees and slipping down in between the warm reef boulders scented with dead crabs, sour seaweed, and barnacles, I would play hide-and-seek all day long. I would ride my bicycle all over the island, as in this photo of me when I was about four years old, sporting the same "ALMOST HEAVEN, KWAJALEIN" T-shirt that everyone in our small community was wearing in 1977.

Granted, these memories are sweetened by nostalgia, but most long-term American residents of Kwajalein and other Kwaj Kids like me share similar recollections.[15] For me, those early years were not only a warm and happy childhood with neighbors that all felt like family; there was also a sort of intimacy with the island itself, with the trees, the sand, the seawater. It was as if the whole environment was teaching me something that could not be spoken in words, something that was not easily understood by my parents and other adults. Many years later, when I finally returned to the Marshall Islands as an adult, I could easily relate to the Marshallese children I met wherever I traveled, because we shared the same appreciation for the smells, textures, and sounds of a coral atoll.

In the 1970s, as has been the case through most of Kwajalein's postwar history, civilian contract workers and their families outnumbered military personnel ten to one. This meant that the civilian majority tended to stay within their little bubble of American small-town comfort and to blame most problems they experienced on "the military," from complaints about strict regulations like being cited for not having a flashlight on one's bicycle at night to the inconvenience of not having enough fresh produce in the supermarket. Civilians likewise took little or no responsibility for the injustices the United States had carried out upon the people of the Marshall Islands, from the horrific nuclear tests of the 1940s and 1950s to the numerous displacements that ensued due to irradiation in the Northern atolls and the ongoing missile-testing project in Kwajalein Atoll. Through our very existence in Kwajalein, we were all directly imbricated in the history of the contemporary Marshall Islands, and yet we disowned the past and lived as if this were all just the military's fault.

Few of the Americans on Kwajalein ever ventured to Ebeye, even though we could see the islet on the horizon. My parents had several Marshallese friends, and so we sometimes took a short ferry ride to Ebeye to attend birthday and Christmas parties. Compared to the perfectly regulated tranquility of Kwajalein, Ebeye always felt wild, exciting, and free, but my parents would never let me play much with the Marshallese children we encountered. It probably seemed too dangerous to them, with broken glass and stray dogs. But for me it was alive and thrilling to see so many people of all ages, speaking a beautiful and strange language I did not understand. Children my age made their own toys, making checkerboards out of bottle caps or surfboards out of planks of plywood (see Horowitz 1983).

These glimpses of the rest of the Marshall Islands came to me also through our housekeeper Neitari, who would sing church hymns in Marshallese with her cousin Arina to my brother and me as she folded clothes and mopped the kitchen floor. She would talk about "Marshallese customs" and teach us about the right way to walk in front of elders or about special foods to eat. Given that we lived in the middle of the Rālik Chain of the Marshall Islands, her cultural musings should not have seemed out of the ordinary, but our community was so American and so alienated from its surroundings that, to me, Neitari's world sounded very exotic.

There were other glimpses, too, of other realities that seemed to exist beyond my little American suburbia, such as the old cannons, concrete bunkers, and mysterious scraps of rusty tanks and other war junk piled in the Shark Pit at the tip of Kwaj. There was also the Japanese Cemetery at the far end of the runway, and another one on Roi-Namur that was even bigger. These places had a strange and unsettling feeling to them, and it was even more disturbing for me to think of the gigantic Japanese warships that rested at the bottom of the lagoon outside my bedroom window. Some nights I would lie in bed looking out at the reflections of the lights of barges and buoys bobbing on the water at night and wonder about what lay below.

We left Kwaj when I was almost nine, partly because my parents wanted to buy a home and settle closer to our relatives and partly because the political climate of the Marshall Islands in 1982 was growing tense. The new Republic of the Marshall Islands was on the verge of deciding its political status under the Compact of Free Association with the United States, and the landowners of Kwajalein were protesting with the conviction that their land was being offered to the Americans without proper compensation or a clear agreement (see chapter 7). This was causing the army commander (effectively the mayor) to react to the Marshallese protesters with harsh regulations, special security procedures, and a number of other extreme measures with which many American residents strongly disagreed.

My adjustment to life in New Jersey was difficult despite being close to my relatives, and I thought about Kwajalein often, but it was impossible to return there. It was a military base, not a real hometown (or so I was told), and I was American, not Marshallese. Oceania was completely alien to my new friends on the east coast of the United States, and so I eventually stopped talking about this distant homeland of mine. The Atlantic was the only ocean I could visit. With its frigid waters and harsh gray surf pounding against the fine, sticky sand, it felt completely alien to me.

After many years in the States, when I was sixteen I finally had a chance to travel back across the Pacific—not to the Marshall Islands, but to Japan. Something felt unusually familiar to me on that first trip, and the more I thought about it the more I realized that the coastal towns where I stayed somehow reminded me of Kwajalein. I felt compelled to study everything I could about Japan, and I decided to return again for a year of exchange in a high school in Miyazaki Prefecture, where I learned Japanese and where my Japanese host grandfather

Mitsuharu would relate his bittersweet memories about spending his youth in the Japanese colony of Manchuria and then serving in the Imperial Navy during the war.

Many years later I worked as a consultant to the local government of Nangō-chō, a small town in Nichinan, Miyazaki Prefecture, on the Pacific Coast. I was taken by surprise when I realized that nearly all the tuna fishing fleet that was registered in the town departed regularly for Micronesia, with many boats based in the waters of the Marshall Islands for several months at a time. This sparked in my mind a strong desire to try to return to Kwajalein; yet I could not imagine how that would be possible. My father's death in 1999, however, convinced me that I needed to go back to the place where he had taken our family, in order to make sense out of my own Pacific past.

◇ ◇ ◇

Starting in 2000, I returned to Kwajalein several times. My understanding of life in both Japan and the United States gave me a much deeper appreciation of the multiple and contradictory realities that existed there. I felt both delighted by being back in what felt like my true hometown and frustrated to see the ways Marshallese were still marginalized in their own country. I especially felt discouraged to see how so few Americans were willing to engage with the world that surrounded them. It was also surprising to see how the victories of the Pacific War were still celebrated and American war veterans were honored year after year, but how little was understood or appreciated about the atoll's Japanese past. For many residents, the Japanese ships in the lagoon were just a place to go diving. No one seemed to sense the magnitude of the battles that had taken place there, aside from the story of American sacrifices or successes; few people reflected on the tremendous losses that Marshallese, Japanese, and Korean families suffered as well.

These returns to Kwajalein raised many questions in my mind and compelled me to begin the journey that would lead eventually to this book. Yet the process has always been fraught with ambivalence, for, as critical as I am in this project of the American histories that dominate the Pacific, I am just as implicated in those histories, and the American community of Kwaj will always be home for me. I deeply understand and relate to the ways many American residents of Kwajalein live their lives, and I have had many friends there, civilian and military. I have been surprised, too, to find how many people on Kwajalein share my concerns. But any military base is a transient space where people do not easily grow roots. In the years since I began returning to Kwajalein, I have been blessed to make and rekindle many more friendships with Marshall Islanders from throughout the atoll, who are capable of seeing the bigger picture of their home and its oceanic, Marshallese context. They are the ones who have inspired my journey and taught me the most.

When I spoke of my predicament of balancing between multiple and contradictory American, Japanese, Korean, and Marshall Islander perspectives to Charlie, a Marshallese friend who had known my family since my childhood, he laughed and said, "It sounds like you are an *aḷap* (designated clan representative) with more than one *irooj* (chief)! Sometimes an *aḷap* has land rights in territories that belong to different chiefs who disagree with each other, you know. You're like someone whose home has a Marshallese *irooj*, an American *irooj*, and a Japanese *irooj*," he explained.

"What am I supposed to do, then?" I asked.

"Well, your job is to tell those different truths as you see them. You tell the truth the way you see it to all your chiefs—not because you dislike them, but because you *love* them. That's the best way to show your respect. You stand between them and tell them what you see, that's all."

So, with the advice from my friend, I decided to study the many truths of Kwajalein as I embarked on the process that led to this book.

Genealogies: Research Background and Influences

My first academic questions about Kwajalein began when I undertook a master's degree at the Center for Pacific Islands Studies at the University of Hawai'i at Mānoa, where I was challenged to explore my own subjectivity in relation to colonialism and indigeneity in the Marshall Islands and all of Oceania. When I took my project to the doctoral level at the Australian National University, I remember being asked by Pacific historian Greg Dening, one of my supervisors, "What conversation are you joining by doing this work?" I am not sure if there is any singular answer to this question; fundamentally this project has been an engagement with multiple voices—indeed, many chiefs and many commoners (both literally and figuratively). It is an articulation of many disparate stories into one larger story. This is, in many ways, what Pacific history is all about, the weaving together of multiple narratives between islands, across oceans. It is the very stuff that Greg Dening himself writes about in his histories of encounter (1988, 2004), which incorporate the subtleties of ethnography and oral history narrative with the tales told by archives and obscure pieces of ephemera.

More important to me than the question of "what academic conversation I am joining?" is the question, "for whom are my words intended?" In trying to relate multiple truths to my multiple "*irooj*," one of the challenges of this project is attempting not only to articulate disparate histories but also to relate those histories between and across borders, between different groups of people. In problematizing and deconstructing the American hegemonic view of history in Oceania, on one level my project aims to excavate multiple buried Marshallese and Japanese narratives of Kwajalein's many histories and bring those marginalized pasts into the consciousness of a wide range of readers. In that sense, I am deeply indebted to the work of Keith Camacho, who has helped to pave this path for me with his book *Cultures of Commemoration: The Politics of War, Memory, and History in the Mariana Islands* (Camacho 2011). On another level, I also hope to provide an alternative to the many histories of Micronesia that cast the Marshallese people as victims of colonialism and nuclear warfare; and in reinvigorating an awareness that stretches beyond the postwar American era, perhaps this project can contribute to a Marshallese sense of continuity, survival, and pride. At the same time, this project aims to recuperate an interest and awareness among Japanese readers, not only for the war but also for the enduring legacies of Japanese colonialism in Micronesia.[16]

I doubt, of course, that this project can be all things to all people. First and foremost it is my own journey, an auto-ethnographic exploration of how I have, through my life and research, made sense out of my own childhood home. Second, this book is written in English, and it is thus mainly intended in its current form for English speakers who might not be aware of Oceanian or Japanese perspectives. Third, although Kwajalein forms the convergent site from which I narrate my island-based perspective of history, I do not claim to be providing an essentialist ethnographic account of "how Marshallese people see the world." Instead my objective is to zone in on some of the encounters that have taken place between different, multiple, intersecting groups of people in relation to Kwajalein as a way of portraying the human stories that exist amidst global tides of politics, economics, and war. I might emphasize very different aspects of those encounters for a primarily Japanese or Marshallese readership, as I have in some of the talks that I have given in Japan and the Marshall Islands over the past decade.[17]

In another sense, it is also true that my words are probably more directed at English and perhaps Japanese speakers for the simple reason that I am most literate in those two languages. I am much less confident about my Marshallese ability, and although I was able to conduct basic research in that language, I needed the help of others for many of my interviews and interpretations at times when my source material was in Marshallese. It is likely the case that I have inadvertently missed valuable clues from the Marshallese context due to my linguistic or cultural lack of literacy, while simultaneously I may have overemphasized Japanese or American viewpoints due to my sensitivity to the subtleties of those languages.

Still, I worked closely with Marshallese historians at Ebeye, Jaluit, and Majuro, and I tried to engage their local perspectives toward the historical time frames I was considering. What was always intriguing about my conversations with these elders was that from their Marshallese perspectives of history, the Japanese or American "periods" were extremely brief and recent (if not insignificant) in comparison to the genealogical deep-time past upon which they based their recollections. I have tried to be mindful of this throughout this book through the use of the coral metaphors of deep time I will introduce next. I can only hope that this book communicates at least some of the multiple but often contradictory truths of Kwajalein, now and here.

CHAPTER 1

Coral and Concrete

Paradigm for Pacific Pasts

> Every one must be struck with astonishment, when he first beholds one of these vast rings of coral-rock, often many leagues in diameter, here and there surmounted by a low verdant island with dazzling white shores, bathed on the outside by the foaming breakers of the ocean and in the inside surrounding a calm expanse of water, which, from reflection, is a bright but pale green colour.
> —*Charles Darwin, from* The Voyage of the Beagle[1]

IT WAS CHARLES DARWIN'S ENCOUNTER with coral atolls when he was twenty-five that first gave rise to his ideas about evolution, radically changing the way humans understood their history as living organisms on the planet (Jones 2007, 2). He theorized that an atoll was formed when coral colonizes the outer rim of a subaquatic ancient volcano that has been worn down by the elements over thousands of years, reaching upward to the surface of the water and piling up layer upon layer to form rings of flat islands that seem to float in a sea of blue. Like the atoll, life on earth and the earth itself were not preordained and unchanging; they were perpetually evolving over time, Darwin argued.

Coral, as many marine biologists and environmental ecologists tell us, is in fact a migratory organism that travels ocean currents over great expanses of the sea, landing upon the edges of submerged volcanoes, amalgamating into communities, forming colonies, dying, hardening, and building layer upon layer upon layer of ancestral heritage to break the surface of the water and make islet after islet, connected by reef, to form atolls—delicate rings of land that can be found throughout Oceania but especially in the Marshall Islands, Tuvalu, or Kiribati.

The Ri-Kuwajleen, the Islanders who first settled Kwajalein, told history through coral long before Darwin did. It is understood in their oral traditions that the entire atoll, this whole ring of islets, originated from one massive coral head in the center of the lagoon, known as Tarḷañ, what anthropologist Laurence M. Carucci has called the "central symbol of Kuwajleen identity" (Carucci 1997a, 163). This coralhead was said to be abundant and teeming with life on one side, but completely devoid of life on the other, and people say that different parts of the coralhead correspond to different parts of the atoll. This is why some islets are lush and others are barren, or why American missile testers bless Kwajalein islet with millions of dollars in land payments for a lucky few while more than thirteen thousand Marshallese workers on nearby Ebeye islet are fated to compete over scarce resources. It also explains why, for instance, some islets of Kwajalein were devastated by the massive battle between Japanese and Americans during the war and why others were left unscathed. Thus the entire atoll, in all its multiplicity and coralloid contradiction, is hewn from the same exact heritage.[2]

Tarḷañ is a symbol for the typhoons of change, the unpredictability of time. In an atoll that has seen wave after wave of overwhelming transformation, from colonization to militarization to nuclearization, Tarḷañ is an icon that stands for "uncertainty, anxious anticipation, 'the rapid beating of the heart in a state of fear' " (Carucci 1997a, 163). For the same reason, the people of Tarḷañ are known to be survivors amidst the typhoons of change; they are always ready for the storms when they come. They know how to make the best of their circumstances "in order to mediate the space between divine grace and disaster" (Carucci 1997a, 165).

"What, where, and when is Pacific History?" asked Matt Matsuda in an essay about the multiplicities of Pacific pasts (Matsuda 2006, par. 3). But, as the Tarḷañ story tells us, does this answer not lie in the substance of the island itself? And is not Pacific islands history the layer upon layer of the organic and inorganic that travels the ocean and forms the reef itself, the rocks and boulders, the coralheads? Is not Pacific islands history the very coral that fuses the Kirin Beer and Coca-Cola bottles of capitalism to the unexploded grenades and rockets of militarism, enmeshing them all with the sunken ships and canoes and bones that came before them? Is not the history of an island's inhabitants so embodied in the land that when that soil is carried elsewhere, as in the tragedy of phosphate mining in Banaba that Katerina Teaiwa describes (2015), part of the spirit of the people moves with it?

This could not be more obvious than in the part of Micronesia that lies north of the equator, what we know today as the Marshall Islands, where over thousands of years people have settled, and especially so in Kwajalein Atoll. In only the short span of the past hundred years, Kwajalein has been sacred Marshallese land and sea, a German and then Japanese copra plantation, a horrific Pacific War battlefield, a support base for nuclear detonations in Bikini or Enewetak Atolls, and most recently a super-high-tech post–Cold War missile-testing and space-surveillance range.

There is another story the Ri-Kuwajleen tell about their atoll, about a flowering tree that sat at the south end of the main islet where the first Marshallese settlers dwelled (Carucci 1997a, 49). It was a tree from which blossomed a type of night-blooming flower (*utilomar*) with such an enchanting and precious fragrance that everyone came to gather its petals to make chiefly adornments.[3]

Some say that this tree did not grow on land but actually out of the reef between two islets (Carucci 1997a, 50). It was a tree that was overflowing with blossoms that could be brought to the chiefs as tribute even when typhoons ravaged the rest of the atoll, and when these white flowers fell into the lagoon they turned into flying fish, enough to feed everyone. *Rū-ruk-jān-leen,* "the people who gather or harvest the fruits [flowers] of the place known as Kuwajleen" is the expression from which the name "Kwajalein" is derived (Carucci 1997a, 49).[4]

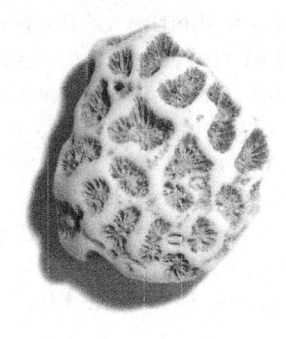

Like the layer upon layer of coral that built up the atoll, myriad Islander canoe voyagers, followed thousands of years later by Spaniards, Germans, Japanese, and Americans, came to harvest Kwajalein's flowers, forming a nuanced and complex genealogy of chiefs, navigators, clans, workers, traders, whalers, missionaries, fishermen, soldiers, and missile testers who all shaped the islands in some way. And since I grew up on Kwajalein, I harvested those flowers too.

Coral Colonizations

> We feel surprise when travelers tell us of the vast dimensions of the Pyramids and other great ruins, but how utterly insignificant are the greatest of these, when compared to these mountains of stone accumulated by the agency of various minute and tender animals! (Darwin in Jones 2007, 14)

In Marshallese, *aelōñ* is a word that means not only atoll and island, but also land and country; it has a deep rootedness in Marshallese identity. Unlike the notion of an isolated, "remote" island, which as the great Pacific islands studies scholar Epeli Hauʻofa reminded us is ultimately a continental view of remoteness and detachment amidst an ocean perceived as a barrier (Hauʻofa 1994), coral is the stuff of migration, ancestry, connectedness, and land. In Marshallese, *wōden kaañal* means "coral drawing force," an expression that alludes to the natural way in which coral attracts fish and all forms of sea life from across the ocean. Lalibjet, the god of the sea, relies upon the power of coral to ensure safety and calm to these islands, to make life possible by balancing the fragile ecosystem, and bringing sustenance and support to all who make these waters their home.

This coral is a sacred, liminal threshold that connects and separates, not unlike Dening's beaches. Marshallese communities harvest white coral gravel called *ḷā* to rake through their villages and around their homes (sometimes as the floor of their homes) as a means of maintaining boundaries between the order of communal domestic space and the wilderness of the ocean. Speaking at the Japan Coral Reef Society, anthropologist Nakazawa Shinichi explained how communities in Okinawa also use coral in this way, as shrines throughout Japan use white gravel stones, to demarcate sacred space. He went further to point out how this is like a symbol of, or border between, life and death as well, that coral is both a primordial womb of humanity and its graveyard all at once.[5]

Coral colonizes: polyps voyage the ocean currents, joining with other coral communities atop subaquatic volcanoes that rise miles above the sea floor to break the surface. They are like seeds that travel from afar to settle upon fertile reefs. Polyps make their journeys with some degree of serendipity. They are swept along with powerful currents and tides, riding the Pacific Current (the Kuroshio, in Japanese), swirling around clockwise; the coral offspring of the Marshall Islands gives birth to the reefs of neighboring Kosrae, Pohnpei, Chuuk, and Yap in the Federated States of Micronesia, which in turn beget the reefs of Palau and up to Guam and Saipan to Ogasawara or over to Taiwan and Okinawa, up to Kyushu, and along the eastern coast of Japan and so on. Coral is all part of a larger genealogy.

Yet, as recent research reveals, their settlements are not at all random, for coral polyps flourish only in favorable places and environments (Dornelas, Connolly, and Hughes 2006, 80–81). When coral spawns, its polyps cross-pollinate between reefs; they deliberately colonize with the intention to thrive. Like coral, human settlers in Oceania were swept along by various currents of migration, driven by politics and other big forces; yet often they have chosen their islands deliberately.

Kwajalein is dynamic and ever-evolving. Like coral, people have also come to this reef called Kwajalein, riding flows, swells, and serendipity. The people who came to this atoll long ago in canoes settled upon the broadest and most plentiful of these islets, becoming the Ri-Kuwajleen (the Kwajalein people) of the islands now known as the Marshall Islands. Other ocean "currents" like trade, science, Romanticism, adventure, slavery, or Christianity would bring other travelers across this reef from across the Pacific, from Europe and North America, and later from Japan. The tide of militarization and empire would wash across the Pacific in the twentieth century and bring other waves of soldiers, civil servants, and engineers, like my father.

Seen from the perspective of marine biology, human beings who travel these waters and settle these islands are all reef organisms. Like coral, they bring their own histories to the reef, territorializing and reterritorializing, adapting to their new surroundings. As Robert Louis Stevenson once related, however, there is a Tahitian proverb that says, "The coral waxes, the palm grows, but man departs" (Jones 2007, 65). Indeed this is true in terms of deep time. The coral endures, but no doubt humans are swept up like the people of Tarḷañ in currents of uncertainty. Still, people leave their mark upon the reef, building upon their predecessors just like other sea creatures leave their histories in the strata.

Insisting "that we make culture and we are made by culture; there is agency and there is structure" (Storey 1996, 11), Antonio Gramsci narrated the dialectical complexity of culture in a way that Edward Said uncannily described as "coral-like" in its approach (Said 1993, 58). Marshall Sahlins tells how anthropologist Leslie White, his mentor, also likened human culture to a coral reef, explaining how human beings are like micro-organisms who all leave behind their small contribution to the greater whole of humanity:

> Lives of great men all remind us
> We can make our lives sublime,
> And in passing leave behind us . . .
> A small deposit of lime. (Sahlins 2003, 13)

In islands across Oceania, this cultural history mixes and cross-pollinates. Into Kwajalein's reef is encoded tens of thousands of years of geologic activity in deep time, followed by thousands of years of voyaging, conquest and settlement, wars and disputes. Layer by layer, new coralheads and islands have formed while others have washed away. In recent centuries, the concrete of Spanish missions has crumbled into the sea with German cisterns, overgrown with flamboyant coral, spongy, brittle, or pinnacled. Japanese ships like the *Shōei* or *Asakaze Maru* nestle upside down, entangled with American Budweiser cans.

◊ ◊ ◊

I do not write this to condone colonialism by any means. Nor do I intend to disregard the immense power discrepancies that have led to the abuse and dislocation of people from their own land. Rather, in thinking about coral as a metaphor for the small, diverse, and marginalized, I am attempting instead to draw attention to the actual participants in the drama of history and show how they are personally implicated, involved, and connected through the larger network of the atoll, and how those histories have sedimented into massive and powerful structures and continued to evolve. Many Japanese or German traders married into local families and stayed in the Marshall Islands until they died; many Japanese families return again and again to mourn the loss of fallen soldiers; many American children who grew up on Kwajalein continue to return in search of "home." It is largely through the mediation of these outsiders that places like Kwajalein have been intertwined into the histories of other localities, through copra traders to Hanover, Germany; through navy sailors to Aichi, Japan; or through missile testers to Huntsville, Alabama.

Some elderly Japanese who remember the colonial period in Micronesia speak of how many children were born of the liaisons between Japanese traders, administrators, or soldiers and Marshallese women. They call these children *otoshidane,* "fallen seeds," a sexual metaphor that refers to the illegitimate child of "a man of rank" (Masuda 1974). Like coral polyps that have traveled from faraway and lodged firmly onto the reef, these "seeds" of colonialism can even be found in the DNA of many Marshall Islanders whose fathers were either killed in the war or repatriated to Japan, often never to return. Though Japan has mostly forgotten this generation of Islanders with Japanese heritage, Marshallese of Japanese heritage often wonder about their ancestors and relatives across the ocean (see chapter 3).

Mauritian poet Khal Torabully writes about the "silenced crossings" of laborers who were sent across the Indian and Atlantic oceans to work as slaves and coolies, and he also invokes the coral metaphor as a way of decolonizing their histories:

> The coral can be both soft, and hard, it can be found in two states, and it is traversed by currents, continuously open to new thoughts and systems. It is a living body with elements which are both vulnerable and solid, it is a symbol of the fluidity of relationships and influences. (Bragard 2005, 229)

Torabully celebrates the creolization and dynamism that resulted from forced migration and points out how colonialism is not just a process of the rich, powerful, and privileged settling on distant shores. Indeed, many migrants who came to Kwajalein and other Pacific places did not do so by choice. There were many "silenced crossings" to Kwajalein that went largely unnoticed.

There were, for instance, the silenced crossings of the Okinawan fishermen who came to the Marshalls looking to make a living. There were the silenced crossings of Korean laborers who were conscripted to work for the Japanese during the war years and who died in the American bombardment.[6] There were also the silenced crossings of the Bikinians and the Rongelapese who were uprooted from their islands and relocated to Kwajalein and elsewhere during the US nuclear tests of the 1940s and 1950s. There were crossings even within the atoll of

Ri-Kuwajleen who were displaced by American missile testing on their own soil and relocated to tiny Ebeye islet.

Each of these crossings left its mark in the atoll, its layer in the reef. Though the history books may have long forgotten these moments, the coral remembers. It is this inclusive and optimistic definition of encounter—the genealogy of coral and its many reefs—upon which I would like to meditate, to create space around the ongoing conversation about indigenous/nonindigenous and the tenacious binary this creates. I am writing here not to delineate who is indigenous and who is a colonizer, but rather to consider the possibility that there is a difference between *actual people* and the "currents" upon which they journey and that regardless of how cruel, contradictory, or accidental, these migrations have sedimented layer upon layer and formed real meanings, emplaced and embodied.

Concrete: Quick-Drying Colonialism

In contrast to the coralline model of history, which acknowledges the agency of individuals in terms of the larger reef, conventional histories usually teach about the victories and losses of nations. I refer in this book to these kinds of layers of history as "concrete." In Kwajalein and many other heavily militarized islands throughout Oceania, coral was literally used as an aggregate, mixed with cement and water to form quick-drying concrete that could be used to construct fortifications or to form roads and runways. Concrete is the pulverization, amalgamation, and flattening of all these coralline histories into one condensed and monolithic mass. Nationalism and historical revisionism are examples of this.

Henri Lefebvre suggests that the production of space is a political process in which space is ultimately homogenized and dominated by hegemonic interests (Lefebvre 1991, 411). Michel Foucault even proposes that "a whole history remains to be written of spaces as the history of powers... from the great strategies of geo-politics to the little politics of the habitat" (Foucault and Gordon 1980, 149). These two theorists developed the idea of "thirdspace," the notion of social, "lived" space, and the constantly negotiated and renegotiated meanings people make about their environments, a concept that has also been explored considerably by Edward Soja (1989).[7]

In many nationalistic accounts of the state, "concrete" narratives are considered "real" and solid, as opposed to narratives that are vague, contradictory, or abstract. Here I am describing the actual physical process by which colonialism and militarism in the Pacific Islands have attempted to reduce the multiplicities of coral into something that is uniform, predictable, and homogeneous. Concrete is a metaphor that describes the dramatic ways in which the organic, abstract, and local histories of individuals are co-opted and *concretized* into compelling (and indeed convincingly "real") narratives that serve the interest of national and global politics. Covered over with streamlined, seemingly authoritative versions of "the truth," the atoll appears to lose its complexity and genealogical heritage.

Take, for instance, how in their quest to possess the Central Pacific, both Japan and the United States in the last century physically shaped Kwajalein Atoll into a military "steppingstone" between the two countries. In the early 1940s, Japanese battalions of *setsueibutai* construction workers, including large numbers of Korean laborers, used dynamite to break enormous holes in the reef around the main islets of Kwajalein and Roi-Namur. These reef rocks were used to build concrete seawalls, buildings, and the first airstrip, still the main islet's most prominent feature. After the war, earth was moved and shifted again later by American military engineers, who blasted even larger holes in the reef, dredged away entire sacred coralheads, and expanded the contours of different islets. At the same time, the US Department of Energy used Kwajalein as a support base from which to conduct sixty-seven horrific atomic blasts in Bikini and Enewetak Atolls, permanently altering the contours of lagoons and poisoning the homelands and bodies of people throughout a wide swath of the northern Marshall Islands.

These traumatic reshapings of reefs and rewritings of land correspond to how hegemonic histories have oversimplified and rewritten the atoll's complexity. The American national memory of invasion and "liberation" of Marshall Islanders from Japanese forces in 1944 has become the official story of what "really" happened. It is a story that effectively inscribed Kwajalein as a "perpetual battlefield" (Carucci 1989, 73), later becoming the pretext for testing nuclear weaponry in the Marshall Islands and using Kwajalein islet for military purposes.

Against the flows of real human bodies in real physical space, these layers of political or public discourse obscure the interrelated and nuanced coral-reef-like connections between people and place. Concrete hegemonizes history. The American victory narrative articulates Kwajalein with the United States and memorializes the land as intrinsically American, simultaneously disallowing the stories of Marshall Islanders, Japanese, and Koreans, let alone ordinary Americans and many others. Likewise, Vicente Diaz (2001, 175) has described how the compelling story of "liberation" in Guam has done more to reinforce American hegemony than anything else.

Concrete has a way of fixing the historical drama of global politics in place. Even seventy years after the Pacific War, the hackneyed triangle of American heroes, Asian foes, and Islander victims is replayed in public narratives. "Liberation Day" is still celebrated by some island communities in the Marshall Islands, even though full compensation has not yet been (and may never be) paid to the victims of US nuclear tests during the Cold War (Barker 2004, 58–59). The US military relocation of its bases to Guam is often portrayed in local media as a positive development and economic boost for island communities,[8] while Japanese overseas development assistance is sometimes seen as a gesture in exchange for increased fishing rights (Tarte 1995). Meanwhile as climate change gets more and more attention, Islanders in low-lying atolls like the Marshalls are described as the losers in the global game: colonized, nuclearized, and now flooded by rising tides (Torrice 2000).[9]

In the deeper history of the atoll, however, even though space may seem homogenized and hegemonized by state narratives and agendas, I am a bit more optimistic about the enduring power of place and the ways in which the "messiness" of the local can transcend the global. Certainly, the impact of these outside influences has been enormous, but for people who have a strong connection to their land, it is possible to see through the surface to the layers below to deeper meanings and pasts. In the deep-time scheme of things, even concrete breaks down. Its surface cracks, the coral breaks through, the atoll's layers get thicker and deeper. Concrete turns out to be but only one of the many entangled and intertwined destinies of the reef. In the perennial deep-time competition between coral and concrete, the atoll always wins.

Atollscapes: The Multilayered Present

An atollic Marshallese sense of time is aware of the many sedimented layers of concrete and coral in the past that make up the present. The power of place remains as an enduring frame around which these competing meanings, identities, and histories are arbitrated. I call these multiply emplaced histories "atollscapes," in mind of Epeli Hau'ofa's point that Pacific histories cannot be read "without knowing how to read our landscapes (and seascapes)" (Hau'ofa 2000, 466).

Atollscapes are layers of historical cultural reality that exist in perpetuity and inform the present. They are neither "sentimental sediment" nor the cultural artifacts excavated in the service of archaeology—not fixed, not essential. Like Appadurai's idea of the ethnoscape and other social imaginaries (1991), they are fluid. Atollscapes are possibilities, different versions and evocations of the past, different rememberings; thus they are dynamic and living, like the ever-evolving coral reef itself. They are multiplicities spreading in all directions.

The migratory multiplicities and nomad histories of coral resonate with the work of Deleuze and Guattari (1988), whose idea of the rhizome suggests an idea of reality that is antihierarchical and lacking a center. Coral is a submarine version of the rhizome, so it is no wonder that the two theorists ask, "Does not the East, Oceania in particular, offer something like a rhizomatic model opposed in every respect to the Western model of the tree?" (Deleuze and Guattari 1988, 18).

I see atollscapes as a rhizomatic way to see the connections between multiple, contradictory perspectives on the past and triangulate collective memories from different groups.[10] Kwajalein is a contact zone (Pratt 1992), a contested landscape in many respects that has been ruled by a long succession of "chiefs."[11] But as my Marshallese friend advised me, one deals with the problem of arguing chiefs and disputed land by "telling the truth *as you see it.*" In other words, I can only relate the multiple truths I have encountered as historian and ethnographer. So it goes without saying that the atollscapes that I narrate in this book are *my own* renderings of different contexts; for I am implicated in some way in each of the histories I tell. As Tessa Morris-Suzuki writes, "Reflecting on our implication in the processes of history does not produce a single authoritative 'historical truth' . . . it does require 'historical truthfulness'—an open-ended and evolving relationship with past events and people" (2005, 27). The atollscapes I provide in this book about Kwajalein are thus not "proof" or "facts" about the past; they are a "truthful" acknowledgment of multiple and often contradictory truths and the dynamic processes by which those truths are remembered.

As Ty Kāwika Tengan explains, Hawaiian oral traditions are

understood implicitly to relate only one aspect of "truth." "The term *moʻolelo,* which itself translates to 'succession of talk' or a 'fragment of a story,' highlights the partiality of any truth and the need to view it as a part of a larger collective knowledge" (Tengan 2003, 90).

Like the Hawaiian context, Marshall Islander *bwebwenato* traditions are filled with multiple versions of the same stories told from different perspectives, as both Carucci (2001) and McArthur (2004) have discussed. These variations of stories are not considered to be contradictory or mutually exclusive, but rather to be integral parts of a larger collective whole. My own research revealed various interpretations of Kwajalein's history, not only from a wide range of indigenous Marshall Islander vantage points but also from Japanese and American perspectives. It would be impossible to account for *all* these narratives in the scope of this project, but I have attempted at least to gesture toward this multiplicity as a way of integrating these many "partial truths" into a larger collective story.

In ethnographic terms, anthropologist Karl G. Heider (1988) uses the term "*Rashōmon* effect," after Kurosawa's film (1950) based on the stories of Akutagawa Ryūnosuke (1917), to describe the disagreement that occurs between multiple ethnographers dealing with the same subject.[12] But while Heider points out that "ethnographies are made, not found" (1988, 73–74), he seems less interested in the value of multiple narratives and discourses (which is arguably what interested Kurosawa) and more interested in trying to resolve the discrepancies that obscure essential truths about a culture.

In this book, I relate a number of atollscapes as part of my ongoing conversation and engagement with a number of archival sources, groups, individuals, and places; yet unlike Heider, I am not as interested in actual events or facts as I am in the various ways in which the past is remembered, related, and sedimented into the ever-evolving coral. Like Kurosawa, I am drawn more to the narratives and the "mythologies" (Barthes 2000) that infuse each atollscape with context and meaning; I am interested in the ways those narratives have become a part of Kwajalein's heritage.

It is not my intention to conflate very different Oceanian epistemologies, but the Palauan model of history that Karen Nero describes (1987) comes closest to the atollscape model I attempt in this study. Choosing to narrate the past through a uniquely Palauan "layered" approach, Nero subverts Western chronological history in favor of one that is firmly rooted in place:

> My understanding of the Palauan sense of history is that it differs fundamentally from a Western layman's sense of history which tends toward a linear development through measured sequences, often individually oriented. In the West the most important dimension is temporal. I believe the most important dimension to a Palauan sense of history is spatial, geographical, and that Palauan history is incorporative rather than individual in concept. (Nero 1987, 44)

In the Palauan model, Nero explains, time is often conceived in terms of a present moment that is related to the eternal, rather than as a timeline model of past, present, and future (Nero 1987, 32).[13] She describes how the past is thus perpetuated into the future through constant negotiation and renegotiation or reconstruction in the present. Local proverbs also point to the multivalence of political discourse, of "double and triple entendres" that are mindful of multiple layers and contexts (1987, 46).

My objective here is to take an incorporative, intersective approach to the past, grounding these conflicting pasts in the solidity of the reef. The Marshallese term *pedped* refers to flat open reef, "the foundation of the island and the atoll," and it is made out of rock-solid coral (called *bar*). I borrow the image of that sturdy foundation, evoking the metaphor of the atoll that can embrace contradiction and still thrive, in an attempt to give priority to the actual place itself, imagining history from the view of the land and lagoon and from the coral teeming with life (and death) that it comprises.

Re-membering Kwajalein

I call my process of considering these multiple atollscapes "remembering the coral and concrete," not only because it is a process of making conscious these many layers, but because it is also a process of acknowledging the wholeness of the entire atoll. In the maelstrom of global political forces that swirls around places like Kwajalein, it is easy to lose sight of the connectedness and relationality of history and memory. Despite the atoll's being firmly rooted to one massive undersea volcano, on the surface we only see islets separated by channels of water that flow between lagoon and ocean. We forget the shallow reefs that connect in much the same way we forget the connections between the present and the past, or between Islander voyagers and the waves of settlers that came after.

I intend the process of remembering to be one of *re-membering* as well, in homage to anthropologist Barbara Myerhoff (1982), whose work with elderly victims of trauma made her conscious of the importance of memory over the course of human lives. She describes it this way:

> To signify this special type of recollection, the term "Re-membering" may be used, calling attention to the reaggregation of members, the figures who belong to one's life story, one's own prior selves, as well as significant others who are part of the story. Remembering, then, is a purposive, significant unification. (Myerhoff 1982, 240)

For the generations of Marshall Islanders who have been displaced from their land; for the Japanese, Korean, and American bereaved relatives of war dead; and for the multitudes of other people who have been connected to Kwajalein in some way, re-membering takes on special importance. Those who have plucked the flowers of the "Kwajalein tree" are linked together through the common heritage of the same place. The atollscapes I explore in this book are stories of that interwoven heritage.[14]

Hokari Minoru, in his groundbreaking book *Gurindji Journey: A Japanese Historian in the Outback* (2015), contemplated the possibility of a cross-cultural history that takes into consideration the agency and interconnectedness of the conversation happening between groups of people at the local level. In his work with the Gurindji people of Northern Territory, Australia, Hokari tells a history in which he personally participates by linking (and re-membering) the space and time of local Japan to that of local Australian country. In the work that eventually led to his book, he wrote, "Local history is a fragment which supposes its implicit all-ness. . . . This fragment gestures toward the complexity and multiplicity of everything without threatening that totality itself" (Hokari 2001, 215).[15]

Like Hokari, in the model of the atoll I imagine integrity in the local, rather than isolation and irrelevance. The orality of personal memory, indeed "oral history," is one in which the speaker *relates* seemingly disparate ideas together. Relating, articulating, and narrating are always about simultaneously telling and linking. Yet there is a big difference between the kinds of articulations made locally and the meta-narratives produced by nations in order to justify power and conquest.

Perhaps it is this atollic view of history, of re-membering Kwajalein's coral and concrete, that has made it possible for Marshall Islanders to triumph over tremendous adversity and rise with dignity above the horrors of World War II, the worst nuclear detonations known to humankind, and perpetual dispossession. There are other stories from other Marshallese atoll communities, both local and diasporic, in which people have dealt with similar adversity and survived. And I would argue that these reefs of history, like Hauʻofa's sea of islands and Dening's beaches, have salience for all of the Pacific in one way or another, not only as sites of encounter but as sites of memory, mixing, and mediation.

CHAPTER 2

Mapping "the Martial Islands"

Imagi-Nations and Mythologies of Kwajalein

> The world we take for granted—the real world—is made ... out of the accumulated thought and labor of the past. It is presented to us on the platter of the map, *presented,* that is, *made present,* so that whatever invisible, unattainable, erasable past or future can become part of our living ... *now* ... *here.*
>
> —Denis Wood, The Power of Maps[1]

IT IS UNCANNY THAT THE WORD MARSHALL—the name of British sea captain John Marshall, after whom the islands were named on European maps in the nineteenth century—should be homophonous with the term "martial." Marshallese land and sea have been contested in battles between Islanders throughout the ages, and throughout the last century they played a large role in the national objectives of world superpowers. From when Japan claimed the islands from Germany in World War I to when the United States used the islands as "steppingstones" en route to Tokyo in World War II; from the Cold War–era nuclear tests to the "Star Wars" missile tests to the present-day War on Terror, the "Martial Islands" have been implicated in some of the most significant military missions of our times.

All too often, the history of Oceania is told through a "Western" optic. In the case of the Marshall Islands, most published histories have been told in terms of the sixty-seven American nuclear tests that took place there between 1946 and 1958, or through the lens of American historians and military planners who regale us with their triumphant tales of victory in World War II. Awash in this tide of American national memory and selective amnesia, we do not learn about the individual lives of ordinary people, the Marshall Islanders, Koreans, Okinawans, Japanese, Hawaiians, and Americans caught up in the actual experience.

Several of my own mentors have shared my concern about the relationship between "big" and "little" histories. This is the question that drives Greg Dening's study of historical narrative in *The Death of William Gooch,* where he unpacks the multiple "big" histories of European empire and Hawaiian interisland warfare as they intersect with the "small" life of one twenty-two-year-old British seaman who was killed on Waimea Beach in 1792 (Dening 1988). It is the same tension that runs through David Hanlon's work as he navigates between American discourses of development and the lives of Micronesians in the postwar period (Hanlon 1998, 2014). Tessa Morris-Suzuki ponders this same historical dilemma in her study of the Cold War repatriation of Koreans from Japan to North Korea when she asks, "What happens when the small stories of personal lives and the grand stories of global politics intersect? How far are we, as individuals, free to choose the courses of our lives, and how far are we the playthings of historical forces too large for us even to see, let alone control?" (Morris-Suzuki 2007, 13).

Kwajalein Atoll, where the same small place has meant so many things in both personal lives and massive global projects, is a productive site through which to consider the ways in which little and big histories, coral and concrete, sediment upon each other to form an interconnected but incongruous past and present. Layer upon layer, different nations and groups have imagined and reimagined, mapped and remapped the atoll in contradictory ways—erasing, obscuring, and co-opting each other's influence. Unlike coral, which is dynamic, gradual, evolving, genealogical, migratory, messy, and in flux, concrete pretends to quickly fix meaning into place and make it permanent. Concrete covers and appropriates the coral; it delimits the ways in which individual actors make sense of their world, streamlining the rough edges and smoothing the contradictions. It essentializes and draws boundaries that suit the political agendas of globalized American power, not the lives of ordinary local people. Kwajalein has been recruited into the narratives of many different countries, sometimes with tragic consequences for the people whose lives have been caught in the middle.

Of course, as I have already explained through the paradigm of the atoll, the relationship between coral and concrete is dialectical;

in a Foucauldian sense the individual is like coral, "the very *material* of power, the thing through which it finds its expression" (Mansfield 2000, 55). In telling Kwajalein's many stories, I have thus chosen to explore themes of both structure and agency by discussing both the "big" global histories and the "small" histories of human actors, to defamiliarize and deconstruct the surface layers of "concrete" while revealing the "coral" underneath. In each of the atollscapes in this book, we will look at Kwajalein's history as a "Martial Island," first by relating some of the most significant public narratives that have figured centrally in American, Japanese, and Marshallese imaginings of the atoll, and then by seeing how those narratives intersected the lives of ordinary people.

Missions and Mythologies

The word "mission" has enjoyed a long and illustrious history in Oceania, where in 1668 Spanish Jesuit missionaries from the Philippines were some of the first on record to bring Christianity to the northern Mariana Islands (Lal and Fortune 2000, 178). Though the Marshall Islands had been a marginal part of the Spanish colonial project in Micronesia and fell under the aegis of the Catholic Church to some degree, it was barely impacted by Christianity in the way that Saipan, Guam, and many other western island groups were. It was not until 1857 that the Hawai'i-based American Board of Commissioners for Foreign Missions (ABCFM) established a Protestant mission in the Marshall Islands at Ebon, and it is that year that Marshall Islanders celebrate as the arrival of Christianity in their country (Hezel 1983, 201–202).

The Church (particularly the Congregationalist Protestant Church) plays a central role in Marshall Islander communities nowadays and there are also an increasing number of active religious missions,[2] but in this book I contemplate the idea of mission in a military sense. Several historians have conducted excellent studies of the Church in Micronesia already; my focus here is on the various other colonial, economic, scientific, and nuclear missions that have shaped the contemporary "Martial Islands" in the twentieth century.[3]

When I was growing up on Kwajalein, the word "mission" carried with it a very specific meaning. As in the 1970s, for today's residents of the United States Army Kwajalein Atoll military installation, it refers to one of the many testing operations that happen regularly.

Nowadays, a "mission" could mean the interception of an incoming dummy warhead from the continental United States, the launch of a new kind of missile, or the testing of a civilian spacecraft by Elon Musk's SpaceX corporation, but for most of American "Kwaj" employees, the word simply means "hard work," whether it involves laboring in the control room, enforcing security, managing communications, or handling an influx of temporary duty specialists from overseas.[4]

There is something prosaic about the way the word "mission" is used nowadays on Kwajalein that is worth further consideration. "We're having a *mission* tonight, so I won't be home for dinner," for example, is the way the term is used by many Americans on the base. For many American residents, a mission is a slight inconvenience that usually means flights might be delayed, parts of the atoll will be closed to fishing or diving trips, and work might be harder than usual. For Marshall Islander residents of other islets in the atoll, it also means that a number of islets are off-limits. Nevertheless, the mission of intercontinental ballistic missile testing at Kwajalein is commonplace and natural. It is so ordinary and ingrained in the everyday existence of the population that it has become somehow innocent; it is all too easy to forget the military nature of the operation involved.

"The very principle of myth," writes Roland Barthes, is that "it transforms history into nature" (2000, 129). Kwajalein is a superb example of the ways in which multiple "mythologies" converge and multiple histories are taken for granted. Reading Barthes, I would argue that the history of America's military mission in Oceania has been "naturalized" into the "mythology" of everyday American life on present-day Kwajalein. It is now taken for granted that the Pacific Ocean is an "American Lake" (Hayes, Zarsky, and Bello 1986) and that Kwajalein is a major hub of national missile defense. It is taken for granted that "the Americans" live on Kwaj and "the Marshallese" live on Ebeye. Few people think twice about why there are ruined Japanese structures throughout the atoll; for those buildings remain as testimony to grand narratives of history in which "the Japanese" were fanatic militarists who held the Marshall Islands captive until they were crushed by American "liberators."

Barthes' project of semiology, while structuralist in many ways, can be a negotiable and fluid reading practice that takes into account the interplay between "texts" and the contexts in which they were produced, and this is most evident in the ways in which a careful reading of everyday mythologies has the potential to demystify public narratives and popular culture. Semiology can be a productive methodology in the analysis of visual images, and as Barthes has exemplified in his earlier work, it also is a useful means of decoding other texts (Rose 2001, 96). *Mythologies,* his tongue-in-cheek critique of popular culture in 1950s Paris, is powerful in the way it defamiliarizes and unpacks those things that "go without saying" (Barthes 2000, 11). Kurt Vonnegut, a former anthropologist turned novelist, undertook a similar project when he satirized his native Detroit in the novel *Breakfast of Champions* (1973), a novel that treated middle-class American consumer culture (and humanity in general) as if it were completely alien to the reader.

Kwajalein is a site where multiple concrete missions have sedimented with the coral of the atoll, leaving behind atollscape upon atollscape of layered history. Throughout the following chapters, like Barthes and Vonnegut, I attempt to decode the missions layered upon my childhood home as they are encoded in maps, photography, art, music, films, and even the land itself. After Dening (1988), I do so by *present*-ing the past worlds from which those mythologies derived, digging down into the depths of the reef.

Concrete Cartographies

Maps are a useful way of getting to the core of the many concrete narratives of Kwajalein and de-naturalizing the mythologies that have sedimented there. Mapping is, after all, mythmaking: "The map is always there to deny that the significations piled on top of it are there at all," explains Wood. "It is only a map after all, and the pretense is that it is innocent, a servant of that eye that sees things as they really are" (1992, 106). Maps thus reveal much about the mapmaker when read with more suspicion or scrutiny. They lead us to a deeper understanding of the context in which they were drawn.

> [The map] is, of course, an illusion: *there is nothing natural about a map.* It is a cultural artifact, a cumulation of choices made among choices every one of which reveals a value: not the world, but a slice of a piece of the world; not nature but a slant on it; not innocent, but loaded with intentions and purposes; not directly, but through a glass; not straight, but mediated by words and other signs; not, in a word, as it is, but in . . . *code.* (Wood 1992, 108)

Wood's argument is reflected by Turnbull (2000), whose study focuses more broadly on the production of knowledge and transnational projections of power. Using the map of southern Oceania based on what the great chiefly navigator from Raiatea, Tupaia, drew for Captain James Cook, Turnbull emphasizes the contrast between European cartographical practices and those of "Polynesians," arguing that the latter used the embodied knowledge of navigation, a "performative" rather than representational modality (Turnbull 2000, 122). Yet Turnbull's portrayal of Pacific Islander mappings is essentialist. By focusing on navigation out of context with Islander notions of land tenure and identity, he makes it seem as if Islanders do not also map their lands and seas with the sort of political intent imbued in the maps of Europeans.[5]

Jolly deconstructed the Tupaia map and proposed that such a geographic representation was likely "*not* his indigenous view," adding that Pacific Islander notions of region around the time of Cook would have been communicated through genealogical stories and chants (Jolly 2007, 509). Comparing Hau'ofa's "Sea of Islands" vision of Oceania (1994) to the "ethnological typologies" of Europeans and American notions of the "Pacific Rim" (Dirlik 1993), she considers the impact of Dumont D'Urville's labeling of Polynesia, Micronesia, and Melanesia on subsequent mappings and understandings of Oceania. Arguing that indigenous and foreign representations of the Pacific have respectively corresponded to codes of "genealogy" versus "cartography," she reminds us of how these two codes created the effect of "double-vision" as foreigners co-opted indigenous navigational practices and Islanders took on "Western" conceptualizations of region.

The D'Urvillian mapping of Oceania is often cited as a regional problematic that has inscribed false and meaningless disparities between island groups; yet the overall colonial and economic "development" of the Pacific Ocean has been most responsible for divergent imaginaries of the area. D'Urville's conceptualization of Micronesia, for example, included Kiribati and Nauru, which lay below the equator but shared some "cultural" affinities with their northern neighbors, but these southern areas were split from the rest of Micronesia in the early part of the twentieth century. Kiribati was settled by British in the 1830s and Nauru, after being colonized by Germany up until World War I, was also administered as a British protectorate. Neither of these island nations was colonized by Japan in the same way as northern Micronesian islands were.[6] They were also never a part of the US Trust Territory of the Pacific Islands. Nowadays, United Airlines services only the Micronesian islands north of the equator, linking Japan and Manila with the "resort" destinations of Guam, Saipan, Palau, Chuuk, Pohnpei, Kosrae, the Marshall Islands, and Honolulu. Despite the proximity between the Marshalls and Kiribati or Nauru, with no regular service other than to Hawai'i or back toward Guam, traveling to other parts of Oceania from Majuro is a time-consuming and difficult exercise. Marshall Islanders are thus aware of their genealogical and historical connections with nearby islands to the south, but few have a chance to venture below the equator. As one Marshallese senior diplomat once said to me about Tonga, "We don't play rugby and cricket like they do down there." American and Japanese projections of power have been so effective that basketball and *yakyū* (baseball) are official Marshallese pastimes.[7]

As Shapiro writes, "To the extent that the nation-state geography remains descriptive (what some call 'realistic') and ahistorical, the ethics and politics of space remain unavailable to political contention" (1997, 16). No map—indigenous, foreign, or otherwise—is innocent. My desire here is to look at a number of different mythologies and examine some of the ways these political agendas have been "mapped" (literally and figuratively) onto the "Martial Islands" from a number of vantage points emerging from both within and without. I will look at the Japanese mission of *nanshin* ("southward expansionism") in the context of the Japanese "Nanyō" regional imaginary of Oceania. I will then move on to explore the American mission of "liberation" during the Pacific War and how it locally transformed, renamed, and reshaped Kwajalein Atoll. Finally, I will consider the ways in which the Marshallese landowners of Kwajalein have remapped and remembered their home islets in response to these foreign discourses with their own mission of "homecoming," a courageous reclaiming of their land, lagoon, and history.

Nanshin: Japanese Journeys Southward

The word Nanyō literally translates to "South Seas," and it is for this reason that it has been described as such in much of the English language literature about Japan's administration of Micronesia from roughly 1914 through 1945 (see Higuchi 1987; Peattie 1988). Yet rarely is there a differentiation in discussions of Nanyō, at least in English, about the difference between Japan's perspective toward

Micronesia versus all of Oceania, or toward the whole frontier that lay to the south of the Japanese archipelago. Translating Nanyō as "South Seas" misses the important point that the *kanji* for Nanyō are actually homologous with Tōyō (the "East") and Seiyō (the "West").[8] In the emerging early twentieth-century Japanese pan-Asian and Oceanic imaginary of empire, later aggrandized by the immediate prewar discourse of the Daitōa Kyōeiken (Greater East Asia Co-Prosperity Sphere), Japan situated itself at the center of the "East" in opposition to Europe and America in the "West." The "South" was thus another "Other" with which to compare the Japanese home islands.

Although it was more a controversial ideal than an official policy, Japan's predominant "mission" in the Marshall Islands before the war was one of southward expansion (*nanshin*) and colonization.[9] As the desire for a robust economy, powerful navy, and maritime presence grew in the burgeoning empire, intellectuals and opinion leaders like Shiga Shigetaka, Hattori Tōru, Taguchi Ukichi, and Takekoshi Yosaburō spawned a new "manifest destiny" to expand into the "South" (Akimichi 1997, 245; Peattie 1988, 37). The "South" that Nanyō actually encompassed was extraordinarily vague and amorphous, corresponding at times to Micronesia (more precisely, Nanyō Guntō), otherwise known as Inner Nanyō (Uchi Nanyō or Ura Nanyō), headquartered in Palau, and sometimes referring to all of Southeast Asia and the entirety of Oceania, otherwise known as Outer Nanyō (Soto Nanyō or Omote Nanyō), which was focused around the Japanese colony of Taiwan. In my research for this book, for example, I would typically search for the keyword "Nanyō" and come up with hundreds of references to Taiwan, the Philippines, New Guinea, Vietnam, Indonesia, Australia, and sometimes even India—*not* Micronesia. Indeed, the prewar concept of the co-prosperity sphere was a grandiose vision that would encompass not only Manchuria to the west but also much of Asia and Oceania in the "South," with Tokyo at its epicenter.

This map, published in 1931, illustrates how Japan imagined the "South" as an extension of the Japanese empire. The straight lines emanating from Yokohama, Kobe, and Hakata in the Japanese home islands represent major transport and shipping routes with hubs at Saipan and Palau, the two major gateways to Micronesia. From Palau, these routes reach farther south and east to the Philippines and Indonesia. In an easterly direction, these sea routes head directly into the Nanyō Guntō, to Truk (Chuuk), Ponape (Pohnpei), Kusaie (Kosrae), and Jaluit, the district center of the Marshall Islands. Undersea communications lines also link Okinawa with Yap, Tokyo and Ogasawara with Guam, and stretch, via Midway, all the way over to connect with the large Japanese population of Hawai'i. According to this map, aside from the fine print subtly indicating US, British, and Dutch territories in a few places, the Pacific is available for Japan's taking.

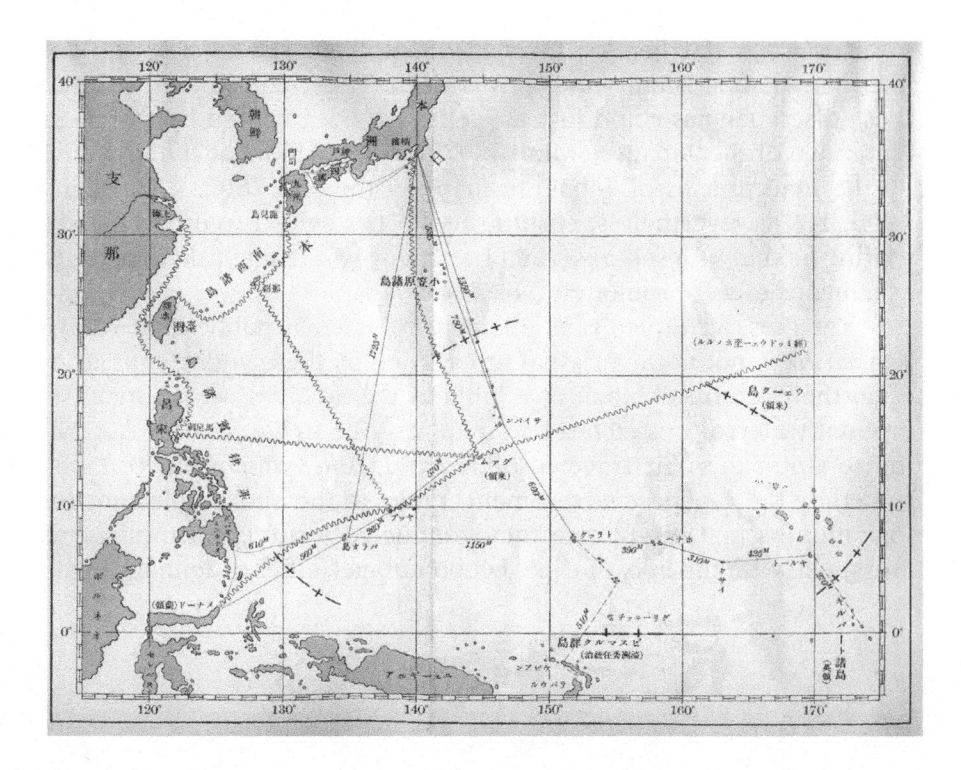

The origins of Japan's involvement in Micronesia began in the Marshall Islands. In 1884, when the British schooner *Ada* reported to authorities in Yokohama that a crew of Japanese pearl traders on their way back to Japan from Australia had been shipwrecked and murdered at Lae Atoll in the Rālik chain of the Marshalls, Foreign Minister Inoue Kaoru immediately dispatched Suzuki Tsunenori (Keikun) and Gotō Taketarō to investigate (Peattie 1988, 9–10). As Peattie describes, there are discrepancies between the reports filed by the two men after they returned to Japan and the several versions of the journey that were published by Suzuki (Peattie 1988, 11). These published accounts were later discredited by Nakajima Hiroshi[10] as being exaggerated or even faked,[11] a foil, perhaps, for Suzuki to conceal the extent of his journeys farther southward to Samoa and other island groups like the Solomon Islands and New Guinea. Takayama Jun argued that these discrepancies could just as well have been caused by the sheer ignorance of the Japanese Ministry of Foreign Affairs at the time and by the inaccuracies of Japanese maps in the late 1800s (Takayama 1995, 189). Nevertheless, Nishino Ryōta has since explored Suzuki's writing as that of a self-absorbed raconteur who embellished his tales as a means of self-promotion (Nishino 2016).

Yet these critiques refer mainly to Suzuki's publication *Nanyō Tanken Jikki*, not to the original report filed by these young emissaries upon their return to Japan, available in the archives, which includes original watercolor sketches and maps on fine tissue paper.[12] According to Gotō, the pair traveled aboard the *Ada* (which was commissioned by the Japanese government) down to the Marshall Islands for four months in 1884, where they conducted a survey of the islands and spoke with the *irooj* of Ujae, Lebon Kabua (father of Jeimata), who

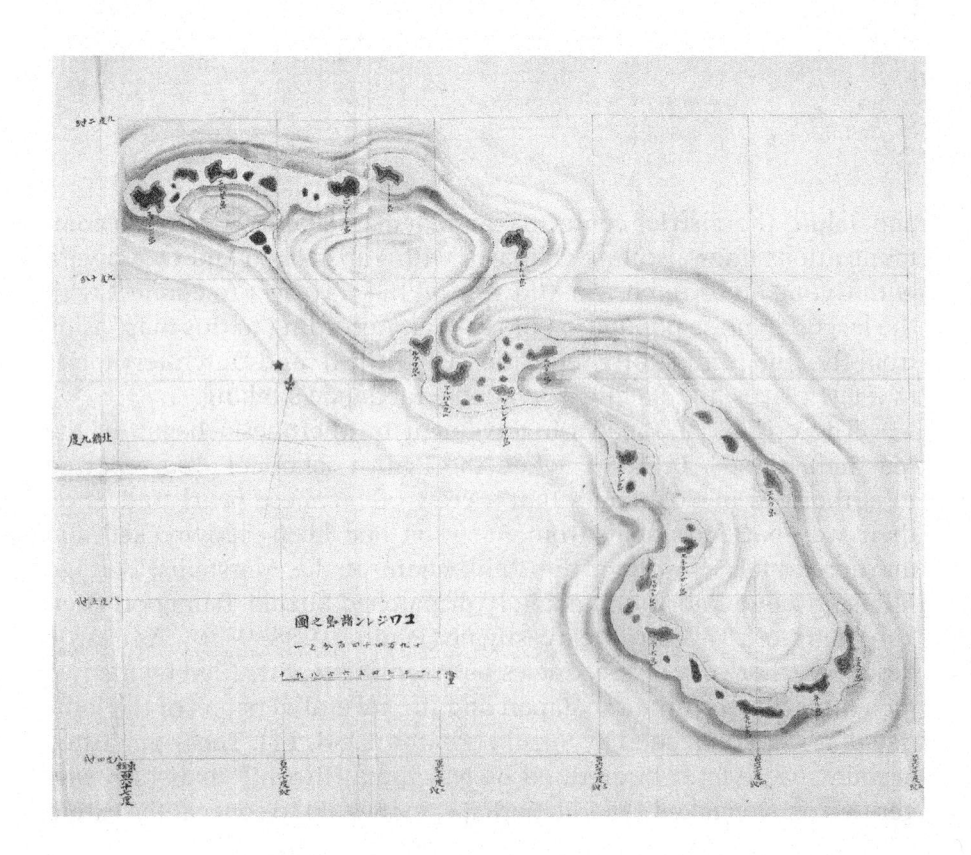

Mapping "the Martial Islands"

told them that Larrelia, a leader of Lae, had probably been responsible for the crime (Gotō and Suzuki 1885). Kabua also apparently told them that there were no Westerners allowed in the Marshall Islands, despite the presence of missionaries and traders (Peattie 1988, 12). Suzuki and Gotō, who only traveled between Kwajalein, Ujae, Namu, Ailinglaplap, and Lae, never saw any European or American presence and thus sensed that the Marshalls could be claimed for Japan, even though Germany would soon annex the islands (Peattie 1988, 12).

Despite the dry and impersonal recollections of the written narrative, the original watercolor illustrations and maps that illustrate this journey in the Marshall Islands provide a strong sense of the fanciful exoticism with which Japanese of that era viewed the islands. Suzuki's map of Kwajalein Atoll (which he spells Kowajiren Shotō) is stylized in an almost dreamy, *ukiyo-e*[13] fashion, with swirly ripples of lagoon and ocean and shapely green islets fringed in red. The atoll, however, while beautifully portrayed, is geographically inaccurate. The names of islets (like Kwajalein and Ebeye) and their geographical proximity to one another are relatively correct. The general shape of the atoll also corresponds somewhat, although the islands themselves are more or less artistic distortions and design motifs.

Suzuki's map and other illustrations, like the aerial landscape painting he made of Kwajalein "port," evoke an exotic faraway southern world of strange but virgin islands that exist for Japan to possess. He uses elaborate painting techniques to Japanize Kwajalein, to incorporate the atoll into a Japanese imaginary that is vague in some respects and precise in others. He is careful to paint lines of longitude and latitude, for example, yet uninterested in the details of which islet is located where. Here Kwajalein is less a specific place than it is a rendering of *any* exotic tropical atoll. Suzuki's writing and imagination of the Marshalls is one that tries to make generalizations about *all* of Oceania, to explicate a "common culture" rather than make claims about any specific island or its customs (Akimichi 1997, 245).

This is consistent with the ways in which Japanese colonial and military discourses authored a sort of uniformity throughout the "Asia-Pacific" imaginary of the co-prosperity sphere and especially in the Nanyō Guntō. Beginning in 1922, the Nanyō Guntō, administered out of a provincial government bureau headquartered in Palau, was treated as a singular entity. There was little sense of distinction in Japanese official narratives between the Marshall Islands at one end of the region and Palau at the other.

This conglomeration of all of Micronesia was further effected when Japan withdrew from the League of Nations in 1933. The Nanyō Guntō increasingly began to be imagined as Japan's "lifeline of the sea" (*umi no seimeisen*), a maritime barrier that would protect against the threat of foreign invasion and influence. The term "lifeline of the sea" appears frequently in the public discourse of the late 1930s. The song "Taiheiyō Kōshin Kyoku" ("March of the Pacific," Kingu Male Chorus 1939) glamorizes the term as a heroic destiny for all young sailors. This militaristic ideal also found its way into the textbooks produced by the Nanyō-chō for Islander schoolchildren throughout the islands.

Such imaginings of the region were depicted most vividly in the film *Umi no Seimeisen,* a propaganda film that was likely hewn from earlier ethnographic documentary footage (Saeki 1932) and edited to promote a more militaristic message by the Japanese Ministry of the Navy in 1938. The animated maps in the film represented Micronesia as "the maritime defense" buffer—sort of a gigantic balloon—while Manchuria and Korea were portrayed as a land-based "continental defense" cushion in the north. The mission of the League of Nations mandate, purportedly to nurture and develop the islands for the sake of their own eventual self-determination, is rendered completely irrelevant in *Umi no Seimeisen*. By the late 1930s, militarization had reversed this rhetoric so that Micronesia existed solely to protect the Japanese home islands. The film portrays the monstrous, clawed hand of foreign enemies (such as the United States) grabbing at the Nanyō Guntō balloon and threatening to pop it instead of attacking the Japanese home archipelago; in this militaristic propaganda, Micronesia became nothing more than one unified amorphous bubble, a decoy to thwart aggression away from Tokyo and the rest of Japan.

Though the Japanese government viewed Micronesia as one consistent and unified political entity, Japanese civil administrators kept highly detailed records from all parts of the Nanyō Guntō, with meticulous statistics about births, deaths, crime, economics, education, and many other items from island group to island group. Rather than making distinctions between specific island populations within each island group, however, the Japanese government typically only reported the amalgamated data collected by each Nanyō-chō administrative capital. Thus, in archives and books related to the Nanyō Guntō region, most of the information about the Marshalls reported back to Japan or to the League of Nations was attributed only to the district capital of Yarūto (Jaluit Atoll), with no nuanced data about each atoll.[14]

Anthropological surveys did chronicle the differences between culture areas, the most notable being the ethnographic work of Hijikata Hisakatsu, the surveys conducted by Yanaihara Tadao, and the literary musings of Nakajima Atsushi.[15] But, like the official records, almost all these concentrated around the western parts of Micronesia in the Caroline and Mariana island groups, particularly Palau, Yap, and Saipan. The islands of the east, including the Marshalls, Pohnpei, and Kosrae, were largely neglected. Those studies that did mention the Marshalls were almost always a marginal part of a larger survey about the overall region.[16]

This shifted in the immediate prewar years when the blurry pan-Micronesia gaze that typified earlier Japanese views of the region gave way to the highly detailed eye of the Imperial Navy in the late 1930s and early 1940s. By 1937, the navy had wrested control of the Nanyō Guntō from the Nanyō-chō civilian headquarters in Palau (Peattie 1988, 250). Advances in aerial technology convinced Japanese military leaders that it would be fruitful to build up the Marshall Islands as their front line of defense against the United States,[17] and in 1939, the Nanyō command headquarters initiated construction in

Kwajalein Atoll, with the intention of transforming it from a rural (*inaka*) copra-trading outpost into one of the most important naval air bases in eastern Micronesia (Peattie 1988, 250–251).

As I will describe later, the military forcefully conscripted Islander men throughout the Marshalls to build up these bases and supplemented that workforce with Japanese prisoner workers and forced laborers from Korean villages. In 1943, at the height of the Japanese military campaign in the Pacific, a year before Kwajalein was invaded, the Imperial Navy issued a top-secret intelligence map that detailed the military installations throughout the atoll, probably for use by battleship commanders or by pilots. This was likely the most detailed map of the atoll ever drafted.

A major evolution had occurred during the Japanese administration of the Marshall Islands from the ambiguous and dreamy aspirations of Suzuki's rendition of Kwajalein in 1885 to the precise military intelligence of the islands sixty years later. The *nanshin* mission had been undertaken effectively: Japan had expanded throughout the Pacific, and Nanyō was no longer a dream but a knowable, controllable, defendable territory.

I used that map in conversations with Marshallese elders from Kwajalein, who were reminded of many of the features of the atoll that had since been forgotten. The map also included an inset of nine points of orientation about the atoll's significant features: military details, poisonous fish and disease warnings, population statistics, and local customs. Present-day American nautical charts of Kwajalein Atoll provide accurate depth soundings, but this Japanese map is, in fact, the only published map that includes the names of coralheads and sites of cultural significance to Marshall Islanders, such as Tarḷañ, the great coralhead from which the whole atoll is said to have originated, written phonetically in Japanese as "Daroan."

Japan's military presence was soon eclipsed by the American invasion campaigns across the Pacific. But more than seven decades after the Pacific War, this military legacy is still remembered and mapped in Japan, albeit mainly by the military and the families of the soldiers who died. A map engraved on the entrance wall memorial at Chidorigafuchi National Cemetery, for example, indicates the large numbers of Japanese who were killed in all the main overseas war zones during World War II. It zones off the "Central Pacific Ocean" (Chūbu Taiheiyō) as one battle theater, encompassing sites that stretch from Hawai'i all the way down to Kiribati and Nauru. Equating region to the number of deaths, it illustrates how the former Nanyō Guntō and its surroundings were the site of some of the most significant losses of soldiers and other Japanese during the war. With an estimated 247,000 deaths throughout hundreds of small islands, the Central Pacific ranks third among World War II overseas battle sites, and when combined with the total deaths in Melanesia and the Philippines, the campaigns of the entire Pacific theater make up the biggest losses out of any region. This is not to belittle the tremendous loss of life or suffering on the Asian continent, but as I will describe later in this book, the symbolism of the Pacific as a place of great sorrow is tremendous in contemporary Japan. In the Chidorigafuchi Cemetery map, unlike earlier maps of Nanyō Guntō, where the Marshall Islands were subsumed into a larger uniform imaginary of Japanese regionality, the islands feature prominently, and Kwajalein is highlighted as one of the key sites of engagement.

But most contemporary Japanese mappings of Oceania today show little evidence of Japan's earlier imperial involvement or engagement. "Nanyō Guntō" has become an obsolete term, replaced by "Mikuroneshia," a phonetic spelling of the English "Micronesia."[18] Destinations popular with Japanese tourists—Hawai'i, Saipan, Guam, and Palau—are highlighted by travel agencies nowadays only for their value as resort locales, divorced completely from historical context and portrayed as nothing more than places to get married, play golf, scuba dive, or engage in *iyashi*, "rest and relaxation." Several years ago, Japan Airlines had a direct charter service to the capital of Majuro Atoll in the Marshalls, which advertised the islands along familiar tropes of a tropical paradise for divers, not unlike other Micronesian destinations, which were also portrayed as "*minami no rakuen*" (southern paradises).

This trope of paradise was also evoked by a now-defunct Japanese nationwide ice cream franchise named Kommoltata. This company, whose name meant "thank you" in Marshallese, played upon the vision of the Marshall Islands as an idyllic tourist destination, sidestepping both prewar colonial and postwar nuclear legacies. Started by a group of ecology-minded Japanese divers who hoped to raise awareness about rising sea levels by drawing attention to the low-lying atolls and islets of the "Marshall Islands Paradise," they named their various ice cream dishes after Marshallese atolls and dive sites. One of its flavors included a special dessert named after Kwajalein, the largest inhabited atoll in the world, Pacific War battlefield, nuclear support site, top-secret missile-testing range, and now a sundae topped with pineapple, yogurt, blueberries, and mango pieces, the flavors of year-round summertime fun in the sun.

Liberation: American Steppingstones

While Japan mapped the "Martial Islands," American policymakers had long felt uncomfortable with Japan's presence in the Pacific. As early as 1921, plans were drafted by E. H. Ellis as part of the hypothetical "Orange Plan" for war with Japan, in which four Marshallese atolls would be used as naval bases for maneuvers against Japanese territories (Rottman 2004, 7). During the Pacific War, military planners decided that US forces would approach Japan in two waves, with Allied operations in the southwest Pacific and the Philippines under General Douglas MacArthur[19] and invasions through the Central Pacific under Admiral Chester Nimitz.

The latter "Steppingstone" campaign took advantage of the scattered topography of small islands and began in Kiribati (the Gilbert Islands) with the battles of Makin and Tarawa in November 1943, where US forces suffered considerable losses but incorporated the lessons they learned about atoll invasions into their planning for the Marshall Islands. Kwajalein Atoll was the main target for American Marine units in the Marshalls, who seized the atoll as part of Operation Flintlock, which began with regular air raids all through December 1943 and early 1944, culminating in an amphibious landing and a "fury of war" (Hezel 1995, 227) that was unleashed on January 31, 1944.

I will discuss the actual invasion in more depth later, but the prevailing mission of the United States at Kwajalein and other Marshall Islands during the Pacific War was regularly described as "liberation," a narrative through which American forces bombarded the region on the premise of freeing Islanders from the clutches of the "evil" Japanese while spreading democracy and security throughout Oceania. The flip side of this mythology, of course, is that US forces have remained in the Marshall Islands at Kwajalein, and at other sites throughout Micronesia, ever since.

Prior to the "liberation" of Kwajalein in January 1944, one of the first things the US Navy did was code name every islet in the atoll, as seen in the following closeup of an invasion map. Interestingly, unlike other atolls where female names were used, in this atoll they named each islet alphabetically after American-sounding male names from A through J, names like Abraham, Benson, Burton, or Jacob (Bryan

Mapping "the Martial Islands" 49

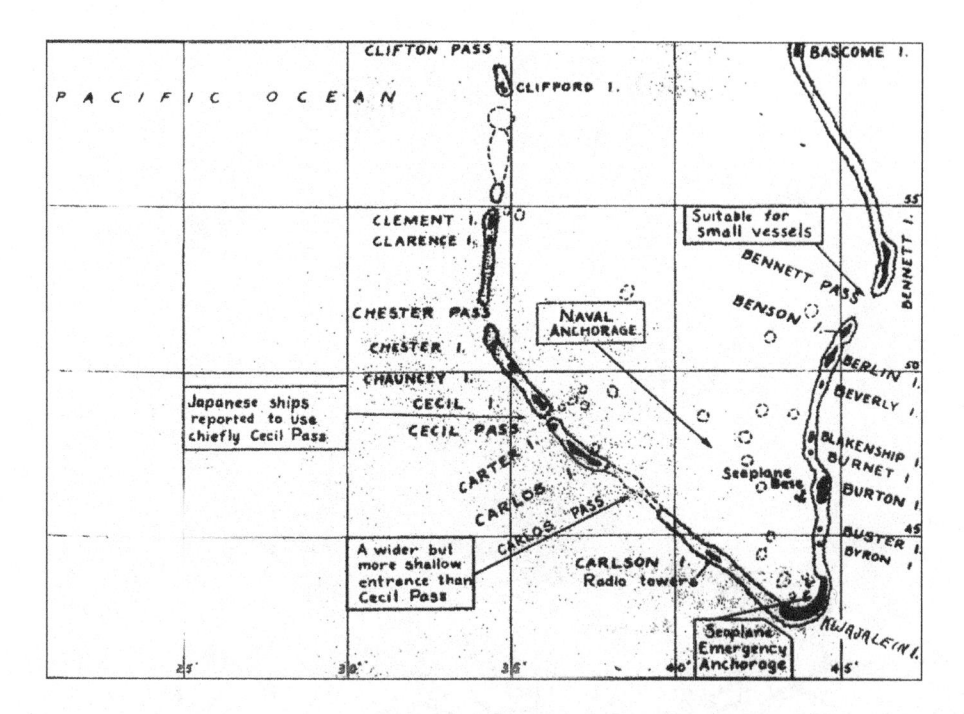

1965, 32–33). This new mapping completely erased the atoll's Marshallese heritage for invading Americans. It situated Kwajalein and the Marshall Islands in an American context, and it also served to masculinize Marshallese matrilineally inherited land that had previously been understood in female terms.[20] Some of these names, like Buster, Carlos, or Carlson, are still used by both American and Marshallese residents of the atoll.

Later "liberatory" maps of Kwajalein from an American vantage point tended to focus on Kwajalein islet, the site of the new naval base, almost exclusively. The military mission of the island was downplayed, as in the following map of the island base in the 1950s that appeared in a handbook for Operation Crossroads.

In this map, the sun shines down merrily, exotic fish surface in the lagoon, and a lifeguard ogles a woman swimming at the beach. Borrowing the 3-D effects used in guide maps for theme parks and tourist destinations, with disproportionate, cartoon-like caricatures, this map's visual treats tell a story about 1950s Kwajalein being a fun and leisurely place to be, rather than what some have called a "Strangelovian"[21] Cold War nightmare.

The freedom earned through the mission of "liberation" is represented by the presumably carefree pleasures of island life. The "restricted areas" are portrayed as blank, innocent spaces, even though they include the zone where planes were dispatched on onward "liberation" campaigns in the Pacific War and later the Korean War and where aircraft were readied for atomic weapons tests at Bikini Atoll. Two separate Japanese cemeteries are labeled discreetly, making them a feature of the landscape, right next to the "skeet range" and the beach. The presence of these mass graves on an otherwise playful map makes them seem more like pleasant tourist attractions than sites of death and loss. Once again, the military project is naturalized as a simple and uninteresting reality of the landscape, less important than fishing and taking a swim in the lagoon.

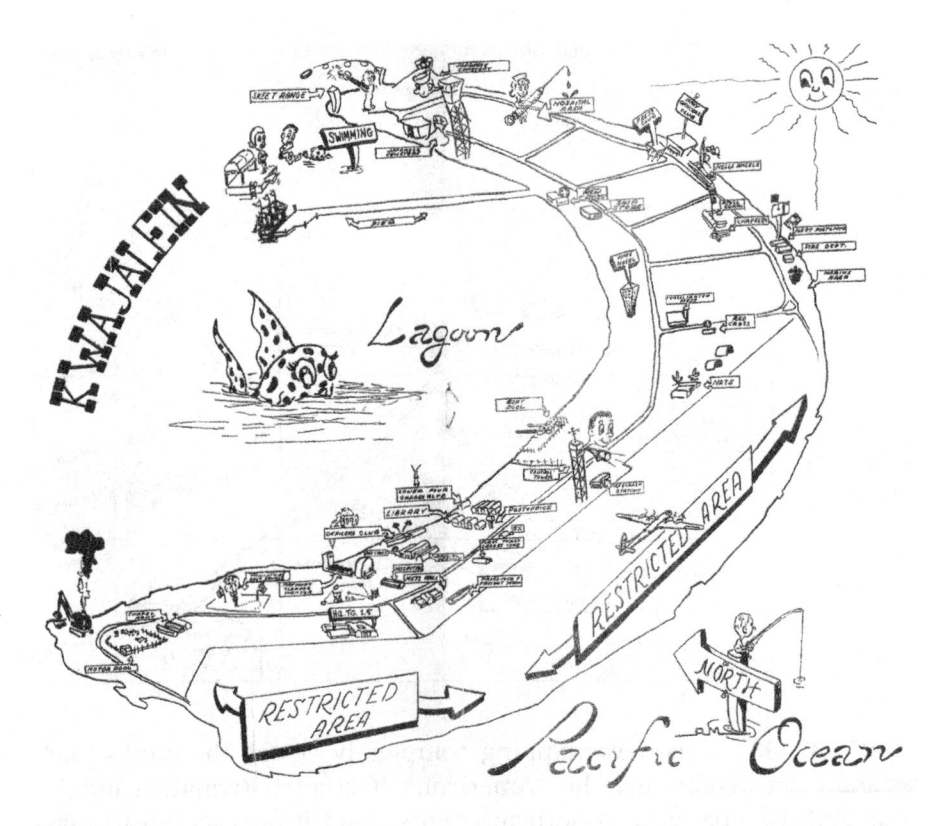

The touristic fantasy of life in paradise is reproduced again in subsequent maps from the 1960s and 1970s, such as in "Places to Go and Things to Do on Kwajalein," printed in an orientation booklet by Bell Laboratories, the main contractor that managed civilian residential life on the island (1972). As the US government developed

PLACES TO GO AND THINGS TO DO ON KWAJALEIN

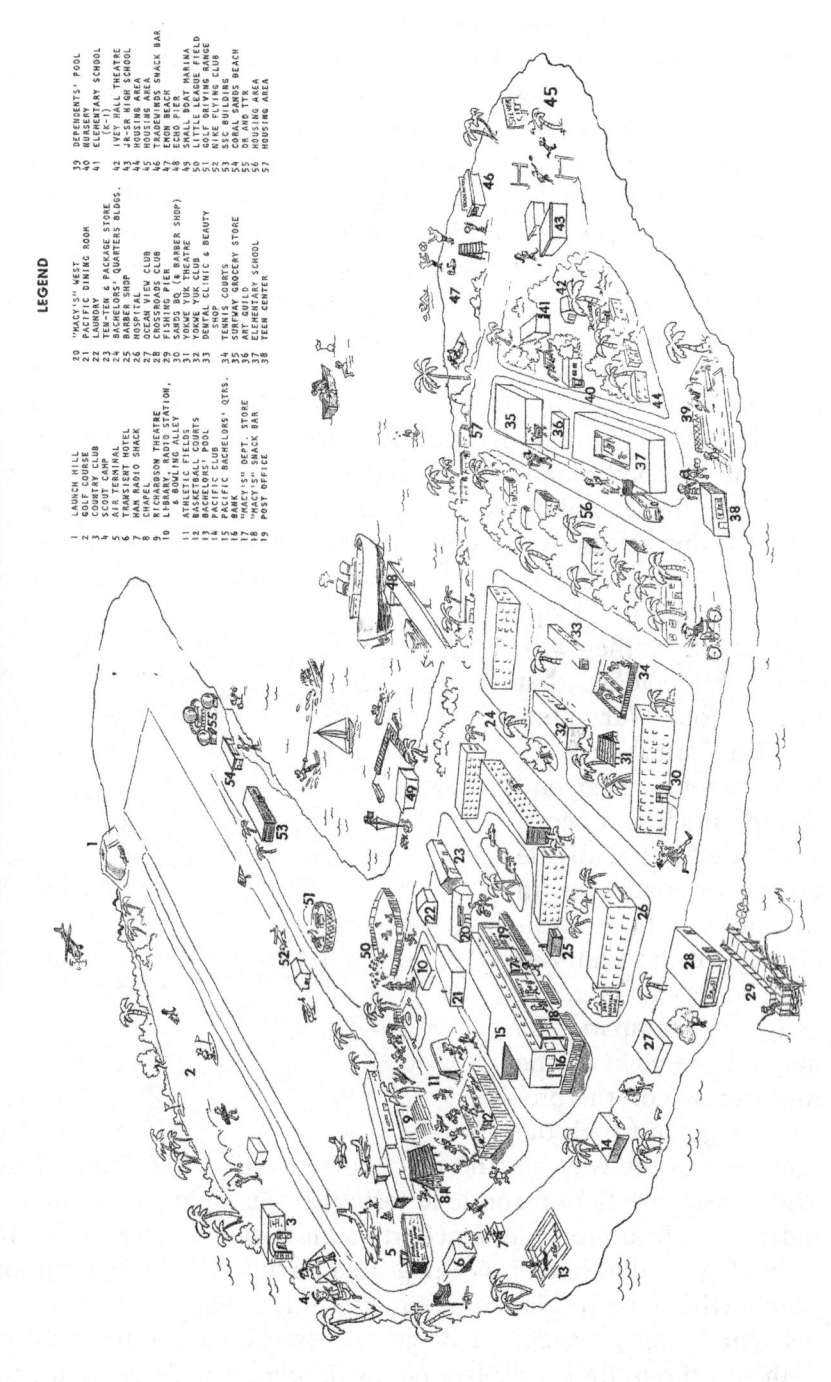

LEGEND

1. LAUNCH HILL
2. GOLF COURSE
3. COUNTRY CLUB
4. SCOUT CAMP
5. AZIMUTHAL
6. TRANSIENT MOTEL
7. HAM RADIO SHACK
8. RICHARDSON THEATRE
9. CHURCH, RADIO STATION, LIBRARY, & BOWLING ALLEY
10. ATHLETIC FIELDS
11. BASKETBALL COURTS
12. BACHELORS' POOL
13. PACIFIC CLUB
14. PACIFIC BACHELORS' QTRS.
15. BANK
16. "MACY'S" DEPT. STORE
17. "MACY'S" SNACK BAR
18. POST OFFICE
19. "MACY'S" WEST
20. PACIFIC DINING ROOM
21. LAUNDRY
22. TEN-TEN & PACKAGE STORE
23. BACHELORS' QUARTERS BLDGS.
24. BARBER SHOP
25. HOSPITAL
26. OCEAN VIEW CLUB
27. CROSSROADS CLUB
28. FISHING PIER
29. SANDS BQ (& BARBER SHOP)
30. YOKWE YUK THEATRE
31. YOKWE YUK CLUB
32. DENTAL CLINIC & BEAUTY SHOP
33. TENNIS COURTS
34. SURFWAY GROCERY STORE
35. ART GUILD
36. ELEMENTARY SCHOOL
37. TEEN CENTER
38. DEPENDENTS' POOL
39. NURSERY
40. ELEMENTARY SCHOOL (K-1)
41. IVY HALL THEATRE
42. JR-SR HIGH SCHOOL
43. HOUSING AREA
44. TRADEWINDS SNACK BAR
45. EMON BEACH
46. ECHO PIER
47. SMALL BOAT MARINA
48. LITTLE LEAGUE FIELD
49. GOLF DRIVING RANGE
50. NIKE FLYING CLUB
51. SSC BUILDING
52. CORAL SANDS BEACH
53. DM AUNTR
54. HOUSING AREA
55. HOUSING AREA

the missile-testing project, more and more civilian contract employees and their families needed to relocate to the island, and in order to persuade qualified, educated, middle-class Americans to do so, recreation and other "quality of life" facilities needed to be built.

This map renders Kwaj a happy, even cute, place to live.[22] On closer inspection, we discover that this map is filled with cheerful tiny comic people who cycle and jog around the paved roads of the island; swim in one of two swimming pools; play golf, volleyball, softball; scuba dive; go shopping at "Macy's" department store; attend school; or watch films at the outdoor theater.

Aside from the large airfield, barely any sign of missile testing is noticeable on this map, unless of course if we zoom in on the large Zeus missile monument depicted near the center of the map. Located near the baseball diamond, the missile stood as a familiar neighborhood icon for several decades until it was removed in the 1990s.

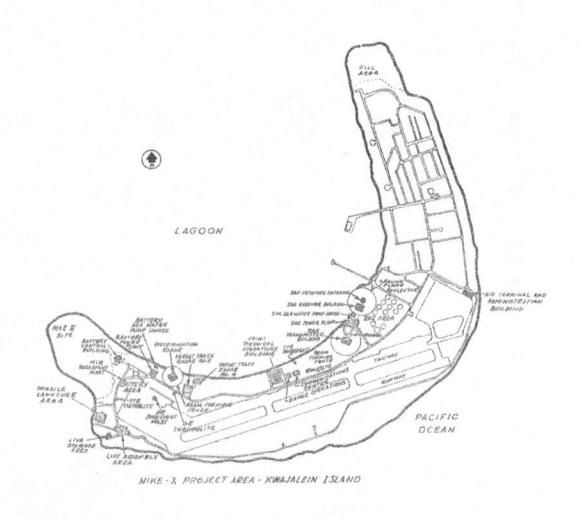

Yet during the very same period, in contrast to these maps meant for the predominantly civilian American population, military and technical maps boasted of another "liberation" ideology, that of the Cold War international arms race to keep America free and thwart nuclear aggression. The Nike X missile project was underway in the atoll, and the western end of the islet was completely layered in gadgetry. Compare the map on the right to the touristic one on the previous page, in which the same end of the islet has the golf course as its only defining feature. With its science-fiction comic lettering and its tight grid of antennas, radars, and beam-forming fences, this military map looks more like a technological diagram or an integrated circuit.[23] The other end of the island, where the residential town area is located, is completely unlabeled and empty, except for its grid of streets and the new "fill area" at the northern tip. Eighty-five nautical miles of undersea cables were buried in 1961 to link the whole atoll to support the Nike-Zeus testing program and connect the islands to powerful antennas, effectively wiring all of Kwajalein into one immense network (Lang 2017).

Maps like these reflect the story of the ongoing American mission of national defense through technological superiority. As the Cold War heightened and the United States improved upon its long-range intercontinental ballistic missiles, the entire atoll was further built up into a testing theater in which to intercept or receive incoming missiles. In 1964, the Mid-Atoll Corridor, a large expanse covering two-thirds of the atoll (see map 3 in the beginning of this book), was established as a splashdown site, and American authorities forced the Marshallese inhabitants of thirteen islets to move to tiny Ebeye islet.

With a massive re-entry zone in the lagoon, bounded by sensor stations, tracking radars, cameras, telemetry units that capture data from incoming missiles, "scoring" devices, and other equipment sited on eleven leased islet locations throughout the atoll and appraised at several billion dollars, Kwajalein seems like the end zone of a space-age military sport. Missiles, test-fired without their deadly nuclear payloads from Vandenberg Air Force Base in California, Kaua'i, and other sites, are intercepted only fifteen minutes later by other rockets fired from Meik (Meck) islet, the most restricted islet in the whole atoll. Massive radars and antennas from space surveillance projects like Lockheed-Martin's Space Fence keep watching the sky. Separate from this, rockets are also launched by civilian contractors like SpaceX from Komle (Omelek) islet. In the map that the US military imagines of Kwajalein Atoll, land and lagoon count for nothing but America's aerospace business and national defense, lending credence to Hayes, Zarsky, and Bellow's characterization of the Pacific as an "American Lake" (1986).

The United States has systematically reconfigured the whole atoll into a full-service missile-testing and space-tracking complex that continues into the present day as a major part of the United States Strategic Missile Defense Command's "Reagan Test Site." At the same time, the American residential community, sequestered peacefully on the main islet, never has had to consider the consequences of this larger testing mission for many Marshallese inhabitants of the atoll, who have been prohibited from residing on their small islets for more than half a century.

Homecoming: Reconnecting Marshallese Genealogies

I now turn to the mythologies and missions of Marshallese people indigenous to Kwajalein Atoll. As I do repeatedly throughout this book, here I am deliberately placing Marshallese narratives after all others. Though I acknowledge the "first-ness" of Islanders in terms of indigeneity, my point in doing this is to emphasize that Marshallese are not only "first" but *now*. Unlike Spanish, Germans, Japanese, or Americans, they have always been present throughout the human history of their islands and have borne witness to all that has taken place there up to the present. Rather than relegate their stories to an exoticized, timeless past, I underscore their relevance to the present and future by telling them in the middle of now and here, in a contemporary context.

Returning to Jolly's characterization of the "double vision" of Islander imaginaries of Oceania (2007), it could be said that Marshall Islander notions of landscapes and seascapes are both "genealogical" and "cartographic" at the same time. Marshallese conceptualizations of place as encoded in navigational chants and oral traditions, for example, represent the islands and ocean currents as a dynamic and ever-changing environment that is tied deeply to the genealogical, matrilineal tenure of land (Tobin 2002). At the same time, however, the value of that land in an increasingly capitalistic world, where America pays lease or compensation money for the use of different islands, has resulted in a desire among Islanders to chart their land and document genealogies to ensure future entitlements.

In Kwajalein Atoll, where Islanders were forced off their home islets (usually without compensation) to accommodate both Japanese and American military missions, the desire both to receive proper remuneration and to eventually recuperate a sense of home has inspired a particular mission that could be called the "homecoming" narrative. Vowing to return to their homelands, the displaced people of Kwajalein have held out hope in a perpetual battle over land rights and justice that has assumed various forms, including a series of peaceful demonstrations from the 1960s to the recent past, all of which have used the same sort of homecoming discourse. I will discuss homecoming in more depth later, but here I will focus mainly on the ways land and ocean is understood in a Marshallese context, and more specifically in Kwajalein Atoll.

Marshall Islanders nowadays refer to their country as Aeloñ in Majel when describing the nation in international terms, but more typically the country is referred to simply as Aeloñ Kein Ad (literally "These Islands"). Though Islanders speak a common language and share genealogical ties between atolls and islands, the idea of a consolidated Marshallese national identity is still a recent phenomenon, as most people identify themselves more locally with a specific series of atolls based on their family land rights. Prior to German colonial administration in the late 1800s, locally the islands were more generally imagined as two separate confederacies divided into island chains, the Rālik (western or "sunset") and Ratak (eastern or "sunrise") archipelagoes. Between these two ran a powerful and vast current called Lolle Laplap, meaning the "big wreath or lei," which was central to Marshallese navigation (de Laubenfels 1950, 259).[24] Kwajalein Atoll was situated on the edge of a broad swath of ocean known as Kapin-Meto ("the Bottom of the Sea"), a region that comprised the northwestern part of Rālik, from which hailed some of the most skilled navigators and powerful *irooj* (chiefs). Because of the unfortunate legacy of Cold War weapons testing that was shared between most of the atolls in this part of the Marshall Islands, Kapin-Meto has gained currency as a common identity for Islanders of this northwest region today. Tobin (2002, 25) provides more about the origins of the Ri-Kuwajleen in this context.

As with most Oceanian cultures, land is central in Marshallese identity politics; as Jiba Kabua writes, "If we do not take care of our land, we will no longer be Islanders and we will die ... the meaning of our names is connected to our land; our identity is our land" (Loeak, Kiluwe, and Crowl 2004, 187).[25] Land may be the foundation of identity, but it is also the grounding in that land that anchors Marshallese people and enables them to travel and migrate far and wide. As Honolulu consul-general Neijon Edwards declared, "Your land is your passport: it is what makes you Marshallese so that you can migrate to the United States, but it's also what will allow you to return home to the RMI."[26] Marshallese land tenure is based on two important matrilineal principles: *bwij* (the matrilineage itself) and *jowi* (the matriclan), the former comprising familial ties and the latter referring to the broader genealogical grouping of *bwij* into networks.[27] These clans extend across islands and atolls and tie the Marshall Islands together (Mason 1987, 9).

Ri-Kuwajleen literally means a "Kwajalein person" (or "Kwajaleinese," just as Ri-Amedka means "American," Ri-Jepaan means "Japanese," and Ri-Pikinni is often translated as "Bikinian"), although in general the term can be used to refer to all the people who have some genealogical affiliation to Kwajalein. This is of course a complex genealogy. Ri-Kuwajleen is more generally the name of a particular Marshallese clan (*jowi*) that had links to Kwajalein. According to Ekpap

Silk, all the people of Kwajalein Atoll were once part of the same clan but they divided into three groups that represented the northwest, the east, and the south of the atoll, and Ri-Kuwajleen came to refer more to the people of the south, where the main islet of Kuwajleen (Kwajalein) is located (Tobin 2002, 25).[28]

The narratives of Kwajalein's land and lagoon that I pursue throughout this part of the book are specific to the experiences and rhetoric of the Ri-Kuwajleen and their histories, and even more specific to those who are considered by the Republic of the Marshall Islands and United States governments to be "landowners." In recent times, Ri-Kuwajleen is a name that is increasingly used in identity politics between atolls to describe the original inhabitants of Kwajalein Atoll prior to the war, to differentiate migrant Marshallese from other atolls who come to work at the US base from the "insiders" who came from Kwajalein or had genealogical ties there through a relative. But although all "Kwajaleinese" share some common experiences or collective histories related to migration, settlement, war, and displacement, Ri-Kuwajleen differ in terms of their specific land affiliations and that land's significance (or insignificance) to others. For instance, simply being a Ri-Kuwajleen does not directly translate into entitlement to land payments from the United States unless one is actually a "landowner" of land that is being leased or used by the US Army.

In this book, in discussing the Ri-Kuwajleen I am generally referring to the large population of people who have land rights at Kwajalein Atoll (which numbers in the thousands by most estimates), and more specifically to the people of all Marshallese social groups whose ancestral lands are explicitly utilized by the United States Army Kwajalein Atoll testing complex. At the time of this writing, the United States currently leases land from the landowners of eleven islets out of the ninety-seven that make up Kwajalein Atoll: Kwajalein, Āne-Eḷḷap-Kan (Ennylabagen or Carlos),[29] Aṃbo (Legan), Likijjine (Illegini), the islands of Ruot and Niṃur (landfilled together by the Japanese military before the war into Roi-Namur), Āne-Kōran (Ennugarret), Kowak-Kan (Gagan), Kiden-Eṇ (Gellinam), Koṃle (Omelek), Āne-wetak (Enewetak),[30] and Meik (Meck). These islets essentially encircle the lagoon from all sides and have the broadest, most usable, best land in the atoll. In addition to people with land rights to these islets, another large group of displaced people and their descendants from the thirteen islets in the off-limits Mid-Atoll Corridor missile-testing hazard zone are considered Ri-Kuwajleen, though most of these people have never been compensated for their losses.

"Landowner," of course, is an English word with a strong European heritage of private land ownership.[31] Such a definition of "ownership" in English falls short of communicating to English speakers what that truly means in the Marshallese sense. "Owning" is an insufficient translation of the concept of being collectively *affiliated* to a tract or a number of tracts of land on different islets, to have a place where one calls home and has rights, rather than a notion of having exclusive domain over that place for one's own private purposes.[32] Stressing Sahlins' "consubstantiality" between the "supernatural," "natural," and "human" as a means of both establishing relationships and differentiating people's ability to have power over other people or land (Sahlins 1985, 81), Carucci explains how the Marshallese concept of resource management differs from American notions:

> [I]n line with the best assessments that can be made of Marshallese custom, no person "owns" anything on Kuwajleen Atoll. Ownership is collective and perduring, transcending the boundaries of corporeal beings and groups. Ownership has nothing to do with economic possession, it is part of being one with the world. . . . Nevertheless, interactions with Europeans and Japanese have led local people to speak in terms of "personal ownership." (Carucci 1997a, 418)

In the Marshallese sense of land rights, where whole clans and multiple individuals have links to the same land, the idea has typically been more one of custodianship, being able to use the land and reap its benefits on behalf of one's lineage. In many ways, it is not that one owns the land, but rather that one is *owned by* that land, that one belongs to it and passes it on to the next generation appropriately. As "Fujio," a Kwajalein landowner of mixed Japanese descent, describes, "in the past, the land used to give Marshallese people coconuts; now it gives them cash, and that's changed everything."[33] Still, it is notable that even the most recent disputes over land are not about the inalienable ownership of property but about how that land is used and who benefits. And though today the defense contractor on Kwajalein cuts the coconuts off the trees to protect the American community from dangerous falling objects, land used by the military throughout the atoll continues to yield a harvest of American dollars for those Marshallese people who belong to that land.[34]

For Kwajalein landowners, the most prominent of whom receive several million dollars annually, keeping track of the land is very important. On one hand, this is crucial in terms of disputes over money and power, as with the struggles between political parties, the national Marshallese government and local stakeholders, and arbitration with US negotiators. Claims to land, however, are just as important in the context of genealogical memory and identity. In an era where American military mappings have renamed and erased Marshallese conceptualizations of land, and where landowners can rarely—if ever—obtain military clearance to visit their own land, many elders recite the names of their ancestral land tracts to recuperate the sense of place and home that has been taken away.

The unit by which land is measured most often in a Marshallese sense is the *wāto*, a land parcel or tract that cuts an islet perpendicularly into slices from lagoon to ocean reef drop-off. A *wāto* can include not only dry land but all the resources that reach out onto the reef, including coralheads and beaches (Tobin 1954, 2). From ocean side to lagoon side, every inch of a *wāto* is significant and can be utilized for a wide range of functions broken down by proximity to fresh water or marine sources, protection from wind, shade, particular crops, and even demarcations of land based on divisions of gender. On Kwajalein islet before it was developed for military use in the early 1940s, for example, the *wāto* near where the airstrip is today were ideal for cultivating taro and breadfruit, which no longer grow anywhere on the islet at all.

Ato Lañkio drew from his memory how Kwajalein islet looked when he last lived there as a child in roughly 1941, before the Japanese military relocated the civilian population to Namo Atoll. He includes every single *wāto*, listing each by name. He draws these in relation to the homes of *irooj*, Japanese traders, the Nanyō Bōeki Kaisha trading post, copra stations, churches, and the schoolhouse. The following map, charted with pen and paper, was conceived first in conversation with anthropologist Laurence M. Carucci for his study of the cultural heritage of each islet in Kwajalein Atoll, commissioned by the US Army, and thus it focuses exclusively on the islet as detached from its full environment (Carucci 1997a).[35] To draw the map, Lañkio and Carucci worked off of an American-drawn geographically "accurate" outline map of the islet as it was in the early 1940s.

Drawing from his memory and from stories he had been told, he filled in the locations of landscape features, houses, churches,

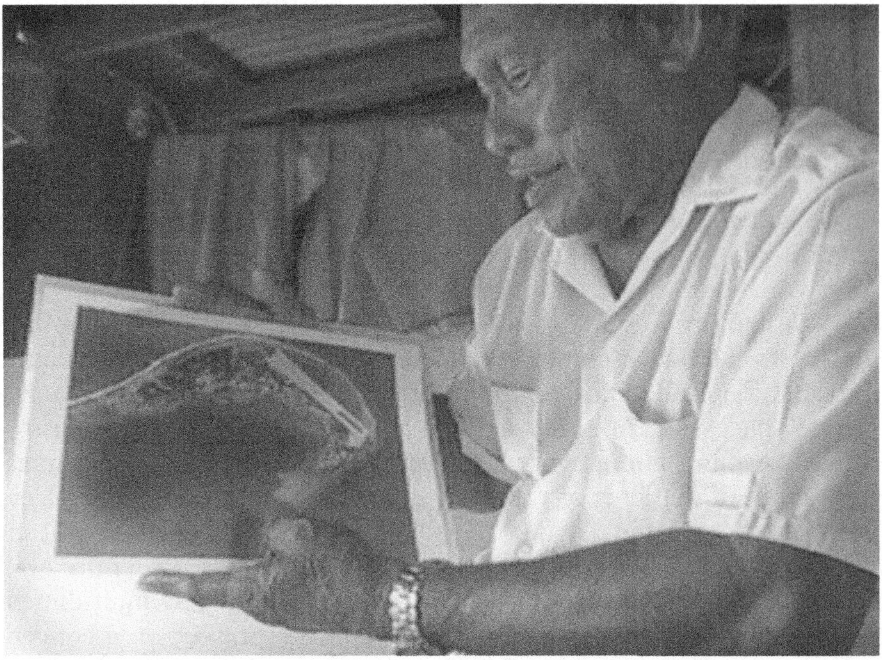

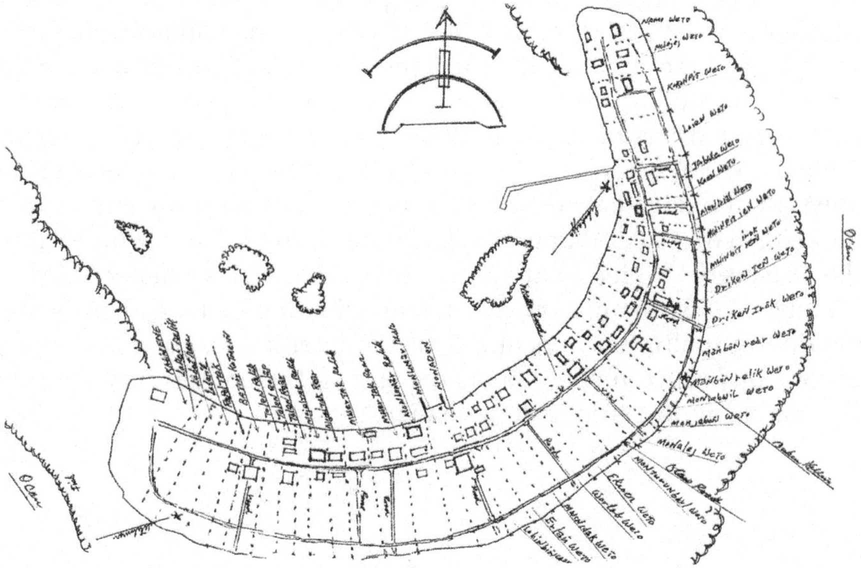

gravesites, roads, and *wātos*. Note how Lañkio corrects this map, though, by adding in coralheads in the lagoon and drawing the reef that runs off the page, suggesting a connectedness with the rest of the atoll. His recollections reference a more robust and multidimensional sense of place that extends beyond the outline of the islet and out into the water. His perspective of *wāto* land divisions is also rooted deeply in genealogies between islands and atolls. As he draws he tells me who is affiliated with each land plot, which *irooj* or *aḷap* is connected to every inch of the land and its surrounding reef.

Lañkio's representations of Kwajalein and Oceania in general are based in a broader context, and the shorthand of the cartographic process is not adequate to contain the layers and layers of meaning across space and time that he communicates to me in the long stories he recounts about every location in the atoll. In Carucci's exhaustive study of the sites of "cultural significance" to the Ri-Kuwajleen, he meticulously proved that *all* places in the atoll were significant (Carucci 1997a). For Ri-Kuwajleen, Carucci contends, the entire atoll is conceived as a dynamic cosmological system that is multidimensional, abstract, and nuanced—impossible to represent on a conventional map. There are even matrices between islets, coralheads, and stars that can only be understood by viewing the lagoon, the horizon, and the sky. For this reason, a linear map like Lañkio's is more useful in present-day land payment negotiations and in communicating with archaeologists, historians, or military planners; it is not fully representative of a holistic Marshallese "sea of islands" understanding of place.

Lañkio also situates his mapping in relation to the other mappings of the atoll, to both Japanese *nanshin* and American "liberation." He speaks not just of "Jabwile Wāto," for example, but also explains: "Jabwile Wāto, where the Japanese built the long pier and had a shop down by the dock called NBK and where the Americans built a road they call Sixth Street that goes straight down to the Tradewinds Bar on the Oceanside, which is my grandfather's land." Like many Marshall Islander elders, his history and his imagination of Kwajalein is thus mindful of multiple layers and dynamic interactions. It is a mapping of coral *and* concrete that honors the past and celebrates surviving and flourishing amidst tremendous change.

CHAPTER 3

Chasing the Chieftain's Daughter

Dancing Japan's Pacific Desires

"Wa-ta-shi no ... la-bā-san ... shū-chō no mu-su-me ..."

ATO L̦AÑKIO WINKS AS HE BEGINS TO SING a Japanese song. Straightening out his freshly pressed orange shirt as he corrects his posture, the elderly Marshallese historian who spent his childhood on Kwajalein wrinkles his mouth to carefully enunciate and draw out each word of the lyrics as he sings slowly and spiritedly. He slaps his palm on his thigh for rhythm, as if reciting a church hymn, and upon finishing the song he breaks out in an extended chuckle, "*Wor-ror!*—ah, damn," he says in a low voice. "I can't pronounce Japanese anymore."

His eyes suddenly glaze over as he raises his eyebrows and looks through the cracks of the doorway of his home on Ebeye islet at the departing US Army ferry headed back to Kwajalein. It is as if he is seeing beyond the atollscape that lies before him in 2006 and into another dimension. "Now, wait!" he says over the receding roar of the boat engines, and he switches back into totally fluent Japanese, "*Ima omoidashita!*—That song is coming back to me now!" He draws a deep breath and continues to sing where he left off, with almost perfect Japanese pronunciation:

> ... *Iro wa kuroi ga*   ... She's black but
> *Nanyō ja*   In the South Seas
> *bijin* ...   She's a beauty ...

"That's all—*emmuij*," he says, clearing his throat and making an embarrassed smile. Ato explains that he learned this song when he was in "*gakkō*," the Japanese public elementary school on Kwajalein, when he was only about six or seven years old. He tells me his teacher used to sing it, and later, when the soldiers came to reinforce the atoll against the Americans and forcefully remove Marshallese from their land, he heard them singing it too.

"Everyone used to sing it, but after the war when the Japanese lost the war and got killed, or when they were sent back to Japan here everyone forgot it," he explains. "I think I know who the song is about, too. There were plenty of Japanese businessmen who came here like that. Married the daughter of the *irooj*, made children, and then they died in the war. So many families connected to Japan today—I don't know," he jokes, "maybe because of this song?"

The prewar popular Japanese song "Shūchō no Musume" (The Chieftain's Daughter)[1] could almost have been a theme song for Japanese colonialism in the Marshall Islands, if not all of Japan's mandated territories in the Pacific, for it emerged at the beginning of the Nanyō Guntō administration and encapsulated a whole worldview of Japanese imperial desires: romanticism, assimilation, and possession. Peattie (1988, 216), Yamashita (2000, 449), and Kawamura (1994, 88) have all made mention of the 1930s version of the song, without tracing it back to its origins or paying much attention to the legacy it produced. As Ato suggests, however, it was much more than a song: The *shūchō no musume* herself was, after all, an icon. I explore in the following pages how as a motif she appears not only in song, but also in dance, art, and imagery throughout the Japanese colonial period, not only in the Marshall Islands, but throughout all of Nanyō and many other sites of encounter. She is, I argue, the quintessential embodiment of the Japanese colonial desire toward the islands and a symbol for the myth of available, alluring virgin territories into which Japan could launch its expansionist "mission" of *nanshin*, or southern advance.

Although this mission unfolded long before imperial Japanese military forces began fortifying rural Kwajalein Atoll as a major frontline commanding base in the war years, the chieftain's daughter narrative of power and privilege foregrounded and legitimated the Japanese military raison d'être by expanding the territory of Japan out into the Pacific. Throughout the Marshall Islands, elders like Ato often recall these lyrics within the context of a time of relatively peaceful cooperation and intermingling with Japanese migrants, along with the bittersweet memories of war they also conjure up. And while younger Japanese today have little or no awareness of the song's existence, for many Japanese people born before the Asia Pacific War, the mere mention of "Māsharu" produces a grin of nostalgia. Long before my conversations with Ato on Ebeye islet, I remember many puzzling moments in Japan when, upon the mention of my childhood in the Marshall Islands, elderly Japanese men and women would begin dancing, arms in the air, swaying from side to side and singing, "*Shū-chō no musume.*"

Despite this, digging around for a recording of the original song in contemporary Japan proved to be quite difficult at first. While I was able to find a disco remix from the 1970s called "Chieftain's Daughter '79," and a newer version by a female *shamisen* player made in 2005,[2] both of these recordings were hard to come by. My quest to find "The Chieftain's Daughter" led me to the old record collections of a radio station in southern Japan, where I first listened to at least three different versions of the song; through old record shops in the back alleys of Jinbōchō, Tokyo; to a farming village in the mountains of Kyushu; to the Pacific Arts festival in Palau; to auction websites and YouTube channels; and to a number of archival sources, in which I finally encountered her, face-to-face, on an unseasonably hot day in Kōchi, Japan, in early November 1923.

Representing Japanese "Tropicalism": The Daku-Daku Craze

With the intense blue of the sky and the warm breezes blowing off the Pacific Ocean, the weather seems more like the tropics than autumn in Shikoku. On the grounds of the new Kōchi Imperial Secondary School (now Kōchi University), the local community has gathered to celebrate the school's opening, with an all-day track and field event, an *undōkai* to celebrate the athletic prowess of the school's inaugural two hundred first-year students, and to enjoy a series of cultural performances (Kisō 1986, 257). The air smells of dry leaves and the overpowering sweet perfume of *kinmokusei* (osmanthus) flowers, and of salty brine and fishing nets off in the distance.

Dressed variously in finely tailored white suits and hats, or in *hakama* with *tabi* socks and *geta* clogs, the well-to-do invited guests and officials sitting on chairs under the red and white tents around the track fan themselves and wipe the perspiration from their brows. Families and other well-wishers from surrounding villages take a break from their farming and fishing to root for these elite students who have come to study from all around Japan. They huddle around *bentō* boxes stacked high with *onigiri* rice balls, fish, pickled *otsukemono* vegetables, and various local delicacies. In the sweltering heat, many of the men have already gone through several bottles of beer and cold *sake*, and they are already quite red in the face as they await the next performance of the early afternoon. In the morning, there have been relay races and sprints, interspersed with brief choral renditions of school songs or traditional dances, like the well-known humorous *yosakoi* dances of the region. Even in the audience, women and men of all ages were standing, clapping, and moving in step with the boys on the playing field as they danced along with these familiar pieces. But a strange hush falls over the enthusiastic crowd when the next group of students steps forth.

A class of forty boys walks out onto the soil of the playing field, barefoot, wearing nothing but red *fundoshi* loincloths covered with "grass" skirts made of straw, with red *hachimaki* bands of cloth tied around their heads. Their skinny teenage bodies are smeared from head to toe in charcoal, leaving only circles of pale flesh around their eyes exposed. Beads of perspiration run down their backs, rivulets of black ink.

With deadpan seriousness, the boys march forth slowly and deliberately with sharpened bamboo spears in their hands, some holding a giant banner emblazoned with a huge skull on it. They form a circle in front of the audience and begin to rotate, kicking their legs inward as they dance. In unison, they start to chant peculiar lyrics:

Sekidō chokka Māsharu Guntō	Down by the equator in the Marshall Islands
Yashi no hakage de daku-daku odoru	She dances *daku-daku* shaded by the palm fronds
Odori odotte yoru o akasha	Dancing all night long
Ashita wa banana no shita ni neru	She'll sleep tomorrow under the banana tree.
Kinō yama de mita shūchō no musume	I saw the Chieftain's Daughter on the mountain yesterday,
Kyō wa izuko de daku-daku odoru	Where will she dance *daku-daku* today?
Odori shiranai hito wa iya	She doesn't like [men] who don't know how to dance.
Dare ga oyome ni yuku mono ka	Who would marry one of them?

Yūkari shigeru Indasu-gawa de	By the Indus River where the eucalyptus thrives,
Yashi no hakage ni banana ga minorya	Bananas ripen in the shade of the palm fronds.
Musume odore ya daku daku odore	Girl, dance, do your *daku-daku* dance
Ashita wa tenki ka yūgata ga akai[3]	Tomorrow might be fair weather, the sunset is so red.

Bobbing their heads back and forth, the boys begin to sway their hips and step from side to side while they sing. As the boys dance and repeat the words, the audience begins to sway with the bizarre rhythm and nod their heads. The line "*daku-daku odoru,*" an unusual expression suggesting a frenzied dance causing profuse sweating or the rhythmic gallop of a horse, is sung in chorus by the audience as they watch and clap, mesmerized by the boys' synchronized movements, delighted by the silliness of it all.

It is a dance with a fanciful and nonsensical, comical feel to it, typical of the sort of "*eroguro nansensu*" of the day, a popular cultural style of art or performance that is simultaneously *ero* (erotic), *guro* (grotesque), and *nansensu* (nonsensical). The lyrics reference the faraway tropical Marshall Islands, which were only subsumed the previous year in 1922 into Japan's mandated Nanyō Guntō islands of Micronesia. Suggesting a chiefly virgin bride who is all at once in possession of erotic beauty and a grotesque otherness, the boys' strange song imagines a backdrop of fanciful islands awash with exotic kitsch, like eucalyptus, banana, and palm trees, or the mystical Indus River. No matter that eucalyptus does not grow in the Marshall Islands or that the Indus runs through what is still in the early 1920s the colonial British territory of India, this is a song and dance with imperial aspirations for all that is out there in the mysterious lands and seas that make up the southern frontier of Nanyō. By the time the black-faced boy minstrels march off the field, the Marshallese chieftain's daughter has made her debut in the popular cultural imaginary of Taishō-era Japan, the alluring damsel of a South Seas fantasyland. Unwittingly, the boys of Kōchi Imperial Secondary School have started a whole sensation and contributed to Japan's mission in the Pacific. Little do they realize that their chieftain's daughter will have a life of her own throughout the twentieth century and will figure prominently throughout Japan's colonial project in the decades to come.

The "Daku-Daku Odori," as the dance came to be known as it was performed again and again throughout the region, was originally conceived by twenty-one-year-old Yoden Tsuruhiko (Kisō 1986, 257). Though he had come to study from Kumamoto Prefecture in Kyūshū, Yoden was clearly inspired by the story of Mori Koben, the entrepreneur from Tosa (Kōchi Prefecture), who had migrated in 1896 to the islands of Pohnpei and Chuuk (Peattie 1988, 28) and become a local legend there, even before the formal Japanese administration of the islands began. Having just moved to Kōchi, Yoden and his classmates were seduced by the real-life tales of Mori, who in fact did marry a local woman from a chiefly family and had already begun an entire Japanese-Micronesian dynasty in Chuuk. Mori's experiences were told and widely celebrated back in Kōchi with much excitement, and the success of his adventures was only further compounded when all the German-held territories of Micronesia were awarded to Japan under a League of Nations Mandate in 1922.

Why Yoden chose the Marshall Islands and not Chuuk as the setting for his song and dance is not entirely clear, except it would be fair to speculate that since the Marshall Islands were the farthest extreme of the Japanese empire in the 1920s, in what was popularly understood as the South Seas, it only makes sense that he would have imagined them to be literally the most "South Pacific" of all those islands (Peattie 1988, 216). Interestingly, even as late as the census of 1937 in the Marshall Islands, there were no Japanese colonists from Kōchi in the Marshall Islands district capital of Jabor (Jebwad), Jaluit, and only eleven residents from the Shikoku region in general (Nanyō Guntō Kyōiku-kai 1938, 11–16). While Japanese migration had begun into Palau, Yap, Chuuk, and Saipan in the western part of Micronesia (Peattie 1988, 186) in Yoden's time, faraway Jaluit in the Marshall Islands was the least known of all the territories.

As I have already described, the term Nanyō was originally conceived as a counterpart to the terms Tōyō (the East) or Seiyō (the West). Literally translated "South Seas," it more generally referred to "the South." It thus follows that, in a typical orientalist pattern, there would be an equivalent sort of dynamic of cultural superiority and simultaneous romanticism taking place from the north (Japan) toward the south, and the further south, the more exotic. Literary critic Kawamura Minato (1994, 88) calls this "tropicalism," a whole genre of popular culture in Japan from the 1920s all the way through the early 1940s that embraced a fantastic vision of tropical islands.

There was also the influence of an American Hollywood version of the Pacific, of alluring but comical girls dancing hula on archetypal palm-studded beaches, and in the mid-1920s Hawaiian music, with ukeleles and slack-key guitars, was quite popular throughout Japan. Unfamiliar topographies, like coconut palms, coral sand and atolls, or celestial constellations like the Southern Cross all figured in this Japanese imaginary. Most importantly with this, however, was a fantasy of the noble virgin Islander princess, typified by the chieftain's daughter.

Yoden's intriguing composition was performed entirely by young men, in the tradition of a sort of comic song or slapstick comedy. The lyrics of the "Daku-Daku Odori" presume that all these "black" boys are in fact the suitors for the chieftain's daughter, who is ever-present and yet never revealed to the audience. This is not, for instance, the sort of cross-dressing parody of hula performed by American GIs at Pearl Harbor and elsewhere in the Pacific later in the twentieth century with the typical coconut bra, plastic grass skirt, and lei (Jolly 1997, 116). It is rather a caricature of a presumed Marshall Islander manhood, stylized into primate-like blackness and danced for the sake of pure comedy. Like drag, the intrigue of Yoden's performance comes from the imperfection of the artifice, from the absurdity of "culturally superior" Japanese boys at an elite imperial school trying to dance a "primitive" dance.[4]

The dance becomes more and more frenzied and amusing as the boys compete, toppling over each other to wag their hips, bob their heads, and shake their thighs in pursuit of the elusive and invisible chieftain's daughter. It is not surprising that with its competitive comic value, requiring participants to outdo each other with absurd dances, this sort of event became popularized (Kisō 1986, 256) at mostly male rural social drinking gatherings in the Taishō period, not only in Shikoku but in other regions as well. The Daku-Daku Odori may not have been the first, but it sparked a trend, since schoolboys at other schools throughout Japan in the 1920s began doing dances like these at their school festivals as well, in a similar style of camp, painting their faces black, wearing headbands, and dancing in straw skirts, in what broadly became known as *dojin matsuri*,[5] or "Native festivals."

The lyrics indicate the impossibility of winning over the chieftain's daughter without knowing how to dance. This prose suggests by extension that men dance properly in order to seduce and marry her. In one sense, imagining the chieftain's daughter as metonym for the Marshall Islands or all of Micronesia, it is possible to interpret this as a dance not only about marrying a woman, but also about annexing and possessing an entire territory by going through the colonialist "motions" of imperial expansion. But at the same time, one must dance the right way to earn the island princess's approval; these lyrics are not just about "possessing" but also about *being accepted* (and "possessed," in a sense) into a chiefly lineage.[6]

Imagining Race in the South Seas: The "Black but Beautiful" Lover

Watashi no labā-san,	My lover
Shūchō no musume	is the chieftain's daughter
Iro wa kuroi ga	She's black but
Nanyō ja bijin	In the South Seas, she's a beauty
Sekidō-chokka,	Down by the equator
Māsharu Guntō	in the Marshall Islands,
Yashi no kokage de	in the shade of the palm trees
teku-teku odoru	She dances lazily [*teku-teku*]
Odore, odore, dobuzake nonde	Dance, dance! Drink up your spirits!
Asu wa ureshii kubi no matsuri	Tomorrow is the happy headhunting feast.
Kinō hama de mita	Yesterday I saw her on the beach,
Shūchō no musume	The chieftain's daughter,
Kyō wa banana no kokage de nemuru	Today she sleeps under the banana trees
Odore, odore, odoranu mono ni	Dance, dance!
Dare ga oyome ni	Who would marry his daughter to
Yaru mono ka[7]	one who won't dance?[8]

Yoden's compelling melody and lyrics spread to other schools, and other festivals in western Japan became so popular that when newly established Polydor Records needed a cheerful song to release on its first album in 1930, it commissioned composer Ishida Hitomatsu to rework the "Daku-Daku Odori" song into an upbeat comic tune (above). The recording (Ishida 1930), performed by well-known Osaka singer Tomitaya Kikuji and played with a *shamisen* and flute accompaniment, was simply titled "The Chieftain's Daughter" ("Shūchō no

Musume"). It is this version that most people nowadays recall and upon which all subsequent versions were based.

It is with Ishida's version that a Marshall Islander first becomes a *"labā-san,"* a humorous Japanization of the English word "lover." This chieftain's daughter is immediately made intimate, eroticized, appropriated as an object of desire, all the while being ridiculed at the same time and imagined in a primitivist scenario of savage headhunting cannibalism and idle laziness. Adding the Japanese honorific suffix *-san* to "lover" underscores the satirical tension with which this love affair is imagined. In contrast to the minstrel dance that accompanied Yoden's earlier version, Ishida's lyrics no longer imagine the bungling antics of a troupe of "black" Islander men competing for the love of a chiefly woman; the presumably Japanese narrator of the song has already claimed her, like Japan has claimed the Marshall Islands, as his own. She is no longer available for local men; she is a "lover," already a prized possession for whom Japanese men must dance. The song becomes a comic invitation for other men to "drink up" their *sake* and dance to win over the heart of a local princess.

In the Ishida version of the song, the expression *"daku-daku"* is changed to *"teku-teku,"* an onomatopoeic term that means "trudgingly" or "slow and laboriously." In a rendering of Islanders as "lazy Natives," much like nineteenth-century European and American representations, the implication here is no longer one of frenzy or sweaty fervor; it is one of laziness and lackadaisical swaying to and fro. In this version, the chieftain's daughter's life is described as idle and frivolous, even boring.

Ishida's line, "She's black but in the South Seas she's a beauty" (*iro wa kuroi ga, Nanyō ja bijin*), serves a similar purpose as the blackface minstrel performances of Yoden and his classmates a decade earlier. It is a satirical device that emphasizes the perceived inferiority of "blackness" within the Japanese imperial racial hierarchies. Russell writes of contemporary Japanese literary representations:

> [T]his tendency to dehumanize and belittle blacks disguises [the] tendency ... to employ the black Other as a reflexive symbol through which Japanese attempt to deal with their own ambiguous racio-cultural status in a Eurocentric world. (Russell 1991, 6)

Indeed, these lyrics carry with them a "black but beautiful" connotation that the chieftain's daughter's appearance would not be desirable anywhere but in the Nanyō Guntō, creating a sort of orientalized, "tropicalized" exoticism that romanticizes and subjugates Marshall Islanders while positioning the Japanese imperial subject as culturally superior, on par with European imperialists. This image of the eroticized Marshallese "lover-san" stands in stark contrast to the grotesque appearance of forty boys smeared black with charcoal. It references another type of "blackness": taking the emphasis away from the primitive African stereotypes performed by Yoden's minstrels and projecting a "dusky maiden" image of the Islander princess as a sexual prize. Still, it is this same marking of blackness itself that makes the chieftain's daughter exotic while also rendering the song comical for the 1930s Japanese listener, who would likely have perceived a liaison with a non-Japanese (and particularly a "black" person) to be deviant, if not "grotesque." This is, after all, probably why the song is categorized into the *ero-guro* genre in the first place. Both "erotic" in its tropical fantasy romance and "grotesque" in its eccentricity, it is a double-edged narrative of titillation and humor.

An image in an August 1930 Polydor newsletter advertising the original recording of "Shūchō no Musume" showed how the chieftain's daughter was transformed into a "black but beautiful lover-san" (Hori 1969). With its photograph of a slender woman in a "grass" skirt with her exposed thigh showing through, with accoutrements like Hawaiian *ti* leaf anklets and a *haku* lei in her hair, the image is less representative of Marshallese femininity and more like a touristic American postcard advertising 1930s Waikiki. It is suggestive in the way that it directly references a European-American primitive fantasy of the tropics, if not Polynesia. An emulation of the trope of the hula girl, her arms are spread back as she gazes out toward a distant horizon. The Polydor image thus fuses the Japanese Nanyō "tropicalistic" optic toward the Marshall Islands in Micronesia with its Western counterpart in Polynesia.[9]

It would not be an exaggeration to say that this image of lazily dancing femininity ultimately becomes a poster girl metonym for the entire Marshall Islands, as she does in this official postal cancellation seal from Jaluit District of the Nanyō Guntō in the 1930s. Whereas similar seals from Palau, Yap, or Chuuk featured traditional buildings, spears, and masks as their motifs, the Marshallese capital of Jaluit was symbolized entirely by a stylized caricature insignia of a bare-breasted chieftain's daughter, standing along the shoreline with ripe coconuts at her feet under text that reads "Yarūto" (Jaluit), as if to make the

Marshallese woman synonymous with the island itself.

Pacific scholars, writers, and artists have long criticized the so-called "dusky maiden" archetype in European and American representations (Jolly 1997; Desmond 1999; Ferguson and Turnbull 1999; Kihara 2005), and the *shūchō no musume* archetype has some resonance with this hula-girl image.[10]

As Teresia Teaiwa (1999) wrote of Paul Gauguin's *Noa Noa*, the artist's depiction of his thirteen-year-old wife Tehaʻamana (the model in his still-life paintings and the inspiration for the character Tehura in his writing) is similar to that of the image deployed by Hollywood and the tourist industry, a conflation of the contradictory "lazy" and "erotically dancing" description:

> Gauguin's Tehaʻamana is inscribed as still life, always in repose, and then made to resignify "polymorphous" mobile "Polynesia." Although an obvious contrast to the image of the "Polynesian" hula dancer, both images are easily absorbed into "Club Med visions," since Hollywood and naïve anthropologists have helped entrench notions that the lives of "Polynesians" come to not much more than languorous days and erotic nights." (Teaiwa 1999, 255)

Looking only at the orientalistic/tropicalistic gaze suggested by the "dusky maiden" and other colonial erotic/exotic representations of "natives," however, can have the consequence of "presuming too much about the gazer," as Kelly elucidates (1997, 76). Focusing exclusively on the colonial gaze also tends to privilege a male optic and presume a facile phallic "penetration" of colonized sites without considering "the realities and fantasies of colonial life" (Jolly 1997, 9). The parallels between "virgin women" and "virgin land" notwithstanding, here we must take into consideration McClintock's (1995) devastating critique of phallic power in imperial conquests. Colonial exploits, not only for Europeans but for Japanese, were not a simple "penetration" of passive and virgin terrain but rather were filled with much more tension, fear, and trouble than is often acknowledged. Indeed, as McClintock writes, the colonial imagination of land as feminine and virgin is:

both a *poetics* of ambivalence and a *politics* of violence. The "discoverers" . . . had stepped far beyond any sanctioned guarantees. Their unsavory rages, their massacres and rapes, their atrocious rituals of militarized masculinity sprang not only from the economic lust for spices, silver and gold, but also from the implacable rage of paranoia. (McClintock 1995, 28)

The chieftain's daughter narrative, while it engages stereotypes of erotic Native women, stresses kinship and the relation to the chiefly father. It is not only a story about dancing erotically to "get the girl," it is more importantly a tale about marriage and union. Effectively, the chieftain's daughter narrative follows in a similar tradition to the hula-girl image, simultaneously denying Islander subjectivity while advancing imperial desires, possession, and colonialism. Yet it plots a different trajectory, one in which Japanese and Islander destinies actually merge. The island princess is not a girl to be taken away as a prize; this is also an alliance between Japanese and Marshallese chiefly genealogies. In Ishida's version of the song and in many later iterations, the princess' father (the chief) is the one who makes the final decision of marrying his daughter to an outsider, thus highlighting the alliance between Japanese and Marshallese patriarchal power.

Still, as McClintock suggests, these fantasies and realities were also infused with a great deal of anxiety. No doubt the allure of the *shūchō no musume* mythology played in the dreams of many of the Japanese traders and colonists who went to the Marshall Islands and other parts of Micronesia, but Yamaguchi Yōji, who was born on Saipan and grew up in the Nanyō Guntō, explains:

Those men were terrified. They went alone to the islands, sometimes to places where there weren't many other Japanese. They didn't know what to eat. They had heard stories about people getting killed in the past. It was a good thing if they could get the protection of the chief, so why get together with a commoner girl if you could find yourself a *shūchō no musume*?[11]

The "Shūchō no Musume" archetype spawned a wide range of images and expectations that could be mapped against the entirety of Oceania, allowing Japanese colonists, soldiers, administrators, and traders to participate in the same sort of imperial project that Europeans had been undertaking in the previous century. The images

Chasing the Chieftain's Daughter   73

produced in the Marshall Islands by Japanese photographers[12] clearly played upon this archetype, singling out the Marshallese woman from other Nanyō Micronesian Islanders as the quintessence of beauty. Typically, like the following image of three Marshallese girls, in postcards and photo almanacs advertising the Nanyō Guntō as an attractive place for Japanese to travel, work, and migrate, there would be a captivating photo of *Yarūto no fujin*, or "woman of Jaluit," in which invariably one or more young and fair Marshallese women would be posed, as if to feature the intrinsic beauty of women from this locale. Often they would be photographed bare-breasted, in a recreation of the Marshalls' premissionary past. These images were produced both to accommodate the narrative of the alluring Marshallese chieftain's daughter, just as much as they were taken to deliver the promise of that beauty and desirability back to the Japanese homeland.

Most Islander women, it seems, were already accustomed to wearing European dresses by the time the Japanese colonial period began, but Joachim deBrum, a Marshallese-Portuguese photographer from Likiep Atoll, also took photographs of his own family members in which many of the models (both women and men) posed in "traditional" attire. It is likely the case, however, that in the Marshalls district capital of Jaluit in the 1920s and 1930s, it was no longer commonplace for women to be topless. It could be argued that Japanese photographers made such images of Marshallese women as a means of ethnologically documenting Nanyō culture, in a scientific effort to portray Islanders as natural and innocent. Lutz and Collins suggest in their readings of *National Geographic* photographs that in fact even such "truthful" representations of women ultimately serve to eroticize and titillate; like American images of indigenous people in the pages of *National Geographic,* these early Japanese photographs only "worked" as both scientific and erotic because they were a racial and gendered subordination of black women (Lutz and Collins 1993, 115–116).[13]

How black, however, could one be while still being beautiful? For the most part, aside from the broad racial hierarchy that placed Japanese above all "lesser races," within the Nanyō Guntō, Islanders were further classified by skin color into two distinct groups: Chamorro (*Chamoro-zoku*) and Kanaka (*Kanaka-zoku*), with most Marshall Islanders of darker complexion categorized in the latter group.[14] According to *Waga Nanyō,* a silent educational film produced mainly by the Japanese navy in 1936, Kanakas were described as "being playfully carefree but of lower cultural level than Chamorros,"[15] while Chamorros were "advanced and of a docile nature with an industrious manner, possessing even pianos and other instruments in some of their wealthier homes" (Nanyō-chō 1936). Chamorro, a term taken completely out of context from the Mariana Islands, where it refers to the indigenous population there, was taken by Japanese to mean "of mixed race" or "of lighter skin." Chamorros were thought to be more intelligent, sophisticated, and advanced, and they were often admired for their beauty. The 1932 photo on the right, for example, labeled "Chamorro Woman of Jaluit," reproduces the chieftain's daughter discourse while drawing attention to her whiteness and mixed-European heritage. The caption under the photo reads, "This photograph depicts the modern style of clothing of Chamorro women today, who do not differ much from European women in that they can not only play the piano but also do contemporary Western dances."[16]

Kanaka-zoku is a word also heavily laden with a complicated heritage. The word *kanaka* originated from Polynesian languages (*kānaka* in Hawaiian, or *tangata* in Samoan, Tongan, and Maori) and simply means "man" or "person." This word most likely came into usage for the first time by North Americans in the context of labor when Hawaiians began to settle coastal British Columbia and the Pacific Northwest as pioneer homesteaders who engaged in manual labor (Koppel 1995, 1). *Kānaka* gradually took on the connotation of "native laborer" when used by American and European (particularly German) plantation owners across their colonial territories throughout Oceania, even outside the Polynesian context. According to the Oxford English Dictionary, Queensland, Australia, where the practice of "blackbirding"—forcing Pacific Islanders from Melanesian islands into labor—had become so institutionalized, was at one point nicknamed "Kanakaland." Gerald Horne writes that in Australia and other parts of the South Pacific in the late 1800s, the term "Kanaka" was used as a racist slur, just as "boy" or the n-word was used in the American South around the same time (Horne 2007, 46). According to David Chappell, *canaque,* the French version of the Hawaiian *kānaka,* which had been popularized aboard ships and in plantations, also was a condescending term white settlers to New Caledonia used to refer to local people, although this word was reappropriated positively by nationalists such as Jean-Marie Tjibaou as a term to consolidate indigenous identity in the movement toward self-determination (Chappell 2013, 2). In turn, indigenous people there began to refer to themselves proudly as Kanaks in the 1970s, calling their territory Kanaky.

Although the etymology of the word's use in Japanese is obscure, it most likely came from the German racial classification *kanake,* which was, like in other European colonial plantations, used to refer to the nonwhite "natives" of German Pacific possessions such as the Marshall Islands and Samoa. Probably this racist term was simply adopted through translations of German ethnological studies and administrative precedent into Japanese administrative practice.[17] Thus despite the term's indigenous origins in Polynesia (where it is still used proudly, for instance, to mean "Native Hawaiian," Kānaka Māoli), *kanaka* carried much baggage by the time it was used by Japanese civil administrators, including the assumption that the Native was meant to do indentured menial labor. It was, as in *kanaka dojin,* often combined with the politically incorrect term *dojin* ("dirt person") in magazines, on tourist postcards, and in various other popular representations.

It is thus unsettling that the Japanese government continues to use this problematic racial epithet uncritically to describe the "race" of the Marshallese people. At the time of this writing, the Japanese Ministry of Foreign Affairs, on at least one of its profile pages for the Republic of the Marshall Islands within its country-by-country fact database, continues to claim unabashedly that the *minzoku* (ethnicity or race) of "the Marshallese people" is *kanaka-zoku*.[18] This was the only island nation in Oceania whose population Japan still considered as *kanaka-zoku* in the official context. It has since updated its profile on some, but not all, materials to describe Marshallese as *Mikuroneshia-kei*, or "Micronesian," in keeping with its profiles for the neighboring Federated States of Micronesia (a nation made up of former Nanyō Guntō districts Pohnpei, Kosrae, Chuuk, and Yap States) and Palau, as well as even Kiribati and Nauru to the south. But the lingering categorization of *kanaka-zoku* suggests that Marshall Islanders have been perceived as somehow racially different from other Micronesians when seen from an official Japanese optic that persists in ethnologically classifying the world's people. The ongoing imposition of such a pan-Pacific plantation-era category (the Polynesian word *kanaka* was never a part of the Marshallese language), moreover, gives an indication of the extent to which Japan still frames Marshallese people in colonialist terms.[19]

Returning to the photographic images of Marshallese, it is important to consider the overall Japanese colonial practice of imaging as well. Morris Low (2003) writes of the way photography was used to support Japanese colonialism in China during the same period. Images were used to produce icons of truth that could convey a scientific "objective" vision of Manchuria as both a site of touristic beauty worthy of "sightseeing" and an unstable, impoverished territory in need of Japanese rehabilitation and military intervention (Low 2003, 110–113):

> Through the use of Western science and the camera, the Japanese sought to impose a modernity on the Chinese and the people of Manchuria as part of their own colonialist project. We can conceive the use of photography as part of cross-cultural communication, a spectatorship that provokes thoughts and action. A certain "look"

involves power relations that can subjugate and empower. (Low 2003, 118)

Granted, photography served similar Japanese imperial interests of subjugation and empowerment in Micronesia, but of course we should keep in mind not to attribute too much power to that gaze itself, as colonial encounters were not so simple. Low writes about images taken by the Japanese government in Manchuria, but he does not take into account the ways such images intersected with popular culture and how this trickled down to the public and to the individuals who actually went to Manchuria. Clearly the intertextuality of popular media—not only photographs but also artistic renderings, music, film, and so forth—created a semiotic "mythology" (Barthes 2000) of representation that cannot be ignored.

In the Micronesian context, tropes of the tropics, primitiveness, blackness, and the available chiefly virgin bride were deeply entangled throughout both official and public representations of Nanyō, ranging from Japanese-navy-sponsored propaganda films like *Umi no Seimeisen* (1932) and *Waga Nanyō* (1936) to the glossy ethnological Nanyō photograph albums, to the observations of Hijikata Hisakatsu and Nakajima Atsushi in the 1930s and 1940s, and indeed to popular songs like "Shūchō no Musume." Settlers, colonial administrators, businessmen, travelers, and soldiers then reproduced these mythologies and assumptions in their own private photographs and memoirs, diaries, poems, songs, and a wide range of other forms about what they observed or wanted to see in the Marshall Islands. This is no different from how Japanese and American tourists today perpetuate their own tropical fantasies on Waikiki Beach in Hawai'i (Feeser and Chan 2006), deliberately framing their snapshots to reproduce the postcard images imprinted in their minds, rather than what they see before their eyes.

Dankichi Dancing

Meanwhile, though Japanese narratives increasingly eroticized and romanticized the Marshall Islander women, they tended to reduce Nanyō Guntō men to comical "black" primitive people who could be enlisted to support the empire.[20] This was particularly evident in the *manga* comic *Bōken Dankichi* (Dankichi the adventurous), created by Shimada Keizō in 1931 and published until 1939 in the popular boys' magazine *Shōnen Kurabu* (Shimada 1976). Read widely by Japanese boys, the comic was a simple narrative of a wide-eyed boy, Dankichi, who, having set out one fine day on a fishing trip with his trusty mouse friend Karikō, falls asleep and finds himself washed up on a tropical island somewhere in Nanyō Guntō.

Wasting no time upon his arrival on this jungle island, Dankichi strips off his shirt and trousers, dons a grass skirt, and, still wearing his shoes and a wristwatch, sets out to dethrone the chief of the island kingdom. He mingles among the "black" *kuronbō* Natives by covering himself in mud and eating bananas, but his cover is blown when a passing squall washes the color away. The chief is enraged by this infiltrator, whom, interestingly, he calls a "whitey" (*shiranbō*). Fearing that he might be eaten by the Natives (an obvious reference to adventure stories of cannibalism[21]), Dankichi easily outsmarts the chief by setting a trap.

Upon supplanting the chief and securing a promise of peace, Dankichi takes the chief's crown and places it upon his head, thereby designating himself the new chief of "Dankichi Island." He immediately and busily befriends the former chief and all the Natives, who happily allow him to paint their chests with numbers, since he cannot remember or pronounce their names. These Natives, who all look exactly the same, are all male, and are drawn as monkey-like black smiley creatures in the tradition of the "black sambo," gladly follow Dankichi and Karikō wherever they go. The Islanders, the *bankō* ("savages") are dressed in grass skirts and wear metal rings around their necks, a comic orientalist appropriation of other indigenous, perhaps African, cultures that further gives the characters a particular kind of "blackness." The boys who danced the "Daku-Daku Odori" no doubt must have been trying to achieve a similar comical primitive parody of blackness when they stepped out onto the playing field smeared in charcoal back in 1923. Accentuating the African motif, Dankichi's island is inhabited not only by the *bankō* Natives, but it is also home to fanciful exotic creatures like lions, giraffes, and ostriches that one might find in the Serengeti but certainly not on a small Micronesian island.

Russell argues that the genre of the "black other" in Japan, as seen in the chieftain's daughter archetype or the *Bōken Dankichi* comic, is in part a legacy of American and European "Negro primitivism" that uses many stereotypes of "Africans." This genre can be dated back to the nineteenth century, when Commodore Matthew Perry entertained

Japanese negotiators in 1854 with an "Ethiopian" minstrel show of white sailors in blackface (Russell 1991, 10). The Dankichi comic was certainly a twentieth-century perpetuation of this genre, yet it could also be said that the "native dances" of the 1920s were also linked to this same minstrel heritage.

Dankichi's glorious adventures in the South Seas continue throughout the comic. He proceeds to wage wars and conquer other islands, all the while tending to the needs of the Natives under his care. Waving small Japanese flags and shouting *"banzai,"* Dankichi leads the men on a march of progress that sees Dankichi in the role of school teacher, chief physician, military general, sports coach, policeman, and various other lead roles. His boyish enthusiasm and innocent playfulness seem to downplay the violence and oppressive coercion he initiates.

Dankichi's is a boy empire, rather like the fledgling imperial project of the Japanese nation itself. It is also a white empire, an articulation of Japanese-ness with European-ness and a narrative of masculine prowess. Essentially Dankichi is the boy hero who, like Barrie's Peter Pan (1928) and Stevenson's Jim Hawkins in *Treasure Island* (1930), is fully entitled to the colonial loot he stumbles upon. Out "fishing" at the beginning of his exploits, like resource-starved Japan in the early twentieth century, Dankichi proudly reaps his rewards as he builds up the economy of his colony. His earnest desire to "civilize" the Natives neatly conforms to the terms of the League of Nations mandate under which the Nanyō Guntō was to be administered. Like economist and educator Yanaihara Tadao, who surveyed the mandated islands and concluded that the Islanders were capable of being educated and nurtured into modernity (Yanaihara 1939; Townsend 2000, 197), Shimada, through his protagonist Dankichi, imagines a paternalistic relationship between "white" Japanese and "black" Islanders, who with proper nurturing can achieve self-determination. Not unlike actual Japanese settler Mori Koben in Micronesia, Dankichi is a colonist who facilitates the expansion of empire but also tends to the needs of locals.[22]

Shimada's narrative represented a shift in popular cultural representations of the Nanyō Guntō away from the dreamy fantasy of a faraway paradise "under the equator" toward a different narrative in which the islands were conquered, controlled, and easily managed by Japanese leadership. Indeed, the Robinson Crusoe–type virtues of rugged survivalism and resourcefulness in the comic suggest a sort of dutiful imperial Japanese masculine ethic that could easily be translated into the national military agenda that was increasing in fervor at the time. It is important to note that other comics of the 1930s that were also serialized in *Shōnen Kurabu* alongside *Bōken Dankichi*—such as Tagawa Suihō's *Norakuro,* about a stray dog that leads a life in the imperial army—had distinctly military themes.

Sudō Naoto points out that the American animation Betty Boop also played a role in influencing both the chieftain's daughter trope and the *Bōken Dankichi* narrative. *Betty Boop's Bamboo Isle,* a 1932 animated piece in which a dark-skinned Betty Boop dances a Samoan dance while clad in a grass skirt, was given the title *Shūchō no Musume* (The chieftain's daughter) when it was shown in Japan, thus aligning racialized and sexualized fantasies for Japan in the the Marshall Islands with those of the United States in Samoa (Sudō 2010, 35). Sudō also argues that *Bōken Dankichi* cartoonist Shimada borrowed heavily from Boop's island and the African jungle setting from another of her cartoons, plus a scene where one character smears himself with mud to pass as a native (2010, 37). This intertwining of American and Japanese ambitions for the Pacific Islands is representative of the conflict and subsequent collaboration that would play out in the decades that followed.

A 1934 propaganda animated short by Komatsuzawa Hajime also fuses American and Japanese popular cultural images in support of imperialism and militarization. It opens with an eclectic bunch of toy-like characters living on a small tropical island somewhere in the Pacific, all of whom are blissfully doing a Nanyō dance in step with the "Shūchō no Musume" melody. Out of the blue, they are attacked by a squadron of grotesque Mickey Mouse look-alikes swooping down from the sky aboard bats that attempt to invade their peaceful haven. The islanders call for help and are rescued by a group of Japanese storybook historical heroes led by Urashima Taro and Momotaro (another inspiration for the Dankichi character), who defeat the Mickey Mouse leader and restore order to the island. Sakura flowers blossom on the trees of the jungle, and the characters all begin to dance to a more Japanese-sounding tune in a traditional Bon Odori style. This cartoon, titled "Picture Book 1936,"[23] was likely meant to stir up motivation for Japan to expand its military in the wake of its withdrawal from the League of Nations in 1933, and a warning of impending war with the United States in 1936 (possibly because of the expiration of a naval treaty in that year). Here, the chieftain's daughter song thus becomes a soundtrack for the Japanese empire itself, an empire that must be defended staunchly by nationalist nostalgia for the home islands.

By 1941, the "chieftain's daughter" style of "Nanyō dancing" had become a trademark for southern expansion (*nanshin*) in general, as could be seen in a photograph printed in the *Mainichi Shimbun* newspaper in 1941, in which Japanese soldiers on the Burmese front were seen dancing a variation of a "Native dance" titled the "East Asia Co-Prosperity Sphere South Seas Dance," *Tōa Kyōei-ken Nanyō Odori* (Hosokawa 1992, 146). As Robertson (1995) argued about this dance, the "theatricality of the colonialist project" is enacted in the crossdressing and caricature of "South Sea Islanders" (974). Yet what is most fascinating for me is how this parody of Pacific Islanders was being performed even on the fringes of the Japanese empire, beyond the Pacific.

These soldiers depicted in the newspaper photo were not only wearing grass skirts, they were also wearing paper crowns, each of them acting out the part of the fictional island king, Bōken Dankichi. The soldiers enacted Dankichi's colonial *nanshin* progression farther south into Southeast Asia, fusing the pursuit of the chieftain's daughter with the comic book hero's colonial exploits. Yet in essence, the myth of the boy king who possesses an island is essentially the same narrative as that of an intrepid Japanese man who dances his way into the heart of a Marshallese princess, marrying into chiefdom as a result. Undoubtedly by the time of the Pacific War, this dancing had become enough of a genre unto itself that Hayashi Kōichi, former Kwajalein Imperial Japanese Army chief of staff until 1943, was compelled to write in his memoirs, "It seems that the main pastime of the Marshallese people was the kind of 'South Seas dancing' made famous by the song 'Shūcho no Musume.' " (Hayashi 1964, 4). But moreover, it was the soldiers stationed throughout the Nanyō Guntō and throughout the empire, often in blackface, who were the ones performing this dance, parodying local people right in front of their faces.

Encountering the Chieftain's Daughter

The mythologies of the chieftain's daughter and *Bōken Dankichi* were so pervasive that they primed Japanese steeped in this popular culture to encounter Islanders in the Marshalls and throughout Nanyō with a certain degree of expectation and ensuing disappointment. For instance, a sailor who worked aboard a naval mail ship that traveled between Japan and a number of ports in the Nanyō Guntō and parts of Asia made a direct reference to the "Shūchō no Musume" song upon seeing actual Islanders in a time when Ishida Hitomatsu's popular song was still a major hit played throughout Japan.

In a photo scrapbook a bereaved elder named Yoshie entrusted to me, I discovered a photo her father had taken in 1932, probably of a dance troupe, with an ironic caption painted beside it in white ink: "Is this what they mean by 'In the South Seas, she's a beauty?' " he asks sarcastically, citing Ishida's exact lines *"Nanyō ja bijin."* His diary and his various descriptions of Micronesian ports of call make the implication quite clear: the realities of the islands and Islanders who inhabited them were different from their romantic preconception.

In fact, there were many men who, like the legendary Mori Koben, became involved with local women (chiefly and otherwise), effectively married, and had children, thus fusing Japanese and Micronesian genealogies. This was compounded by the fact that most of the Japanese men who were sent to the Marshall Islands (even more than other parts of Micronesia) were either unaccompanied or young and single. Kobayashi Izumi researched how many *nikkeijin* (people of Japanese descent) there were in the Marshall Islands and discovered that about 30 percent of the population is part Japanese, most of whom are from chiefly families (Kobayashi 2007, 88). Writer Nakajima Atsushi, a fan of Robert Louis Stevenson's *Treasure Island* who traveled around the Nanyō Guntō in 1941 and wrote a travelogue of his journey,[24] described in his memoirs his encounter with "Young Paramount Chieftain Kabua" upon arrival in Jaluit Atoll in September of that year. He wrote:

> The [Kabua] home is a bungalow that looks like a small trader's shop. At the entrance is a sign with Japanese characters on it that read "Yashima Kabua . . ."[25]
>
> Explaining that the master of the house is not home, two young women greet me. At first glance, I know by their faces that they are of mixed Japanese blood, but even judging them by Japanese standards, they are certainly beauties [*bijin*]. I can tell immediately that they are sisters. The older one tells me she is Kabua's wife.
>
> Soon her husband is called home. He is black but is a young rather intelligent-looking fellow of about thirty years old who looks rather hesitant, as if he is perpetually on guard. Apparently he speaks enough Japanese to understand me, but he says nothing

but quiet words to express his comprehension of what I am saying. For a moment, I cannot believe that this is a Paramount Chieftain with an annual income of at least 50,000 to 70,000 [yen] . . .[26]

On my way back, I learn from one of the civil servants working there that the young Kabua had recently fathered a child with the younger sister of his wife (whom I had just met), and it was causing quite an uproar in the village. (Nakajima 2001, 200–201)

Nakajima's description of his brief exchange with an actual "Chieftain," Iroojlaplap Kabua Kabua, and two beautiful women is another episode that says much about how Japanese perceptions of Marshall Islanders were shaped by an ongoing, intertextual narrative of race and exoticism. Nakajima, who was only in his early thirties himself, was not much different in age from Kabua Kabua, and yet he paternalistically describes the chief in his writing as "Young Kabua" (*Kabua Seinen*). The women he encounters are "of mixed blood" but they are "beauties" (*bijin*) by Japanese standards. Again, this statement is like a rehearsal of the "Shūchō no Musume" narrative of "black" (or in this case mixed-blood) but beautiful in the South Seas, "even by Japanese standards." Likewise, Kabua is "black" but intelligent. Unpacking these statements, "black *but* beautiful" and "black *but* intelligent" of course reveals the author's underlying racist equation of blackness with unattractive simplemindedness. Finally, his anecdote about Kabua Kabua's involvement with his wife's sister and the birth of a child, incidentally yet another "chieftain's daughter," ridicules the chief as a promiscuous—even incestuous—savage.

Yet flipping this encounter around and listening to a Marshall Islander perspective on the same moment tells a very different story. Possibly unbeknownst to Nakajima, the two Japanese-looking sisters he writes about were in fact the daughters of Noda Tetsuzō, a Japanese businessman who had been dispatched to the Marshall Islands in the 1930s by Nanyō Bōeki Kaisha. Noda, who fathered three children in Kosrae with a woman named Srue,[27] was then transferred to Jaluit Atoll, where he subsequently partnered with a woman of chiefly descent named Eline, from Mejit Island. Like Mori Koben in Chuuk, Noda thus literally had a Marshallese "lover-san," a real "chieftain's daughter."

Noda and Eline had three daughters in the Marshall Islands: Yamato, Kimie, and Tamai. It is the elder two daughters that Nakajima meets in his narrative. Kabua married Yamato and the two lived together, but in keeping with the Marshallese *irooj* custom of being free to have more than one partner, Eline allowed Kabua to cohabit with their daughter Kimie as well; hence the birth of the child that Nakajima describes. As this sort of practice was quite common in the Marshall Islands among chiefs, it is worth questioning whether this "uproar" (*ōsawagi*) happened in the overall Marshallese community or in the Japanese expatriate community that was shocked by this custom.

According to Kimie's granddaughter Fumiko, the *real* "uproar" for the *Marshallese* community of Jaluit at the time had ensued many years earlier, when Kabua's father-in-law Noda went back to Japan, entered into an arranged marriage with a Japanese woman, and returned matter-of-factly with his new bride, who moved into the family home and lived together alongside Eline and the rest of the family, much to Eline's dismay.[28] While the Japanese wife generally kept to herself and helped out with the household, most family members ignored her and did not speak to her, to the extent that her name is not even remembered by Marshallese descendants, who only knew her as *okusan* ("the wife").

Kaname Yamamura also reflected upon this sort of mixing in his childhood at Wotje Atoll. His father, Hiroshi, another Japanese businessman with Nanyō Bōeki Kaisha, like Noda Tetsuzō, also had a Japanese wife, whom Kaname affectionately referred to as his "Japanese mother" (in Japanese, he called her his "*Nihon no okāsan*"). Granted, the idea of fathers having more than one partner is perhaps less stigmatized in the Marshalls, where there are expressions like *mamaan maj* ("men [are like] sea worms")[29] and *jined ilo kōbo, jemād im jemā ro jet* ("our mother is ours forever; our father also the father of others").[30] Pollock (1970) also shows how dynamic the Marshallese extended family structure is in accommodating children from different unions. Yet, as in the case of the cold reception of Noda's Japanese wife by his Marshallese family back in Jaluit, clearly such marital arrangements were not taken lightly if they crossed racial borders in certain ways.

The stigma of such unions with local women was even more pronounced back in Japan, where presumably most businessmen or officials on assignment in the Marshall Islands often chose to keep quiet about their Islander lovers or children and perpetuate family obligations by marrying other Japanese, even if it resulted in complex arrangements in their Nanyō lives. Former Nanyō administrator Yasutake Seitarō reflects that:

> Concerning marriage between Japanese and islanders, it was said that marriage with foreigners would make our blood polluted or make our family record dirty because the Japanese were a so-called "Pure" race. Furthermore, the Japanese prewar family system was very restricted. In case of a union between a Japanese and an islander, if the Japanese father acknowledged a child of this union as his own, then the child was given a Japanese name, which was registered in the government's record as an adoption. (Higuchi 1987, 62)

Many Japanese fathers refused to register the children they produced with Islander women, resulting in those children being seen as *otoshidane*, "fallen seeds" (illegitimate) by Japanese authorities. At the same time, from a Japanese standpoint, common-law marriages to Islanders were not legally recognized, so it was likely that the family obligations of Yamamura or Noda back in Japan required them to engage in an arranged marriage (*omiai kekkon*) with a Japanese woman, regardless of circumstances. In the case of Marshallese-Japanese Kaname, who was recognized by his father and traveled with him on various errands to Japan, the extent of his father's local relationship was accepted and understood.[31] Here Kaname poses (second from left in back row) with his relatives at a family gathering in Nagasaki.

Kobayashi Izumi has argued that from an Islander perspective of matrilineal land tenure and power, intermingling with the Japanese colonizer was acceptable, if not desirable. In a matrilineal society like the Marshall Islands, he explains, where women have traditionally been in control of the assets and all children born become a part of the mother's family, the identity or background of the father is not very important. This, added to the need for small island communities to avoid consanguine relations and ally with colonial power, compelled many chiefs to marry their daughters to the single Japanese men that were posted in their islands, which explains why so many chiefly families throughout Micronesia possess some degree of Japanese heritage (Kobayashi 2007, 89).[32]

Izumi's argument highlights the agency of Islander communities in relation to Japanese settlers, who were in the minority, compared to places like Palau or Saipan. But it is also important here to note the agency of women in the Marshall Islands, first and foremost, in the sense that a chiefly daughter would be a very powerful chief in her own right, a *lerooj* (female chief), not simply the property of her father to be brokered and traded. Her position afforded tremendous power in that *she* could negotiate on behalf of her matriline. From a Marshallese perspective, it was not the whim of Japanese or Marshallese men nor the chauvinism of a patriarchal Japanese colonial system, but rather the wisdom and authority of chiefly women who were able to influence the colonial power structure and turn the odds in their favor. From this Marshallese perspective, the *Shūchō no Musume* song takes on a much more nuanced meaning, not one in which a destitute Islander Cinderella awaits her prince, but one in which an empowered *lerooj* princess sweeps the powerless Japanese businessman off his feet and gives him access to her land in exchange for higher status in the empire.

Thus, despite the comedic, bizarre, and romantic narrative of Ishida Hitomatsu's song, the reality of mingling with a real-life woman of chiefly status was in fact a complex and problematic endeavor. I wish to draw attention to the broader, complicated contexts that superficial narratives like the "Daku-Daku Odori" and the "Chieftain's Daughter" betray. Like the coral reef, these are messy histories with multiple trajectories. Traders like Noda were much like coral polyps riding the currents, following along with the trends of colonialist culture but deliberately settling the reefs of the Marshall Islands and leaving their traces in the atolls they traversed.

Yet Noda did establish himself as the father-in-law of a major *iroojlaplap* of the Marshall Islands (indeed, a major leader with land claims at Kwajalein). His children and grandchildren went on to become significant local leaders, including his grandson Kimilang (Phillip), a diplomat who served as the Marshallese ambassador to Japan. Like many other Japanese men who settled and started families, Noda and Kaname's father are remembered positively by their many descendants and larger communities. Although the popular narratives of prewar Japanese colonialism were about incorporating and possessing Nanyō, nowadays, when Japan has all but forgotten its erstwhile tropical Other, it could be said that Marshall Islanders of Japanese descent still "possess" Japan proudly through their own genealogical heritage.

Dancing Back the Memories: The Mission Continues

Driving up from the city of Kobayashi in Miyazaki Prefecture, Japan, I am struck by the sight of a Micronesian building off to the side of the road approaching the Ikōma Highlands. Standing next to several rows of greenhouses and surrounded by bales of hay is a traditional Palauan meeting house, a *bai*.[33] I pull over to the side of the road and notice a plywood sign in the shape of an Islander woman: "Welcome, Free Entry."

The *bai* has been erected, I soon learn, by the local residents, a small community of farmers who all relocated from Palau at the end of the war, when they were forced to repatriate to Japan. The youngest of the village's residents, Kubo Matsuo, takes a break from his farming, bowing and wiping sweat from his forehead as he approaches me with soil on his hands. Looking at me cautiously he explains, "We don't get many visitors here. Most people don't care about the past anymore, but for our families it was bad enough just to have to come back to Japan at the end of the war.... That place in Palau was our home, our place. It was part of Japan. We needed to remember it somehow, so before all of us die we decided to go back to Palau and find someone who could build us one of these."

Kubo tells me he is already in his seventies and was born in Palau, the former capital of the Nanyō Guntō, in a time when Japanese outnumbered Palauans and other Micronesians. His parents were among many from large families who took advantage of the Japanese government's out-migration and settlement (*kaitaku*) scheme in the mandated territories as a way of starting a new life and making more income. He was still a young boy when the Pacific War ended, but he had gone to school together with Palauans and other Micronesians, and he even knew some Marshall Islanders who had been sent to study there. When American forces finally reached Koror, the capital, many civilians, including Kubo's family, survived by surrendering and sailing back to Japan on US naval vessels.

"Returning" to Japan for Kubo and many other youth, however, was like settling in a strange country. All the people from his village in Palau had to apply to the government under yet another agricultural development and settlement scheme, buying cheap land in Miyazaki Prefecture, where the population was sparse. Southern Japan, with its subtropical climate, seemed ideal to these families. Yet the city of Kobayashi, a rugged town at the base of the Kirishima mountain range founded on the logging industry, is a long drive from the coast. In the winter, the icy breezes from Mount Takachiho-no-Mine come sweeping down the plateau.

"So, we had to make it feel like home," Kubo says, smugly pointing to a framed photograph on the wall of the *bai*. "We had to dance!" I am surprised to find an image of a younger Kubo, together with three other men from the village, two of them shirtless, in plastic green grass skirts. They are thrusting their right legs forward and raising their arms in synchronization. They look a little red in the face, and Kubo laughs as he explains that they had been drinking.

He tells me that whole village has been doing this Palau-inspired dance ever since they returned to Japan in the 1940s, and they often perform it in small, intimate drinking circles and social gatherings like weddings. In the beginning, they used to paint their faces black with charcoal, he says, but that was "too much trouble," so these days they just use the grass skirts and that suffices. "*Chotto odoru dake de omoidasu wa*—Just a little dancing and the memories all come back," he says, lovingly hugging one of the beams in the meeting house.

While I have not found a similar example of a whole community of postwar returnees to Japan from the Marshall Islands, the elderly dancers of Kobayashi are not alone in their Nanyō nostalgia. Another group in the Ogasawara Islands has popularized their "Nanyō Odori" as cultural heritage (Tomita 2005). It was at the Festival of Pacific Arts in Palau in July 2004 that I first observed them as they made their first public appearance in Micronesia, dancing on stage in front of large crowds of Islanders from all over Oceania.

Beginning their dance with the incantation in English of "left, right, left, right . . . ," the dancers moved their bodies in a peculiarly stiff fashion. Their movements were awkward, childlike, and deliberately exaggerated, a bit like toy soldiers. The music sung by a woman in the background was also unusual, a hybrid of Chamorro and Palauan words mixed in with Japanese, yet jumbled together and impossible to comprehend. The "nonsense" lyrics and the marching, childlike movements, I would argue, were probably not all that different from the "Daku-Daku Odori" of the 1920s. The military-like marching, moreover, seemed like a reference to the regimented marching exercises first introduced by Germans and later enforced by Japanese authorities throughout Micronesia, even echoed in cartoon form when Bōken Dankichi marches the Natives off to war.[34]

There was a solemnity on the dancers' faces, however, a noticeable austerity with which they performed their well-rehearsed steps. Undoubtedly this was not mere entertainment for the dancers; it was part of their own heritage. There was a bittersweetness and nostalgia that underscored the spectacle, and the audience seemed to notice this as well, for many people nodded in empathy and seemed strangely to connect with these visitors from Japan. While the mockery of the dance was potentially offensive, it was more than made up for by the earnestness of the dancers, many of them young and genuinely passionate about their art.

I traveled twenty-five hours south of Tokyo by ferry to Chichijima, Ogasawara, in the summer of 2009 to meet with these dancers and hear their stories. Our ship was greeted by their dancing as it came into the harbor. Their Nanyō Odori, they told me, had been taught by members of their community who had returned from Saipan before the war, and the elders of their community had proudly passed it on to younger generations. Their dance was preserved as part of Tokyo's cultural heritage, yet when I asked about its deeper origins, they spoke about it in romantic terms, saying that all they knew was that it was a "traditional" dance taught to their ancestors by Nanyō Islanders. Many of the people of Chichijima and Hahajima are themselves mixed-race ancestors of whalers from the United States and Hawai'i who were the first settlers of their islands. For them, the dance gave them a sense of belonging to an island heritage, much like other members of their community earnestly danced hula. Still, they referred to the leader of their dance group by using the outdated and orientalist term *shūchō,* a clear reference to "The Chieftain's Daughter." One of the dancers invited me to her home and showed me photographs of other Nanyō dancers on Hahajima, dancing with their bodies covered in soot. "They still do it the old way," she remarked with a giggle and a hint of nostalgia.[35]

Once again, it is as if the chieftain's daughter makes her appearance in the postwar Japanese imaginary, yet she has transformed many times over. She originated in the 1920s as a faraway colonial exotic dream, metamorphosed into a seductive "lover" and bride, and eventually symbolized entwined Japanese-Micronesian genealogies. Yet in the postwar period she has become an object of forlorn longing rather than fanciful desire. Like the islands lost when Japan was defeated during the war, the chieftain's daughter is a lost "lover-san," never to return. Whereas the prewar "South Seas" dances and narratives triumphantly and romantically celebrated Japan's expansion into the Pacific, the postwar Nanyō dances like those in Miyazaki and Ogasawara, or the song sung by the leader of the dance troupe, mourn the loss of a tropical homeland.

For Islander elders, the song and dance has a different meaning, of course. Kurata Yōji, a Japanese settler who spent his early adulthood in Palau before and during the war, confirmed my suspicions that the original Nanyō Odori was not a traditional dance by any means, but song and dance that was often done to entertain men while drinking, whether it be comical or erotic.[36] When I asked Humiko Kingzio, an elderly Palauan woman whose father was an Okinawan settler, if she knew about this dance, she immediately answered by explaining that it was the dance that accompanied "The Chieftain's Daughter" song, generously—if hesitantly—agreeing to dance it for me that evening. Explaining to me that it was the dance that she used to dance for the soldiers during the war, she locked the front door, let down her long hair and began to sway her hips and sing as she slowly glided around the room.[37] Back in the Marshall Islands, Emlain Kabua, widow of first president Amata Kabua and a *lerooj* female chief herself, explained to me that as a child growing up on Jaluit, children were disciplined if they sang the song, explaining to me that "It was a culture for grown-up men, not for us children to know about."[38]

In Japan, despite the nearly universal memory today of "Shūchō no Musume" among the elderly, few of the younger generation, including the Japanese tourists who flock to resort hotels, have any awareness of the link between Japan and Micronesia. They do not see how prewar Japanese colonialism is related to tuna fisheries, to development aid and construction, to elections, or to postwar nuclear testing (Kawamura 1994, 7). They are often not even aware of the war between the United States and Japan and how it shaped the future of all Micronesian islands, let alone the Japan-US Security Alliance that still allows for American bases on Japanese soil. Kwajalein or the Marshall Islands, let alone the Pacific Islands in general, do not enter into the awareness of most people in Japan today.

But while Japan lost its South Sea islands, America gained power over the Pacific and the Japanese home islands as well. Though Japan had long eroticized its colonial other in the form of the chieftain's daughter, now it was Japanese who became the object of America's imperial desire.[39] As Dower writes, after the war, "the eroticization of defeated Japan in the eyes of the conquerors took place almost immediately, creating a complex interplay of assumed masculine and feminine roles that has colored US-Japan relations ever since" (1999, 137). Similarly, in the Pacific Islands, American popular culture narratives also began to emerge. The US military presence throughout Micronesia added a new layer of "concrete" to the atollscapes of Kwajalein and other "Martial Islands," and soon American representations of both Islanders and Japanese began to take center stage.

In these new currents of empire that spread out across the ocean, the chieftain's daughter gradually disappeared from view, but her history was sedimented deep into the coral reef. Gone but not forgotten, her song can still be recited by the declining numbers of elderly people in Japan and in the islands, who watch her dance across their memories.

CHAPTER 4

Bones

Confronting the Atollscapes of War

> Full fathom five thy father lies;
> Of his bones are coral made . . .
> *Shakespeare,* The Tempest

A CASUAL WALK AROUND MOST OF THE ISLANDS throughout the Marshall Islands immediately reveals the scars of fighting from the Pacific War. In atolls like Jaluit, Wotje, Maloelap, and Mili, many people have returned to their land and built upon the remains of Japanese military bases. Some Marshallese residents have made use of old Japanese buildings, cleaned them up, and returned to their own land to live in them. Children sometimes swim in rainwater collected in the craters from American bombs. At Kwajalein Atoll, where US military installations have reshaped the landscapes and shorelines of some islands and displaced the indigenous population entirely from many others, these old structures stand out—abandoned—amid the silent manicured lawns and picket fences of the base. The adjoined islets of Roi-Namur (Ruotto and Nimuru in Japanese), in the north of the atoll, almost serve as a museum for Japanese prewar concrete defense architecture, their desolate gutted-out and bullet-pocked old buildings standing amidst the postwar American missile-testing facility buildings, radars, and antennas.

As I walk around taking photos and footage of these machine-gun-etched structures close to where my father once worked on Roi-Namur,[1] I remember how I used to climb on these concrete bunkers when I was a child, as in the photo on the next page with my mother from 1976.

I flash back to being seven years old and going on a picnic with

Bones: Confronting the Atollscapes of War 93

my father one Saturday, listening to his stories as we bicycled around the island together, the smell of barbecuing hot dogs, salt spray, and jet fuel from the runway on the ocean breeze. My father had just bought me my first camera, a Kodak Instamatic, and we were taking pictures together around the island.

"See that thing over there?" he points, gesturing toward a mossy concrete mound in the middle of the Kwajalein golf course. The structure's iron reinforcements are protruding, blood-like rust oozing down the sides. "That's a bunker. It's where the Japanese soldiers used to hide during the war." He squints as he looks into the viewfinder, painstakingly adjusting the aperture and fine-tuning the focus before snapping a shot of me standing in front of the crumbling old fortification. He pats me on the shoulder and waves at one of his work colleagues rolling a golf bag across the grass. We ride around the runway, past a big C-141 cargo plane, pushing hard against the wind. "And see?" We stop our bikes at the southwest tip of the islet near the Japanese Cemetery. "That's where our soldiers came onto the island when we came to free this island from the Japanese," he says, pointing toward the reef between the southern tip of Kwajalein and the neighboring islet we called "Carlson," which I later learned was really named Ānebouj (Enubuj).

My dad also shows me the impressive collection of white globes and radar antennas gathered along that end of the islet. "I control a radar like this one at my company, too," he says as he squints up into the afternoon sunshine with an obvious sense of awe and pride in the technological creature that rotates above our heads.

"What's that for?" I ask.

"We use these radars so we can see if other countries like Russia are trying to invade us or shoot missiles at us. And we use them to test our own missiles. You know like when we have a mission and I stay at work late so we can shoot one of those rockets into the lagoon?"

"Why do we test missiles?" I would ask him.

"It's not easy, son," he would say. "But there's always a war going on somewhere in this world, and you or I might have to go and fight someday. And that's why I work here, so that we don't have a big war, so that we're all safe."

My father and I would have conversations like these as I grew up on Kwajalein in the 1970s. The stories he told left images in my mind from a world I didn't understand. They seeped into my dreams at night, dreams in which my father was taken away by the Russians or the Japanese. Dreams in which Japanese soldiers, who all somehow managed to live in little concrete boxes, pulled me underground into their hideaways.[2] Dreams in which missiles rained down from the sky. I knew what that would look like, after all: We used to sit outside drinking lemonade while watching the missile tests once a month at night. The colorful streaks of unarmed warheads re-entering the atmosphere and crisscrossing the sky before they entered the lagoon are imprinted in my mind.[3]

My father's folksy explanations of our island home in the 1970s and 1980s, though well-intended and gentle, likely had their roots in the American victory narratives of World War II that have come to dominate most contemporary Micronesian histories. He had probably heard the stories from colleagues at work and other fellow American residents and had taken them for granted. They innocently reflected the paternalistic martial masculinity that was emblematic of American power in modern Micronesia.[4] Through his stories, I learned that we all lived perpetually under the threat of an unseen enemy, but that my father and the other American fathers of Kwajalein would use their Buck Rogers–like radar beams and missiles to protect us. I began to assume that before the Americans came, "The Japanese" were sneaky but ultimately impotent men who suddenly captured and held these islands like fortresses, and that "the Americans," for the sake of freedom, came marching onto the island in 1944 just like we Boy Scouts used to march in the annual Kwajalein Parade, waving the American flag and setting things straight.

Kwaj Karnival

We celebrated liberation every year when I was growing up. Commemoration of liberation was always part of the biggest event of the year, the Kwaj Karnival, a huge attraction held around Memorial Day and planned for many months in advance.[5] It culminated in a full-scale fairground on the playing fields between the air terminal and the racketball courts, in a part of Kwajalein Island known by the original Marshallese inhabitants (Ri-Kuwajleen) as the stretch between Minpit-ien Wāto and Riken-jen Wāto.[6] This area was also close to where Japanese military barracks and the admiralty area once stood.[7]

The Karnival included a wide array of games and attractions ranging from bingo to "dunk the mermaid"; food stalls selling corn dogs, fish and chips, and many delicacies from all over the world; and even a number of rides like a carousel (which my father once let me operate) and a small Ferris wheel. I was not aware, nor probably were most children, that the main focus of the event was not mere community entertainment but the institutionalized celebration of American military sacrifice and victory in the Marshall Islands. There was, however, usually a display of photographs in a tent somewhere near the entrance. Posters lined up on bulletin boards were covered with black-and-white photographs labeled with all the stages of Operation Flintlock, the invasion of Kwajalein Atoll.[8]

Though I was much more interested in getting in line for cotton candy and going on the rides, I remember these images vaguely. They were the same images that also appeared annually in the *Hourglass* military newspaper,[9] pictures of devastated smoky landscapes and palm trees with no fronds. There were images of American soldiers disembarking in droves from amphibious landing craft on the beaches, lying bravely on the ground with guns pointed at an unseen enemy, or carrying wounded comrades. There was one image of a Japanese man with his hands raised high in the air in surrender, and another image of a Marshallese woman being given water from a canteen by Marines. There was also a picture of indistinct bodies, blurry and unrecognizable, face down and mixed in with the coral debris.

As I will discuss later, such photographs and others served to capture these moments of victory and liberation and act as proof of American military might at a time when morale was flagging amidst a major world war. As testimony of the US campaign they also became illustrations for future battle planners and became historical evidence lest there be any doubt about American hegemony in the Pacific. To me as a young American child, they were part of a bigger narrative that taught me to picture Marshallese as happy bystanders, singing and cheering elatedly as these victors arrived, hands outstretched to receive chocolate bars and Spam—on the sidelines, watching the real world pass them by. Flattened like the characters of a children's story, all the characters in the drama looked like good guys, bad guys, and some extra guys on the side (and all guys no less). Indeed, the drama of Kwajalein, let alone the history of many former US Trust Territory Micronesian islands, is a relentlessly, often exaggeratedly androcentric narrative in which Islanders have been cast as "emasculated" damsels in distress, Japanese as wicked imperialist menaces, and Americans as benevolent bearers of justice and freedom.

These kinds of strong sentiments about American victory and liberation persist today on Kwajalein, especially since the United States has been waging a perpetual war in the Middle East. The Karnival ceased in the early 1980s due to the high costs and various liabilities to contractors, but Operation Flintlock continues to be observed annually, often with the visit of many American veterans and a wide range of solemn ceremonies. With the fiftieth anniversary of the invasion in 1994, the battlefields of Kwajalein and Roi-Namur were commemorated with the installation of memorials, such as the chapel's stained glass window depicting a soldier kneeling on one knee with his face to the American flag and his back to the Marshallese flag. Later in the 1990s, the ruins of Japanese fortifications and structures on Roi-Namur and Kwajalein were included in the registry of US national historic landmarks under the US National Park Service as relics of that battlefield and American victory. As always, today the *Kwajalein Hourglass* publishes many of these war images to remember the invasion and to honor troops (such as on American national holidays like Memorial Day or Independence Day), and they are displayed prominently throughout the base installations of the atoll.

With all this commemoration and fervor, it should not come as a surprise that many Marshallese observers would be inclined to characterize the US initiatives in World War II as a mere part of an endless war that has never stopped (Carucci 1989, 76–77). The atomic bomb tests during the Cold War at Bikini and Enewetak, followed by the missile testing at Kwajalein, the mobilization of the military in connection with the Korean War and Vietnam War, and even the present-day global "wars on terror" would likely all be included in this Marshallese idea of their islands and oceans being used as a "perpetual battlefield." But many Marshallese leaders describe the sacrifice of their land in terms of the global security it provides. Jack Akeang, former Kwajalein councilman involved in the drafting of the Marshallese constitution, once stated that Marshallese "export [their] peace and love to the rest of the world" (*Kwajalein Hourglass,* March 23, 2005, 4).

Still, the liberation narrative throughout the Pacific and elsewhere tends to legitimize US military versions of history while downplaying the experiences and hardships of the people who experienced that history. In the case of Kwajalein, it reinforces American postwar power and rationalizes the ensuing marginalization and displacement of Marshall Islanders on their own lands and seas. It disallows Marshallese agency and renders unimportant the various Marshallese legacies of survival and resistance to colonialism that came long before the Americans or the Japanese. It also disallows the histories of a relatively prosperous and positive prewar era under the Japanese administration. Japanese wartime militarism caused its own share of horrific violence, including strict discipline toward Islanders in general; yet the story of the war is not so simple. In focusing exclusively on American victory, the liberation story denies the non-American memories of Marshallese, Japanese, Okinawans, and Koreans for their loved ones who also sacrificed their lives in one of the bloodiest confrontations of the Pacific War.

Capturing Kwajalein: The Larger Context

The invasion of the Marshall Islands was, of course, much more complex than the simplistic narratives I had gleaned from my childhood and my high school education in the United States. As I have described already, it figured largely in American plans for securing power in the Central Pacific, even before the League of Nations had awarded Japan the mandate to govern Micronesia as the Nanyō Guntō.

In the early 1940s, Japanese plans, meanwhile, entailed the reinforcement of the Central Pacific as a barrier against invasion. Japanese forces were reconfigured by September of 1943, the eighteenth year of Shōwa,[10] under a new line of defense in the Pacific that crossed through Chuuk (Truk), known as the "Tōjō Line," after wartime prime minister Tōjō Hideki. Much of that year was spent building up and fortifying Kwajalein Atoll and other sites in the Marshalls to be the front line of defense. The Marshall Islands were seen as "unsinkable aircraft carriers," and Admiral Koga Mineichi, Combined Fleet commander, saw their role as being to delay and weaken the Americans, after which airpower from the Combined Fleet would be sent from Chuuk to end the struggle in a "decisive battle" (Rottman 2004, 21).

These plans to take to the high seas and defend the nation's "Lifeline of the Sea" (Umi no Seimeisen) were romanticized in naval songs like the military song (*gunka*) "Taiheiyō Kōshin Kyoku" ("March of the Pacific," Kingu Records 1939), which captured the spirit of pride as young conscripted soldiers and sailors were sent to the Nanyō front. It was both a glorification of the Imperial Navy and a theme that sailors sang on ships. The song celebrates a prewar ideal of victorious manhood, sort of a repetition of the adventurous imperial boyhood enshrined in the *Bōken Dankichi* comic series. Even today many elderly Marshallese can sing it in Japanese, and several proudly sang it for me, explaining that they had learned it in school or heard people singing it around the Kwajalein base:

Umi no tami nara,	If you're a seafarer,
otoko nara,	if you're a man,
minna ichido wa akogareta	your day has come
Taiheiyō no Kuroshio o	to sail the Japan Current
tomo ni isande	o'er the Pacific of your yearning
ikeru hi ga	bravely together,
kita zo, kanki no	with a thrill that
chi ga moeru.[11]	makes your blood boil.

These heroic lyrics belied the darker realities of the Japanese militarization of the Marshalls. To build up and fortify the base, authorities established the Fourth Fleet Construction Unit, which was made up of civilians employed by the Japanese military, mostly Korean laborers and Japanese who were unfit for military service. The main task of these workmen around the time of the battle was building the runway: blasting and pulverizing coral from the reef and compacting it onto the airfield. If the laborers who were at Enjebi in Enewetak Atoll were any indication of the makeup of the construction battalions at

Kwajalein, this unit would have included not only Koreans but also many Okinawans from poor rural villages. Peattie reports that more than two thousand prisoners were mobilized for labor (1988, 252), although the number of these that went to the Marshalls was much smaller. In 1940, 104 inmates were transferred from Abashiri Prison in Hokkaido to Yokohama Prison, where they were sent with additional prisoners aboard the *Kokushima Maru* in battalions with names like *sekiseitai* (patriotic corps) to work on building airstrips in Tinian (Shigematsu 2002, 32). Three hundred were then sent onward to work at Wotje Atoll in the Marshalls to build airstrips there (Ogiu 1966, 179). An additional wave of prisoners was sent from Yokohama later in the war to fortify the defenses at Weno (formerly Moen), Chuuk. Many of these laborers were actually intellectuals, artists, and activists, many of whom had been arrested by the Kenpeitai Special Police on suspicion of being communist or being a general threat to the war effort. Many of these laborers died of heat exhaustion before the rest were sent back to Japan. The remainder stayed in Micronesia and most were killed when they were caught up in the ensuing military conflicts.

The roughly 1,200 *tanki kōin* (short-term) Korean laborers at Kwajalein and Roi-Namur were conscripted for their labor under threat of imprisonment, like the father of Yi Won-Sun, a South Korean woman who returned for the first time to the Marshall Islands in August 2007 to mourn the loss of her father (Yun 2007). Documents translated by JICPOA (1944f) indicate that there were 19,916 *tanki kōin* laborers throughout the Japanese-occupied Pacific, mainly Koreans. The inability to replace these men, who were supposedly on one-year contracts, eventually led to changing their status to ordinary workmen (*kōin*). As of December 1943, the largest numbers were at Chuuk (10,326), Nauru (1,657), Kwajalein (1,253), Mili (1,196), and Wake (1,196).[12] And though details are scarce about the lives of the Koreans who lived and worked at Kwajalein, some of the hasty intelligence interviews conducted immediately after the battles later on at Enewetak Atoll give us some indication of how this story unfolded. For instance, twenty-two-year old Korean laborer Kang Ko-kae at Enjebi islet, Enewetak, was the eldest son of six who had been working as a civil servant in a rural town in central Korea. On November 23, 1942, he, along with many other Koreans taken forcefully from agricultural regions, had been sent from Busan aboard the *Hakosaki Maru,* which unloaded laborers throughout Nanyō Guntō en route to various atolls in the Marshalls (USMC 1944a, 2).[13]

These laborers were referred to locally as *"ninpu,"*[14] or "coolies," and their battalions were often supplemented by local Marshallese labor as well. Though most Islanders were relocated to smaller islands, and the civil administration and school were relocated to Namo Atoll, men like Handel Dribo and Manke Konol in Kwajalein were recruited to work with the *ninpu* as teenagers. They recalled being given Japanese nicknames, and they proudly described building barracks out of wood for soldiers shipped from Japan or constructing Japanese-style communal *ofuro* baths for soldiers to bathe in together.[15] Working conditions were harsh, but these men developed a rapport with their Japanese superiors. Separated into different battalions from their Korean counterparts—who often suffered even worse discrimination and violence from military leaders—the Marshallese laborers observed the radical differences between the aggressive military authorities and the amicable civilian authorities and businesspeople who had preceded them.

Marshallese were typically separated from Koreans and other laborers in wartime construction battalions, but even earlier, during the civilian administration, there was a general policy of segregation in matters of labor and schooling.[16] Tomiyama, citing a report by Umesao Tadao from the 1941 Nanyō Research Team, points out that most Micronesians were fluent in Japanese—often more than Koreans who had been forcefully recruited from mountain villages of Korea—and this sometimes even created a sense of Islander superiority and racial hierarchy toward these laborers, whom they saw as lower-class citizens of the Japanese empire (Tomiyama 2002, 62).[17]

Thousands of Japanese personnel, mostly from the Imperial Navy, were deployed to Kwajalein in two waves, one in around 1941, and a second, larger wave in 1943, which came down from other Japanese-held territories via the Philippines (Hayashi 1964, 22–23). Some of these soldiers had already seen intense combat in Manchuria, where new recruits were often initiated into military culture by executing prisoners of war with bayonets (Kawano 1996, 187). On many atolls, Japanese soldiers were deeply suspicious of Marshallese clergy or affiliates of mission schools, believing them to be allied with the Christian enemy, and in some cases, church leaders were severely punished or executed on suspicion of being spies.[18] Prewar chief of staff Hayashi Kōichi claimed that younger soldiers from the Shanghai Special Forces Unit were ordered to conduct an execution of American prisoners of war, nine captured Marines, on Kwajalein on October 16, 1942, an event that later resulted in several convictions during the war crimes trials (1964, 20–21).[19]

The shift between civilian and military rule was traumatizing not only to Marshall Islanders but to Japanese civilians as well. Yamaguchi Yōji, who was born in the Japanese community of Saipan and spent his early childhood there, described to me his horror upon first meeting a Japanese soldier when the war reached the Mariana Islands:

> I had never met any Japanese soldiers before. We used to pretend to be soldiers in school and we'd watch movies and all of that during the early 1940s, but then when the war actually came to Saipan and we had to go into hiding, that's when I actually saw them, because the civilians didn't really have much to do with those soldiers.
>
> I remember how we were all hiding in a cave when the Americans were invading, and we had to keep as quiet as possible. I was sitting there with my mother. And then all of a sudden, this baby started crying and it wouldn't stop. Everyone wished the baby would just be quiet, but they knew how awful it must have been for the mother. But then this soldier suddenly got up from where he was sitting and he pointed a gun right at the baby and shouted

at the mother in really harsh, military-like language, "If you don't shut that baby up, I'm going to have to kill it right this instant!" It scared all of us so much, and I couldn't believe it. It made me feel sick to my stomach. He didn't kill the baby, but just the thought that he would have done so without hesitation was horrible.[20]

At the same time, however, the rapid militarization of the Marshall Islands was also traumatizing to the young soldiers who were drafted and deployed suddenly to an unfamiliar environment. In war diaries confiscated from Imperial Navy ships during the war, many of the men posted to Kwajalein write about feeling bored or tremendously homesick, despite the camaraderie they felt with other sailors. Increasingly required to act as tough and resilient as possible, these men were expected to swallow their fear lest they be perceived as weak by the enemy. This photograph on the previous page, presumably taken on Kwajalein in one of the years prior to the American invasion, gives a sense of some of these complex emotions.

"They weren't allowed to say anything girly [*memeshii*]," explained the widow of Satō Shigeru, a civilian engineer who had worked repairing submarines on Kwajalein until 1944 and had even once traveled back to Japan before he died in the invasion of the atoll.[21] Reading Shigeru's self-censored letters of 1943 and 1944, one gets little sense of his everyday existence. He asked his wife to send a deck of playing cards, inquired whether their baby son had gotten fatter, and mentioned in passing how hot it was. He wrote about the outdoor theater where the soldiers were shown *samurai* films, and about how soldiers used to wash their laundry by hanging it out in one of the passing squalls, but not much else (Satō 1942).

Most of the young draftees had never seen tropical islands before and had no idea how to survive from the land and sea, unlike the earlier Japanese colonists, who not only knew how to fish and gather local food but also how to speak Marshallese and other local languages. The soldiers were also strictly forbidden from eating most local foods for fear of poisoning, so they relied on Japanese rations, which became scarce as supply routes were blockaded (Hayashi 1964, 12–14). As the Japanese troops became more desperate, further violence and strict martial regulations were implemented on both Marshallese and Japanese populations, including civilian labor crews, and the Koreans and Okinawans they comprised. This resulted in a general sense of friction and discontent on all sides.

Crushed Jewels

Despite all these preparations, Japanese airpower was unexpectedly so diminished in the southwest Pacific and other places by the middle of 1943 that it became clear that the Marshalls would be left largely undefended. The Japanese Fourth Fleet also had not expected the Americans to attack its new immediate headquarters at Kwajalein Atoll, which was still an incomplete base, but rather the more populated and fortified atolls of Jaluit and Mili, and base commander Admiral Akiyama Monzō had mistakenly shipped many troops from Kwajalein to Mili (Peattie 1988, 267).

As American plans became apparent to Japanese commanders, the order was given for the Marshalls to be "sacrificed" for the empire on behalf of the rest of the Fourth Fleet and ultimately the Japanese home islands. Hayashi Kōichi writes in his memoirs that even as early as May of that year and in the months before the American invasion, all of the Marshalls and Kiribati were already seen by the Japanese military as a potential *gyokusai* mission (Hayashi 1964, 24–27).[22] *Gyokusai*, a euphemistic word literally meaning "crushed jewel," was a term coined to make "total annihilation" (Dower 1986, 231–232) more palatable to the Japanese populace.[23] It was first used only months earlier in May of Shōwa 18 (1943), in the arctic confrontations at Attu Island in the Aleutians, to glorify the sacrifices of 2,600 imperial Japanese soldiers who fought to the death.

The ideal of *gyokusai* was that a soldier was to offer his life for the emperor rather than become a prisoner, even if it meant killing himself with a grenade or engaging in another form of suicide. Keene notes that sometimes *gyokusai* was carried out even when it would have been possible to continue resistance. After personally witnessing the *gyokusai* at Attu, he notes that soldiers were taught to believe that this practice was the way of all Japanese soldiers and that no Japanese soldier had ever been taken prisoner in the history of the empire; yet this was a complete fallacy, as even as recently as the Russo-Japanese War, high-ranking Japanese military officials had been prisoners and returned to Japan "without suffering disgrace" (Keene in Oda 2003, viii).

Granted, *gyokusai* was not desirable for many soldiers, who naturally wanted to return to their families, and the ordering of mass suicides by Japanese commanders in civilian communities in Okinawa and other sites later in the war are excruciating memories that continue to undermine relations between Okinawans and the central government in Tokyo.[24] But many soldiers feared being taken prisoner not only because of the shame they imagined they would be greeted with back in Japan, but because of the animosity and resentment (and likely retaliation) of their fellow soldiers. The kind of resentment Japanese soldiers felt (or were expected to feel) toward "deserters" who chose not to die with their comrades is encapsulated by an entry in a captured war diary from Hirobe Kiyoji, a first class maintenance seaman attached to the 952nd Air Group on Kwajalein, who was killed in the bombardment: "There was another deserter today. . . . I cannot understand the psychology of the kind of heartless individual who would desert at such a time when every single person is working to the utmost of his abilities. 17 February" (JICPOA 1944d).

It was in this mood of anticipation and expectation of an exhaustive fight-to-the-last that Japanese forces throughout Kwajalein Atoll began to prepare for the battle. Plans were drafted hastily for final fortifications: all Marshall bases' emplacements and fortifications were to be completed immediately; trenches were to be dug; all usable iron and concrete supplies were to be rallied together for further defense and weapons; food was to be secured; and local food sources were to be surveyed in case supplies ran out (Hayashi 1964, 25–26).

Even before the American land bombardment, the air raids were so severe over Kwajalein that a feeling of impending doom hung over the entire atoll. Marshallese describe hiding in bunkers for days and days on end and still remember the trauma painfully. One woman described to me the sound of the sand rushing like an avalanche down the sides of the dugout concrete shelter she hid in every time the American planes would come, certain that she would die. Some Japanese soldiers were also unnerved, as recounted in this diary entry from December 16, 1943: "I have a terrible headache. My toothache is getting better—still bothers me, however. I wonder if I'm getting another nervous breakdown from the bombings" (JICPOA 1944e, 3).

In other diaries of Japanese soldiers captured after the battle there are often comments about how the soldiers were so anticipating their demise that they consumed all their rations without budgeting for a long conflict, as in the case of the crew of a submarine chaser (*tokubetsu kusentei*) who within a week had downed the several cases of *sake* they had received when in port in Kwajalein. A seaman named Takizawa laments about a similar problem in his diary entry of January 9, 1944:

I read a story in a magazine (*The General*) today, describing how certain soldiers at the Burma front said, "We may be dead tomorrow;" smoked all the *Homare* [brand] cigarettes that had been distributed to them; and later wished they had saved some. Our situation is very similar. We couldn't bring ourselves to try to keep four months' supply of canteen goods while undergoing enemy air attacks and so we finished the supply in ten days. Here it is only January and we are already completely out of tobacco. The common feeling among the men is that since we are on the front lines in the service of our country there isn't much that we can do except to put up with everything. (JICPOA 1944c, 2)

The northern part of the atoll was the site of an airbase at Roi and Namur (Ruotto and Nimuru)[25] with almost three thousand personnel, only four hundred of whom were trained for combat (Peattie 1988, 267). In the south, there were about five thousand people on Kwajalein (Kuezerin) and another five hundred at the seaplane base on Ebeye (Ebize). The Japanese Sixth Base Force had only been on Kwajalein since August 1941 and at the time of the invasion it included a submarine base, communications unit, a guard force, a large number of civilian military contractors (*gunzoku*) such as submarine repairmen, and various other people who were passing through the area (Rottman 2004, 31; Hayashi 1964, 22–27; Fukushige 1987, 35–45).

American forces, frustrated by the losses suffered in Kiribati, were not willing to take any chances in the Marshalls, and so they sent 46,670 troops to Kwajalein—the Fourth Marine Division, which was to attack in the north of the atoll around Roi and Namur, and the Seventh Infantry Division, in the south around Kwajalein and surrounding islets. Between January 31 and February 3, Roi and Namur were invaded. Americans met with intense resistance on Namur, where island defenders hiding in the jungles fought from their various concrete emplacements with "light automatic weapons, mortars, and grenades against tanks, flame-throwers, satchel charges, armor-piercing shells, naval broadsides, and aerial bombs" until they were defeated (Peattie 1988, 267).

On "banana-shaped" Kwajalein Island, a newsreel from the Seventh Infantry Division described how they divided their operation into two regiments: "Each had half a banana and a day to peel it" (USMC 1944b). There were many more combat-ready Japanese troops on Kwajalein, so the fighting was even more intense, and it lasted from

February 1 through February 5,[26] in a climate of fraught struggle. The 61st Naval Guard force, 2,600 naval personnel, maintenance crews, construction workers, Koreans, Okinawans, Marshallese,[27] and others who were on-island at the time tried their hardest—sometimes even with swords—to resist the overwhelming attack that was raining down upon them. Even those who were not combat-ready and were hiding in bunkers were sometimes blasted out with torches. Though most Marshallese in Kwajalein Atoll had gone into hiding on nearby islets in the atoll at the time of the battle, American soldiers in the latter part of Operation Flintlock, which continued onwards to Enewetak Atoll and was just as gruesome, even knowingly attacked Marshall Islanders on occasion, as one elder describes: "They knew [we were Marshallese]! The soldiers called out to the leaders, 'Kanaka! Kanaka!' and waited until they responded, and then threw in the hand grenade. Such was the measure of their [insanity]" (Poyer, Falgout, and Carucci 2001, 124).

On February 2, Commander Akiyama issued the final order of *gyokusai* to all personnel, to die in their positions rather than be captured, and most remaining soldiers followed the command (Peattie 1988, 268). By the second week of February 1944, the main islets of Kwajalein Atoll had been reduced to rubble and charred terrain, and "The entire island [of Kwajalein] looked as if it had been picked up to 20,000 feet and then dropped" (quoted in Hezel 1995, 227). At the end of the conflict, out of the total 8,782 "Japanese" (Fukushige 1987) estimated to be in the atoll before the conflict (a number that included Koreans and Okinawans), 8,410 had died.[28] Among the dead were some of Japan's most elite commanders, but notably among those killed on Kwajalein was a high-ranking naval officer related to the imperial family, thirty-year old Otoba Tadahiko. Also killed in the invasion was twenty-six-year old Ishibashi Kazuhiko, the son of Japan's 55th prime minister, Ishibashi Tanzan (1956–1957).[29]

There were 332 dead and 845 wounded Americans, while 130 Japanese and 167 Koreans were taken prisoner (Walker, Bernstein, and Lang 2004, 55–67). There is no record of how many Marshall Islanders died in the conflict. Perhaps the invading forces neglected to count this number, or perhaps—for the same reason Korean or Okinawan statistics were not recorded—the American military did not want these numbers to be known. Former Kwajalein archaeologist[30] Leslie Mead suggested conservatively that a comparison of prewar and postwar Marshallese demographics indicated an aggregate loss of at least 244 individuals, but that this number may have actually been as high as 700.[31] Poyer, Falgout, and Carucci estimate at least 200 deaths (2001, 121).

In the United States, the successful invasion of the Marshall Islands was announced immediately on the front pages of newspapers nationwide and celebrated as a turning point in the war. On February 6 of Shōwa 19 (1944), in what would become a convention for all *gyokusai* defeats, the mournful patriotic ballad "Umi Yukaba" (If I go away to sea) was broadcast solemnly to the public over the radio back in Japan.[32] But throughout the Marshall Islands, even in the former Japanese capital of Jaluit, Marshallese still hiding from American bombings on distant islands throughout the Ralik and Ratak archipelagoes did not even know for many months that Kwajalein had fallen.[33]

Kwajalein and Enewetak were the only atolls subjected to a major amphibious landing, but the majority of Marshallese atolls were bypassed by American forces. This did not mean, however, that they were left untouched; most atolls and islands with military fortifications had already been subjected to bombing since the beginning of the war. Each site throughout the Marshall Islands—indeed throughout the entire Pacific theater—experienced and remembered its own timeline of war.[34] Marshall Islanders and Korean laborers were forced to endure long months of starvation and brutality by Japanese military on the most fortified of the bypassed atolls. On Jelbōn islet in Mili Atoll, long after Kwajalein had surrendered and Americans were already building it into their own naval base, Japanese soldiers reportedly killed two Koreans and passed off their flesh as whale meat, serving it to unsuspecting laborers who were suffering from starvation and fatigue. When Korean laborers discovered the bodies of their colleagues, it sparked a revolt in the middle of the night from both Koreans and Marshallese, who managed to kill most of their Japanese captors and escape to nearby American warships. This story, related to me in person by survivor Lee Inshin,[35] was first reported by Kim Jae-ok to his American rescuers in March 1945. According to Lee, nearly 170 out of about 400 laborers were shot to death for their involvement in this uprising (Lee 2006). The account of Elson Ebel, a Marshallese elder of Mili, also corroborates this story, adding that this rebellion would have been successful had the Japanese cook not escaped to a nearby island and summoned other Japanese soldiers. In all, Ebel claimed that 84 Marshall Islanders, including women and children, were also killed in the conflict and the ensuing punishment (Poyer, Falgout, and Carucci 2001, 226–229).[36]

In the aftermath of the invasion of Kwajalein Atoll, the dead were buried in haste in a race against the tropical heat and humidity. Americans killed in action were carefully placed in marked graves on Āne-Ellap-Kan (Carlos) islet in the south of the atoll and Ane-dikdik in the north, for safe transport later back to the United States, but Japanese, Koreans, and others—most of whom were affiliated with the Imperial Navy and did not wear dog tags—were likely buried in at least nine mass graves around the islet of Kwajalein, which were later partly consolidated, and in many other graves around the atoll.[37] No sooner did the battle end and the bodies were buried than bulldozers began to build Kwajalein islet up to be a major US base for launching further attacks in the Marshalls and across Micronesia.[38] Dealing with survivors, however, was a completely different issue. A guide to the Marshall Islands published for American residents in 1972 explains the "liberation" of these people quite succinctly:

> As each island was taken during or after the war, the Japanese control ended and it became subject to United States authority in accordance with the international law of belligerent occupation. The first task confronting the occupying forces was to capture all units of the Japanese armed forces. These people were disarmed, collected in prisoner of war camps, and treated as prisoners of war in accordance with the rules of international law. At the same time, the civilian population had to be dealt with: Japanese, Koreans, and Okinawans, as well as local islanders....
>
> The local inhabitants of the islands presented a still different problem. Though they were first regarded as having the status of Japanese subjects, a lack of clarity in the mandate definition of nationality made it possible for the United States to treat them instead as liberated persons under American wardship. (Bell Telephone Laboratories 1972, 28)

Kwajalein and the Marshallese people were oxymoronically "liberated" directly into the "wardship" of the United States.[39] Islanders felt relieved to breathe free after the torment of war and strict Japanese military operations in the atoll, and in many cases they greeted the occupying American forces with gratitude (mixed with a fair share of trepidation). "Freedom" was granted to them, but they were also shocked and deeply saddened by the destruction of their land and the loss of their loved ones. Though they welcomed the food rations and "liberties" of not having to comply with strict regulations as they did in wartime, many were not sure what this freedom actually meant in an American political context; they were happy that the war was over but uncertain of their future (Poyer, Falgout, and Carucci 2001, 279–283).[40]

Reflections

At night Kwajalein feels enormous: The blinking lights and revolving searchlights of distant antennas and radars throughout the entire atoll twinkle incredibly far across the void of lagoon and ocean, and the horizon is visible for nearly 360 degrees. There is a devastation as well, a sense of forlorn sadness and death, and something deeply spiritual and all-encompassing, the infinite endlessness of ocean, swirling and lapping and roaring, breathing life into the memories, submerged and buried there. I knew and always felt that something happened there, even as a child, but what?

Reviewing 3,300 American war images from the invasion of Kwajalein that I have gathered for my research from various collections is painful and deeply troubling, and it has taken me months to complete the process. My own experiences of life on Kwajalein, my familiarity with the landscapes and atollscapes of my childhood home, or on Roi-Namur, where my father worked at the other end of the atoll, makes these photographs intimate, as if I uncovered them in a family album in my own home. The images are unnerving, for they would look like any other "battlefield" image if it weren't for the familiar shorelines, the recognizable Japanese buildings, and even the names of soldiers and leaders after whom many landmarks were named. Looking at these images fills me at times with a gut-wrenching and conflicted sadness that I cannot easily explain.

Perhaps there is no need to explicate this sadness, but it comes from the experiences of hearing many sides of the same story, of having experienced all these places called "America," "Japan," and the "Marshall Islands" in my own life, and knowing the common humanity of all that transcends nation. For me these images are personal. I feel the island and reef, precious Marshallese land, ripped and scarred, trees defoliated, the sea contaminated. I sense the anger, fear, and pride of both the American and Japanese soldiers. I resonate with what antiwar novelist Oda Makoto wrote about *gyokusai* and all the Koreans who suffered and perished as a part of the invasion of Kwajalein, or the way American soldiers later "dumped" more Japanese and Korean bodies as their campaign waged on in Enewetak Atoll, only to conduct thermonuclear tests upon their graves in the years that followed.[41] And of course I empathize with the ambivalence and sorrow of the Ri-Kuwajleen.

Nonetheless, the American men who invaded and "liberated" Kwajalein were of my grandparents' generation, and they had come from all over the United States. Most of the soldiers had grown up listening to Glenn Miller and Billie Holiday. Like the majority of the Japanese and Korean men who were on Kwajalein at the time of the battle, they had traveled for weeks across the ocean on warships or had trained as pilots. They were ordinary people like my great uncle, who was accidentally killed in an aviation accident while training for a mission. Had he not died, he could just as easily have been deployed to Kwajalein. My late father, named after his uncle, was deeply invested in the American military mission of Kwajalein. Though he was a civilian who had never fought in a war, he took great pride in the power of the military and in the job he did in the defense of the United States. I feel inextricably linked to the American military through my father's job and my childhood at Kwajalein, and also through the stories of my grandparents who reminisced at times about how they too had cheered when headlines were received with elation all across America that the Japanese had been defeated in the Marshall Islands. Before I knew of the atoll's tragic history, the suffering of its people, and the stories of those deployed there by Japan's mission, I just thought it was a happy little American town.

When I lived on the atoll in the 1970s, Kwajalein still had a roughness about it that put the past within reach. The rusty machinery of war—the tanks and cannons and sunken ships—was a familiar sight to me, but so too were the newer military machines. Children growing up on Kwaj like me often took a fascination in the massive military aircraft that would land on the airstrip, or the enormous cargo barges, the landing craft reutilized for passenger use, the heavy loaders, the cranes. Despite being a so-called "tiny" island in the Pacific, Kwaj and some of the other islets in the atoll were a virtual showcase of defense technology and contraptions. We lived our utopian small-town lives as if they were partly American suburbia, partly an exciting military operation; in fact, they were both. There was a domesticity and a simultaneous commando-like thrill to it, the comfort of home-cooked food and easy days at the beach combined with the constant arrival and departure of aircraft and the occasional nighttime missile test. At the age of six or seven, I was already pretending I was a plane as I sped alongside the exposed runway on my candy-apple-red bicycle, delighting in the suffocating stench of jet fuel combustion mixed with sea salt.

I first set foot at Kwajalein Atoll only thirty years after the photographs I work with in the next chapter were taken, a short span in view of the deep-time of the atoll. In retrospect, little had changed aside from the landscape. The gutted-out and bombed Japanese buildings in the images look almost as they did when I lived there, despite the decay. Even today, aside from the paint that has eroded away, there is not much difference between these photos and what I have witnessed or touched with my own hands. But now when I walk through the ghostly architectural remains of Kwajalein I am transported to buildings I have also known in Japan. I think of places where I have studied and worked, built in the 1920s and barely refurbished since, strong old cool concrete walls smelling of musty mildew and sweet chalky *sumi* ink and paper. Shattered and nearly unrecognizable in the rust and rot of the ruins at Jaluit or Roi-Namur are light bulbs in porcelain fixtures just like those I have known in old Japanese homes where I have stayed. And as I walk through the ruins of Kwajalein today, I think of the fathers and brothers of the bereaved families I have met in Tokyo, whose photos I have seen and letters I have read.

The images that follow are not proof of "truth," but their violence hints at an unspeakable horror that was no doubt shared by all who experienced the war, including the various Americans of different backgrounds who landed on these islands. In the images, I see the denuded palm trees; the beach where I once played, barren and lined with bodies; the sea boiling black and burning with the carcasses of sinking Japanese ships, ships I would visit sixty years later while scuba diving to the depths of the lagoon. Like the big chunks of reef that were pulverized into the concrete that covers Kwajalein's airstrip, coral is terribly delicate, vulnerable stuff.[42] It is sobering, if not terrifying, to envision the tragic layers of bone that lay hidden and entangled in the coral strata beneath the concrete and the lawns, under my playground and elementary school, under the supermarket, the bakery, and the swimming pool. By approaching this history vulnerably, I hope to show the vulnerability of *all* the human beings involved in the conflict, as separate from the bigger dramas in which they participated.

CHAPTER 5

Capturing Liberation

American Imag(in)ings of the Battle of Kwajalein

> The camera is a weapon against the tragedy of things, against their disappearing.
>
> —*Wim Wenders*[1]

> All war photography can potentially suggest parallels between gun and camera. It can also make visible atrocities that would otherwise be hidden.
>
> —*Lutz and Collins*[2]

IN THE IMMEDIATE DAYS AND MONTHS AFTER the US bombardment of Kwajalein Atoll in late January and early February 1944, when the war against Imperial Japan's military forces was beginning to turn in America's favor, photographic depictions of victory boosted morale at home and throughout the Pacific "theater." Combat photographers shot thousands of images, rivaling the many bullets shot by their compatriots. They were ordered to do so partly to chronicle the battlefield and partly to disseminate to the media, where they could provide evidence of American triumph to the public and the world at large. These photographs related a crystal-clear, black-and-white narrative of the American mission of liberation in the Pacific during the war.[3]

World War II was the first major conflict in which both still and moving photographic images figured so heavily as a means of intelligence, testimony, propaganda, and dissemination.[4] The Battle of Kwajalein, like all battlefields of the Pacific War, was photographed deliberately to provide proof of American victory and tell a story to the larger population.[5] Its amphibious tactics became the stuff of military textbooks and the visuals from the attack fed the American propaganda machine at home to encourage the public to invest in war bonds while boasting of American strength and Japanese weakness to the world at large. The still images taken during the war were distributed widely through the media and printed in magazines, books, and newspapers throughout the United States and the world, and are still used to perpetuate a particular American reality today. Film footage of Operation Flintlock was also edited into newsreels and propaganda films. Here I explore this imaged and imagined American atollscape of Kwajalein in order to understand its many dimensions.

Re-Imaging/Re-Imagining the Battle of Kwajalein

Photographs, as many theorists have asserted and I have begun to illustrate in the previous chapters about Japanese colonial image making in Micronesia, are a constructed and mediated form of representation. Yet Young elaborates, "as a seeming trace or fragment of its referent that appeals to the eye for its proof, the photograph is able to invoke the authority of its empirical link to events, which in turn seems to reinforce the sense of its own unmediated factuality" (Young 1988, 58).[6] Culled from various armed forces public relations branches, the thousands of photographs of the war in the Marshall Islands housed today in the US National Archives in College Park, Maryland, are a rich resource that bespeaks a particular factuality of battle as seen from an American optic.[7] Some of them have been used again and again as evidence of the particular truth that interested the American military in 1944, and as such they dwell on the extent to which Japanese casualties were inflicted, on the treatment of prisoners, and on the friendships forged by soldiers with the "exotic" Marshallese "natives." They also meditate on the clear transformation of "Japanese fortress" into "free American territory." These images were captioned with text that described the spectacle of the battle in terms of an inevitable American victory. The images and the text that accompanies them depict an impossibly clear but reassuring story of winners versus losers, finders and keepers, a story in which only the American male heroes have names and histories, and nearly all Others are either just dehumanized and written off as Japanese, "natives," or women.[8] Most of the captions and archival texts quoted in this chapter included the offensive and racist term "Jap," which was used commonly in the 1940s by American officials as a way of justifying violence and dehumanizing Japanese people. Where possible, I have chosen to either omit this term or replace it with "Jap[anese]," in order to indicate the original racism without reproducing the violence.

The caption, explained Barthes, works to "anchor" an image; it "serves to 'rationalize' a multidimensional image; it 'loads' the image, 'burdening' it with a culture, a moral, an imagination" (Lutz and Collins 1993, 76). By consciously taking this into consideration, it is possible to decode the "mythologies" of the Kwajalein war images by analyzing the captions alongside the photographs they describe. I would argue that much can be learned from studying the story these captions tell in the bigger context of what we know about the invasion from the stories told by Americans, Marshallese, Japanese, Koreans, and Okinawans.

Many of the Kwajalein liberation photographs and their captions were released to the press and then used (often with caption intact) in media representations in the United States. These image commentaries actually primed American soldiers and helped to create their impressions of Japanese people (and later, "Natives"). Veteran Bruce Muench, who arrived on Kwajalein in 1945 in the aftermath of the battle, describes in his memoir *Spam Cans, Rice Balls, and Pearls* how pervasive these sorts of media texts were in preparing him for his time in the Marshall Islands:

> Other than what I had read in the newspapers and seen in the movies, I had no conception of what the Japanese were like.... The stereotype image we got from the movies and cartoons typically showed the Japanese soldier as some sort of single-minded fiend, bent on murdering whoever got in his way. The Japanese culture was as foreign to me as if I had been parachuted into a tribal community in Nepal. (Muench 2002, 78)

Muench's self-reflexivity is rare among war accounts of the invasion and ensuing occupation of Kwajalein, perhaps because of his late arrival on the atoll. His narrative about the relations he developed with a Marshallese man and with Japanese after the war critically reminisces about many racial stereotypes American Marines held, not only toward Japanese but toward Islanders, whom most soldiers referred to as "gooks" (2002, 56).[9] Muench explains that such terms left his and others' vocabulary the more he became familiar with Marshallese people.

What, however, do these photographs tell us when we consider the larger global and local contexts that unfolded around the moments they were taken? What can these images say about the actual individuals, living and dead, portrayed in them? What can they tell us about the war and Japanese/American militarism in the Pacific? What stories—whose stories—do they not tell? I now explore through captioned war photographs and edited/narrated film footage how the liberation story framed the Battle of Kwajalein by smoothing over—and continuing to obscure—the tragedies of war on all sides, not only for Marshallese, Japanese, and Korean civilians and defenders,[10] but also for American soldiers themselves.

For the purposes of this book, in "re-membering" and deconstructing the liberation of Kwajalein, my intention is to reflect upon the intersections between individual lives and the larger historical and political contexts in which they participated. I have thus selected images from the archives as a way of exploring, like Barthes, the "mythologies" and power relations involved in America's production of history in the Pacific War. I am aware of my own participation in the production and reproduction of this history, not only as an American consumer of these images and narratives, but also as a photographer and (hi)storyteller. I therefore aim to be as self-reflexive as possible and to contextualize my own contradictory and sometimes ambivalent relationship to these mythologies as I confront them. Here I take Gillian Rose's invitation to use multiple methods to interrogate the power of images, conscious that "the visualities articulated by producers, images, and audiences may not coincide, and this may in itself be an important issue to address" (Rose 2001, 202).

In analyzing the making of these images, it is important of course to differentiate between the actual photographers, military public relations officials, and the different forms of media that then disseminated the images (both still and moving).[11] All the photographers who took images of the northern and southern bombardments of Kwajalein Atoll were soldiers themselves, following orders. It is likely that few had traveled outside the United States prior to the war. The photographs they took were processed and studied far away from the battlefield, removed from context, and then recontextualized when certain photographs were chosen for publication on the merit of their impact. The ways those images were then used (or not used) by the media is another crucial consideration, and one I only touch on in a preliminary way here. But it is clear that these images found their way into numerous publications, from *Time* magazine to metropolitan and local newspapers worldwide, where they were subject to further editorial authorship. Nevertheless, there was a deliberate authorial and editorial process going on at all stages of the documentation and dissemination of the battle, in varying degrees. The military ordered these images for their own intelligence and documentation, and also partly for public consumption; yet for exactly the same reason, any images that may have reflected poorly on American soldiers or officers, and any depictions that complicated the simple and dehumanized story of a resounding American win and Japanese loss, were censored or not disseminated.

The photographer was shooting on the fly alongside his comrades during the action of the battle, but even then, moving with his battalion, he would only have been able to take pictures from an American vantage point. Once the battle was over he was freer to compose shots of battlefield casualties or of prisoners of war that told the story most effectively. Thus there are piles of photos of dead, wounded, or captured "Japanese" as if to provide reassuring evidence of the massive losses for the Japanese side.[12] American losses, while in the hundreds, were never depicted in the same manner. One sees, for instance, a postbattle shot of a dead white American Marine, lying alone, his head turned to the side, his right arm outstretched, his left hand propped on his chest, displaying a wedding ring (NA-70414). This photo, shot by combat photographer Marine Sergeant Andrew Zurick of the Fourth Marine Division, shows a soldier whose face is clean, eyes gently closed, his mouth open, as if peacefully asleep. Such a compassionate portrait amidst so many contradictory images of mangled, bloated, faceless "Japanese" bodies piled on the battlefield or unclothed prisoners of war suggests countless questions.[13]

The combat photographer was instructed in what to take or what not to take, and he no doubt practiced a significant amount of self-censorship based on what he knew might even get him into trouble when the film was developed later. Like American military censorship, earlier Japanese photographers' censorship of their own war images was just as deliberate and careful. As Morris-Suzuki explains of Japanese military censorship of the Nanjing Massacre, rules governing which images are likely to be "banned" are quickly internalized by war photographers and their superiors: "Their sense of survival taught them when they should and should not take pictures, and which images were not even worth submitting to the censor" (2001, 175).

"Doesn't the photographer," asked Walter Benjamin, "have the obligation to expose the guilty with his photos?" (Sontheimer 2005). And whether the blame rested entirely on Japanese imperial militarism itself or the furious bombardment by American military might upon a relatively defenseless atoll, the devastation surely impacted the cameramen who witnessed the drama unfold. Perhaps it was this "obligation of exposure" that led many photographers to document the sheer horror of *gyokusai* in the Battle of Kwajalein as extensively as they did, taking "messy" images that did not suit America's cleancut discourse of "liberation." As evidence of this, many of the images in the archives were boldly stamped "RESTRICTED" by military authorities or scribbled with the words "NOT RECOMMENDED FOR RELEASE." One might speculate, however, that there were other forbidden images that were never archived in the first place.

Not surprisingly, the most frequently restricted images appear to have been those that complicated the tidy legend of "good Americans," "bad Japanese," and "grateful Natives." For instance, there is a series of images that depict Marshall Islanders in compromising situations, emerging terrified, naked, and emaciated from Japanese bunkers (such as image NA-74284, of a young, partially clad Marshallese man obviously in shock, surrounded by American soldiers), and many that show young-looking Korean or Japanese prisoners of war in pitifully humiliating conditions, unclothed, wounded, and dazed while being interrogated at gunpoint by big Americans. See for instance image number NA-70420, of a naked soldier caked in sand, sitting dazed on the ground with outstretched legs as he is accosted by a group of four US interrogators.[14]

As Lisa Yoneyama writes of the "traces" of Hiroshima, there is a tendency to "tame the memory" of the war (1999, 44–45), something I wish to avoid. My aim here is not to place blame on any individual, but rather to show how the "big history" of war and nation betrayed and "concreted over" the "little histories" of the people whose lives were caught up in these events. It is not my interest to be complicit in this narrative of liberation by reinscribing the valorization of massive death and destruction, or the dehumanization and loss of dignity depicted in the close-up images of Japanese, Korean, and possibly Marshallese bodies. A careful appraisal of such powerful images, however, can in fact restore dignity and humanity to the dehumanized. Anne Perez-Hattori has, for example, chosen to reproduce the disturbing medical photographs taken by US Navy officials of the bodies of Hansen's-disease-inflicted Chamorros interned in "colonies" in early twentieth-century Guam. Her decision is a deeply respectful way of restoring the dignity and memories of these Chamorros as "members of our island community" (Perez-Hattori 2007).

My own effort, likewise, is to humanize and remember all the lives lost during this "liberation" process. These images, taken entirely by Americans for whom the Pacific, Islanders, Japanese, and Koreans were all mostly unfamiliar, show a tendency to dehumanize, exoticize, or eroticize the Other, all the while redeeming and celebrating American individuals throughout the campaign. I therefore have chosen a number of captioned images from the archives (and some from print and film media, for the sake of comparison) that I felt were most representative of this uneven power relationship. They represent each of the framings of the stages of "liberation" that I found to be most prevalent.[15]

I present these framings under five rough categories: (1) Capture, where the changeover between Japanese and American power was documented through the looting of national symbols like flags and other artifacts, or by images of mass death and carnage[16] that indicated the island had fallen; (2) Dehumanization, in which Japanese and Korean prisoners are shown disrobing or fully stripped of their clothing and possessions; (3) Cleanup, whereby the battleground is sanitized and American soldiers are vindicated through tropes of washing or domesticity; (4) Gratitude, in which Marshallese are portrayed in the aftermath of battle as thankful, happy, and free as they celebrate freedom, work alongside Americans, receive aid, and accept American gestures of kindness; and (5) Romance/Ridicule, wherein the Marshallese people (mainly women) and their islands are either romanticized as exotic/erotic people and places in the imagined Pacific paradise, or ridiculed for their failure to live up to those expectations. There is often some crossover between these themes within each photograph, but in the following sections I will attempt to unpack the liberation narrative by following the battle mostly in the order in which it was photographed.

Capture

> As I thought of the landing that I would be making on the morrow, I was both excited and anxious. Yes, I thought of death, but I wasn't afraid. Somehow I couldn't see myself as dead. "Why wasn't there fear," I wondered. Even

though I was nervous, it was with excitement, not fear. Instead there was a thrill. I was headed for great adventure, where I had wanted to be. This was just an adventure. It was "grown up" Cops and Robbers. . . . Thoughts of glory were in my mind that night. Now it was my turn to "carry the flag" into battle. It was my turn to be a part of history.

—*Private First Class Robert F. Graf, U.S. Marine Corps, upon invading Kwajalein Atoll (in Chapin 1994, 4)*

In this fading image, three American Marines, probably in their late teens or early twenties, stand in the bright sunshine of Namur islet in the aftermath of invasion. The military photographer's caption explains that they are holding up the bounty of their exploits: a "small Jap[anese] flag" and some paper currency. Their faces beam with boyish delight and enthusiasm. Two of them have removed their shirts, probably sweaty from the intense tropical heat. The one in the foreground flaunts his silver watch and what looks like a wedding ring. Together, they are a wholesome vision of 1940s boy-next-door white masculinity. Despite their military fatigues, they look more like three cheerful friends who won a rigorous game of basketball than three soldiers who waged a bloody battle through the jungles of Kwajalein Atoll that left thousands of Japanese men dead. The message is clear: The hard work is over, it was a job well done, and the liberation of the atoll has been achieved. The Japanese enemy, absent from the photograph, is represented by the loot he has left behind for lucky American

"SOUVENIRS—Marines hold a small Jap[anese] flag and money they found after capturing Namur, Kwajalein Atoll, Marshall Islands," 2 February 1944.

servicemen to take home: his small (and therefore trivial) flag, his worthless cash (perhaps pulled from the pockets of a uniform), and—as many other images attest—swords, helmets, and a wide range of other exotic treasures.

It is the historical narrative told by the captioning of these photographs that is the most interesting, because the ideas that accompany these pictures create a third language of juxtaposition between text and image. Indeed, in Young's terms: "One of the reasons that narrative and photographs are so convincing together is that they seem to represent a combination of pure object and commentary on the object, each seeming to complete the other by reinforcing a sense of contrasting functions" (1988, 57–58).

An otherwise violent image of dead bodies, ruined landscapes, and expended artillery thus becomes a celebratory declaration of victory when coupled with a clever headline or catchphrase. The Public Affairs Office of the Department of Defense was no doubt conscious of this, for their wording of the captions typed on manila index cards on the back of each photograph and later released to the media sometimes reads like advertising copy. Even an "innocent" photo like the one above assumes ironic significance when comically entitled "Souvenirs" and labeled with the explanation that these men have just completed the invasion of the northern part of the atoll and taken some mementos from the Japanese soldiers they killed.

CHANGING OF THE GUARDS

As in this image of captured Japanese artifacts, many of the war photographs taken at Kwajalein Atoll and subsequent battle sites throughout the Marshalls deploy the sign of national flags to downplay or belittle Japanese power and herald the installation of an American regime. Repeatedly, as the Hinomaru[17] was triumphantly supplanted by Old Glory, the persistent comparison between "small" Japanese flags like the one above and the hearty, fresh, new American flags like those raised on Iōtō (Iwo Jima) could be seen in still photos and film all throughout the Pacific War campaigns. Similar to the image above, there are many images of Marines at Kwajalein covetously holding tarnished, damaged Japanese flags. Given the rituals and performances surrounding the American flag and its installation from island to island as the United States advanced victoriously through the Pacific, it cannot be underestimated how meaningful it

Capturing Liberation 121

"THE FLAG RISES ABOVE THE SMOKE—the Stars and Stripes waves over a Marine position and the smoke of battle on Namur Island, Kwajalein Atoll in the Marshalls."

would have been to military officials that the "captured" Japanese flag also appeared cheap, ruined, defunct, and pitiful. These photos declared that the empire had been defeated and, like the Pledge of Allegiance American children are made to recite toward the American flag, the glorious mission of "liberty and justice for all" had been served.

Hoisted on a lone trunk of a palm tree on Namur islet, the image of the Star-Spangled Banner rising "above the smoke of battle" is an emblem of victory amidst complete destruction and devastation. It is, like the flags that announced freedom from British rule in the American Revolution, the ceremonial heraldry by which America's own liberation was displayed. On Kwajalein islet, the destruction was even more thorough, with observers describing that only one palm tree was left standing, as symbolized in the sort of image below.

Japanese history (likely owing in part to such "lone palm" photographs) also incorporated these semiotics of defeat. For bereaved family members of the Japanese soldiers who were killed during the bombardment, the strong contrast between the utter beauty (*utsukushisa*) of the present landscape and the complete and unimaginable obliteration of war is central. Even though there were close to three hundred Japanese and Korean survivors of the battle, Kwajalein, in Japanese histories, is described as nothing less than a complete *gyoku-*

sai in which all were lost. Suzuki Yukiko reflected upon her second visit to Kwajalein:

> It's unimaginable to think that here, so far away from Japan, there was a *gyokusai* so severe that only one tree was left standing . . . and the blue of the outer ocean and the bright blue of the inner lagoon . . . the blue of the sky . . . such a beauty we can't find back in Japan. It's just so beautiful.[18]

CRUSHED JEWELS

What was *gyokusai* for Japan was a "textbook battle" for the United States, but even so, the sheer scale of the death and destruction created complications in depicting the American victory, depictions that might otherwise have been sanitized. Kwajalein was one of the first full-scale "crushed jewel" American soldiers would encounter in the war, and the "messiness" of the confrontation there was hard to downplay. The photographs taken in the immediate wake of the fighting in the north and south of the atoll seem to meditate almost exclusively on the overwhelming loss of life.

Print media capitalized on these images, using them to narrate a story of Japanese vulnerability and American invincibility. A layout from *Yank* magazine was particularly blunt in its use of dehumanizing and racist images of mass death, in which two combat images (which also appear in the archives) were contrasted with each other, one on top of mainly Japanese carnage, and one on bottom featuring American bodies. The image, boldly captioned, "We Killed A Lot of Japs" [sic], depicts at least four Japanese bodies, one with his outstretched foot still clad in a *tabi* boot, another one face down, unclothed and covered in blood. An exploded fuel barrel and a wrecked tank join other shrapnel and junk on the battlefield. Five American soldiers stand around in what appears to be casual banter. One smokes a cigarette. A sixth soldier seems preoccupied with the damaged tank. The relaxed pose of American soldiers in the background seems to imply that somehow the job was effortless and instantaneous, and the corpses in the foreground seem ordinary and commonplace, naturalized into the landscape of the liberation mythology. In comparison, the image on the bottom of the page, captioned "But Some of Us Died Too," is more somber and respectful of death, as white American bodies are laid out one by one on stretchers, covered in blankets. More than twenty servicemen stand around the bodies, mourning their loss.

Despite the actual events that unfolded at the time these images were taken, the contrast of these two images—one violent and impersonal, one reverent and humane—is no doubt deliberate and strategic. The top photo depicts slain foes, the bottom depicts fallen heroes, creating a visual text for the reader that says Japanese troops were ruthless inhuman barbarians not worthy of respect while "a few good men" of our white military died in honor for their country. The text in the article that accompanies these images also illustrates this message and the overall American military context of early 1944:

> Although there is still some occasional rifle fire and the smoke still curls from the ruined concrete pillboxes, the veterans of the Army's 7th Division are now sitting under the trees or lying on the ground with V-mail blanks, writing their first letters home.... The men cannot say that they are on Kwajalein, cannot give details of the action they fought here, cannot name friends who were injured, cannot give the date and cannot say where they came from and where they are going. They can't say much of anything except "I'm still alive and well." But that is enough.... There are heated arguments about whether the 1st Platoon of Company A killed more Japanese than the 3rd Platoon of Company L. Hardly anyone knows for sure just how many Japanese he did kill. "When it gets past 10, you lose count and lose interest," says Pfc. James Carrigan of San Aba, Texas, ... who accounted for 12. (Miller 1944, 3)

Newsreel film footage also dwelled on this postapocalyptic battlescape. Like captioned photos, this footage was edited, narrated, scored in compelling ways, and then recycled in a number of propaganda films produced during the war. The most significant of these films was a short produced by the US Army Pictorial Service in 1944 titled *What Makes a Battle,* which was clearly directed at the American public to promote the war effort, sell war bonds, and rationalize the production of weapons. The film's impassioned male narrator proclaims:

> Without [weapons], no battle is possible. You the millions of workers, men and women, young and old, high school kids and grandmothers, Democrats and Republicans, Protestants, Catholics, and Jews. White and colored. You who make them know their purpose.

WE KILLED A LOT OF JAPS

MARINES STAND BY A WRECKED TANK AND TALK ABOUT THE BATTLE FOR KWAJALEIN ATOLL WHILE IN THE FOREGROUND REST A FEW OF THE 8,122 JAPANESE KILLED. THESE MARINES DIED ON ROI IN THE KWAJALEIN CAMPAIGN. OUR LOSSES WERE COMPARATIVELY LIGHT: FOR BOTH ARMY AND MARINES, 286 DEAD, 1,175 WOUNDED.

BUT SOME OF US DIED, TOO

Give them to our fighting men and you give them the overwhelming power of the world's greatest industrial democracy, the power we are now using to rid the world of the Nazis, the power that will break the empire that produced the Jap[anese] executioners and murderers.

Superimposing the Japanese naval ensign over a map of the Nanyō Guntō Micronesia and the territories held by Imperial Japan, the narrator describes Kwajalein in the Marshall Islands as "Centergate in Jap[anese] Fortress Pacific," as depicted in an animated map from the film. In this still frame of the map, the rays of the Japanese flag reach out like deadly and threatening tentacles, filling an imaginary bounded expanse of Oceania. Previously unknown by most Americans and even by most Japanese (for whom the islands were the farthest away and least colonized), the Marshall Islands are visualized as the dead center of the ocean, the ultimate prize in the empire.

Depicting Americans as nothing but heroic and humane and Japanese as nothing but suicidal and fanatical, extremely graphic long shots of severe casualties and deaths are shown in succession, with equally violent narration and a sinister musical soundtrack that sounds as if it belongs in a Hitchcock film. The narrative then focuses on the plight of prisoners of war and how they were treated (as I will discuss in the next section). It closes on yet another flag image: an American Marine with his back to the camera, with the vengeful narration, "Yes there will be more battles, harder and fiercer battles, until all of these honored dead are avenged with a terrible justice."

But the vindictive pursuit of "terrible justice" made it easy to ignore the nuances and contradictions of battle, as well as the simple fact that, at Kwajalein, the Japanese military forces—not anticipating the American strategy of bypassing some of the more heavily fortified atolls like Jaluit—were outnumbered by the Americans nearly five to one. That the defenders of the atoll were able to resist and hold out as long as they did was quite a remarkable feat.

Meanwhile, writing off suicides and sacrificial "banzai charges" as ridiculous and "pointless," as is done in *What Makes a Battle*, also devalued what would have been acts of heroism[19] seen from the Japanese military perspective of 1944. Such characterizations of Japanese masked the complicated cultural context in which *gyokusai* had become not only the honorable way to die for one's country when resistance became futile, but a way of avoiding the severe torture anticipated at the hands of the enemy (Kawano 2001, 175–177).[20] For American soldiers encountering these mass suicides, however, the experience was deeply unnerving and traumatic, as former soldier and Japanese literature expert Donald Keene notes of his experiences:

> After putting up strong resistance, the Japanese decided to use all their remaining strength to stage a final attack. Perhaps they hoped that a sudden onslaught would sweep the Americans into the sea, but in fact American casualties remained light. Half the Japanese garrison died not from enemy action but from an act of mass suicide.
>
> Most of the Japanese soldiers who were not killed in the final assault killed themselves, often by pressing a hand grenade to their chest. I was baffled by their determination to die, to use their last grenade against themselves rather than the enemy. Of course, the end of Japanese resistance on the island was welcome to the Americans, but the sight of the exploded corpses was sickening, and I found it impossible to reconcile what I interpreted as mindless fanaticism with what I knew of the Japanese from their works of literature. (Keene, in Oda 2003, viii–ix)

ONE SMALL FLAG

Another photograph taken on Kwajalein islet seems to suggest the darker realities of *gyokusai*, alongside the overt symbolism of captured flag. It is an image simply titled "Members of the Burial Detail on Kwajalein" and features thirteen (possibly fourteen) soldiers squinting toward an unseen photographer, their grim faces covered in sweat, soot, and stubble. In the immediate background is the burnt grass and shrubbery of Kwajalein's jungle stripped away and piled up with the dugout rocks and boulders of a bomb crater, its coral mud exposed and whitewashed in the equatorial sunshine. The decapitated charred trunks of three coconut palms stand in the distance. Three men in the foreground solemnly hold a ripped Japanese flag upside-down, its bright red Hinomaru surrounded by brush-painted Japanese writing that can be seen if one looks closely enough. An initial look at the

Capturing Liberation   127

"MEMBERS OF THE BURIAL DETAIL on Kwajalein, Marshall Islands, 8 February 1944."

captioned photo (the looted flag together with the "burial detail" caption) would suggest that these men who have gloriously defeated the Japanese and liberated Kwajalein Atoll are now burying their enemy by the thousands.

Yet in this photo, the men's expressions speak of fatigue and heat exhaustion, and perhaps even revulsion, for the air is likely filled with the stench of death. The thrill and gaiety of winning is not present whatsoever here; it is replaced by the burden and trauma of the battle's aftermath. Some of the men do not even face the camera; others look almost disgruntled and disheartened. The eighth of February, when this photograph was taken, was already several days after the US invasion of Kwajalein islet was complete, and the cleanup of the islet was underway. Even by the middle of the battle, wrote military historian Samuel Marshall, American troops had already tired of killing: "The slaughter seemed to them to be senseless though it was unavoidable. The taking of one Jap[anese] prisoner cheered a company more than the killing of fifty" (Marshall and Dawson 2001, 84). Having lost many of their friends in the battle but also having to deal with the bodies of so many dead Japanese and Korean bodies undoubtedly made a powerful impression on these men.

Muench relates the experience of one of the soldiers who came before him and participated in the invasion:

> Following the battle, this man was assigned to picking up the enemy bodies for burial at the north end of the island. A trench was excavated by bulldozer, the bodies dragged into it and lined up in rows. They were bloated and decomposing by this time.... Later in 1945, in an effort to conceal the stench, or perhaps to provide a more fitting burial grounds, the island administrators decided to re-bury the Japanese bodies, which had been simply lined up and bulldozed under the coral rubble along the north end of the island... It had been a year since these bodies were initially buried, so there was not much left but the bones, however there was apparently enough organic material to make a pungent odor once the bodies were exposed to the air. We were surrounded by that odor for at least a week afterwards. It was like no odor I ever experienced, both sweet and sickening. Once you smell it, you never forget it, because it penetrates your brain. (Muench 2002, 65–67)

Muench's vivid and disturbing description expresses a sense of the horror and "messiness" of war, as well as evoking the humanization of the American soldiers involved. As I describe later in this chapter, American propaganda was interested in communicating a clear-cut story that dehumanized the Japanese while it propagated an earnest and wholesome vision of US soldiers.

Like Muench's narrative, however, the portrait of the burial unit undercuts this message as it evokes a sense of the ambivalence and hardship of war for all parties. This is one of several images in the archives where the subjects of the photograph subvert the prevailing narrative or intention and instead allude to some of the more unsettling realities of the battle experience. While at first glance it would appear to depict a crushing victory over Japan, through the expressions of the men it becomes a moment of what Christian Metz would call "instant self-contradiction" (1985), in that there is some "slippage" in the signs: We wonder if this "liberation" is happy after all.

Yet undoubtedly the most significant slippage here comes not from the hapless countenances of the soldiers, but from the Japanese

Capturing Liberation 129

flag they hold. Flaunting the spoils of their military exploits, the image is composed not unlike a portrait of hunters returning with game or fishermen proudly holding up their catch. The Hinomaru would have meant little to these soldiers (and to most non-Japanese) other than a symbol for Japan itself, at the very least, a token captured from the enemy. Like *any* slain deer or giant tuna, the flag would seem at first glance to be a symbol for the generic bounty of the American campaign: it is a surrogate for *any* Japanese person.

But this is a special flag. Upon closer inspection, it is clear that this *nisshōki* Japanese flag is covered with brush-written characters. And while the American soldiers are probably oblivious or unaware of this layer of meaning, since they hold the text upside down, the Japanese writing is quite legible. Zooming in on the flag and turning it right-side-up, one can easily tell the flag is covered with *yosegaki*, or messages from a number of people, radiating out neatly from the red rising sun in the middle. The bold, proud, polite characters painted on the left edge of the flag translate roughly to "Dear Oki Kiyoshi-kun, we all wish you good luck on your departure for the front."[21] The suffix *–kun*, after the first name Kiyoshi, is an intimate, diminutive form used for boys and male colleagues. It tells us that Private Oki was probably fairly young. It also suggests that the people who have signed this flag for Oki are within his inner circle of workmates, family members, or community.

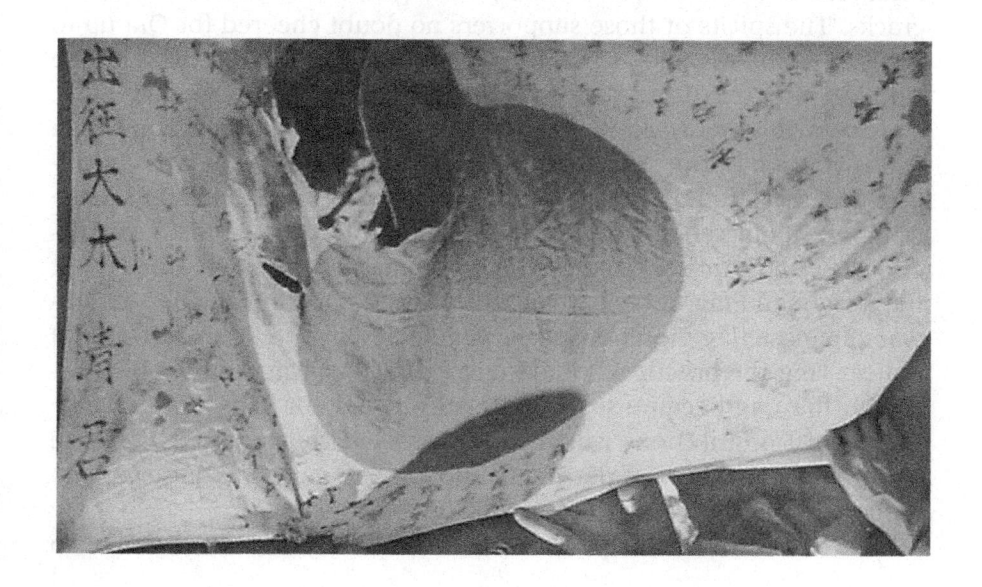

A well-known Japanese proverb, *"ji ga hito o arawasu"* (literally, "calligraphy [i.e. handwriting] reveals the person") is helpful in reading this flag. The quality of this image is too poor for us to read the actual inscriptions with much accuracy, but it is abundantly obvious to the viewer familiar with Japanese calligraphy that Oki's flag reveals the personalities of a whole regiment, school, community, or family. There are some names and messages that are brushed thinly and delicately onto the flag, the mark of an elegant and humble person or perhaps a gesture of femininity. Others sign the flag bluntly but passionately with deliberate calligraphic blots of ink in an expression of bold and almost rebellious individuality. Others write with more "manly" pointy and straight-edged *katakana*-like characters, similar to the way many of the soldiers penned their self-censored letters to families back home.

Whereas typically American flags are draped over the caskets of soldiers killed in action, then folded and presented to family members on behalf of the nation, in wartime Japan, a soldier would carry with him a *nisshōki* like this as a talisman and memento to bring him protection and security in his mission and good luck to ensure his safe return home. Such flags were emblematic of the intersection between the national and the personal, hinting toward a more familiar, more human, and more emotional side of the war, such a warm and intimate reminder of family that they were often worn against the body of their owners for security and reassurance. Upon the national "text" of the flag, these inscriptions were like human faces behind the depersonalized national rhetoric, subtle messages that slipped through the cracks. The spirits of those supporters no doubt cheered for Oki up to his final moments just as much as the letters from family back in the United States encouraged the American soldiers as they fought.

Ironically, *yosegaki* writing on the Japanese flag was actually in contravention of the Japanese Imperial Public Code, as it was considered a desecration of the national symbol.[22] One could make the same criticism about the "abuse" of the US flag by, for example, advertisers or by patriotic Americans who wear flag-patterned clothing.[23] But the American Flag Code is a voluntary set of guidelines, whereas prewar Japanese flag violations were punishable by the Kenpeitai special police. That the practice of making good-luck charm gestures by writing on the flag became so widespread throughout Japan in defiance of national prohibitions was indicative less of resistance to Japanese nationalism as it was of personalization of the national war effort, so authorities probably overlooked such infringements.

So here is thus a Japanese flag, ostensibly a national symbol to the Americans who hold it, but entirely different from the American flags raised on makeshift coconut palm flagpoles, for it is signed, well-worn, personalized, possibly even loved. The gaping hole in the upper left-hand corner indicates where a bullet may have pierced or a grenade may have detonated. It is creased and ragged from being folded and rolled up again and again, and it is stained by blots of what likely is the blood of its owner, the bodily signature of the flag's owner himself, which merges into the blood-red Hinomaru at its center.

We can only wonder where this flag is now. Perhaps it went back to the States with one of the soldiers in the burial unit where it was coveted as a prize, framed or folded away in a box, forgotten in someone's attic as worthless war paraphernalia. Perhaps collectors have auctioned it over the Internet: A typical web search on a given day of the American online auction site eBay reveals at least twenty such so-called "battle flags" (or "Kamikaze flags") for sale, some fetching hundreds of dollars. A compassionate few Americans have tried to repatriate the flags to Japan. One woman in California, via the Japanese government, managed to locate the family of the soldier whose flag her father had kept in his collection of souvenirs from his time as a pilot in the war. She discovered that through returning the flag she had provided a man with "the only tangible link" to his father, who had died sixty-two years earlier in the Philippines (Seitz 2007).

Each of these flags represented an individual human being. Captured in February 1944 in the Marshall Islands and photographed for us to witness is Oki Kiyoshi's flag. We can only imagine what Oki was doing on his final day on Kwajalein, or what route brought him there. Had he been drafted into the Imperial Army, deployed to the unfamiliar Pacific front? What was his life like in the wooden barracks on Kwajalein built by Marshallese construction workers or Korean laborers? Did he look across the lagoon on quiet nights like I once did as a child? Oki's flag calls out from the archives like a story within a story, reminding those who can read its messages that this was a real human being with a past, a family, a hometown back in Japan where loved ones were waiting. This flag still speaks to us across the decades to all those who will listen.

Dehumanization

Although most Japanese histories of the invasion of Kwajalein tend to write it as if there were no survivors, nearly three hundred people,

"Hands held high, the Japanese soldier tells his Marine captors that there is another inside who is afraid to give himself up."

over half of whom were Koreans, were taken prisoner throughout the atoll. For those who survived the bombardment but who had been told they would be tortured if they became prisoners of war, surrendering to Americans was probably more terrifying than it was relieving.

Image no. 72003 appears to have been taken near the Air Operations building on Roi islet, judging by the remains of the building in the background. Three helmeted US Marines seem to tower over the slender Japanese soldier, his hands raised in the air, his fingers splayed as widely as possible. The Marines could easily be twice his age, likely no more than twenty-one or twenty-two. The man on the left holds his rifle firmly in place, pointed at the soldier, a paternal but stern expression on his face. The Marine in the foreground with his back to the camera seems to be holding something up to his own face, possibly even a camera of his own. The soldier's eyes are wide and anxious as he looks at him, completely exposed and vulnerable. His fellow soldier, the caption tells us, is too "afraid to give himself up."

This "soldier," on closer inspection, does not even seem to be wearing a typical Japanese military uniform; he appears, rather, to be clad in a workman's shirt. In fact, not only is he not in uniform but he is completely unclothed from the waist down. Of the several thousand war images of Kwajalein, there are countless pictures of dead or captive "soldiers" in nothing but loincloths. Perhaps, hiding in their sweltering concrete fortifications, it was too hot to wear full uniforms. But another possibility is that these images are of the "*ninpu*" (mostly Korean or Okinawan) laborers, for whom this was normal attire while working outdoors or on the reef.

More importantly, it is also likely that at the time this photo was taken "Marine captors" had asked this "soldier" to strip. There was apparently no formal American military policy of making potential "Japanese" POWs strip, but by January 1944 this had become standard operating procedure because of a deeply ingrained belief that the enemy would hide grenades in his clothing and then feign surrender. Although this was based on isolated reports of such incidents in Guadalcanal and Tarawa, American soldiers felt intense fear and distrust that Japanese would turn themselves into human bombs. Thus, all prisoners, including at least some Marshall Islanders,[24] were typically ordered to remove all their clothing.

The US military was quite invested in advertising its benevolence toward soldiers through the medium of propaganda films, probably as a tactic to encourage Japanese in later battles to honor the Geneva Conventions. Despite the cruel conditions under which Japanese forces held many Allied prisoners (or even executed them on occasion), making prisoners strip and holding them unclothed for long stretches of time would seem inhumane. Article 2 of the Third Geneva Convention of 1929 (which pertained to the treatment of prisoners and was applied during World War II) states that POWs must "at all times be humanely treated and protected, particularly against acts of violence, from insults, and from public curiosity"; Article 12 requires that clothing and footwear must be provided to all POWs.[25]

Yet there are many photographs in the archives of naked "Japanese" in compromising poses being interrogated on beaches, surrounded by Marines pointing guns in their faces. Predictably, most of these were restricted. Although the Japanese, Koreans, and Okinawans would indeed eventually be clothed and fed, given cigarettes and medical treatment, they were first made to march unclothed across the battlefield where they were held naked in confined holding pens before being taken aboard ships. This is when many of the photographs that ended up in the archives were taken.

"Battle of the Marshalls," 2 February 1944.

It could be argued that in the complex context of radically different battle tactics, ignorance, cultural and linguistic misunderstandings, and the need for up-to-date intelligence, American soldiers were simply "following orders," and the war photographers, as military personnel, were also just documenting "reality," strictly for their own files. Yet if this were the case, why would the most explicit of those scenes then be used in the propaganda film *What Makes a Battle,* which was fully meant for public consumption and watched by audiences all across the United States?

In one scene from the film, a skinny young man in a loincloth emerges from a pillbox emplacement, pulling back his long hair and bowing deeply. The next shot is a scene of naked prisoners crouching on the ground, while another ten men, who from their attire and hairstyles look distinctively like laborers, are forced to strip at gunpoint. One American Marine even forcefully yanks off the trousers of one of the men. The narrator boasts, "[T]hese sullen human beings were in terror that they would receive the same fate that *they* had given *our* boys at Bataan. Instead, we gave them cigarettes, food, and water.

Soft, eh? Well, the record *shows* who's soft.[26] We just happened to be *civilized*. That's the difference."

As the narrator speaks, footage of a wounded Japanese soldier being given cigarettes is shown, but this is immediately contradicted by a scene of at least twenty naked "Japanese" marching down a road and then later being made to sit unclothed on the ground in large groups in fenced-in pens while American troops smile off to the side.

Given the context of 1940s America, where exposing almost any part of the body was strictly forbidden in motion pictures, the idea of filming naked Japanese being herded around Kwajalein and making the film available to the general public is exceptional, especially given the emphasis on Americans being "civilized." But this only draws more attention to the ways in which racial stereotypes played such a large part in American encounters with the enemy. Asian men were depicted as barbaric, nearsighted, short, immature, and uneducated—the complete opposite of what Americans and Europeans imagined to be a noble enemy. We do not see, for instance, in images taken from Europe at the same time, footage or still photography of white German troops being stripped and subjected to the same humiliation by Allied soldiers, although of course scenes of stripping, nakedness, and violence were commonplace in Nazi photographs of Jewish people, ethnic minorities, sexual minorities, and others in concentration camps. It was only possible for Americans to make public these graphic images of "the Japanese" because they were considered to be completely Other: nonwhite, incomprehensible, exotic, inferior, and ultimately inhuman.

Cleanup

MOPPING UP THE MARSHALLS

On Namur, the thick jungle has been burned down to a cratered moonscape, and the bombed-out holes in the earth have been filling up with seawater from below. Far in the distance on the horizon is the roofline of the damaged Japanese air operations building. Also faintly visible are the skeletal remains of the hangar at the Roi airbase. In the foreground, one Marine walks from crater to crater, spraying down the contorted remains of Japanese, Okinawans, and Koreans with sodium arsenate.[27] Countless bodies already seem to be floating in the swampy crater. Two Marshallese men unload another body off of a canvas

"NAMUR ISLAND—Natives help U.S. Marines move dead Jap[anese] bodies on island," 5 February 1944.

stretcher.[28] One Marshallese man, his back to the camera, leans on a shovel or a stick in his right hand as he rests, watching this macabre scene unfold. "Natives help US Marines move dead Jap[anese] bodies on island," the photograph is bluntly titled.

On Kwajalein islet, the army used burial squads of eleven or more men, all of them Americans, who were assisted by a burial detail of fifty-five Marshallese (Poyer, Falgout, and Carucci 2001, 239), and burials followed most of the proper procedures. In the north of the atoll, however, at Roi-Namur, the picture (literally) seems to have been quite different. Archaeologist Leslie Mead indicates that although some images and records suggest that some of the "Japanese" bodies were treated in the proper manner, as at Kwajalein (lining the bodies up, carefully interring them in canvas, and burying them after spraying them with an embalming fluid), "the situation apparently deteriorated very rapidly," and "quite literally everyone on the island was drafted into working to remove the bodies, both Marines and Marshallese."[29]

The way this burial photograph is titled, one gets the sense that these Marshallese men are just lending a helping hand to the Marines.

Apparently these men were volunteers who had been gathered by the Marine Corps Civil Affairs Unit (Poyer, Falgout, and Carucci 2001, 238), but the scenario of an American soldier walking near the crater, with other American Marines marching around like supervisors, some in the foreground and some in the background, while Marshall Islanders toil in the hot sun shows that perhaps these "liberated" Islanders are not just "helping" but are actually working under the command of the military itself. Lindstrom, in his analysis of Pacific Islanders depicted in Allied war photographs from the South Pacific taken around the same time as those taken in Kwajalein, points out how the framing of Islanders in this manner works to pose them as "Allies" fighting alongside Americans for the same "just" cause:

> The natives also volunteer to defeat the Japanese. They join labor corps and defense forces. Pictorially, they line up; they raise their right hands; they make their marks on induction papers. And their allegiance legitimates the Allied presence. The cause is just. The natives join with us rather than with the Japanese. (Needless to say, images of native allies were also common in Japanese productions.) . . . The loyal native redirects his cannibalistic zest and jungle savvy against a common Japanese foe. (Lindstrom 2001, 118)

At the same time, in the contrast of white supervisors and "colored" Islanders, this image is one of untold others that recall the racial tensions of black and white throughout American history. On one level, this framing recruits the Marshallese man as an Allied colleague while it simultaneously inscribes him as "hired help." Lindstrom points out that this is entirely consistent with the ways the US military itself was segregated and African Americans were assigned only to low-ranking support battalions: "Military photographers situated dark Islanders within the overgrown discourse of American racism, as South Seas versions of Black Americans" (2001, 114).[30] And while the exotic "natives" are "domesticated" through this predictable categorization, Japanese, Koreans, and Okinawans are only further dehumanized as they are dumped one by one into the brine of Namur Island's craters of coral, sand, and wilted vegetation. Unlike previous photographs where bodies were still recognizable, in this image they have completely become inanimate objects, the road kill of liberation.

And so began the ugly process of "mopping up," literally and figuratively. Throughout the rest of the atoll, American soldiers swept each small islet, looking for stragglers, capturing remaining Japanese ships at sea, and even diving down to the lagoon floor to seek valuable documents to translate for intelligence purposes. For more than a year after the conflict, new batches of soldiers were mobilized strictly for mop-up purposes in the Marshalls: disposing of bodies, capturing remaining Japanese, dealing with prisoners, and forcing the surrender of other atolls still under Japanese control.

LAUNDRY

In cleaning up the atoll, bulldozers and heavy equipment were used to clear the landscape, but on another level, there was arguably another kind of "cleaning" process going on, one meant to purge the atoll of the stench of death and sanitize its history into a blank slate upon which America could project itself. Thus a clear theme emerges in the postwar

"In commemoration of Mothers' Day 1944 crew members of the 7th A.F. B-24 Liberator, *Come Closer*, based on Kwajalein in the Marshall Islands, mix the practical aspects of the laundry problem in with a touching sentiment."

photographs on Kwajalein, not only of neatening the land, but of household cleaning and ultimately the cleaning of the body itself. There is, for example, a surprising preponderance of images of soldiers washing and devising different ways of doing their laundry with windmills and other gadgetry. These images served not only to report on the day-to-day austere living conditions of the soldiers, they also worked to weave Kwajalein into 1940s Americana, a time when "family values" and middle-class domesticity featured centrally in the mainstream culture.

Images like the following photo of pilots "mix[ing] the practical aspects of the laundry problem in with a touching sentiment" communicate the multiple meanings of "cleaning up" on a number of different levels of irony. Ten men in uniform, some shirtless, labor over their laundry in front of their airplane, scrubbing clothing in buckets and hanging it out to dry, while laughing. Two men hold up the banner that reads, "Mothers' Day: Dear Mom . . . Cleaning up in the Marshalls. Sure wish you were here. Love from 7th AAF [Army Air Force]." One wonders, given the context, whether the "laundry problem" is just a joke about not being able to keep clothing clean and dry in the frequent squalls of the tropics, or if the "problem" is a chauvinistic joke about these men not having mothers and wives to take care of them. Such a reading makes the line, "Sure wish you were here," all the more relevant.

But this image, presumably taken in May of 1944, three months after the invasion of the atoll, is obviously also playing off the double meaning of "cleaning up" on a more symbolic level: ridding the Marshall Islands of Japanese. What was only recently a catastrophic scene of death, mass burial, and anguish is thus systematically disinfected, freshened up, and bleached into white middle-class America.

BATHTIME

In line with such mythology, the theme of cleanliness can also be found in several images that portray American soldiers showering outdoors or bathing in the sea. In contrast to the humiliating images of prisoners of war stripped naked and made to wait in barbed-wire pigpens, nudity in the white American context of postwar liberation takes on completely different meanings of purity, wholesomeness, and renewal. The image below, taken immediately after the battle, has an almost baptismal quality to it, as Marines eagerly strip off their uni-

"ON JAPAN'S SANDS, Marines cool off on former Jap[anese] Beach," 2 February 1944.

forms and frolic past the detritus of war and into the lagoon to "cool off" after their campaign.

"The imperial act of discovery," writes McClintock, "can be compared with the male act of baptism. In both rituals, western men publicly disavow the creative agency of others (the colonized/women) and arrogate to themselves the power of origins" (McClintock 1995, 29). Here Kwajalein lagoon itself becomes not only a restorative site of cleanliness for the atoll's liberators, but also a site through which they "rebirth" the atoll into the territory of the United States. With their bodies they mark the transition from Japan to America on this former Japanese beach. Stripping away their uniforms, they commune with nature and return anointed by Kwajalein's waters, "naturalizing" America's mythology of seizing Japanese (but really Marshallese) land and sea. In doing so, they also render their Western (and Christian) imaginary of the Pacific onto their environment. As Lutz and Collins write, "beaches are the essence of the Pacific for many Westerners, as travel posters attest; the beach should be a scene of pleasure, not of work or unpleasant sights" (1993, 140).

Never mind that at the time of the invasion of Kwajalein, nearly one hundred years had passed since the first American Christian missionaries came to the Marshall Islands at Ebon and admonished the original inhabitants for not wearing enough clothing, and that (despite Japanese customs of swimming in *fundoshi* loincloths) Marshallese of

1944 no doubt would have found swimming in the nude obscene. Just as Teresia Teaiwa wrote about the cruel irony of the bikini swimsuit being named for its "explosiveness" after the nuclear testing in Bikini, one of the bitter ironies of colonialism in the Pacific is that now it is the Islanders who frown on the scantily clad tourists who help themselves to their beaches (Teaiwa 1994, 97).

In all these images of bathing, soldiers are shown celebrating the great outdoors, splashing happily in the sea or hosing themselves off outside. It is worth also considering the way American military masculinity is naturalized via the countless photographs of bare-chested soldiers that appear in the archives. Like the bare-breastedness of Marshall Islander women that was fetishized so often by Japanese and American photographers, the toplessness of American soldiers is eroticized in these war photographs. In most of these images, American male bodies are portrayed as natural, pure, and masculine, celebrating the soldiers' virility.[31]

Gratitude

From the time of the WWII liberation, and the US occupation, which inoculated the Marshalls with canned SPAM

"K-RATIONS A TREAT TO HIM . . . A Marshallese boy perches comfortably on a wind-twisted coconut tree and prepares to open a box of K-rations. He found the Marines' field rations a welcome change in his usual diet of rice, fish, and coconuts. Picture was taken soon after the Fourth Marine Division's invasion of the Island," March 1944.

and westernized thinking, Marshallese have valued their
relationship with the US and looked up to the Americans.

—*Aenet Rowa, 2005*

A significant component of the American liberation story during the war, not only in the Marshall Islands but also in Japan, involved the provision of food. The US provisional military government was only to supply "enemy populations" with enough food, shelter, and other supplies to avoid health problems and social unrest, but in the former Nanyō Guntō, where Islanders were not "indigenous" Japanese, this order was "interpreted liberally" (Richard 1957, 183). This image of a young Marshallese boy relates the story of Islanders being showered with new and desirable American food while it also exoticizes Marshallese as pristine, "traditional," unspoiled (and even childlike) people. The field rations he receives, say the caption, are "a welcome change in his usual diet of rice, fish, and coconuts." Given the posing of the boy "perching comfortably on a wind-twisted coconut tree," there is a suggestion here that this "native" child wearing a knit ski cap is in his natural habitat, suddenly confronting the modern world through the good grace of American liberation. Yet not only was rice a major influence on the Marshallese diet ever since it was introduced by Japanese colonists as a staple in the 1920s, so were many other Japanese foods, which were traded at nearby Jaluit Atoll and sold in local shops on Kwajalein. By the time of the American invasion, Marshall Islanders were already well-accustomed to Japanese canned foods, such as mackerel (*saba*), and preserved pickles like *umeboshi* salted plums and *takuan* made from *daikon* radish.[32] They were used to using *shōyu* (soy sauce) on their food as well, to the extent that in times of scarcity, people would survive by pouring it on rice and eating it with coconut. To this day, the per capita average consumption of Kikkōman brand soy sauce is actually higher in the Marshall Islands than it is in Japan.[33]

Indeed, the Americans introduced many new (and many extremely unhealthy) foods to Micronesia, and most Marshallese recollections of the invasion are preoccupied with this influx of food in abundance, "reflecting," say Poyer, Falgout, and Carucci, "both the privation of war and the important symbolism of food in Marshallese culture" (2001, 243):

> While Americans undoubtedly thought, correctly, that their gifts were signs of good will and gestures of friendship, they were less

Capturing Liberation

aware that Marshallese also interpreted them as the customary distributions of chiefs—very powerful chiefs with a seemingly unlimited source of goods. Joined with the invasion's overwhelming display of military might, Americans came to be seen as "the parallel of traditional conquerors writ large—that is sacred chiefs."[34] The political implications of this abundant initial generosity would emerge later in the American administration. (245)

Walsh has also considered the implications of this generosity in her study of American-Marshallese power relations, arguing that Americans may have intended to liberate the people but instead became the new *irooj* (chiefs) within the larger political sphere, a relationship that suited American strategic imperial needs in its establishment of the US Trust Territory of the Pacific Islands and

"Magode, Chief of the natives on Carlos Island, Kwajalein, accepts a cigarette from Pvt. Loren V. Fager of 241 Vermyo, Raton, New Mexico. Marshall Islands, 26 April 1944."

made Marshallese independence a complicated affair in the 1980s (Walsh 2003). And although the Marshall Islands is an independent republic in "free association" with the United States, at Kwajalein Atoll, where the military has occupied most key islands nonstop since the war, I would argue that these "chiefly relations" are still in place, to some extent.[35]

In the next image, we see yet another "chiefly" exchange between an American serviceman and "Magode, Chief of the natives" on Āne-Eḷḷap-Kan (Carlos), two islets up the west reef from Kwajalein. Framed not unlike early American portrayals of exchange between settlers and Native Americans, or European voyagers and countless Pacific Islanders, the American soldier makes a peace offering, here in the form of a Camel cigarette. It is important in this image that this is person is referred to as a "chief"; in fact, "Magode" is one of the only Marshallese individuals appearing in the archives who is properly identified with a name other than "native."[36] This is telling, given that American military and later civilian administrators, like Japanese and previous colonial powers, were keen to negotiate only with traditional leaders, preferring to govern the populace through those people they identified as kings.

Of course, much to the frustration of these officials, Marshallese land tenure and traditional leadership is much more sophisticated than this: all Marshall Islanders have claims to land, with multiple affiliations crisscrossing between atolls and islands. This image would suggest, however, that somehow this American soldier is on even terms with or even superior to this traditional leader, that through his generosity he is made both welcome and powerful. Lindstrom also writes about similar images between Allied soldiers and Islanders in the Solomons:

> Images of shared effort intimate that the native is like us, or at least somewhat like us. In pictures at least, natives and servicemen work together for joint goals, muscling artillery up a mountainside, unloading PT boats. Poses of shared endeavor and everyday experience connote a common humanity. These shared experiences include having a Coke together, playing checkers, lighting up one another's cigarettes. This last pose is very common in the archives: servicemen and Islanders again and again give each other the courtesy of a light. (2001, 120)[37]

Capturing Liberation 145

"MONDAY IN THE MARSHALLS: With a cigarette dangling from her lip, a native woman on Kwajalein Atoll, Marshall Is. does her family's washing. Rocks make a good scrubbing brush. Note the bucket provided by the Marine Corps. Picture was taken shortly after the Fourth Marine Div. invaded the Japanese-held islands."

Romance and Ridicule

The picture on page 143 shows how Marshallese men, who were not usually given access to alcohol or cigarettes during Japanese times, are granted these "freedoms" through the paternalistic intervention of American men, who offer these pleasures as a gesture of shared manhood. By the same token, however, scenes of Marshallese women smoking cigarettes or engaging in other activities that did not fit the stereotypes of the eroticized "hula girl" were ridiculed in some of the images as unladylike. The following image, of a young woman doing laundry "with a cigarette dangling from her lip," is a perfect contrast to the previous image. It implies through its sarcastic captioning and grotesque framing not only that smoking is unbecoming for a woman but that Marshallese women are somehow primitive and unclean enough to indulge in the habit.

"Rocks make a good scrubbing brush," the caption explains of the

"NO GLAMOR GIRLS . . . Native women of Kwajalein Atoll in the Marshall Islands shun sarongs, favor "Mother Hubbard" dresses, as this photograph illustrates. They do not wear shoes, either," March 1944, Kwajalein Atoll.

woman's method for doing "her family's laundry."[38] Cross-reading this image with the series of soldiers doing their laundry with buckets and scrub boards, another parallel is drawn in terms of the "shared everyday experience" that Lindstrom alludes to in the above quote. Yet the caption also directs the viewer to the bucket that has been provided by the Marines, emphasizing once again that American goodwill and advanced technology are making a big difference in the lives of the "natives" and that these gestures are received with immense gratitude.

It was only a short time before military authorities began to strictly regulate interactions between American soldiers and Marshall Islanders. Soldiers were prohibited from visiting Marshallese villages on other islands, likely in part out of fears that soldiers would become sexually active with locals. As I have already mentioned, defeated Japan was eroticized "in the eyes of the conquerors," as evidenced by the fetishization of *geisha* (Dower 1999, 137). Arguably a similar trend could be said of all military campaigns, as discussed by Enloe regarding the prostitution that inevitably springs up around American bases (1990, 81).

The eroticization, or attempted eroticization, of Kwajalein women can also be seen in the gaze of military photographers, setting the stage, perhaps, for depicting postwar Micronesians during the Trust Territory era. Lutz and Collins analyze this in depth in their study of the images in *National Geographic,* pointing out, for instance, how the magazine's images of Micronesia "emphasize the 'toplessness' of its women, the exoticism of its dancers, the romance of its navigators, and the juxtaposition of things native and things modern or Western" (1993, 136). But unlike the images of "bare-breasted beauties" that feature in military photography from parts of western Micronesia like Palau and Yap, where Islanders tended toward customary attire, military photographers seemed disappointed by Marshallese and Kosraeans in eastern Micronesia, where the influence of nineteenth-century American missionaries had been the most pervasive.

In an image mockingly titled "No Glamor Girls," eleven Marshallese women pose for the cameraman with their backs to Kwajalein lagoon. The caption explains that these women "shun sarongs," as if to suggest that Islander women should wear sarongs and go topless, in line with the Hollywood fantasy of the premodern South Pacific. The image ridicules the women, portraying them as somehow inferior in their disappointingly modern "Mother Hubbard" dresses, cheap substitutes for the exotic Pacific "dusky maiden" archetype. "They do not wear shoes, either" is another characterization of their lack of "glamor."

On one hand, soldiers' invasion narratives expressed a sense of kindred values around the awareness that most Islanders were Christians (Poyer, Falgout, and Carucci 2001, 237). For Marshallese, too, even though Americans had never been in an official colonizing role in the past, the return to the islands of fellow Christians was cause for celebration, since missionary activities had been severely limited during Japanese times and religious ceremonies had been outlawed during the war. And judging from some of the images in the archives, on occasion soldiers were even serenaded with church hymns. Yet on the other hand, soldiers' fantasies of the tropical island Pacific framed their expectations of Islanders and fixed them in the premodern past, so the Marshallese women's Christian-influenced attire may have been disappointing.

"Pfc. Louis A. Avial of Gilroy, Calif. (left) and Cpl. James Riddick of Everest, N.C., attempt to purchase a grass skirt from young native girls on Carlos Island, Kwajalein, Marshall Islands," 26 April 1944.

In contrast to the prewar Japanese romanticization of the Pacific, in which Marshallese women were framed erotically by the "chieftain's daughter" discourse discussed in chapter 3, American depictions of Marshallese women were typically disparaging. For Americans, Paradise had already been found in European exploration literature and in the territory of Hawai'i (which the United States eventually made into a state after the war in 1959). It was this imaginary that set the standard for the American Pacific; anything that did not fit the eroticized fantasy of slender hula dancers with light skin was not authentic enough.[39]

It was, nonetheless, probably the "hula girl" fantasy and the American fetishization of the "grass skirt" that led to scenes like the one above, in which "grass" skirts are apparently being sold to two soldiers on Āne-Ełļap-Kan (Carlos) Island. In this image, four girls and a mature woman (perhaps their mother or aunt)—all of whom wear cotton dresses—display "traditional" garments for the Americans. The young woman in the center appears to be laughing, either out of amusement or embarrassment as the soldier on the right looks at her intently. Meanwhile, the older woman on the far right models one of the skirts on top of her cotton dress.

From a Marshallese perspective, because this "traditional" clothing had not been worn since the late nineteenth century, these "grass skirts" would have been quite extraordinary objects. It is important to note, first of all, that Marshallese women did not customarily wear "grass" skirts made from loose strands of fiber like these; up until the late 1800s and on some ceremonial occasions thereafter, they wore elaborate and intricately woven mats that typically covered their knees.[40] Women would never have worn the skirts shown here in this photograph. In fact, they look like *in*, the kind of skirts that were once worn by Marshallese *men* (Spennemann 1998). They also resemble the skirts worn by male dancers during the sacred and chiefly *jebwa* dance.

Taking this cultural background into consideration, it is likely that the women in this photograph were either weaving "traditional" male Marshallese attire for the soldiers themselves to wear, or perhaps they were producing order-made skirts to meet the soldiers' demand for hula paraphernalia. In either case, this exchange is a moment in which Islanders sell "traditional" culture and "dress up" to meet Americans' expectations of authenticity. The "cross-dressing" of the woman on the right is also an intriguing moment of inversion in which she dresses in premodern Marshallese menswear and simultaneously plays along with American "Hawaiiana" stereotypes of the Pacific (see Desmond 1999).

Of course here we could also say that by purchasing grass skirts, the soldiers are on the verge of "going native" and engaging in their own "ethnic cross-dressing," what Lindstrom calls the "collapse of boundaries and convergence of once disparate identities: the self as other" (2001, 120). These playful moments are not to be taken seriously; they are entirely ironic if orientalist in their composition. What is interesting to me, however, is the multiple layering of gazes (indeed, perhaps a convergence of atollscapes) that takes place in this image. While the two soldiers project their fantasies of the Pacific onto the Marshall Islanders as they literally gaze at the young women, the older woman on the right gazes straight back into the camera. She parodies the American fantasy (and caption) of the photograph by jokingly drawing attention to her own "drag" performance as a "native," the old-fashioned man's skirt layered on top of her modern dress.[41] Is this a Marshallese inside joke?

In collapsing these boundaries and finding affinities between "lib-

"SALES TALK—Sergeant Brooks pauses for a moment in a native village to view with curiosity a tiny, elderly native woman. In native villages such as this one, members of the patrol found many traces of Japanese such as pictures and ammunition; and yet the natives were very much against the Japanese," June 1944.

erated natives" and their "liberators," the postinvasion narrative of Kwajalein also needed to eradicate all traces of "Japaneseness" from the atoll. In the midst of their fascination with atoll Pacific life, mop-up units also had to contend with the possibility of Japanese hiding away in the jungles of small islands or with Islanders who might be pro-Japanese. The following image, in which two soldiers view "with curiosity" an elderly Marshallese woman in a village, explores these encounters with "natives" on the remote small islands of Kwajalein Atoll.

The photograph is posed quite evocatively, with foliage draped over the immediate foreground. The setting is a very "traditional village" with thatched structures and a sense of a quaint and timeless era. The soldiers in full uniform, with helmets, smile as they greet the elderly woman, who is only about half their height. She wears a white gown and seems to look up to them, with a smile on her face. It is a peaceful scene that looks like an illustration from a children's fairy tale book. As such it elegantly carries the liberation narrative of heroic knights coming to save a peaceful kingdom helplessly mired in the evildoings of another empire. The woman seems to welcome the soldiers, and the soldiers seem to present themselves as perfect gentlemen just making a courteous neighborhood visit or, as the caption jokingly suggests, a "sales" call.

Yet these so-called salesmen probably were not on a business mission but rather a mop-up operation to small islets in the atoll to check for Japanese stragglers or pro-Japanese "natives." As the image's caption indicates, there were many "traces" of the Japanese, such as "pictures and ammunition." What sort of pictures might have these been? Perhaps these were images of friends and loved ones? In light of the fact that many Marshallese had worked alongside the Japanese and there had been romantic liaisons between Japanese soldiers and local women, as well as generations of children born of mixed Japanese-Marshallese heritage, it would be strange if the departure of the Japanese were not also accompanied by ambivalence and melancholy for many people. As the caption of this photo suggests, Americans felt a need not only to justify their own presence, but also to reconcile the notion of Marshallese as subjects of the Japanese empire by reminding themselves that the "natives" were "very much against" the Japanese at the same time. Meanwhile, according to many accounts, these Japanese artifacts were confiscated by American authorities and never returned. Former first lady Emlain Kabua, whose father was Japanese, spent the war years on one of the small islands in Kwajalein Atoll. She explained that her family hid many of their possessions, since the American soldiers made these house calls and literally took away many important family heirlooms, documents, and photographs of personal significance (interview, March 14, 2010). For many Marshall Islanders, especially those with Japanese heritage, it was as if the Americans were actually trying to confiscate their memories.

For Americans, it may have seemed contradictory to the script of liberation from the "enemy" that Marshallese would cling to some Japanese customs and keepsakes. As I have mentioned elsewhere, however, many Marshallese in Kwajalein old enough to remember the Japanese colonial period do so with a fair degree of nostalgia and as a time of productivity, cooperation, and generally positive change. Those same elders, though, make a clear distinction between the civilian administration of the atoll up until the late 1930s and the ensuing time of military rule that followed. They also distinguish between "Japanese civilians" and "Japanese soldiers," the latter group being characterized as unreasonably hostile and harsh or "crazy." Indeed, Marshallese were against military occupiers, period. Muench reminisces about his conversations with a Marshallese worker he befriended during his time on Kwajalein, when he first came to terms with indigenous ambivalence toward the American presence as well:

> Once I asked Caleb if he was happy that we had taken the islands from the Japanese military. He said, "Yes, and we'll be happy when you go home, too!" At first I was affronted by his candor, but after awhile I could see his wisdom. These islands were theirs, not ours, nor the Japanese, nor the Germans. They knew how to survive and be happy in their environment—we didn't. (2002, 54)

But happiness in one's environment is relative. Following ostensibly the same logic, in what has been characterized as a policy of "benign neglect" (Kiste 1993, 70), the subsequent US Navy administration of the Marshall Islands in years to come would pursue a strategy of leaving Islanders to go back to their "traditional ways" of subsistence living, supposedly because they would be "happier" this way, all the while militarily exploiting the islands for a decade of Cold War nuclear testing. After more than a century of colonialism and encultur-

"MARSHALL NATIVES HAIL THEIR LIBERATION ON FOURTH OF JULY—Native girls of the Marshall Islands stage a colorful dance before hundreds of Marines and Sailors at an impressive 4th of July celebration. . . ." Majuro, 4 July 1944.

ation, during which Marshallese got used to the pleasures and pains of Spanish, German, and Japanese empires, the idea of being "liberated" back into the premodern era made little sense to anyone.

Post-Liberation: An Ongoing "Special" Relationship

"In the Pacific Islands," writes Keith Camacho, "the making of history is a vibrant process of contestation and celebration" (Camacho 2011, 177). At least in the early days after the invasion, the liberation of the Marshalls was celebrated with much fanfare. Marshallese staged various cultural performances, including the *beet* dance performed in this image taken in Majuro Atoll, featured in an "impressive 4th of July celebration." Young barefoot Marshallese maidens dance merrily in the center of the photograph, led by the enthusiastic cheering of a man raising his arms and clapping off to the left, and an older matriarch on the right. In the background, a large group of soldiers in uniform are visible, and more than one of them is taking a photograph of this momentous event.

Captions from other photos taken this same day explain that "hundreds of natives" did performances, including one performance in which Marshallese men "staged a colorful dance" in which "the American eagle (made from cardboard ration boxes) [conquered] the Rising Sun" (image NA-93270). Here Marshallese rehearsed the narrative of liberation through performance, playing out the story of an almighty America that was strong enough to conquer Japan's empire. In light of Carucci's argument about "sacred chiefs" (1989, 85), however, this "colorful dance" could be read less as a story about Marshallese emancipation from Japanese rule than as a story about the dueling of two chiefly powers and the ultimate hegemony of America's military brawn. This pageant bears a striking resemblance to a parade I witnessed on Ebeye to commemorate the Kwajalein invasion: one carnival float was decorated as a jungle where young Marshallese boys brandished swords and wore headbands emblazoned with the imperial rising sun insignia (the *kyokujitsu-ki*); the next float signaled American postwar superiority with a mock control room in which children dressed in lab coats and spectacles maneuvered a gigantic papier-mâché missile with "US Army" painted on its side (see Dvorak 2004, 59–60). In either case, "before and after" are not much different; military muscle is the common catalyst for rupture.[42]

It is also highly significant that the celebrations featured in these photographs take place on the Fourth of July, the date the United States celebrates its sovereignty and liberation from England. Thus the celebration could be seen as a celebration of America and American independence, a Marshallese gesture of solidarity with the United States' mission of spreading freedom in the world. Yet from an American perspective somehow in these representations of "happy natives" rejoicing the end of the war and Japanese military rule, it is as if the camera collapses thousands of years of "free" Marshallese civilization into the brief span of American history, rendering that earlier memory obsolete.[43] Thus this fanfare marks the beginning of an era of American quasi-colonialism in the Marshall Islands and throughout Micronesia, in what policymakers aptly titled "strategic trust."

It is in fact this collapse of histories that continues to resonate throughout the postwar years in the relationship between the Marshall Islands and America, causing many leaders, both Marshallese and American, to euphemize this unequal alliance of interdependence as "special." After American abuse of the Marshall Islands for decades as a nuclear proving grounds and the lease of Kwajalein Atoll as a missile-testing site, the fact that many Marshallese still consider the United States to be their best friend makes this a very "special" relationship indeed, even with the millions of American dollars in aid.

It is arguably these representations, these oversimplified images of cut-and-dried liberation, that have helped to obscure the memory of other pasts that came before the invasion and set the tone for the present day. Through the veneration of this kind of erasure, Japanese human connections to Kwajalein and the Marshalls or Micronesia in general were severed, replaced by images of fanatic subhuman militants and their subsequent demise. The memory of Marshallese genealogies, lands, and sacrifices, meanwhile, got mired in the force of the American mythology, buried beneath a concrete-coated atollscape filled with "benevolent white chiefs" and their loyal "native" subjects.

Marshallese loyalty to the American cause has remained strong ever since the Pacific War, and it is renewed nowadays when thousands of Micronesian soldiers are fighting alongside Americans in Iraq and other sites (Hezel 2005, 5). On Kwajalein in 2005, when a particularly military-minded commander installed a speaker system to broadcast army bugle calls throughout the base, the largely civilian American community protested in letters to the editor of the *Kwajalein Hourglass* and in other public forums. Base residents, expected to stop their activity to turn and face the flag by the air terminal as an expression of appreciation for "our men and women of the armed forces," laughed at the prospect, some pledging to ignore the bugle calls altogether. But it was the Marshallese base workers—citizens of an independent republic and trusty best friends of the United States—who stopped whatever they were doing, placed their hands over the hearts, and patriotically stood at attention until the bugle broadcasts would come to an end (*Kwajalein Hourglass,* March 30, 2005).[44]

The American story of spreading democracy through liberation and postwar power is not unique to Kwajalein, of course. It has taken on different inflections in other places globally, as well as in other parts of Micronesia (see Diaz 2001). Yet in the Marshall Islands, where the United States has from the Cold War to the present aimed to justify its presence in the Central Pacific as benevolent and essential, liberation takes on a special meaning. As Lazarus Salii pointed out in 1972, Micronesians have always been well aware that the United States has been both "conqueror" and "liberator" in their islands (Poyer, Falgout, and Carucci 2001, 289), and the slippery terrain between these contradictory extremes requires maintenance and reinforcement of the liberation legend.

It is this American double standard, no doubt, that brought local Marshallese leaders in Kwajalein Atoll to finally change the name of "Liberation Day" to "Memorial Day" in the early 1990s, around the fiftieth anniversary of the battle.[45] Unlike the Americans who live today on Kwajalein as temporary transplants from the States, the Marshallese of the atoll have strong and painful memories of the war and all the people they lost. Mindful of the deep sorrow and anger most Islanders also feel about nuclear weapons tests in northern atolls and the sickness and displacement they caused, paramount chief (*iroojlaplap*) and former president Imata Kabua was known to say sarcastically, "why don't they just liberate us from the radiation already?"[46]

"I always want to say to Americans, you'll never find any more true and loyal friends than the people of the Marshall Islands," says "Wesley," a Ri-Kuwajleen resident of Ebeye. He insists how pro-American and devoted Marshall Islanders are but is quick to point out that Marshallese were also very pro-Japanese in certain contexts. Along with their loyalty and fondness for Americans, there has also been anger and bitterness over the many trespasses the United States has committed:

> Once, an American official came up to me and said, "Hey, did you know the Japanese finally apologized to us for bombing Pearl Har-

bor?" And I said, "Wow! That's great! I really take my hat off to those Japanese to apologize like that, they are such gentlemen!" And then I said, "And what about you guys, when are you going to apologize to us about all those nuclear tests you did here?" And the American guy just turned around without saying anything and walked out of the restaurant.[47]

Whether for defense, offense, or "just testing," Kwajalein is today the uncontested epicenter of the "Martial Islands." Encoded in the American discourse of the present day, from the battle tales and iconography of commemorative historical plaques and memorials to the ways the current missile-testing range justifies its mission, are the legacies of this liberation narrative set into motion more than half a century ago. Yet the images captured of the atoll's "liberation" hint at deeper stories that lie just beneath the military base's manicured surface.

Every so often, someone comes across dangerous unexploded ordnance from the war sitting in his or her backyard or nestled among the multicolored coral thickets of the reef. Yet we are not asked to remember the mass graves where Japanese, Korean, and Okinawan bodies were buried by the thousands, not implored to know where the houses of Marshallese chiefs once stood, and not reminded that this is Marshallese land. When the US Army digs new trenches to repair its water pipes or replace a street lamp, the public rarely learns about all the bones they find. These histories are sanitized and landscaped over by peaceful grassy lawns, idyllic beaches, and, of course, concrete. The US Army refers to this as "beautification." Indeed, Kwajalein today is strikingly picture-perfect. Amnesia is bliss.

CHAPTER 6

The Haunted Bathtub

Encountering the Spirits of the Atoll

Long-term American residents of Kwajalein speak about how their children see ghosts of Japanese soldiers, the most notable being "the Japanese commander," an apparition who has befriended many American children but never seems to visit any adults. For American "Kwaj Kids" who knew of them, the Japanese ghosts were about as real as Santa Claus, except for that parents didn't seem to like it when we talked about such things. They thought that it was just their children trying to rationalize the frightening realities of war.

But Kwajalein is a place of many spirits.[1] Like all Marshallese atolls, it is a place where the souls of ancestors live in the land, and where a whole world of "demons" also thrives. Many Islanders accept and embrace this world, and they speak also of various kinds of magic, both good and bad.[2] I cannot say that I thought of these things very much as a child, but I did always sense that Kwajalein was alive and that the entire atoll was a being in its own right. It is a dramatically beautiful and devastating place, teeming with life but equally filled with death. It always seemed that there were dimensions to the atollscape that I could not see with my eyes but could feel somehow.

I have my own vague recollection that I might have seen a ghost when I was eight and lying in my bunk bed at night; it smiled at me and I felt intrigued and terrified all at once, though I had no direct association with the war at the time. Back then I knew little about what had happened on Kwajalein, nor about how many thousands of people had died. I told a few people at school about what I had seen, and they joked that I must have seen the Japanese commander. But I soon forgot about all of this, and it faded from my consciousness.

It was 2005 when I first became aware of the haunted atollscape of Kwajalein again. I had flown up to Roi-Namur on the early flight and spent most of the morning walking alone through the ruins of the battlefield there. It was my first return to that part of the atoll since I had been a child and since I had lived in Japan. The whisper of the trade winds rushing across the reef and through the jungle evoked a sense of eeriness as the breezes swept between the bombed-out concrete buildings that still stood there. Two stingrays swam in the waters at low tide as dark storm clouds mounted in the west. I felt an overpowering sense of melancholic fear mixed with an inexplicable sense of fatigue, and I suddenly realized I needed to return to Kwajalein as soon as possible and rest. In fact I could barely stand. I flew back and fell into a deep sleep.

As I slept I had a sudden realization of how deeply painful and emotional the collective wounds I was visiting were. I knew all at once that these had been terribly *frightening* times. Connecting with the place where so many people had perished, it became clear to me how these men had come here and they knew they were going to die here, in this beautiful and yet devastating place. The sound of coral shards rolling in the surf, the relentless sun. . . . I saw glimpses of soldiers separating from loved ones and making their way across railroads and high seas, resigning themselves to do things they did not want to do. I sensed the fear of local people lamenting an impending doom from which they could not escape, the pale sweat of the Japanese and Okinawans escaping in convoys over the ocean, dodging the American torpedoes below.

This dream changed the way I viewed Kwajalein. I had always felt some sort of haunting presence, an awareness that the past was still alive in the form of Marshallese, Japanese, American, Korean, and other ancestral others who had died there, but this was different. It was my first true understanding of how it might have *felt*. It was an unveiling of what had been completely buried and hidden from view, my first realization of just how huge and tragic the past was and how many spirits there were. I could no longer scuba dive to the depths of the lagoon to look at old sunken Japanese wrecks without imagining the lives that had been lost there.[3] As I scaled the masts of gigantic warships like the *Tateyama Maru* and the *Akibasan Maru* more than fifty meters beneath the surface of the water, I began to hear the *gunka* military songs I had heard elderly Marshall Islanders sing echoing in my mind, songs like "Getsu-Getsu Ka Sui Moku Kin-Kin" and "Taiheiyō Kōshin Kyoku."[4] As if I had become a ghost myself, I floated

The Haunted Bathtub

past those eerie ladders and hallways and peeked into portholes into the cabins within. It was not hard to imagine sailors scurrying as their ship entered South Pass into Kwajalein lagoon, blasting its horns. My eyes and all my senses seemed to be retuned to a new frequency, to an atollscape that had previously been invisible to me.

A month later, when I was in Jaluit Atoll, I had an even more powerful experience. Unlike the gutted ruins of the military buildings of Kwajalein Atoll, which sit abandoned on high-security US missile-testing grounds, the prewar military and civilian structures of Jaluit felt alive and real; they sat right next to Marshallese dwellings and churches, between basketball courts and laundry hanging out to dry in the sun. Since I had already seen photos of many of these buildings from the 1930s in various Japanese archives, I instantly recognized some of them as I strolled out of the village of Jebwad, the former Japanese district capital. The peculiar shape of this building, for instance, caught my attention.

Recalling its fanciful zigzag decorations, I instantly remembered a black-and-white photograph I had seen of the old weather bureau at Jebwad. Squinting, I could easily imagine the wooden buildings that used to stand beside it. I could imagine the dozens of copra schooners and steamships in the harbor nearby, the sound of coal being unloaded and uploaded. I could imagine the Nanyō-chō officials in their white uniforms, the Marshallese men in the *seinendan* young men's association practicing their marching, the Marshallese women singing hymns as they worked hard at weaving hats, fans, and cigarette cases out of pandanus leaves for sale back in Japan.

Like my explorations of Roi-Namur, my encounters with the ghostly atollscapes of Jaluit haunted me and filled my mind with images: ghosts of buildings, ghosts of people. I felt this even more strongly when I crossed Jaluit lagoon to the small islet of Iṃwej (Imiej), site of the former Japanese naval base. My hosts, who had relatives living on the island, insisted that I would learn much about the Japanese period if I went there, and so I went enthusiastically. My host-brothers loaded a motorboat with fresh water, canned food, and rice, and we sped out over the choppy inlet to the other side of the atoll.[5]

The Bathtub: Trademark of Japanese Settlement

Arriving at Iṃwej we are greeted by Jina, the boys' uncle. He shakes my hand vigorously and says *iọkwe,* and then proceeds to lead me to his house, a small, sturdy shack built atop the concrete of the former Japanese seaplane ramp. The boys go off to play basketball with their cousins and I sit down on a woven mat on the beach with two women strumming ukeleles and grating coconut. I notice a large, oddly shaped object jutting out of the sand and realize that it is the propeller of an airplane from the war, caked with coral and debris.

Jina serves me a fresh green coconut to drink and then pats me on the back, saying gently in elementary Marshallese, *"Kwoj jambo?"* (you want to take a walk?), so that I will understand. I follow him into the jungle, where we pass a rusty prewar Yanmar brand electric generator overgrown with vines and then approach the underground Japanese hospital. It is a gigantic mound covered in shrubbery, palm trees, and a corroded cannon. The door of the infirmary is tightly shut and barricaded with a rock. It looks like no one has touched it since the war, and I do not even want to imagine what lies within.

"You don't go there, okay? It's a place for ghosts," Jina says, with a stern look.

We travel further into the jungle. There are massive craters in the center of the foliage, still remaining from the air raids of the 1940s. They are filled with rainwater and breeding mosquitoes. An enormous pig that was bathing in the mud awakens, startled, and lumbers back in the opposite direction toward the beach. Jina thrashes his way through # The Haunted Bathtub

the thick of the jungle, wielding a machete, and it seems that at every turn in the path we encounter yet another decaying piece of war machinery—a ruined tank, airplane fuselage, concrete bunkers, guns.

Entering a clearing we come upon a two-story concrete building. Its windows are missing and half of the building has completely caved in. Rain from the morning's storm drips into puddles all around the inside of the structure, cascading down like a waterfall in some places. There are shards of broken glass, possibly blown out by explosions from the bombing, and piles of old junk lying together with chunks of concrete that have fallen from above. Bony chickens scamper through the shrapnel, followed by dozens of fuzzy chicks that chirp incessantly as they escape our path.

Jina leads me inside. It is a dormitory for pilots, he explains. "*Lale*—look at the *mun cook,* the kitchen," he says, pointing at a crumbling old stove with two holes carved out for charcoal fires. "And look at the toilet," he says, leading me into a room where urinals are lined up against the wall. They look eerily too contemporary to belong in this scene of war wreckage, as if they had come from any public toilet.

I rest for a moment on a low wall, and then I realize how that wall forms a large square basin. I am shocked to discover that it is an *ofuro*, a Japanese communal bath. I have soaked many times in similar baths in Japan and I know them well, but I had never expected to find one in the middle of a Marshallese jungle. Like the toilets, the bath looks out of place on what otherwise seems like a small and remote rural island. It is littered with chunks of crumbling concrete and scribbled with graffiti, but it is no doubt a Japanese bath.

The *ofuro* is somehow so human, so everyday, such a domestic and personal space. Inside the bath is a low bench where the soldiers probably sat for hours after a long day of training exercises, dangling their legs into the hot water and pretending that they were home, back in Japan. I can smell the soap and the burning firewood. When was their last soak?

Jina, who does not know the thoughts that are racing through my head, comes up behind me and laughs. "Ah, and this is a Japanese . . . swimming pool!" He is only in his forties, of a younger generation that does not remember the war or the colonial period before it. I am younger than Jina, and yet my years in Japan create in me an inexplicable nostalgia for an era that I never experienced. I smile at Jina's joke, but something about the bath makes me feel incredibly sad.

Baths like these, I would later learn, were built at most Japanese military bases, and many private homes also heated water each night for a long soak. During the colonial period, Marshallese boys were often recruited to gather tinder around the island in exchange for money or sweets, and many also were allowed to take a hot bath as well, after the Japanese were finished with their ablutions. Hatfield Lemae, the former high school principal of Jaluit High School, who was a little boy during the latter days of the Japanese colonial era, recalls what a fondness he developed for hot baths. Even in his old age, he would fill up an old oil drum with water and heat it, despite the hot and humid climate.[6]

Baths were also a common feature on naval ships, where seawater was heated. In Kwajalein Atoll, for instance, one such bathtub remains deep below the surface of the lagoon aboard the wreck of the *Asakaze Maru*.

Kawazoe Katsuki, captain of the *Dai-Roku Kyō-Maru* submarine chaser, was transferred back to Japan shortly before the bombardment of Kwajalein Atoll. In his memoirs, he reflected that he had to abandon "those boys," whom he had come to know as brothers and sons. After writing about how he drank for two whole years with those sailors and knew them well, he described the scene of his last bath in an *ofuro* on board the ship in October 1943:

> The day before I left the ship, early on the 11th, I heated the water for my *ofuro*. I tried to wash away all the filth that had built up on my body for nearly two years circling each island of the Marshalls and the Gilberts, but it goes without saying that the *ofuro* was filled with hot sea water anyway...
>
> As usual, my subordinate, lance corporal Kanda, diligently washes my back. As he is doing this I notice some drops of warm water splashing on my back. The door of the bath is open for ventilation and there is no condensation on the ceiling. When I look back behind me I realize to my surprise that Kanda is making a tearful face and his eyes are overflowing with tears.
>
> "What's wrong with you, you're crying, what happened?" I ask.
>
> "It's just that you're leaving us, sir, and I just suddenly felt very sad and can't stop crying," he says, and I feel a heavy sensation in my chest as I hear this. (Kawazoe 1990, 223)

The *ofuro* in Japan is often a place for fraternization, a peaceful safe world where men can form close brotherly bonds. Men in Japan use the expression *hadaka no tsukiai* (naked relations) as a figure of speech that means "heart-to-heart" communication but also has a literal meaning when referring to the shared nakedness of bathing. In the context of Japanese military culture this could have had the additional meaning of being unarmed and therefore both unthreatening and vulnerable.

The bath is also a comforting, soothing sanctuary. During the invasion of Kwajalein, Japanese American soldier Ben Honda, an intelligence officer, describes how the first Japanese soldier he had to interrogate was found in an *ofuro* during the invasion.

> He was out taking a bath when . . . they captured him and I said, "How come [you were] caught?" Because when they brought him back all he had on was his loincloth. He said . . . "For days you had your landing and the navy kept shelling us and I was constantly hiding. Finally you came ashore and I was taking a bath and I decided the hell with it, I was going to give it up." So they captured him. (Blum 2001, 40)

The *tokkōtai* (suicide bomber or *kamikaze*) pilots also made a point of taking a long soak in an *ofuro* before they flew off on their missions, as a gesture of purification.[7] Perhaps the prisoner mentioned by Honda was also enjoying this one last pleasure, assuming that he would die while bathing. Perhaps similar thoughts crossed the minds of the pilots who were using the bathtub in the dormitory I visited in Imwej. But it was an island that was bypassed by American forces, and Japanese and Marshallese starved for lack of food. More likely their baths (if they were able to take them at all) must have been increasingly plagued with anxiety.

Their fear seems to reach out across the distance of time and grab hold of me as I stand there in that moment with Jina, staring into the crumbling, moldy bathtub.

One Hundred Kilograms of Sand

It is nearly a year after this episode in the Marshall Islands that I encounter the spirits of Kwajalein again, but in a very different way. It is a fine April day in Tokyo and the *sakura* cherry blossoms are in full bloom at Yasukuni Jinja, the national shrine for all the souls of the soldiers who served Imperial Japan. I have been invited here by the Marshall Islands War Bereaved Families Association (Māsharu Hōmen

Izokukai), the main group that represents the 35,000 Japanese who died during the Pacific War in the Marshall Islands and Kiribati. It is my first time to enter Yasukuni Shrine, a place filled with controversy and imbued with nationalistic—often militaristic—symbolism.[8]

Roughly one hundred elderly people have assembled from all over Japan. Some are wearing formal black funeral attire, but others are dressed quite casually. Over their reception desk outside the shrine, cobalt-blue banners are displayed with a symbol of the Southern Cross constellation on them, the emblem of the bereavement group.[9] As more and more members of the group assemble, they laugh and chatter happily. It seems like a big reunion of good old friends.

One of the executives of the association explains to me, "This is exactly how our bereavement association started in the first place back in 1964. All the families of the Kwajalein war dead kept gathering at Yasukuni year after year on the sixth of February, the day of the Kwajalein *gyokusai*, and then we decided it was time, twenty years after the battle, to form ourselves into a proper organization. It was too cold in February, so lately we have been meeting in April when the *sakura* are their most beautiful."[10]

We enter the shrine after an hour of waiting among the crowds of other bereaved groups who have scheduled ceremonies that day. Each group waits politely, each representing another battlefield, and we are summoned over a loudspeaker, as if waiting to see a doctor in a clinic. A *kannushi* (Shintō priest) leads us into the inner sanctum of the shrine and plays a taped version of "Kimigayo," the national anthem, from a hidden stereo system. Then we walk single file into the main hall, where we sit on the *tatami* mats on the floor. I sit next to the president of the association. The air smells of old wood, what seemed at first like a hint of incense or burning wood, and fresh leaves and vegetables.

On wooden elevated platters, there are heaping mounds of fresh sweet potatoes, *daikon* radishes, turnips, and other vegetables. There are other offerings of food and *sake*. Recorded military marching music plays in the background as the priests keep bringing in new wooden platters to place on the table, including one upon which a bright red sea bream sits. Behind this table is a classic icon of Shintōism, a gigantic mirror, an oval framed with elaborate carvings of phoenixes, various leaves, and crests.

The music stops and the main priest sits on the floor with his back to us, facing the altar. He begins to call out to the 35,000 spirits who died in the battles of the Marshall Islands and Kiribati, beginning with Commander Akiyama Monzō. It is a long chant in archaic Japanese, but I can clearly distinguish the names "Kuezerin" (Kwajalein), "Ruotto" (Roi-Namur), "Mili," "Buraun" (Enewetak), and other atolls.

After imploring the spirits to be at peace, the priest hands us ceremonial branches of leaves tied with sacred strips of white paper hanging from them and asks us to place them on the altar. All of us bow once, clap twice, and then bow twice together.

Back outside the shrine, I notice as another bereavement group representing another Pacific War battlefield begins to enter the shrine and repeats almost the same procedure. We are served ceremonial *sake* to complete the ritual, and a cheerful woman comes up to me and says, "I think the spirits would be very happy you are telling their stories. . . . I didn't even know where my father died until the 1950s. All of us wanted so badly to know what really happened."

She explains to me how within a year after her father's death, her mother had received a small, cheap wooden box, in which a small strip of white paper with the name of her deceased father was written, and nothing else. They had known that her father had died somewhere in the Pacific, but they did not know it was Kwajalein until they had searched for some time. In lieu of the cremated remains of soldiers, the bereaved families placed these empty boxes into their family graves.

"It was a long while before any of us knew about Kwajalein, and much longer before any of us got to go there," she tells me. "I still have never gone myself, but at least I have touched Kwajalein sand. All of us *izoku* (bereaved families) keep some in the grave or in our family altars. I wish I could have seen my father again, but that sand makes me feel like a little piece of him is close by."

Later I learn more about how all of these families had gotten their own collections of Kwajalein's coral sand. In 1965, Ukita Nobuie, the president of the newly formed bereavement society,[11] sent a letter to the US Army commander of Kwajalein politely requesting access to the island so that family members—especially parents—could at least touch the soil where their loved ones had died.[12] He received a terse letter in response, explaining how Cold War missile-testing security issues prevented any such visit or the construction of a memorial. Ukita wrote back, pointing out that the elderly parents of the deceased wanted one last chance to be with the spirits of their children. Again, the group was declined entry. This correspondence was repeated several times, all with the same negative result.

Undaunted by these rejections, Ukita wrote to request instead that if they could not access Kwajalein because of security issues, at the very least the families would like to receive Kwajalein sand so that they could inter it in their family graves. Given their initial uncooperativeness, it was remarkable that by the end of that year, the US military finally gave an order for one hundred kilograms of sand to be delivered "to a port or airfield in Japan." News reports in Japan celebrated the arrival of the Kwajalein sand as if the actual soldiers themselves had finally come home, as in a photo in which the sailors of the Self Defense Force vessel *Amatsukaze-Maru* delivered the Kwajalein sand to the bereaved families in several boxes, as if they were caskets of fallen soldiers.[13] In response, Ukita expressed the group's gratitude:

> During these three months, we sent this sand to over three thousand bereaved families who desired it earnestly for a long time. When we sent it, we [put] about 20 grams of sand in a small vinyl bag for each family. One old mother received this sand as if her most dear, dead son [had come back to her] and she held it tightly in her hand for many hours.

Years later, even before the bereaved were allowed access to the base, they finally were allowed to have a small memorial erected on Kwajalein, assembled by Japanese American residents of Kwajalein out of a kit that stonemasons crafted in Tokyo.[14] It was not until 1975 that any of the Japanese bereaved families were allowed to set foot on Kwajalein, after many of the younger soldiers' parents had themselves already died. Nowadays the family members—mostly the children of soldiers who were old enough to start families when they went off to war—return again and again to pay respects to these spirits of Kwajalein, and the US military generally welcomes them (with some exceptions) as a part of their close partnership with Japan.

And so most Japanese soldiers who perished at Kwajalein never really returned home to their families, nor did the Korean laborers. Though the coral of the atoll migrated north to Japan where it settled into tens of thousands of cemeteries all over the country, the spirits and memories of the Pacific War continue to linger in the atollscapes of Kwajalein lagoon.

Perhaps I have made peace with these spirits, but still I am haunted by a past that I cannot see. I want to learn more of these men who traveled so far upon the ocean currents—these men whose bathtubs lie coated in coral at the bottom of the sea.

CHAPTER 7

Dislocations

Moving Land, Moving People

ALTHOUGH IN THE FIGHT BETWEEN the United States and Japan, Kwajalein was little more than a steppingstone, for the Marshall Islanders who had strong ties to that land, the war was completely devastating. Ri-Kuwajleen twentieth-century history is in some ways turbulent, in other ways triumphant, but it has unarguably involved much displacement, replacement, upheaval, and change. Not only did colonial and military authorities from Japan and the United States move people off their tracts of land and relocate them to different islets or parts of islets; both Japanese and American forces actually moved, zoned, and restricted the land itself. This moving of both land and bodies is deeply etched in the Ri-Kuwajleen worldview, as Carucci (1997a) has explained in great detail, and it is reflected powerfully in the discourse produced by landowners.

Today, what is known as United States Army Garrison Kwajalein Atoll (USAG-KA) and Reagan Test Site (RTS) has a long and complicated postwar history, from Japanese command base in the 1944 to US naval base in the 1945; from Korean War support base in 1951 to command center for the nuclear tests at Bikini and Enewetak in 1954; from Zeus missile testing commanded by the navy in 1959 to Nike-X missile testing commanded by the army in 1964; from one defense support contractor to the next: Transport Company of Texas, Global Associates, Pan-Am, Raytheon, Kwajalein Range Services. Yet behind the scenes of this elaborate Cold War and post–Cold War military endeavor, Marshall Islanders made countless sacrifices. Homes were destroyed, lifestyles were abandoned, families were separated, and human beings were sickened by radiation.

Bombing, Dredging, Filling

In a physical sense, too, land was completely moved, shaped, and transformed all throughout Kwajalein Atoll, and this scarred and reconfigured Ri-Kuwajleen identity as well. In a comparable Pacific island context, Katerina Teaiwa has written of the entangled destinies of Islanders and their land on Banaba, Kiribati (Ocean Island), where people were moved by Japanese and then British authorities in order to facilitate the mining of their island for phosphate (Teaiwa 2015). Displaced into exile far south to the island of Rabi in Fiji and made to pay for their new island home out of the compensation money they received from the British Phosphate Mining Company, the Banabans were forced to begin a new life while their own land, literally, was taken in vast amounts to be sold as fertilizer in Australia and New Zealand. With land being of such central importance to Pacific Islander identity, Teaiwa argues that this mining not only devastated the island of Banaba but corporeally eviscerated and essentially "mined" the heart and soul of the Banaban people.

Kwajalein, which at one point in its past was also called "Ocean Island," experienced a very different history from Banaba but shares in the legacy of concurrently displacing earth and bodies. Though American and Japanese military powers relocated Marshallese people in Kwajalein Atoll to suit their needs, they also moved and shifted the land and the coral itself, reshaping the contours of several islets and reefs and obliterating others. Before the war, the Japanese construction corps *setsuei butai*—including Marshall Islanders, Koreans, and Okinawans described in the previous chapter—used dynamite to blast out enormous sections of the reef around Kwajalein islet and to fuse the islets of Roi and Namur together with a causeway. This coral and limestone rubble was then used as aggregate to pave the airstrips, build sea walls, and, in some cases, mixed with cement in the construction of military fortifications.[1]

The subsequent air bombardments and heavy fighting throughout the atoll during and prior to the invasions in 1944 decimated the surface of many major islands. Their bombing blasted huge craters in the reef, such as these pools near Ebeye, used by Marshallese children nowadays as swimming holes to play in during low tide.

During the early 1940s, when Japanese troops forcefully removed Marshallese from their lands, they did not pay any form of compensation to any of the people whose lives were completely transformed by this relocation. In the words of the former Kwajalein Negotiation Committee, which recounted this history from landowner perspectives for review by Marshallese national government and American government negotiators,

> American forces basically picked up where the Japanese left off, using Islanders to work as laborers and relocating them to suit the needs of the expanding base.... They were dispossessed of their lands by the very people they were assisting, and were shorn of the right to regain access to their traditional means of eking a subsistence. (KNC 2002b, 57)[2]

In 1947, after the land had been cleared and Kwajalein became an American naval base, the US Department of the Interior took responsibility for the US Trust Territory of the Pacific Islands, a "strategic trust" that included the Marshall Islands and several other island groups in Micronesia. Marshallese who had been living on Kwajalein and nearby islands prior to and during the war, and those who returned to the atoll, were rounded up and encouraged to work for the Americans to help build storage facilities, airstrips, hangars, and other structures. A labor camp was hastily constructed on Kwajalein (at the site of the current golf course) to house these workers, and their family members came to live with them there.[3]

Meanwhile on Kwajalein in the late 1940s, various maneuvers were being undertaken to support the nuclear testing projects underway at Bikini Atoll, in what was known as Operation Crossroads. Kwajalein provided logistical support during these tests. US military personnel offloaded materials from ships that had been tested in Bikini lagoon, assembled photographic and other testing or measurement equipment, and worked in the command center. Kwajalein also served as a base for aircraft involved in the tests, and there were decontamination tanks and other facilities on the main island. Crossroads was one of the first detonations of nuclear weaponry after the bombings of Hiroshima and Nagasaki, and it destroyed the homes and the livelihoods of the Marshallese inhabitants of Bikini, who were forced into exile on Rongerik Atoll and later relocated to Kili Island.[4] Later, further tests would be conducted that would unleash the same hardship upon the people of Enewetak Atoll. Between 1946 and 1958, the equivalent of seven thousand Hiroshima bombs[5] were detonated at both Bikini and Enewetak Atolls, even vaporizing three of Bikini's islets (Jones 2007, 37).

The sheer awe of the nuclear project fascinated scientists, policymakers, and other onlookers. The fetishization of atomic power in the 1940s and 1950s was such that European designers Jacques Heim and Louis Reard named a swimsuit "L'Atome" (the atom) after the mind-boggling "sexiness" of these atomic blasts, and the latter decided to call his skimpy creation simply "the bikini" (Teaiwa 1994, 91–92). I cannot emphasize enough the audacity and violence of this crude and perverse naming: what if, for instance, this swimsuit—named after the trauma of a whole population of human beings—had been named "the hiroshima" or "the nagasaki" instead? A *National Geographic* reporter who observed the first tests of the original Crossroads detonations *Gilda* and *Helen* called the colossal wall of water that swallowed up all of Bikini lagoon in 1946 "a wet caress, a kiss of death" (Weisgall 1994, 264).[6]

The massive dislocation of land that resulted from American nuclear testing in the Marshall Islands gave geologists the opportunity to test Charles Darwin's theories about atoll formation, to find out once and for all if in fact atolls were made from coral polyps that attached to sunken volcanoes. Up until the Cold War, many scientists had doubted Darwin, believing the idea of underwater mountains and

Dislocations: Moving Land, Moving People

volcanoes completely preposterous. Yet when, during the Bikini Resurvey Project, scientists dug through 1,411 meters of coral at Enewetak Atoll and discovered a basaltic volcanic material, Darwin was finally proven right (Jones 2007, 38).

While these experiments may have inspired new respect for coral polyps, they certainly did nothing to respect human beings. On March 1, 1954, as part of the Castle Series of tests, the "Bravo shot" was detonated in Bikini Atoll, originating from a relatively small cylindrical device that would form the basis for the MK-21 nuclear bomb.[7] The resulting nuclear explosion was the largest that had ever taken place in history, fifteen megatons, equal to the force of roughly one thousand Hiroshima bombs, distinctly visible from Kwajalein, a full four hundred kilometers to the southeast, where "the buildings shook as if there had been an earthquake" (Juda 2004). Raining fallout all throughout the Marshalls, especially in the northern atolls of Rongelap, Utrik, Ailuk, and surrounding waters, Castle Bravo caused more displacement and unprecedented suffering as some (but *not all*) of the most irradiated populations were eventually evacuated to Kwajalein Atoll for treatment. While the subject is beyond the scope of this book, the people of Rongelap and other nuclear-affected atolls contend that the United States deliberately exposed them to radioactive fallout by not evacuating them swiftly, and then proceeded to conduct experiments on them as human "guinea pigs" under the guise of medical care, part of a secret government project called Project 4.1 (Horowitz 2011).[8]

While the nuclear testing was underway, on Kwajalein American authorities had decided in January 1951 to relocate the Kwajalein labor camp, describing it as an eyesore, "a squalid, shantytown appearance contrasting sharply with the spick-and-span buildings of the adjacent military establishment" (Tobin 1954, 3). The Ri-Kuwajleen, who had already been "herded into labor camps hastily hoisted together with material at no cost to the United States," were pushed further off their land to Ebeye, where "there emerged the beginning of the making of what [was] to be called three decades later . . . the 'ghetto' of the Pacific" (KNC 2002b, 57). The US Navy constructed a new labor camp three islets removed from Kwajalein on Ebeye islet, at the site of what had been the Japanese seaplane base and the former barracks for the Japanese 952nd air unit. Using cheap plywood boards to construct housing, cooking buildings, and outhouses, the Navy Seabees built a low-budget village of bungalows and other buildings that was meant to house 370 people. These were crude structures that were not designed to withstand the harsh tropical elements of the Marshalls, and they soon began to fall into disrepair.

In the beginning, according to "Clara," who grew up on Ebeye in the 1950s and 1960s, the islet resembled a pleasant "outer island," with peaceful streets, trees, and a warm and friendly community. Yet even at the start of the relocation project, more than 559 Marshallese people were moved from the Kwajalein labor camp to Ebeye (KNC 2002a, 34), so from the beginning there was not enough infrastructure to handle the transplanted population. Soon the flimsy structures built by American crews (especially the outhouses that were lined up along the ocean shoreline) broke down from the salt air and the wear and tear of overuse by a growing population. Sanitation problems began to emerge, worsening a massive fly problem that already existed from long before the war[9] and contributing to the outbreak of various diseases and health problems, including a severe polio outbreak that actually started from an American on Kwajalein.

Conditions on Ebeye worsened severely through the 1960s and 1970s, with serious epidemics, water shortages, sewage backups, severe sanitation problems, power problems, and overcrowding. The population swelled from 981 people in 1954 (with 160 housing units and an average of six people sleeping in one room) to 8,000 people in 1977 (with 588 homes and nearly fourteen people sleeping in one room), a "development" problem that became a thorn in the side of Trust Territory administrators, who were highly criticized in the US press (KNC 2002b, 53; Tobin 1954). Many Marshall Islanders from other parts of the country came to live with their Ri-Kuwajleen relatives in the new settlement at Ebeye in hopes of finding higher-wage jobs on the base. Others came simply because they wanted imported supplies and food that were available at Ebeye because of the base at Kwajalein, including construction supplies.[10] Riding on the copra boats that regularly stopped at Ebeye, many people traveled to Ebeye and decided to stay (Tobin 1954, 19–20). Access to better medical care on Ebeye (at least in comparison to outer islands) was another major factor in people's decisions to migrate. The proximity to the airport at Kwajalein (and thus the link to Majuro and Honolulu—or Pohnpei, Chuuk, and Guam) was ultimately yet another reason why people came.

Around the same time buildings on Ebeye was being built with makeshift plywood structures, Kwajalein was being gradually built up as a small American town. To support the increase in personnel during the nuclear tests and the Korean War, construction crews built hard housing with sturdy cinder-block concrete. Later, in the 1960s when Kwajalein became the testing site for the NIKE-ZEUS antimissile programs, they would add more durable housing and bring prefabricated aluminum trailers built to withstand the elements. They would begin installing facilities to improve the "quality of life" for the "affluent, educated, middle-class" American missile-testing workforce and their family members on Kwajalein (Linka 1977), including various shops, a kindergarten-through-high-school education system, swimming pools, sports fields, and so on. Potable and waste water systems were meticulously constructed. A massive power plant was erected and the whole islet of Kwajalein was wired, but, tellingly, Ebeye was not linked into this American power grid. This was in sharp contrast to Japanese times decades earlier, when power stations had been centrally located and lines had been strung across the reefs between islets for both electricity and communication, and Marshallese living in these vicinities had access to these services.[11]

And while Ebeye was starting to grow from displaced labor camp to a major population center, in 1960 yet another labor camp was established for Marshallese workers in the northern part of the atoll. When the former Japanese base of Roi-Namur (Ruot and Niṃur) was chosen to be the site of a major complex of highly advanced missile-tracking radars, the Marshall Islander residents of that islet were also relocated to an islet called Āne-bōn (Enniburr, known in Japanese times as Santō, hence its current English nickname, "Third Island"). This islet has a history similar to Ebeye's in some respects—it was built up in a similar fashion, is crowded, has few natural resources or channels of obtaining fuel and affordable foodstuffs, and so forth—but because the population is significantly lower and it is so far from Kwajalein, the Marshallese who live there are often completely neglected, not only by American authorities but by the Marshall Islands local and national governments. Nowadays, living so close to the massive radars of Roi-Namur (the ALTAIR radar is one of the largest and most sophisticated of its kind in the world), Āne-bōn Islanders also face a potential radiation hazard if they climb to too high an elevation or go to some of the small islets that lie in the beam of the radars (Wilkes 1991, 160).

Beginning in 1963, Americans, together with Marshallese and Hawaiian workers,[12] also dynamited the reef and dredged up massive amounts of the sea floor, including whole coralheads, mainly to provide material for use in building landfill and adding to the size of the islet. In the 1960s and 1970s, more than two hundred acres was added to Kwajalein islet and also to Meik (Meck) islet. This added significantly to both the northern and southern ends of the main islet of Kwajalein, and it thickened much of the lagoon shoreline, but while American military engineers literally enlarged the islet, they also destroyed many culturally significant Marshallese trees and landmarks, and they changed the islet's shape markedly.

From a landowner perspective, this mining of rock left large rectangular holes in the reef and removed important coralheads that were not only valuable fishing and food-gathering sites, but also places of sacred importance to the Ri-Kuwajleen. Lañkio explains that the American bombings destroyed an important beach rock pillar more than one meter in height, a matron deity said to be able to predict coming storms with great accuracy. This deity, named Libar Wāto (literally "Ms. Coral Rock Land Parcel"), was said to carry a drum, and in many legends she was understood to be one of the core "island support posts" that held the atoll together (Carucci 1997a, 199–200).[13]

In the Marshallese sense, as land is measured not only in dry areas but also underwater, in *wāto* parcels that stretch perpendicularly across the atoll from lagoonside shallow depths to oceanside reef drop-offs, many landowners were upset about the losses to their ancestral reef zones as well, such as a major coralhead called Wōdeḷattiliej (Carucci 1997a, 199). Handel Dribo, who would later play a major role in the demonstrations for fair compensation and treatment in the 1970s and 1980s, angrily complained that the American landfill dredging project was destroying valuable marine resources on his part of the reef. Lamenting that the American contractors had carelessly vacuumed up a valuable coralhead where his lineage had always been able to gather fish, lobsters, clams, and octopus, Dribo lamented, "They've stolen my icebox!"[14]

The shifting of the land disadvantaged many landowners who lost land through the process, but it benefited others, whose land expanded. Where land mass increased between islets along the atoll, for instance, the *wātos* from which the landfill began were actually extended further. This was in keeping with Marshallese land tenure practices in the past when islets grew larger due to the shifting of sand from storms or other natural phenomena.[15] One of the biggest increases in land was to Namo Wāto, the northernmost on Kwajalein islet, which nearly doubled in size when American construction crews filled in the reef in order to build an area on the American missile range where the Kwajalein High School, Emon Beach park, and a residential zone of aluminum-sided trailers were placed. This whole tract of land, with its perfect contours, white coral dirt, and bright reflective buildings, had a surreal quality; it was nicknamed "Silver City."

In other parts of the atoll, the US government literally wrote off the land it seized by condemning it as worthless and unusable, thereby avoiding paying compensation altogether (Crismon 2005, 127). This was consistent with what American authorities had done in Guam (Maga 1988, 187–193) and various other locales in Micronesia, with condemnation statutes being formalized under the Trust Territory administration (KNC 2002b, 58).[16] Conveniently landscaping and reconstructing some islets and totally neglecting others, American officials created vast disparities between different parts of the atoll that had not existed before.

In 1964, the US military established the "Mid-Atoll Corridor," a giant section of the atoll (two-thirds of the atoll, in fact) that divided the lagoon in two halves and provided a splash-down target and hazard zone for incoming missiles. For Ri-Kuwajleen, this enormous stretch of land and water contained many small islet villages, countless marine resources, thick protected jungles rich with crops, and several sacred chiefly sites, such as the *mọ* (taboo and forbidden to all except *irooj*) islet of Enṃaat. Yet in the parlance of defense contractors and engineers, it was a playing field for a Cold War game of catch, shooting missiles into space from Vandenberg Air Force Base in California and watching them arrive nearly eight thousand kilometers away only fifteen minutes later, earning Kwajalein lagoon the sporty nickname of "The Giant Catcher's Mitt."

In order to use this zone, a contract was drawn up between landowners and US authorities called the "Mid-Atoll Agreement," although landowners had little choice in the matter. Under this agreement, American authorities relocated whole villages of people: five people from Kā (Gea), thirty-nine from Tar-wōj,[17] nine from Āne-kaṇ-liklaḷ, sixty-one from Murle, thirty-eight from Wōnmak, twenty-three from Wōje-jāirōk, fifteen from Nōḷ, thirty-nine from Enṃaat, thirty-three from Ero, twenty-eight from Kurōr, and thirty-eight from Pikeej (Bigej) (Wilkes 1991, 155–165). Of this experience, Anjain Rowa explains:

> I was nine years old, we were asked to leave our island, the island of Tar-wōj, way out there [he points across the atoll]. I think it's five

islands down from Carlson [Āne-bouj] Island . . . it's surrounded with a reef, beautiful beach, we call it Tar-wōj. That's where I grew up. I lived there, I loved the life there. You were really free to do anything you wanted to do. You could walk from one end to the other end. Nobody bothers you. You pick up the coconut, you grind it, and you eat it, throw a net, get some fish and eat, you know it's a free life. But then we were asked to move because they wanted to do these missile tests in Kwajalein lagoon. So we left our island and there were so many promises that they made to us. They promised to pay us, they promised to give us fuel, they promised to give us food when we come to Ebeye. But they didn't keep those promises for very long. (conversation, May 6, 2005)

The bitter and unsettling experiences of this evacuation are portrayed in some of the US Army photos taken at the time, although most of these images are posed shots of military officials happily sipping coconuts alongside the Islanders as if it were a happy process. Ri-Kuwajleen of all ages were moved on military ships and small motorboats from thirteen small, rural, relatively abundant islets of the Mid-Atoll Corridor and promised a better life on Ebeye. Some of these "mid-corridor" landowners had already been living and working at Ebeye and were using their land to grow food. In order to be counted as eligible for compensation, these individuals had to return to their islets in order to be "relocated" by American authorities, who—not caring about Marshallese land tenure practices and complex interrelations—labeled such people as "opportunists" (Crismon 2005, 299).[18] One Pacific Missile Range brief summed up this apathy and condescension best by saying, "Marshallese land-tenure customs are, to an American, both curious and feudal in concept and operation" (Bauer 1960, 26).

In one shot, Irooj Kabua Kabua (whose Japan-era prominence I mention in chapter 2), Irooj Albert Loeak, and Iroojlaplap Lejolan Kabua are shown watching as residents are moved from one of the Mid-Atoll Corridor islets. Military authorities enforced the relocation with the assistance of landowner elites like these *irooj*, many of whom protested in later years together with the displaced Islanders.

Elderly people, who were used to living off the land and using Marshallese traditional medicine, were given the promise of better medical care. Families were told they would be able to eat like kings from all the food the Americans would supply to them, and given the bounty of rations American military forces had showered on the Ri-Kuwajleen in the immediate postwar years, this was likely credible to them. When the "Mid-Atoll Corridor People" were brought to Ebeye, although they were provided with housing and some degree of support, this was insufficient and not designed for the long term. Seventy-eight concrete housing units were constructed, along with a power plant, sewer system, and fresh/salt water distribution system. According to a study commissioned by landowners in 2002, American officials calculated that only 194 of the 319 individuals who were relocated received any financial compensation whatsoever, and the United States did not consider that more than 1,000 people had customary land rights in the Mid-Atoll islands. To make matters worse, only a token $300 a year was provided to each person, and this amount only increased to $480 a year in 1966 (KNC 2002b, 58–59).

Displaced Ri-Kuwajleen entered a steadily urbanizing cash economy on Ebeye, where insufficient land payments were not enough to pay for monthly utility bills or home rentals. Agriculture was close to impossible in Ebeye's postwar rubble and crowded setting. When "mid-corridor" children were born after 1965, they were not eligible for compensation. And though there were many positive aspects of living on Ebeye (for instance, the proximity to job opportunities at Kwajalein or access to different aspects of modern convenience), what was most troubling for all Islanders was that they were prohibited from returning to their land. Despite homesickness, most people never returned, even to visit, fearing severe punishment. Others felt that returning would be pointless, given that the only times they were allowed back, between missile tests, was barely enough to engage in growing crops or fishing.

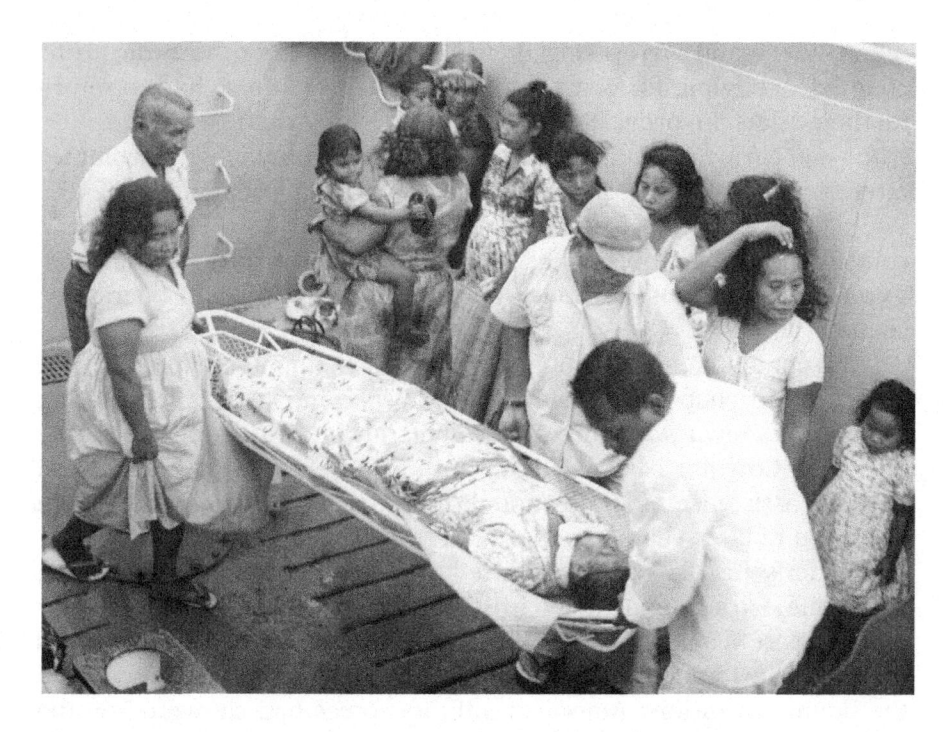

These displacements were only a part of the major impact to "home" that the Ri-Kuwajleen were to experience; at the same time, the atoll itself was changed as it was metamorphosed into a strategic ballistic missile testing "theater." The formation of the Mid-Atoll Corridor left whole islands uninhabited and unused. It also made it difficult to access marine resources and travel easily throughout the lagoon. Whereas the long boat journey from Kwajalein islet all the way up to the northern islets of Roi-Namur or Epatōn (Ebadon) and Mejatto in the far northwestern corner of the atoll could once be broken up by stopping at small islets and visiting relatives along the way, this new testing zone prohibited free movement during missile tests and made it impossible for anyone to reside on these small islets. Meanwhile, the new restrictions on movement placed by American military "chiefs" into this no-trespassing zone arguably instilled in Islanders a new kind of *mǫ* (taboo) that would only have been attributed in the past to places that were the exclusive domain of the *irooj*, and this likely bolstered the authority and influence of American military officials throughout the atoll.

Through the 1960s and 1970s, the deteriorating conditions on Ebeye had become a textbook study of "development" gone awry and all that was wrong with American strategic policies toward the postwar Pacific. In response, in 1966 the Trust Territory government ordered the Department of Defense to rebuild the islet entirely, under a poorly designed scheme that could only be executed when the Trust Territory administration repossessed all the private land from the Ebeye landowners (Hanlon 1998, 194). This only infuriated these landowners[19] and further exacerbated the situation when those landowners had to pay rent to live in the new housing structures. The population continued to grow, however, and a lack of proper infrastructure, funding, and implementation perpetuated the problems that had existed in the 1950s and continued through the several decades that followed. One report and article after another was written in increasingly miserable terms about Ebeye's "squalor" and segregation from the middle-class community of Kwajalein. As social commentators around the world fixated on how to "fix" Ebeye, however, the displaced Ri-Kuwajleen landowners were looking back across the lagoon to their home islets, frustrated that they were not receiving any meaningful compensation for all that had been taken from them.

No doubt the biggest change that the Kwajalein missile-testing complex generated from all these displacements was the disparity and imagined distance between Ebeye and Kwajalein. Despite the physical closeness of the two islets and the fact that Kwajalein and Ebeye were once linked in Japanese times by power lines and a narrow-gauge railway that ran across the reef (Sims 1993, 40), the postwar American influence on the atoll created an ever-growing contrast, a binary that is difficult to reconcile. Ebeye and Kwajalein are not even on the same telephone exchange: Kwajalein is patched by satellite into the Paso Robles, California, telephone network and shares an area code with Santa Barbara, while Ebeye is serviced by the National Telecommunications Authority of the RMI. Despite the slight, three-mile span of reef that separates the islets, calling Kwajalein is an expensive long-distance call.[20]

To bridge this gap, ferries have shuttled the Marshallese workforce back and forth between Ebeye and Kwajalein on a regular basis ever since the Kwajalein labor camp was relocated. One of the early commuter crafts was the *Tarlang*, a decommissioned naval landing craft that was converted into a passenger ship, inaugurated in 1964. Even today, the 900–1,000 Marshallese worker commuters have to adjust their lives to this boat schedule, waking up as early as possible to secure a seat on one of the predawn crossings in order to be at work on time. The constant rumble of boat engines churning in the water as the ferries make their way back and forth between these two islands from dawn until midnight has become a familiar background noise in the atoll soundscape. Like the powerful landing crafts, aircraft carriers, tanks, bulldozers, cranes, and airplanes that radically altered the Ri-Kuwajleen homelands, the mournful drone of the ferry as it crosses the lagoon at night is a song of constant moving, change, and relocation.[21]

"Writing Back" The Land

I have already visited the ways in which the land and water of Kwajalein were carved up and reimagined in both symbolic and physical ways, but now I shift paradigms by looking at how these movements of land and bodies were part of a *writing* process as well. Here I recall again Epeli Hau'ofa's poignant remark that reading Pacific Islander histories requires a literacy in landscapes and seascapes, that history is "written" in the environment (Hau'ofa 2000, 466.) Ty Kāwika Tengan expands upon this in more detail in his study of *mo'olelo* in the Hawaiian context, considering landscapes and seascapes to be a site through which "Oceanic peoples trace their genealogies of families, place, and travel" (Tengan 2003, 90; Diaz and Kauanui 2001). In the example of Kwajalein Atoll, Carucci (1997a) shows through a detailed study of the cosmologies of Ri-Kuwajleen elders how the name of each *wāto* represents an important part of atoll history.

Some examples of this on Kwajalein islet itself would be Namo Wāto, likely named after the settlement of very powerful *irooj* from nearby Namo Atoll. It is the legendary site of origin of some of the most prominent Ralik *irooj*, who apparently settled that part of Kwajalein at some time in the distant past (Carucci 1997a, 206–207).[22] Būkien kālōñ and Lo̧-pat Wāto, respectively "the fishing shallow where (they) fly upward" and "the location (where [they] strike) the reef foundation," are exactly the land tracts where the military and commercial aircraft alight and land daily upon Kwajalein's airstrip (Carucci 1997a, 195). Thus many elders point out the wisdom of their ancestors in foreseeing the future, although this is also an example of how historical meaning is constantly being written and rewritten onto the land.

In other words, the land and sea can be read as a historical text that holds the Ri-Kuwajleen narrative together, but, after Barthes, I would argue that this text is constantly being negotiated and cowritten by multiple actors, not just in terms of Islander narratives of place, genealogy, and movement, but also in terms of colonial, military, and other global political influences. The concrete layers of Kwajalein Atoll form a text on top of the coral that is both politically legible and politically written. As Michel Foucault writes, "the military and the administration actually come to inscribe themselves both on a material and with forms of discourse" (Foucault and Gordon 1980, 69).

For Barthes, landscape is the quintessential example of what a text is, "a space in which there is a weaving together of symbols to create an irreducible plurality of meaning" (Duncan and Duncan 1992, 27). So physically, Americans and Japanese both rewrote the atollscape by shaping land and forcibly removing Marshall Islanders from their homes, and they also wrote through the "concrete" meanings that they layered onto (or attempted to erase from) the land.

For example, Namo Wāto—the land tract mentioned earlier—is written and imbued with Marshallese histories of chiefly conquest and genealogies that stretch back to Namo [Namu] Atoll (Carucci 1997a, 207). But at the same time it has literally been "written" by American engineers, who, as explained in the previous section, nearly doubled that *wāto*'s size when they dredged the reef and tacked on another broad stretch of land at Kwajalein islet's northern tip. In recent decades a tradition has evolved in which the graduating students of Kwajalein Junior-Senior High School (located in the middle of Namo Wāto) actually spray-paint their names onto the asphalt as a way of leaving their mark on the land. Even if these names are erased by the next school year's end, this is an innocent but equally valid example of the ways in which meaning and history are repeatedly layered, told and retold through the medium of land.

The playful writing of American teenagers is sharply contrasted by the traces of the Korean conscripted laborers who were ordered to build the causeway that connected the islets of Roi and Namur during the war years. The son of one of these men, a Korean immigrant to the United States who worked at Kwajalein in the 1980s, described how he discovered the names of workers etched in Hangul script into the concrete of the causeway deep in the jungles of Roi-Namur.[23] These writings, probably the only mark left behind by the Koreans of Kwajalein, are lost in the entangled vines and foliage of the atollscape. I searched for several days but could not find them.

Land can also be erased. Kwajalein Atoll, if not all of Micronesia, has been "disappeared" at certain times in its history due to the secrecy of military endeavors. Both Japanese and American operations completely concealed the locations of their deployments in the lead-up and aftermath of the Pacific War, for example. For decades after the war ended, many Japanese families did not even know where their loved ones had died. Kwajalein's use as a nuclear support base and subsequent missile-testing range has also kept it out of the public eye until relatively recently. Walsh comments on how rare it is for news reports to ever mention Kwajalein or the Marshall Islands when discussing missile testing, disguising the location of such exercises as "somewhere in the South Pacific" (Walsh 2001, 4). Such stealth has consequences at the local level for landowners, whose plight does not get taken as seriously as it might if the atoll were more visible.

The boundaries of land, while originally written or disputed by landowners, are also rewritten and policed by colonial and military power. Crismon's 2005 study of borders at Kwajalein, from a largely American military perspective, proves the point in both anthropological and geographical terms that American authorities write and shape the land by arbitrating access points, boundaries, and security. Simply calling Kwajalein "a base" gives it a certain significance that ties it to other bases worldwide and detaches it from its local surroundings (Dvorak 2004). Access—and subsequently what it keeps in (American base residential life) and locks out (Marshallese landowners, workers, and other nonbase residents of the atoll)—is at the core of the Ebeye and Kwajalein divide. In some ways it is as if the ferries that shuttle back and forth between Ebeye and Kwajalein trace lines on the lagoon—a linear narrative arc that seems to tell of either one extreme or another—of great riches at one terminus and great poverty at the other.

A young Ri-Kuwajleen landowner and *irooj* explains this contrast:

> At times, we come over to Kwaj to play softball and eat pizzas and have fun with our American friends and after that we go back to

Ebeye where it's all cramped up and basically if you open your door you hit another person's door. It's like living in . . . New York where you have upstate New York and then you've got the Bronx. Kwajalein is perfect for the Americans, and Ebeye is like the ghetto.[24]

Americans living on the base, like many writers and activists who have critiqued development, often look upon Ebeye as "the other side of the tracks," as the "skid row" that lies on the outskirts of the perfect American dream. Kwajalein, they presume from this standpoint, has it all; it is the Shangri-La of the Pacific, like the "Almost Heaven, Kwajalein" T-shirts once worn by Americans in the 1970s proclaimed. Ebeye, in this comparison, is seen as the "Slum of the Pacific," as it has been labeled throughout much of the postwar period. Journalist Harold Jackson encapsulated this view when he wrote:

> In American eyes, the base is the honey pot around which the Ebeyeans swarm. The contrasting Marshallese view is that the largest and most inhabitable island in their atoll has been taken from them. Recognizing that they are not likely to get it back, they want to continue declaring their rights and to seek proper compensation. (quoted in Johnson 1984, 20)

In this way, the "text" of Kwajalein Atoll began to emerge in postwar development discourse. Americans called Ebeye a "slum" that they thought Marshallese desperately wanted to leave so they could taste the pleasures of American suburbia; Marshallese landowners, on the other hand, realized wisely that they needed to discursively frame Ebeye as a slum in order to emphasize to the international community the real neglect they had experienced and stress the point that their land had been taken without proper compensation. This is not to say that Ebeye wasn't in fact suffering from severe infrastructure, sanitation, and population challenges, but that describing Ebeye in such bleak terms was one of the only ways local leaders could call attention to the injustices that American militarism had created. Regardless of the broader implications of the whole atoll and the dynamism of Ri-Kuwajleen and other Marshallese understandings of relations between islands and Islanders within and beyond Kwajalein, over time a sharp boundary was drawn. Thus, Kwajalein Atoll became a virtual "Tale of Two Cities," a binary in which the whole atoll was collapsed into the black-and-white story of two islands (Johnson 1979).

Returning now to the Ebeye-Kwajalein dialectic that local Marshalls reporter Giff Johnson once described as "apartheid" (Johnson 1980, 1), there is no question that these two islets have been imbued with semiotically negotiated layers of "concrete" meanings—mythologies—that have come to almost precede the places they reference. In the same way that geographer Sasha Davis describes the way the tourist industry has reimagined the abandoned nuclear test sites of Bikini Atoll as a tropical dive ecotour "Pacific Eden" (Davis 2015), over the years, observers have reimagined Kwajalein and Ebeye respectively as "paradise" and "hell." Ebeye exists in the post–Cold War discourse of development as if it were Kwajalein's dirty little secret. In order to write his powerful novel about the nuclear and missile tests and their impact on Marshallese lives, former Kwajalein resident Robert Barclay portrays Ebeye as a nightmarish "playground of demons" in his book *Meḷaḷ* (2002). Japanese author and war activist Oda Makoto visited Ebeye and described it as an island of forgotten spirits, a "graveyard" of fallen and forgotten Japanese and Koreans who lie together with Marshallese victims of nuclear weapons (Oda 1998). Journalist and scholar Ōno Shun has also written about Ebeye as a *Taiheiyō no Gettō* (Pacific ghetto), translating the slum discourse into Japanese (Ōno 2001, 168). The apocalyptic visions of the Pacific

(Cowell 1992) that the Ebeye "text" contains have become so compelling that some writers find it perfectly acceptable to write about the island without ever setting foot there, such as when Oliver Sacks describes it as a "shantied hell," based only on his brief layover at Kwajalein's airport (Sacks 1996, 27).

Before Japanese militarization in the 1930s, Ebeye was a rural small island with a population of only nineteen people (Hatanaka 1973). Even when the labor camps were first relocated, many Marshallese who spent their childhoods at Ebeye recall that the island was lively, fun, and filled with *iokwe* (love).[25] Only through the rampant militarization of most major islands in the atoll after the war was it remade into a crowded urban sprawl, crowded with cars, that was no doubt uncomfortable, unhealthy, and congested but not necessarily a "ghetto" or a "slum" in the truly impoverished sense. Ebeye's crime rate is also extremely low despite its population density. Even today the island has retained many of the social protocols and community traditions that make it feel more like a well-loved rural neighborhood than an inner-city "shantytown." It is an island that is cared for by its residents, many who work hard to sweep the surroundings of their homes clean every morning, maintain their churches and schools, and cooperate with each other. Few have written, as LaBriola (2006) reminds us, of the vibrant sense of sharing and celebration on Ebeye even during the worst of the overcrowding, at a time when many American commentators complained of the stench of raw sewage and children playing in trash. And so, it is worth wondering, even with respect to the many hardships people have endured over the years, if Ebeye is a nightmare, then whose nightmare is it?

As LaBriola writes, ever since Tobin's scathing critique of the Trust Territory's treatment of Marshallese in Kwajalein Atoll in 1954, "American discourse surrounding Ebeye has been laden with colonial assumptions about not just development and progress, but also about Marshallese people and culture, as well as so-called cultural loss (LaBriola 2006, 71). Writing on the power of America to "develop" Micronesia in the postwar period, historian David Hanlon explains:

> The discourse of development coming out of the West constituted a form of Orientalism in which the underdeveloped world of the postwar period came to be known and controlled through the writing, describing, interpreting, and teaching of it and by experts whose tools of measurement reflected the rationality and logic of

their own very privileged, powerful world. . . . Development, then, offered the prospect of a more effective hegemony in its discursive homogenization and systemization for knowing and hence controlling the 'Third World.' " (Hanlon 1998, 10)

Hanlon builds on this argument, however, warning us against a simplistic reading of hegemony and domination in Micronesia and urging us to consider how Islanders have made sense of their "subjugation" under colonial rule in creative and powerful ways (Hanlon 1998, 131). He also elaborates upon this theme by focusing on the elaborate and navigator-like statecraft of Tosiwo Nakayama, first president of the Federated States of Micronesia (Hanlon 2014). Arguably, the people of Ebeye, and particularly the Kwajalein landowners, are a perfect example of this kind of creative diplomacy. To suggest that Marshall Islanders are "becoming professional victims," as Hezel insinuates in a pamphlet of the same title (2000), is to misconstrue the agency with which Ebeye residents and displaced Ri-Kuwajleen landowner elites make sense out of their island home in relation to the military base at Kwajalein, the other islets of the atoll, the national government, and the world at large. Walsh responds to Hezel by pointing out that in the legal framework of American civil rights and democracy,

> the discourse of victimhood is as close to Western notions of resistance that Marshallese get. Calling attention to their situation at the hands of powerful others is equivalent to a demand for justice and for *others* to take responsibility to look after the weaker (less powerful) more seriously, as chiefs provide for their people, mothers protect their children, and coaches guide their teams. It is obvious to Marshallese that they have been wronged. By pointing it out to the world they are insisting on justice. (Walsh 2003, 407–408)

Ebeye is often visualized in development statistics and literature, or in antinuclear campaigns, as Kwajalein's shadow side. It is often (mis)imagined as the ideological antithesis to the Kwajalein "paradise country club," the site of literal and metaphoric "dumping," as Hanlon writes:

> Dumping and other related and employed metaphors such as "slum," "ghetto," "reservation," "cesspool," and "festering sore" are not only cruel, but sometimes dangerous. Rooted in colonial

perceptions and values, such metaphors, even when used by sympathetic observers to call attention to the abuses of American policy in the Marshalls, can denigrate inadvertently the subjects of their concern.... The risk in writing about dumping on Ebeye is that it can invite further dumping on Ebeye. (Hanlon 1998, 188)

"Writing" and "writing-off" Ebeye as nothing more than a tragic outcome, a big mistake of development and colonialism does little more than further reinforce the Kwajalein/Ebeye dialectic and perpetuate the clichéd binaries of us versus them, First World versus Third World, "the West" versus "the Rest." It is significant to appreciate this background and wider contextual world when considering the "homecoming" story of the Kwajalein landowners, their resistance, and their frustrations. Too many scholars and journalists, usually with good intentions, have framed the story of the landowners within a larger anti-missile-testing, antinuclear, or antimilitary rhetoric and gone no further. Many of these journalists and writers are people who have never been to the Marshall Islands, people who feature the Kwajalein story as a mere case study, part of a bigger project of protesting nuclear weaponry or militarism.

Although such projects have their own merits, what often happens when the Kwajalein story is written in this way is that Ri-Kuwajleen and Marshallese in general begin to look more and more like pitiful, passive victims who (even foolishly) put up with one misfortune after another, victims who, in the long run, only exist in the fatalistic antinuclear narrative to show "us" (in the "developed" world) the consequences of our mistakes so that we can "wise up" before we destroy ourselves. Some writers turn Marshallese into the nuclear martyrs of the Cold War, in order to show the world, with their unfortunate death, sickness, suffering and "squalor," what will happen if "we" don't stop making nuclear weapons.

This tendency in writing about the Pacific is typically orientalist; as Cowell writes, such representations show that "paradise is . . . finally inferior to the true 'best of all possible worlds' (if not paradise itself)—the West" (Cowell 1992, 151). Most recently, this can also be seen in media narratives of climate change, wherein the low-lying Marshall Islands, Kiribati, Tuvalu, and the Maldives are portrayed as the canaries in the coal mine that must be sacrificed in order to warn the world of the doom that awaits lest we not salvage New York, Venice, and Amsterdam. In such scenarios, history always ends miserably for

Islanders and other people from "Other" utopian and faraway locales: They are the martyrs who perish for the sins of the rest of the world.[26] In short, these kinds of histories would seem entirely to condemn the Marshall Islands as uninhabitable, worthless, futureless, just like land the US military condemned throughout Kwajalein atoll in an effort to avoid paying for it. Like the "fatal impact" narrative advanced by Alan Moorehead in the 1960s of the utopian Pacific Eden being destroyed by contact with explorers and colonists, the agency of Islanders and the possibility of a positive future are not possible in such renditions of history (Moorehead 1966). As Bikini representative Jack Niedenthal points out, however, the threat of climate change is tangible as more and more islands flood during extreme tides each year. Islanders are beginning to grapple with the equally undesirable realities of possessing irradiated or militarized islands versus having even less accessible underwater islands.[27]

At a local level, many of the Americans who live and work on Kwajalein have also participated in the "writing" of Ebeye just as they have "written" their small American hometown version of "Kwaj" into existence as well. Crismon argues that "while Americans on Kwaj may be able to physically and discursively separate themselves from Ebeye and the Marshallese, the two islets and peoples are inextricably linked" by the very borders that keep them apart (Crismon 2005, 10). The American community can choose to be apathetic to Marshallese community issues in the atoll by rationalizing that their gated existence on the base has nothing to do with Ebeye, or by foreclosing Ebeye as an unfortunate but inevitable consequence of failed development. In the imaginary of the suburban lifestyle of Kwajamerica, Ebeye thus serves as a metaphorical "dump" that helps many Americans to rationalize a colonial lifestyle. This critique is echoed in the keen observations of "Joan," a long-time Kwajalein resident and former academic who takes an active interest in Marshallese history. She goes one step further by tying in the issue of race:

> This is a very nice life, largely unavailable to most Americans living in the States, but the American residents of Kwajalein must somehow deal with the mentally uncomfortable construct that they are exploiting people for their personal benefit in a manner that would be completely unacceptable in the States. So the myths of Kwajalein, beginning with the "saving of the natives from the Japanese" became fact. Layered on to this is the fact that their conscience is

further soothed by being able to shrug their shoulders and maintain that the situation exists because of Army regulations and that no one individual can do anything to change it. Finally, the last layer on the cake is the ease with which Americans blame the Marshallese for being incapable of sustaining their society, even with American assistance, and they point to Ebeye as an example of this. In the end, most of them have to swallow and believe that whole message in order to be able to live here.[28]

As Hanlon writes, "dumping on Ebeye" thus serves to reinforce American hegemony and reduce the "homecoming" resistance of landowners as irrelevant and futile. But ironically, although "dumping" still goes on today, it is also done by the landowners themselves, who actively "write back" their own legitimacy by adopting the "slum" metaphor into their own discourse. There are many Kwajalein leaders nowadays who turn the balance of power around by feeding this "development-speak" of slums and shanties right back to their own national government and the United States in their renewed campaign for justice. Marshallese spokespeople also make genuinely passionate and compelling arguments at US congressional hearings, at the United Nations, and at other bodies, testifying against the basic violations of human rights they have endured in their lifetimes. In the Compact renegotiations, the Kwajalein Negotiation Commission's survey even included statements like this, with all the ever-familiar comparisons and tropes of disparity:

> Ebeye has a history of deprivation, of its people being treated as second-class citizens, of unremitting and perpetual health hazards and epidemics, of makeshift housing, and of over-crowdedness. It stands in sharp contrast to the island next door: Kwajalein with its luxurious lawns, comfort, modern schools, well-equipped hospital, clean beaches, abundant ultra-pure drinking water, golf course, and social clubs. (KNC 2002b, 49)

Recent Kwajalein leaders reproduce this discourse tactfully, drawing powerful linkages between the nuclear testing program of the 1950s and the missile testing that followed. They speak of Ebeye as not only the "Slum of the Pacific" but, even today, as a "labor camp." Citing the painfully high male teenage suicide rates on the island, their representatives have referred to it as the "Suicide Capital" (deBrum 2007). Reclaiming their land symbolically by using this discourse to serve their own political mission of "homecoming" and fair compensation, the landowners revive decades-old images of development and put them to new uses.

There are many landowners, though, who have long felt resentment that they are being "dumped" upon by their government in having to welcome Marshallese migrants on their land from all over the country. The influx of workers into Ebeye over the past half-century has produced an increasingly exclusionist view among some landowners who insist that Ebeye and other islets in Kwajalein be the exclusive dominion of the displaced Ri-Kuwajleen and Ebeye islet landowners. Marshall Islander migrants from other atolls, they explain, do not always pay rent for the land they use on Ebeye for their homes, so the legitimate landowners do not receive any compensation for their land, either from the United States or from the Marshallese residents some describe as "squatters."

In turn, these migrants from around the country make up at least half the population of Ebeye, and part of the stress they experience is that landowners demand that people living on their property, even if they are paying rent, contribute some of the little money they have for birthdays, weddings, funerals, and other ceremonies. Tenants, in turn, feel obligated to keep quiet and comply with these expectations. This has led more people to push recently for monthly leases or rental agreements with all conditions spelled out in writing. The Committee of Five, a working group made up of landowners from Ebeye, also reviews the intentions of each lease and all plans for construction before these plans are passed on to the *irooj, aḷap,* and *ri-jerbal* leaders of the land concerned. This can be intimidating for many renters, who perceive this group as bullies and fear that everything they do is subject to the whim of the landowners. As "Bella," an elder woman leader in the Marshall Islands government who has lived on Ebeye, explains, "If you do something bad on Ebeye, they'll chase you out. If you refuse to do something you'll get sent back to the outer islands. And you can't repair your house because your existence on Ebeye is supposed to be *temporary.*"

An offshoot of this is a sense of cultural nationalism, if not separatism, among younger Kwajalein landowners toward their fellow Marshall Islanders, insisting that only "pure" Ri-Kuwajleen should be allowed to live on Ebeye and other key islands in the atoll. From a Marshallese genealogical viewpoint, this is problematic, given that the intersecting *bwij* and *jowi* of families gives most people extensive ties to land in numerous atolls and imbues each individual with a transatollic identity. Some who ascribe to this form of cultural nationalism have nonetheless advocated building schools in the atoll that would only be available to "Native" Ri-Kuwajleen. This controversial rhetoric of purity builds on the precedent of the largely unsuccessful "Operation Exodus" in 1975 and 1976 (Hanlon 1988, 202–203), an initiative launched by the military to forcefully "deport" unemployed non-Kwajalein Marshallese back to their home islands to reduce crowding. Yet it also draws upon the United States Department of the Interior's racist policies regarding adjudications of Native American and Native Hawaiian land title claims on the basis of "blood quantum," a controversial measurement for indigeneity that has been rigorously critiqued by Hawaiian scholar Kehaulani Kauanui (2002).[29]

There are, however, many constructive ways in which the "country club/slum" binary is being reconciled by landowners. One Kwajalein leader representing landowner interests has recently proposed to finally link the two islets together, merging the land and its meanings into one. Explaining the failure of a road link built to alleviate population pressure in the early 1990s by connecting Ebeye with the nearby islets to the north, former foreign minister and Kwajalein senator Tony deBrum proposed that the community could be "integrated" by building a causeway south to Kwajalein:

> [T]he separation of the Marshallese population from our American friends is a vestigial remnant of the unenlightened policies of the forties and fifties. It does not fit in today's world. Integrating the power, water, and communications systems, the building of a land connection between Ebeye and Kwajalein . . . will result in immediate improvement. (deBrum 2007)

Indeed, this is the sort of creativity that many American "developers" have lacked (and perhaps dreaded), for no doubt it springs from an ability to navigate the atoll as dynamic, interconnected, and fundamentally Marshallese. After all, Epjā (the original name for Ebeye) references a Marshallese navigational proverb, *Epjā, bwe en jā,* or "approaching Ebeye, it will jibe" (i.e., the sail of the outrigger canoe will swing to the other side), a phrase that suggests radical changes in the wind and weather (LaBriola 2006, 69).[30] This can also refer to the threat of capsizing. The notion of "jibing" (*jā*), LaBriola explains, is often perceived by some observers as avoiding danger, implying that Ebeye is somehow a negative or unapproachable place because of this. But she challenges this assumption by suggesting that "jibing" could just as easily be a positive technique by which the complexity of Ebeye can be reimagined on a much more "human and personal" level (LaBriola 2006, 70–71). Jibing with the winds of change, one could also say, is what is required in surviving in Ebeye and the whole of Kwajalein Atoll, perhaps.

Likewise, Irooj Michael Kabua, who spent much of his life on Ebeye and is an avid outrigger canoe racer, explains that the meaning of Epjā is "to literally capsize your situation, turn things upside down, to make something out of nothing" (conversation, March 14, 2005). Thus creatively inventing and making sense out of their world, the landowners and the thirteen thousand people who live on Ebeye jibe into the wind, navigating their precarious lives with great dexterity and sensitivity, holding together as a community against the great storms of chaos that swirl around them. Harnessing the tremendous winds of change they face, they sail in new directions on their journey back home.

CHAPTER 8

Homecoming, 2016

The Ri-Kuwajleen Revolution

> We own land because we are born. The island has belonged from generation to generation. That land is not really ours—it belongs to the next generations too. That means you cannot give it away. We have our way of sharing land with friends or someone who has done good to you, just like when you share your food. Just like a plate and you say, "You will eat this plate with me." The plate you will never have for your own. Just to share it. Your kids and my kids will share the land. But sometimes some people who you invite to eat with you like to take all the plate themselves. There will be problems then.
>
> —*Lijon Ekniling*[1]

IT IS A SWELTERING DAY IN 2005 in the bustling center of Majuro Atoll, and I am walking along the dusty road after buying a bottle of water from a grocery store. A white luxury sedan with smoked windows cruises gracefully toward me and pulls over into a driveway. Prominently displayed between the dashboard and the windshield is a macramé mat crafted out of plastic green and white beads. It reads:

IROIJ IMATA KABUA
THE BUCK STOPS HERE
2016 KWAJALEIN[2]

The window rolls down on the passenger side to reveal an energetic slim man with spiky gray hair, a beaming smile, squinting from the bright light that pours in from the outside. He is wearing a bright blue aloha shirt adorned with fishing motifs. From his neck dangles a massive golden marlin pendant suspended on a heavy chain. "Hop in—why don't you come along for a *jambo*[3] with us? We'll give you a ride," says Imata Kabua, the paramount chief (*iroojlaplap*), former president of the Republic of the Marshall Islands, and most powerful landowner of Kwajalein Atoll, as he calmly motions to the back seat. I climb into the cool interior. Marshallese music pumps out of the stereo, a harmonized trio of female voices processed with echo effect sliding and lilting rhythmically between the notes of an upbeat country-western electronic keyboard melody. The air smells of the leather upholstery of a new car and the sweet but musky fragrance of the pandanus-leaf handicrafts that adorn the rear window.

"You like that message I put on the dashboard?" he asks, barely raising his voice above the music, as his driver smoothly pulls out onto the main road. "Some ladies made that sign for me. It says 'The Buck Stops Here,' because I'm serious. We landowners are tired of arguing anymore about Kwajalein. In 2016, when the current Land Use Agreement runs out, the US military is gonna have to go and finally we're gonna go back to our islands!" He raps his left fist victoriously on the plush armrest and winks at the driver, who nods reverently. "Isn't that right, Senator?" he leans around and looks at the plump, elderly man sitting next to me in the back seat.

"That's Ishmael John, the senator from Enewetak," Iroojlaplap Imata tells me.[4] "We're gonna go barbecue some of those radioactive chickens he brought me from Runit tonight, you wanna join us?" he jokes. The two politicians and the driver have a good chuckle.[5]

"*Iọkwe*," the jovial Nitijelā veteran senator smiles at me and extends a firm handshake.[6]

"*Iọkwe*," I respond.

Imata introduces me, "Oh, and this *ripālle*[7] guy here is studying about the history of Kwajalein, and he grew up there; it's his home, too. He was eight years old when he saw us doing our peaceful protests back in 1982, when we went back to our land during Operation Homecoming. You remember when we did that?"

The senator takes a deep breath and nods with a knowing expression as he watches me from his side of the car.

We ride slowly, listening to the music, through the only main road, past the College of the Marshall Islands, basketball courts, Momotaro Store (run by the Momotaro family, related to settler Noda Tetsuzō), Chinese shops and new building projects funded by the government of Taiwan, the national telecommunications satellite, the national government complex, the movie theater. The two men make small talk in Marshallese about elections and recent court cases, peppering their conversation with gossip about old friends and fishing tournaments. Every so often kids run out into the street and wave as our car passes by, shouting *"iọkwe!"* A big hand-painted sign on the side of the road says *"Moña in Majel"* (Local Marshallese food), and two teenage girls walk away from the restaurant stall holding paper plates loaded with fish, rice, and pumpkin and small plastic bags of *bwiro*.[8]

It is hard to believe that Kwajalein Atoll, nearly an hour away by a commercial airline flight, is part of the same country. In contrast to this modern capital, the main island of Kwajalein is a highly regulated, landscaped place where only a thousand some middle-class American civilians live in the confines of their residential and working environment at the military installation—working hard during the week, mowing their lawns, scuba diving, and playing tennis on the weekends—while the vast majority of the population, the thirteen thousand Marshallese of the atoll, live packed into the 1.5-mile-long stretch of treeless land at Ebeye islet. Of those thirteen thousand, only about one-tenth have jobs working for the base. Kwajalein Atoll is so dominated by the American presence that Marshall Islanders often seem relegated to the background, despite their population. On Majuro Atoll, however, the radio features Marshallese DJs, political commentary, and Marshallese hip-hop. It is clear that Marshall Islanders are in charge of their own world.

"I'm getting sick of this place," says Imata. "I've been stuck in Majuro for the past several months, and I haven't gone back to Kwajalein or any atolls for ages. But you have to stay here if you want to make the Marshall Islands national government listen to you."[9]

We pass the American embassy, which, ever since the terrorist attacks of 9/11, has been refitted with a tall and imposing wall. It looks like a fortress, with surveillance cameras, a guarded gate with metal detectors, and police cars parked nearby, an aberration on this laid-back narrow stretch of land in rural Majuro. From lagoonside to oceanside the Rairok district of Long Island, where the embassy sits, is not much wider than the length of one football field from shore to shore with a single road running down the middle. Not far beyond is the embassy of Japan, which pales in comparison: It is a nondescript office in what, aside from the Japanese flag outside, looks like an old motel somewhere in the American Midwest.

Our driver pulls into the Long Island Formosa Resort, and we all get out. It is the farewell party of a women's convention, with representatives from all the atolls. As we walk into the Taiwanese-run hotel, Imata greets various people of all ages, several of whom instantly decorate him with leis. One young man steps forward and greets us, and I notice he is wearing a bright green T-shirt with the shape of Kwajalein printed in white on the breast pocket. The back simply says "Kwajalein Atoll" with an illustration of a missile taking off and the number 2016 framed by a cloud of rocket smoke, to symbolize the imminent departure of the missile range. "Nice shirt," Imata winks.

He leads me to a woman with several crowns of flowers (*wut*) piled in her hair: "This is my sister, Queen Seagull, visiting from Ebeye." She leans forward and gives my hand one firm shake up and down and looks politely to the side, smiling and enunciating as she says "*io̧-kwe!*" He introduces me to her in much the same way he introduced me to the senator. "He was eight when we made those *peaceful* protests in 1982." He draws out the word "peaceful" as he grins at both of us, as if he has said it many times on many occasions. Her eyes soften as she looks at me once more and nods, "*emman,*" that's good.

We walk into a large ballroom decorated with balloons and women's rights slogans, where women representing all the atolls and islands of the Marshall Islands are gathered.[10] Imata comes up to me and explains that he has asked them to sing a song for me. "It's the song we sang back in the 1980s when we took back our land during Operation Homecoming. You should hear it." After a series of speeches, the convention participants stand together and begin to sing loudly in perfect harmony, as if reciting a church hymn:

Jutak lon tak kin tu jo i kijiem bwe je monono,	Stand up with us to share your happiness
ke e jor tok molo ilo ad emman-tata	and your devotion in all that is good
im ejelok ejelok e ewaj maron in ton	so good that no one, no one can express how much happiness
kemelele ki joñan monono e ao,	we feel right now
oh	oh
Io̧kwe, io̧kwe bwe en kar bo ilo ra-dar	I truly wish a radar,
Radar kan remon im delon ilo movie,	a radar would capture this moment in a movie
Movie pija kan,	a moving picture

Pija kan remon kin an	a picture so good that
Emman tata enaj kar limo im lale	it becomes all the rage to see
Ejelok jonan emman.	And nothing could be so good.[11]

"That song just says it all," Iroojlaplap Imata tells me when the singers have moved onto their next piece and we have finished applauding. "That's why we call it the official Kwajalein song and lately we sing it during Memorial Day as well to remember all the sacrifices everyone has made for their land. And that's why we're singing it again now, because we haven't forgotten."

At this point, a line of women holding big baskets and plastic containers of food begins to form. The line grows longer and longer as the women dance with the rhythm of the band on stage. They sway back and forth as they approach a long table and lay down their various offerings of rice, chicken, pork, coconuts, breadfruit, pumpkin, papaya, cake, and other treats. Another small group of women breaks off from this line and approaches with more leis of small red flowers and spiky bright green leaves, and, seeing us standing with Imata, they come to the senator and me and decorate us with the same chiefly regalia. Three more women approach us, dancing and smiling as they carry big plates, one for each of us, loaded down with the best selection of all the food from the buffet. No sooner have the chief and former president taken a few bites of food than another woman comes strutting up to him, grabs his arm, and pulls him off to the dance floor. He happily obliges and dances off with her as the hall darkens and erupts into a disco-like scene with strobes and multicolored beams of light shooting in all directions.

Dancing under the Radar

Islanders who reinhabited their land throughout the atoll during "Operation Homecoming" in the 1980s sang the "Iọkwe Radar Song" as a declaration of their immense happiness in going back to their islands in spite of continuing American military use. Poetically coopting American missile-testing technology, the song's lyrics call on Kwajalein's powerful surveillance and tracking radars to "take a movie" and bear witness to their own joyous moment of bravely resisting American power and coming home to their land. It is a subtly subversive, even playful, critique of the American military presence that champions Marshall Islander agency and power, not through vengeful tactics but through humor, community-wide mass mobilization, and an overall mood of celebration in protest of injustice.

On another level the "Iọkwe Radar Song" is testimony to the nuclear heritage of a population that has long borne the burden of the Cold War and post–Cold War eras. For the Marshallese people of Kwajalein, colossal radars are as commonplace as breadfruit trees, coconut trees, and coral reefs; they are a part of the atoll as well, as in this photograph taken on Āne-Eḷḷap-Kan in 2016, where decommissioned radar housings share the same space as a village, church, and cemetery. Radars are, in many ways, physical monuments to Marshallese displacement, for they stand on soil where Marshallese houses once stood and inhabit islands that were once the domain of chiefs. As Kwajalein is the only remaining US military base in the Marshall Islands, the radars are also emblematic of the people of Kwajalein, as distinguished from people of other atolls. In the same way they assist American defense engineers to successfully track and shoot down incoming missiles, the radars also symbolize the savvy of landowner elites to discern the motives of outsiders. Like missiles launched from Kwajalein, such elites are "interceptors," as Walsh writes, not only of "fast approaching foreign forces," but indeed of the increasingly globalized policies of the Marshall Islands national government as well (Walsh 2003, 40).

Despite its tone of elation, the "Iọkwe Radar Song" is also a song of resistance that confronts the ongoing military use of Kwajalein.[12] I use it here to introduce a particular Marshallese mission in Kwajalein that might best be labeled the "homecoming" narrative, a story about how landowners have historically reacted to the displacement they experienced due to missile testing: fighting bravely for land rights and compensation and attempting to return home. "Homecoming" is a proud narrative of Marshallese solidarity and dignity in the face of the kind of treatment Islanders endured in their encounters with both Japanese and Americans. It is a direct reaction to both Japanese expansion and American "liberation," but at the same time it is also an affirmation of land, identity, and continuity. It is an avowal of perseverance in spite of extreme hardship, a celebration of survival.[13]

"Homecoming" is rooted in a strong sense of Marshallese land and identity that stretches far into the distant past, and in postwar Kwajalein it is a resistance movement that began at least as early as the early 1960s, when landowners literally "came home" to their lands in a series of "sail-ins" and "sit-ins" to protest the occupation of their atoll. As I suggest with the above anecdote and describe in more detail later in this chapter, the "homecoming" mission has been a major motif of the latter twentieth and early twenty-first century for the people of Kwajalein, and it is still at the heart of many Ri-Kuwajleen efforts for compensation and justice. From 2003 to 2011, during which time I was conducting the bulk of my research, landowners strongly resisted the RMI national government about the continued use of Kwajalein Atoll by the United States beyond 2016. Rejecting the terms of a new agreement that the US and the RMI claimed to be "internationally binding," and vowing to return home to their islands when the original lease expired in 2016, the landowners stood their ground and created a stalemate. They were willing to forfeit their prospects of future land rental payments rather than endure an uncertain future of what some of the landowners characterized as total "insanity" in the atoll (deBrum 2007).

Vowing to go home, Ri-Kuwajleen landowners believed they could leverage influence over their national government and petitioned for better treatment and compensation. The installation at Kwajalein is a major source of revenue for the Marshall Islands, not only because of the money paid for its military use through the Compact of Free Association, but also because of the taxes paid by all base workers, both Marshallese and American. By threatening to "invade" their own homelands or discontinue the lease, the landowners thus asserted their own power over the nation. What seemed to some like a battle against the United States was actually a battle between Marshall Islanders over land and power that had been going on long before Japanese or Americans, or Spanish or Germans, landed at Kwajalein.

To some extent the latest scuffle over Kwajalein land payments represented a battle for more money, no doubt, but more importantly the struggle over land in the atoll was part of an ongoing war of wit, a war of attrition, and a war of survival. It was part of a fight between concrete and coral.

The Deep-Time Battle over Land

The RMI is too young an entity to really speak of a Marshallese state narrative that could be mapped against that of the United States or Japan, at least over the span of the past century. The story of Kwajalein landowners' resistance efforts is not simply a "Marshallese" narrative, for there are many Marshallese people from different atolls and backgrounds who would not relate to this story. Yet this story has a long legacy in terms of the battle over land rights and entitlements in the Marshalls, nowadays between traditional leaders and the national RMI government, and previously between powerful Rālik chain chiefs. This is an older story than is usually acknowledged.

Rālik *irooj*, the chiefly genealogies from which the "Kabua dynasty" (Frankael 2002, 308) and other Kwajalein-area *irooj* hail, had established some degree of dominant power in the Marshalls through their interactions with other chiefs and colonial powers. These "patterns and results of their interactions reverberate in contemporary Rālik relationships with the United States, particularly in the lease of Kwajalein Atoll" (Walsh 2003, 166). Likely due to the empowerment they gained from US military involvement at Kwajalein, Rālik *irooj*, especially around the Kapin-Meto area, are often considered to have more influence over their people and land than their counterparts in the Ratak chain.[14]

The legacy of Lebon Kabua, or "Kabua the Great," whom Germans pronounced "king" of the Marshall Islands in the late 1800s, may have contributed to the contemporary practice of *irooj* and *lerooj* in Kwajalein Atoll describing themselves to Americans as "king" or "queen." According to some Japanese historians, at the time when Suzuki Keikun visited the Marshall Islands in the 1880s, Lebon was referring to himself by the English word "governor," which he pronounced "Kabua," hence the origin of this name, although this is difficult to verify (Takayama 1995, 168). Many Americans remember how Iroojlaplap Lejolan Kabua, adoptive father of first president Amata, would make frequent cameo appearances in the Kwajalein base, carrying a cane and wearing a badge emblazoned with the word "KING" as he made his rounds, shopping in American retail shops and presiding over cultural gatherings (Crismon 2005, 126).

The drawing of analogies between European monarchy and Islander "chiefdoms" is a common motif in the colonization of Oceania. In Hawai'i, the *ali'i* (ruling chiefs) have long been represented by Americans as "powerful warrior chiefs" that were analogous to European royals, if only "lagging behind in the march of progress" (Ferguson and Turnbull 1999, 52). In the context of the buildup of the US Armed Forces in Hawai'i, such analogies have been used to make it seem as though there were a precedent for militarism that justified the American agenda. As Ferguson and Turnbull have noted, memorials and museums like Fort de Russy in Honolulu tell a narrative that reduces the complex precolonial history of Hawai'i to a story about warring tribes and suggests that Hawai'i was already a militarized zone long before the Americans arrived (1999, 52).

Colonial narratives from European, American, and Japanese perspectives typically represented Islander "warriors" as primitive relics of the premodern, "uncivilized" past. Such narratives suggest that modernity, Christianity, and foreign influence were responsible for "taming" the perceived belligerence and wildness of Pacific men. A US Trust Territory Handbook for the Marshalls District of Micronesia in 1965 puts it this way:

> The salient characteristics of the Marshallese personality are dignity, courtesy, kindness, and generosity. "Ejoij ke" (Is he kind?) is usually the first question asked about a newcomer. Although only three generations ago the Marshallese warriors were renowned throughout the Pacific for their fighting prowess, today the Marshallese are far from a war-like people. (TTPI 1965)

Such commentaries celebrate Marshallese kindness but relegate their proud "fighting prowess" to the ancient past. Ethnologies like these replay the wartime "liberation" portrayal of grateful "happy natives" and "noble savages" while depriving Marshallese of agency. They are not innocent descriptions; they deserve our suspicion precisely because these narratives were written by American administrators in the wake of the Pacific War, where two unquestionably "warlike" nations—Japan and the United States—waged a devastating battle on Marshallese sea and soil. In 1965, when the comments above were written, American "warriors" had long supplanted Marshallese and Japanese "warriors," and had just conducted sixty-seven atmospheric and thermonuclear atomic weapons tests in the Marshall Islands. Kwajalein had already been an active and busy American military base for twenty years.

European or American military and missionary forces are often credited (often by themselves) with bringing peace to the Marshalls and quelling the flames of battle between island groups and clans. In fact many land wars and disputes simply changed character and became more nuanced as Islanders strategically aligned themselves with different outside forces in their confrontations against each other. Many histories of Micronesia describe the gunboat diplomacy of naval commanders and colonial forces in the late 1800s. For example, describing how colonial authority spread and took root in the Marshalls and other island groups, Hezel and Berg (1985) write in *Micronesia: Winds of Change* (their seminal textbook for use in classrooms in the former Trust Territory of the Pacific) that foreign naval commanders used violence to coerce local chiefs to stop fighting and allow copra trade or mission work to begin (340). But although the violence and coercion of outside forces on local chiefdoms was certainly a major influence, from an Islander point of view it is still important to acknowledge the cleverness and agency of local leaders in allying with colonial forces to consolidate their power.

The battle over land and power in the Marshall Islands continues into the present day, even if without bloodshed. For the landowners of Kwajalein nowadays, and more broadly speaking, the Ri-Kuwajleen in general, the battle over land is nothing new; it is ongoing. Collective memories of Islanders from all around the area relate the stories of powerful *irooj* who fought and died in wars between different clans for domination over different atolls and islands.

In the case of contemporary Kwajalein, where so much of the "homecoming" discourse is politically entangled with national politics in Majuro or internationally in Washington with high-profile lawyers and lobbyists, the story of land rights has become extraordinarily nuanced. Many Marshallese are quick to judge the Kwajalein landowners' campaign for compensation as political chicanery or gambling with public funds by paying costly lawyers to sue the United States. Many Americans working on Kwajalein who have no understanding of the broader history sometimes presume that landowners are just "looking for free handouts" or that this is merely a matter of poor financial management and corruption on the part of "the Marshallese." In response, one of the landowners' representatives, Tom Kijiner Jr., stressed that on the contrary, not only do these landowners deserve much more compensation than they have received to date, but that "getting proper compensation is hard, hard work" (Walsh 2003, 409).[15]

Many Americans I interviewed about impressions of Marshallese on Ebeye expressed dismay about how "traditional leaders" and landowners "waste" money. Citing the example of Ebeye "looking like a slum," they talked about how landowners should use their money to improve "their island." This perspective, however, conflates landowner payments (which landowners understandably equate with "rent" paid to a landlord of an apartment) with infrastructure or "development" funding, two completely separate issues. Additionally, although some receive substantial amounts of money, landowners share most of their income with their own extended family network. And, as I write elsewhere, since many of the landowners and other residents of Ebeye are actually displaced from other islands, they rarely have either the motivation or permission to "improve" upon their environment.

At the core of landowners' discourse, however, is a bigger story that has more to do with identity, home, and dignity than it does with material wealth. It is rooted in clan wars of the Rālik chain that stretch back into deep time, long before Captain John Marshall passed through the islands in 1788 en route to Australia. The last great war of Rālik described by oral traditions was waged between Jemāluut and Ḷañinni from the reefs of Kwajalein, across the seas to Namu Atoll, and all the way down to Ebon in the far south of the chain, where the latter emerged victorious. Jemāluut, meanwhile, was killed and all his descendants were pushed off the land and treated as commoners (Tobin 2002, 330–331).

In 1823, some of the first recorded paramount chiefdoms were established, pulling together the atolls of the Rālik and the Ratak chains. Lomade became the first *iroojlaplap* of Ratak and northern Rālik; Kaibuke became the first *iroojlaplap* of southern Rālik (Loeak, Kiluwe, and Crowl 2004, 234). In 1863, when Kaibuke died of typhoid fever, the two most powerful *irooj* of Rālik, Kabua and Loeak, began a tense and angry battle for the paramountcy, and Kabua ultimately prevailed in 1880 in a bloodless confrontation, earning him the distinction of "Kabua the Great," eventually recognized as the "king" by German authorities when they set up their colonial government (Hezel 1995, 125). This bloodless battle between Kabua and Loeak was described by German observer Otto Finsch, who said that "There were indeed no bloody scenes, but ever so many laughable ones, and of valor and heroic exploits there was none at all" (Finsch 1893, 35). Once again, the European view of the martial practices of Islanders as "laughable" and backward should be noted here. In fact, reading Finsch's observations more closely, the war between Kabua and Loeak was extremely nuanced, strategically elaborate, and deliberately designed for Kabua to regain the part of his domain he believed had been wrongfully taken by Loeak. Perhaps it was not *meant* to be a deadly battle:

> When [Kabua] appeared, like his retainers all gathered together, in the national costume, there was much drumming and acting, eye-rolling, and all the old weapons, spears, whale spars, etc., were hunted up. Finally, the enemy fleet, 20 canoes strong, drew near. Kabua mustered his army, 85 warriors all in all, graybeards, cripples and boys included, and valorously advanced against the foe, armed with Spencer-rifle and lance; the dauntless women came along. They brought provisions, cocoanuts, in little baskets, but also stones and "pain-killer," an American panacea which had already been introduced among the natives. Loeak landed with his troops, some 150 strong, women included, but Kabua, according to the customs of war, might not yet attack him, since his own district proper had not yet been violated. With remarkable dispatch, however, there was erected a redoubt of coral stones, four to five feet high and of the same width, over the whole width of the island, which at this spot was only a few hundred feet, for these earthworks appear to play a special role in the conduct of war by the Marshall Islanders. Despite the presence of sentries, the soldiers of the enemy could pass through unmolested to visit their wives and to purchase powder and lead from the white trader. In the evening, by the light of the fire, when the women made a fearful noise with drumming and singing, there was, however, much blind shooting into the darkness of the night, in order to scare the foe and inspire courage in their own men. But despite all the shooting there were no wounded, and since both sides were exhausted, did not receive

any more cartridges . . . were out of provisions, peace was made, only after months to be sure. (Finsch 1893, 35–36)

Arguably, Rālik land wars were quite sophisticated, and they also evolved and took on new forms as Islanders appropriated some of the tools or modes of fighting used by foreigners, such as the rifles Finsch describes above. In subsequent decades, Islanders also adopted European models for resolving land disputes through the legal system. Hezel explains that the early part of the twentieth century in the Marshalls would have been "tediously placid" had it not been for the rekindling of the conflict between Kabua and Loeak when the latter died in 1904 and his successor, Litokwa, took up the struggle over land again (Hezel 1995, 125–126). This eventually led to threats of war between Kabua and Litokwa that the Germans found highly problematic, and different government and church figures sided with each.

Ultimately, whereas earlier disputes would have been resolved by all-out battle between *irooj* and their supporters, both parties instead hired legal counsel and pursued a court case, Kabua hiring an agent of Burns, Philp & Company and Litokwa hiring Eugen Brandeis, a former German commissioner (Hezel 1995, 127.) Through these legal proceedings, presumably the first major Marshallese court case over land with foreign attorneys as counsel, Kabua retained and reinforced his status as a charismatic and diplomatic but highly expansionist leader, while Litokwa and the Loeak family managed to retain a significant amount of land for future generations. And though not everyone was happy, this set a precedent of brokering land disputes through foreign legal mediation.[16]

It is not my intention here to provide an exhaustive history of these sorts of exchanges through the twentieth century. Rather, I intend to point out that not only have land disputes and courageous and complex battles been waged by Marshall Islander leaders for centuries upon centuries, but that those battles evolved and transformed into the "homecoming" discourse. Though many commentaries on landowner resistance presume that court cases are a recent development, as the example of Kabua and Litokwa shows, it has been more than one hundred years since the first major court dispute over land was waged in the Marshall Islands. Strong or clever chiefs on certain islands may have used their wits and martial strength to expand their territory throughout the Marshalls, but as times changed, *irooj* and their representative *aḷap, rijerbal,* and others strategically adapted to

European modes of resolution and structures of authority. The battle over land and power, nonetheless, persists into contemporary times, in increasingly globalized ways.

A Chick without Its Mother

Jojoḷāār is a word that roughly approximates to "a chick without its mother," and it is an analogy used to describe people who have been evicted from their land, like the people of Enewetak, Bikini, and many of the islets of Kwajalein (Tobin 2002, 332). Without its mother (the land), the chick is left to starve and suffer. Losing one's land thus means losing one's identity, power, and "face." Marshallese historian Ḷokrap on Ebon related to anthropologist Jack Tobin the additional significance losing land has in the case of *irooj*:

> After the land is lost, the *irooj* rank is lost. That is, rank depends upon the possession of rights in land . . . if the United States took away all of [an *irooj*'s land], he would still have *irooj* blood, but he would not be respected as *irooj*. He would just be like *kajoor*.[17] Blood does not count; the land is the criterion.
>
> Long ago, the *irooj* were respected as gods. Not like ordinary people. But once they lose a war (*jipokwe*), they are like ordinary people. They have lost their *ao* or dignity.[18] (Tobin 2002, 331)

This image, taken on Kwajalein islet in the 1890s by Joachim deBrum (the Marshallese-Portuguese son of a copra entrepreneur on Likiep Atoll named Joseph deBrum), shows a deposed chief named Langju posing with his family. According to Leonard deBrum, Langju had been an *irooj* at Ujae Atoll but was defeated by the warriors of Kabua "the Great" and subsequently lost his title (deBrum et al. 2005).

It is largely in this bitter context of loss and demoralization that the Kwajalein landowners—led by a small group of Rālik *irooj*—pursued their "homecoming" protests. So although many observers, both Marshallese and American, suggest that the landowners are covetous and proud, that they only are "making trouble" and trying to glean as much money as possible, it is crucial to consider the severe consequences of losing one's land as described above. As one landowner indicated to me,

> As for the *irooj*, it's also about "face." This is true in the Pacific Islands all over, and also throughout Asia: You make me really hurt, and I'm gonna lose face. Face is important. It's more valuable than money.

In the premodern past, *irooj* and their followers were often killed if not at least dispossessed of their land when defeated by others (who subsequently gained the title of *irooj*). Nowadays, even if land is only being temporarily leased to the United States, the term of eighty years is still a span of several generations. Losing land to the United States, or having it somehow taken away by the Marshall Islands' national government, would be the epitome of disgrace. Throughout the ages in the Marshall Islands, from a genealogical perspective, such a loss would have represented a total erasure of a lineage's past, a rupture in history; by the same token, it would have been a forfeiture of future generations' birthright. Thus, reducing the problems of Kwajalein landowners to mere squabbles about money and pride is missing the atollscape that lies beneath the surface.

Invading Home: The Postwar Ri-Kuwajleen Battle

Like the American and Japanese public narratives I have been relating through my exploration of the tensions between "coral" and "concrete," the story of Kwajalein landowners' resistance is multifaceted, political, and complex. It is a story that is unfolding in the present tense, but it involves contested land claims between multiple parties and many turbulent and personal disputes. It is not my intention to provide an authoritative legal strategy or framework that could be used to argue landowners' claims to various parts of Kwajalein Atoll. This is, rather, a look at an important Marshallese atollscape of heroic resistance and self-determination.

In Marshallese, *jodik* is the word many leaders use to describe the demonstrations staged by thousands of people from the late 1960s to the early 1980s at Kwajalein to protest the American use of the atoll without proper compensation for their land, as well as the poor living conditions of Ebeye. Interestingly, *jodik* originally meant "invasion" and is a word that comes directly from the Japanese word *jōriku* ("invasion" or "landing"), used by the Imperial Navy to describe the American amphibious invasion of Kwajalein Atoll.[19] The *Marshallese-English Dictionary* even offers this tongue-in-cheek example sentence to describe the word's usage: "*RiAmedka raar* jodiki *Kuwajleen im pād ie m̧ae rainin.* The Americans *invaded* Kwajalein and have stayed on it ever since" (Abo et al. 1976, 113).[20]

The Marshallese postwar "invasions" of Kwajalein Atoll of course had their precedent in the deep-time battles of the Ri-Kuwajleen atollscape, back in the days when *irooj* planned the invasions of different atolls to increase their territory or avenge past wrongs. But using the Marshallese appropriation of the Japanese word *jōriku*—a term that had been used to describe the US bombardment of the atoll—suggests that these protests were meant in one way or another to be a counter-invasion that would give the Americans a taste of their own medicine.

The *jodiks* were never violent; in fact they emulated many of the democratic tactics of free speech gleaned from the American civil rights movement that was unfolding around the same time as missile testing began on Kwajalein.[21] Always with the intention of protesting that they were not being properly compensated for the use of their land, starting in 1969 the landowners used civil-disobedience strategies like "sail-ins" and "sit-ins" in an attempt to get the attention of both Marshallese national leaders and American authorities who could improve the situation.

As Johnson (1984), Hanlon (1998), Toyosaki (2005), and others have chronicled, the landowners in Kwajalein waged a long and hard battle for compensation. After the war, the fact that no compensation whatsoever had been paid to them (even to *irooj* and other traditional leaders), combined with military regulations and the increasing problems and pressures of Ebeye life, brought this issue to a head by the 1960s.

The first official lease for Kwajalein land, often known as the "99-year lease," was signed by Lejolan Kabua in 1964 and provided for $10 per acre per year to the landowners, for the use of the 750 acres of Kwajalein islet only, on the condition that the United States "improve the economic and social conditions of the Marshallese people, particularly at Ebeye" (KNC 2002b, 58). To give a sense of how this trickled down to the landowners, it is worth noting that $1,000 was distributed to each of the four *irooj* for Kwajalein and the rest was given to the many others who had rights to the land (Kahn 1966, 80). In other words, the United States offered no retroactive compensation for its use of Kwajalein from 1944 onwards. More importantly, it took no account of its military use of the various other islets in the atoll.

When the Mid-Atoll Corridor was formed in the same year as this new lease was signed, and only some of the landowners were given nominal stipends of a meager $40 each, the landowners' anger began to grow. The mid-corridor landowners repeatedly petitioned the Congress of Micronesia (COM), and when the Trust Territory government ignored the COM's resolution to negotiate a proper lease, the COM encouraged the landowners to resettle their lands, even sending a representative along to facilitate the process (Johnson 1984, 27).

This planted the seeds of the first true "homecoming" in 1969, when key landowner Handel Dribo,[22] one of the leaders of Ebeye and the owner of significant land in the Mid-Atoll Corridor, launched the first "sail-in" with thirty-one Islanders to reinhabit parts of the atoll and interfere in missile tests if necessary. Dribo, who had once worked as a carpenter building Japanese barracks in the early 1940s, had a strong sense of justice and discipline, and after having to rebuild his life after the devastation of the war, he was not willing to stand by and watch his land and livelihood be taken away from him.[23] His persistence resulted in a new five-year agreement for the use of these islets that amounted to only $285 annually for each of the landowners there (Johnson 1984, 27).

In the mid-1970s, Senator Ataji Balos of COM, another major protester, argued at a US congressional hearing that the promises of the original 1964 lease agreement to improve conditions in the atoll had not been kept. Stating that "the people of Kwajalein do not recognize the validity of the lease," Balos helped to spark yet another resettlement in 1977, in which Dribo led forty landowners to occupy three of his mid-corridor islets near Meck, on the east reef (Johnson 1984, 28). When American officials did not honor their promises to renegotiate after this demonstration, Dribo went right back to his land again in March of 1978 and stayed until he and other landowners felt that their demands would be met.

These protests and negotiations continued through the 1970s, and they typically followed a pattern of landowners making deals with American lawmakers, only to find that those deals were not fully implemented later. This was particularly the case with promises securing the support of the United States to help develop and improve the standard of living on Ebeye. Again and again, landowners protested by trying to "come home," then negotiated for more compensation, and ultimately felt as if they were not being taken seriously (Johnson 1984).

Johnson explains that the Pentagon has never dealt directly with the landowners, always preferring to negotiate via the Trust Territory government or the Marshall Islands government (Johnson 1984, 29–30). This is true on the surface, and it is even replicated today in the ongoing "government-to-government" dealings that take place under the Compact of Free Association with the United States. But Ri-Kuwajleen have indeed historically engaged directly with one colonial and military authority after another.[24] In Japanese times, landowners communicated directly with military officers in the admiralty (Hayashi 1964), and during the immediate postwar years, direct communication between the military and local leaders was a standard occurrence. Throughout the evolution of the military installation at Kwajalein, local landowners and Ebeye leaders have had some semblance of dialogue with the military leadership of Kwajalein.[25] Some of the more sympathetic Kwajalein commanders have forged deep friendships with the landowners and worked hard to amplify their voices to influential parties in the Department of Defense; yet commanders have a fixed two-year tour on Kwajalein, as do many military officials. Even the recent corporate management by Kwajalein's main contractor is cycled on a regular basis. With all this institutional amnesia, the enduring patience of these landowners, despite their frustration, is quite remarkable.

Homecoming: The Second "Liberation" of Kwajalein

In 1982, when the new Republic of the Marshall Islands government negotiated a fifty-year lease with the United States for only $4 million a year, without meeting landowner expectations, the landowners were enraged and decided to launch their biggest *jodik* ever. As a child, I actually witnessed the early stages of Operation Homecoming, which began around the same time that my family left Kwajalein to move to the United States. More than a thousand Marshallese, mostly women, sat on the grass in front of the open-air theater near the air terminal—the same area where the Kwaj Karnivals (where we Americans commemorated the US invasion) had been held every year. They sat quietly on the ground, legs folded, talking, singing, staying in place, making their presence felt.

In retrospect, I can see how the presence of all those dedicated Marshallese bodies reclaiming the green grass lawns of Kwajalein looked like the March on Washington that took place upon the lawns of the American capital in the 1960s, as it was partly after this movement for civil rights that Operation Homecoming was modeled. Some young Marshallese today who know this history even reflect upon the movement's leaders, calling one spokesperson or another the "Marshallese Martin Luther King."[26] Indeed, for many landowners, these protests were a campaign for their true postwar "liberation."

Fred Pedro is a former political consultant for the Marshall Islands government who, at the time of my research, was in charge of V7-EMON, a Majuro radio station that used the slogan "Rockin' the Missile-FM" and represented the views of Kwajalein landowners and nuclear-affected atolls. Growing up on Ebeye and observing the demonstrations, he reflected,

> You know, with America you try to be nice and you get sidestepped and pushed aside. In America, people speak up! It's like "the wheel that squeals gets a little oil." And that's why the Kwajalein money got proposed as part of the first Compact . . . because of the demonstrations and what have you. And people said then as they do now, "why are you guys anti-American, for criticizing the US and wanting more?" But I say you must be out of your mind! It's *very* American to go after what is right. In fact if anything, we've been taught by the Americans to stand up for what is right. But if you just wanna be trampled on, that's not American! So I believe the Kwajalein landowners are actually representing the *core* of [American] values! Do what is right, stand up for what you believe is right. It has nothing to do with anti-Americanism whatsoever! No not at all.[27]

Ataji Balos, who helped execute Operation Homecoming, explained what it was like to be a part of this massive invasion.

> The men were afraid. They thought they would be killed, and they wanted to see what happened first. So we took mostly women and kids; they were really brave. Kwaj was ready for us when we came, because they knew we were coming. We landed at Camp Hamilton on lagoonside, and there were already police waiting there for us. Five days later, and this was in July or August of 1982, I think, we took Emon Beach. People in riot gear with guns, bulletproof vests and shields met us there. I told them, "Don't do anything to us, we just go peacefully."
>
> On Emon Beach, they arrested us in a big van and took us to the jailhouse. Imata and the five boys that were on his boat and me were taken there. They only kept us in jail one night, maybe from 5 p.m. until the next morning. And then Julian Riklon led a march from the Camp Hamilton site, followed by many women, down to the jail. He was beaten in the jailhouse when he got there, but the women protested and cried so much that they finally let him go.
>
> We stayed at Camp Hamilton from June to October of 1982. We brought food over from Ebeye and boats came and left back and forth. The authorities didn't want any Americans to come near us. We were lucky because there were lots of fish just that time in the lagoon, and we were able to survive off the fish we caught. (conversation, May 5, 2005)

The scene of the protesters camped at Camp Hamilton Beach (part of Erlañ Wāto) on Kwajalein on the next page provides a sense of how many children were involved in the demonstrations. What looks at first like an innocent youth outing is actually being monitored by an American police officer (in the center of the photograph) taking notes on his observations and taking the names of children where possible.[28]

The army's reaction to the protests on Kwajalein, which ultimately lasted three and a half months, was to shut off all water at the camp sites,[29] to bar gardeners or housekeepers from going to work, and to ban access to telephones and banking services (KNC 2002b, 62). The commander of Kwajalein erected concertina wire and klieg search lights on the reef to ward off any further "trespassing," and the Pentagon ordered a complete press blackout, which required Balos to fly to Honolulu to speak with the media and report on the situation to humanitarian groups (KNC 2002b, 62). He concluded that the hardline reaction from the military was not only because the protests had successfully blocked the test of an MX missile but because "the presence of many Marshallese people throughout Kwajalein Atoll [was] simply offensive to the US military" (Balos 1982, 2).

Filmmaker Adam Horowitz chronicled this first major *jodik* in his film *Home on the Range* (1983) and featured Handel Dribo as he returned to his land to hunt and fish with his grandchildren, sat on a missile launch pad, and built houses. At one point in the film, Dribo sings along with his old Japanese records, expressing a nostalgia for the days before the Americans came and took away his land. In some respects, *Home on the Range* is less about the issues of landowners than it is about protesting the nuclear arms race and weapons testing. It does, however, provide a powerful portrait of Kwajalein Atoll from a landowner perspective in the early 1980s, at a time of the Marshallese nation's formation as a sovereign state. It is also the only cinematic representation of Operation Homecoming.[30]

Operation Homecoming was brought to an end by the involvement of President Amata Kabua, whose charisma and power as *iroojlaplap* was powerful enough to break up the protest and organize a new land-use agreement that would only last a provisional fifteen years (with an option to renew for a total of thirty-five years through 2016). The landowners, however, were still very displeased (KNC 2002b, 61), but the Compact of Free Association with the United States had not been concluded at that point, so a three-year interim lease was negotiated and signed until the compact went into effect.

Disputes about distribution of the money and lack of any clear initiatives to fully rebuild Ebeye eventually led Balos and Dribo to once again lead a protest to Kwajalein in 1985, when the interim lease expired. Balos recalls how they came from oceanside behind the Snack Bar restaurant around the adult swimming pool and the hospital.

> Except that time, the US military deployed over a hundred military men from Honolulu with machine guns and riot gear. The whole protest altogether lasted for months, and all these communications went all the way up to Washington, DC. But the colonel on Kwaj couldn't arrest us, because it was our land. He put up yellow tape and told the Marines to shoot to wound but not to kill if anyone exited.
>
> But it was peaceful, you know. Women and children just sitting there and playing, and they invited the Marines to come and drink coffee and have cookies. Many Marines got sent back because they realized we weren't dangerous. (conversation, May 5, 2005)

Ataji and other landowners' stories sound so local and familiar, small-town stories about neighborhood disputes as opposed to clashes between nations. They are the small histories of coral making sense out of the big, blanketing histories of the concrete coating of global politics. What for the Pentagon was perceived as a major security breach was played out at a local level as peaceful activism in which Marshallese women welcomed onto their own land the soldiers who were guarding it, plying them with refreshments.[31]

For the new Marshall Islands' national government and its representatives, however, many of whom had significant stakes in the land themselves, the Kwajalein issue was a sensitive balancing act between honoring the sacrifices of the Ri-Kuwajleen while also acting in the best interests of the nation. Once President Amata Kabua had persuaded the landowners to sign the land-use agreement, the Compact of Free Association was fully implemented in October of 1986. This was not done effortlessly. Ataji Balos and the protesters were first removed from Kwajalein by force, and later the fledgling RMI government used laws of "eminent domain" to make Kwajalein comply with its agreement with the United States (Hanlon 1998, 212).[32]

The right of eminent domain, a concept inherited by the Marshall Islands government from the Trust Territory era, allows the government to condemn and then appropriate private land in the national interest. This became a critical concern for Kwajalein landowners in their campaign of resistance against the unauthorized offer of their land to the United States by their national government, in that they feared that the RMI might attempt to invoke this power. Senator and foreign minister Tony deBrum testified in 2010 to the US House Foreign Affairs Committee on Asia, the Pacific, and the Global Environment, arguing that invoking eminent domain in the Kwajalein situation, as happened in the 1980s, is unconstitutional, and that the only remaining option if the United States and the RMI could not find a way of increasing land payments and compensation for the displaced Ri-Kuwajleen would be for the United States to dismantle its installation and rehabilitate the land to its original condition. DeBrum pointed out that in the drafting of their constitution,

> [T]he people of the Marshall Islands sought to define the governmental privilege of eminent domain in such a manner that it would be almost impossible to exercise. . . . For over a hundred years, our country had been under the colonial rule of one nation or another and the practice of taking land from our people was always perceived with suspicion and in some cases outright repugnance. . . . Basically, the definition of public use versus economic use must be irrefutably established, and secondly, a clear and definitive assessment of value must be completed. But yet another requirement must be met. That is, land substantively similar to that which is condemned must be provided to substitute for that which is taken, and ceded to the dispossessed. As hard as we have thought this over, we fail to find land which matches the size of Kwajalein, the largest atoll in the world, to replace it should it ever be taken successfully in eminent domain proceedings. (deBrum 2010)

The events of the 1980s set a precedent that showed the lengths to which the RMI government was willing to go to preserve the integrity of the country and enforce its "special relationship" with the United States. Though land rights were eventually returned and payments were made in full in the 1980s, a bitter aftertaste was left with landowners, who began to feel a sense of distrust toward their new national government and its "government-to-government" dealings with American officials.[33]

Lejman jūri: The Women Have Their Say

It was no coincidence that the majority of the people involved in the *jodiks* were women, even if the most outspoken leaders were the men. Indeed, in keeping with the Marshallese land tenure custom of *aḷap*-ship, in which land inheritance is matrilineal but senior males act as clan heads on behalf of women, men represent many of the landowner families. The Marshallese expression *lejman jūri* is a term that means "when a woman speaks, the men must give way." Women are the arbiters of disputes, the final word, and in the customs of Marshallese land inheritance, it is through the mother that land is received. *Maman maroñron*—"women are the protectors of the land"—is another expression of relevance here. Throughout my research, while trying to find elderly people who remembered Japanese times, I wound up discovering many Ri-Kuwajleen women who had also participated in the demonstrations. One of these women, "Clara," explained to me,

> When our male leaders came to us women and asked if we should go back to our land on Kwajalein and stay there, we went right away because we knew that it was right. And that is what you do in the Marshall Islands. We support our brothers, we back them up and we stand up for the land when we agree with them. We knew it was a problem between the American military and our leaders and we knew it was our job to stand in the middle and resolve the conflict. That is why we went. But it's true a lot of the men who worked on Kwajalein were afraid of losing their jobs if they participated in the demonstrations, and some of them were really scared to go in the first place, so we went, and many of us were very old women and little girls, too.

The military and colonial influences that made *irooj* into kings in Rālik are also responsible for strengthening and stylizing patriarchal power and diminishing matriarchal power at Kwajalein (Walsh 2003, 170–172), but this does not necessarily mean that women have lost the power and influence they have over the land, nor does it diminish women's role in decision making. Clara's comments above point to this responsibility to "stand up for the land" and step into the battle zone when the time is right to resolve conflict. As Lijon Eknilang explained after the protests in 1985, "Men don't have the power. They will talk about it and take it to the community and the women will make all the decisions. Without women nothing will happen. If women want men to do something they will tell them to do it" (quoted in dé Ishtar 1994, 28).

As Enloe emphasizes, women around all military bases worldwide play a huge role in mediating the balance of power and working in many ways as arbiters of peace (Enloe 1990). Walsh (2003) points out that on Kwajalein, where so many Americans hire "maids" to clean their homes and sometimes take care of their children, Marshallese women play an important role as ambassadors for the Marshalls and the Ebeye community. Traveling back and forth between Ebeye and Kwajalein daily and having everyday relationships with American families, Marshallese housekeepers have always had much more of a direct influence on the American community than have men, who typically have worked in maintenance, grounds, and other manual labor areas. In her analysis of local women from the environs of military bases, however, Enloe also looks at the relations between military men and local women and focuses considerably on sex workers (Enloe 1990, 81–84). The Kwajalein Atoll context is different from other bases, though, as it is mainly a civilian population where families live and a large number of American women also hold supervisory roles. Romantic liaisons do exist between Americans on the base and Marshallese on Ebeye, but not to the extent that a significant sex industry has formed, as in the case of many other bases around the world.[34] Nevertheless, the fact that Marshallese still use the word *kōkan* (Japanese for "exchange") to mean "prostitute," or *Mādke* ("America") to mean "venereal disease," is evidence of a long legacy in which Marshallese women's (and men's) bodies have been exploited in previous conflicts over land and power.

The "homecomings" of the 1970s and 1980s were a very different story. The women who resettled Kwajalein lands during the many "homecomings" of the 1970s and 1980s were deliberate and conscious of their ambassadorial roles. These women literally laid down their bodies and their lives in the defense of their land. Handel Dribo and the other organizers of Operation Homecoming were so conscious of women's role in conflict resolution that they didn't think twice about sending so many women to defend their position.[35] And although some of the younger women who participated in the demonstrations reflect nowadays upon their experiences with some ambivalence,[36] many of the elders who had strong memories of their original displacement were eager and determined to see justice served.

The association between *lejman jūri* and "homecoming," or women and land, is most strongly felt in the ways Dribo and other landowners perceived American responses to the protests. Many landowners feel that the United States has historically deliberately installed women in positions of power in the Marshall Islands as a tactic to influence the Kwajalein situation and quell resistance. Fred Pedro explains this theory:

> Back in the eighties at the height of the protests, when the Kwaj *irooj* were standing there and saying, "let's just end these demonstrations," Handel said, "no, I'm not gonna let you down, I'll take on these Americans. I'll fight for us, for my chiefs." But then at the time, right in the middle of these protests in 1981 the US suddenly appoints this lady to be the Trust Territory High Commissioner and they sent her out here. So this lady comes and pleads with Handel to stop the protests, and he said, "Hey, who taught these Americans our custom?" Cuz when the ladies ask you, you gotta stop![37]

During the Land Use Agreement standoff, Kwajalein landowners believed that history was repeating itself. In 2004, at exactly the time when a new compact was being implemented and a new lease for the atoll was being deliberated, the United States sent its first woman army commander to lead the USAG-KA installation. This was around the same time that a woman ambassador was also appointed by George W. Bush to head the US Embassy in Majuro.

Regardless of whether or not American strategists implemented a *lejman jūri* plot of their own, in the past, justice was mediated through the sacrifices and strength of more than a thousand Marshallese women from Kwajalein who helped to come home, "invade" their land, and push for proper compensation. "Trespassing" on their own soil, the Ri-Kuwajleen women rallied against their marginalization and pressured officials to reflect upon the many trespasses that America had committed against the Marshallese people. "You know," says Pedro, "if I were to resolve it myself, I'd just try to get the women to negotiate on behalf of everyone. Our women aren't afraid to talk; they'll take on a man anytime."

The Battle Continues

> We're happy we're contributing to world peace by allowing our land to be used, but in return, we'd like the world to work with us, especially the US government, about how we can solve the problem of Ebeye.
>
> —*Irene Paul (Ebeye resident)*[38]

Around the turn of this millennium, more than two thousand years after humans began to settle Kwajalein, and at least tens of thousands of years since coral began to migrate to the shores of the submerged volcano that became the atoll, American and Marshallese lawmakers began the arduous process of renegotiating the Compact of Free Association between the RMI and the United States. The new compact included an amendment to its previous Military Use and Operations Rights Agreement (MUORA) of 1982, due to expire in 2016, that would entitle the US military to continue using Kwajalein Atoll for another fifty years through 2066, with the option to renew its lease through 2086. In anticipation of this extension, fearing that the events of 1982 might be repeated, the Kwajalein landowners joined together as a new entity called the Kwajalein Negotiation Commission (KNC), headquartered in Majuro and chaired by Kwajalein *irooj* and senator Christopher Loeak, who would become RMI president in 2012.

The KNC launched a series of public relations campaigns to make their voices heard. Unlike in 1982, before the Internet era, when the US Department of Defense could issue a press blackout, this time around the landowners could make use of the world wide web, e-mailing press releases all over the United States, staging various protests in Majuro and at Vandenberg Air Force Base in California (where some missile tests are launched), and even setting up a website devoted to telling "the Kwajalein landowners' view of their displacement by . . . the lease with the US from post WWII to present times." The site included profiles of prominent landowners, several downloadable documents (such as "The Plea of Kwajalein Landowners"), and a brief history of the displacements. The top page featured an outstretched hand, from which a fiery missile was launched. Images of four Caucasian hands emerging from black suits pointed sternly at Kwajalein, likely representing American lawyers and politicians determining Kwajalein's future. On the left-hand side, a forlorn, homeless figure sat dejectedly on a sea of graves, representing the displaced spirits of ancestors.

Meanwhile, as renegotiations went on in Honolulu and Washington, the landowners worked with researchers and consultants to prepare detailed statements and proposals to the RMI for a renegotiation of the Land Use Agreement that would better suit their needs for the future. Arguing that landowners had been sorely uncompensated for the use of their lands, that the living conditions on Ebeye were completely unacceptable, and that continued use of Kwajalein would require careful renegotiation, the KNC generated its own assessment of the value of the Kwajalein installation. Using an elaborate system of calculation, it concluded that the $11 million the landowners had been receiving annually was extremely insufficient and that "taking annual inflation and population growth into account," the "total fair rent" for 2003 should be closer to $33 million (KNC 2002a, 44). This figure was calculated partly out of the commonsense approach that all Kwajalein "natural resources" were in fact being leased to the US military, and that not only the land but the lagoon was being used.[39] It also took into consideration the total loss of subsistence income due to severe access restrictions to various parts of the atoll.

The KNC proposed that this amount for America's proposed fifty-year lease be compounded and paid upfront into a trust fund account by the United States, for a total of roughly $1.4 billion. This would allow the landowners to invest the money in advance, in consideration of the "unusually long period of fifty years" and the fact that the value of Kwajalein to national missile defense was far greater than this figure. The landowners pointed out that in spite of this, rent had never been paid for Kwajalein land used by the United States prior to 1964. Explaining that previous lease payments had never been enough to distribute income fairly to all "non-titled" landowners, they argued that this trust fund would then generate annual payments that could sustain all landowners fairly.[40]

Overall, however, the commission proposed a number of major improvements that were meant not only "to serve as a means whereby the Kwajalein landowners affirm their fullest support for the continuation of the defense related activities in Kwajalein Atoll" but also "to establish a process of strategic and rapid development aimed at a systematic transformation and improvement of the socio-economic conditions of all Marshallese communities in Kwajalein Atoll" (KNC 2002a, 32). To meet these ends, the KNC proposed that in addition to rental payments, the United States should pay to deal with the environmental impact of missile-testing and space operations; to pay a separate amount to help build infrastructure; establish a housing fund, health plan, and scholarship fund; and provide an insurance policy for each landowner in the event of disaster from testing initiatives.

This proposal was debated along with many other proposals from different parts of the Marshall Islands. Ultimately, however, US and RMI negotiators came back to the landowners with a "lowball" compromise for the whole country (Aubuchon and Hezel 2003) that paled in comparison. The US offer regarding Kwajalein was that in order to use the atoll between 2003 and 2066, with an option to renew through 2086, it would simply increase land payments to Kwajalein from $11 to $15 million annually and adjust this amount for inflation.[41] In addition to this, the compact generally set aside another $3.1 million annually to use as "Special Impact" funding for overcrowded Ebeye, and an additional $200,000 annually that could be channeled into development projects in response to specific grant proposals.

Though the Marshall Islands national government was disappointed that their proposals for the whole country were not met, they negotiated until the RMI as a whole was offered roughly $33 million per annum, part of which would be invested in a trust fund over twenty years, by which point the United States would begin to withdraw its funding altogether in 2023. Kwajalein landowners, however, were outraged by what they considered to be the failure of their own government to push hard enough for a better deal for them, even though their land was a central part of the package and was being promised to the United States for eighty years, a full sixty years longer than the terms of the end of the renegotiated compact.

According to the landowners, the RMI government concluded the compact "without consulting with them," even provisionally promising the United States it would later negotiate domestically with the landowners until a new Land Use Agreement (LUA) based on the US offer was agreed upon. Many landowners believed that the administration of President Kessai Note was eager to pay off national government debts and was willing to ransom Kwajalein's future to do so. The incumbent Note administration disputed these allegations, arguing that landowners had a fair chance to push for their terms (Zackios 2007), but in the end negotiations closed with landowners being offered much less than what they asked for. Moreover, Imata Kabua's biographer Jim Philippo contends that the actual amount of money the United States was willing to spend on the RMI or Kwajalein was never really negotiable, and the United States masterminded a sort of coup d'état based on the tactic of "divide and conquer," pitting two opposing parties in the Marshalls against each other in the expectation that the landowners would finally relent (Philippo 2015, 216).

The landowners immediately refused to sign a new LUA and put forth a petition with more than one thousand signatures on it, vowing not to yield to pressure to allow continued use of their land unless a better deal could be reached. As a concession, the KNC determined that an annual $19.1 million would be the minimum acceptable amount in land payments to which they would agree, in addition to other proposals that would rebuild Ebeye and improve the welfare of the atoll.[42] This proposal, however, was not entertained by the RMI, nor did American authorities make any comment for quite some time. In response to a general reticence from the RMI government, the landowners staged a series of rallies, including a "The Buck Stops Here" rally in front of the Nitijela (Parliament), which pressured the RMI government to clarify its position on the use of Kwajalein ("RMI Protesters Disrupt Nitijela Session," Yokwe Online, August 4, 2003).

At the same time, government representatives were divided about the Kwajalein issue. Though many officials privately admitted that they felt the Kwajalein landowners were sorely undercompensated for the value of their land and their continued sacrifices, publicly their mandate to secure funding for the stability of their nation had to take precedence (Aubuchon and Hezel 2003). In a country where US government funding accounted for 60 percent of the national budget, the RMI negotiators did not want to take any chances.

"Even Friends Must Draw the Line"

In 2005 Iroojlaplap Imata Kabua adamantly expressed his views about the renegotiated compact on behalf of the Mojen of Jeimata[43] to then US ambassador Greta Morris in a letter that was published in the *Marshall Islands Journal* and later publicized on various websites and news services.[44] Kabua sarcastically and pointedly clarified the position of the Kwajalein landowners within the framework of the Marshall Islands constitution:

> Our constitution prohibits the taking of land without the consent of the owners of the land and fair compensation. The RMI government

owns no land. For the legitimate use of Kwajalein beyond 2016, a Land Use Agreement between the RMI and the people of Kwajalein is required by law and by the Constitution. No such agreement exists and we have proclaimed our intention not to agree to a new one and to return to our lands in 2016. Your condescending public statements ignoring that reality go beyond acceptable standards of international relations and, to us, reflect systematic taunting on the part of a powerful partner bullying a less powerful one. So pervasive is your attitude among other American representatives in our country that now an army colonel on temporary duty to oversee housekeeping chores there calls Kwajalein "my island!" (Johnson 2005)[45]

Kabua accused the ambassador (and, by extension, the United States) of "threatening a sovereign nation" by taking land without compensation and "abusing" the Marshallese people. Explaining that "we do not subscribe to your world policy that might makes right," he vowed to legally confront the United States in order to "protect our homelands." He pointed to American hypocrisy about putting American and Marshallese soldiers' lives (in the US military) at risk to "establish democracy in Iraq" while "undermining the very foundation of... Marshallese constitutional democracy." He concluded by writing:

Make no mistake about our physical and spiritual ties to our lands. Our forefathers fought and died to provide us with this peaceful home, sovereign and free. Our right to live here peacefully and to pass it on to our heirs, whole and intact, is a fundamental right you and your government cannot take away. We have been your friends for the longest time in spite of the outrageous things your government has done to us. But there comes a time when even friends must draw the line... treating us as if we are just grass for the American elephants to stomp on does not augur well for a mutually beneficial tomorrow. (Johnson 2005)

Anthropologist Caroline Lutz picked up on this letter in an article about the need for anthropology to tackle problems of American global hegemony and empire, in which she used the Marshallese example to show how American quasi-colonialism and military regimes still exist throughout the world underneath the veneer of the world being happily "divided into sovereign nation-states" (Lutz 2006, 3). She framed this argument in terms of other bases throughout the Pacific, pointing out how the Korean military is still under US command, how Japanese taxpayers were largely responsible for paying the US armed forces to relocate many bases from Okinawa to Guam in recent years, and how the Philippines is "one of the more vivid examples of the inequalities and tensions produced in places where US imperial projects are underway" (Lutz 2006, 6). Pointing toward the ways American power is projected throughout the world in specific and peculiar ways in different locales, with many places around the globe sharing some universal experiences, she emphasized the ways the local is mapped into the global through the organizational structures of the US military itself.

The importance of studying American empire notwithstanding, it is essential to observe that Kabua's letter did not constitute a critique on behalf of the nation against the United States or its armed forces, as Lutz implied. Conflating Kwajalein with the Marshall Islands national government, Lutz also suggested that "the Marshallese" are strongly opposed to American military or political involvement in their islands, when in fact most Marshall Islands leaders speak of the base at Kwajalein as a "national asset" and the Compact of Free Association as a "special friendship" (Zackios 2007).[46] Lutz's reading therefore misses some of the unique nuanced dynamics of what it means to be a "landowner" in Kwajalein Atoll. It is extraordinarily rare among military bases worldwide that local landowners can engage in dialogue with military and government officials in the first place, so Kwajalein landowners are exceptional in this regard, even if that dialogue is not always productive (Crismon 2005, 504).

Likewise, Kabua's comments may have been addressed to the ambassador, but they were also a veiled protest against the RMI national government and its "government-to-government" alliance with the United States. His sharp words stemmed from the fact that in the past, Kwajalein landowners and traditional leaders had audiences with Pentagon officials and American lawmakers and, at the very least, with base commanders who had the authority to answer to their requests. In another respect, comments like these also represented resistance by local traditional leaders against the democratically elected national government, such as the administration of then-president Kessai M. Note, Kabua's successor and the first commoner to become head of state.[47] The Note administration was criticized on many occasions by Kwajalein traditional leadership for presuming too much influence over land and money at the local level, a domain that had previously been controlled mainly through chiefly authority.[48] During German and Japanese times, and indeed all throughout the Trust Territory period, as Walsh has pointed out, power was brokered from colonial authorities down to *irooj* (2003, 173–189). Even from the formation of the RMI in 1979 until when Note was elected in 2000, the country was led by presidents who were also paramount chiefs, namely Iroojlaplap Amata Kabua and Imata himself, who succeeded his cousin after his untimely death in office.

Kabua's comments to the ambassador were not the disheartened words of an ethnic minority leader futilely protesting the military; they were the words of an experienced former president and paramount chief who stood firmly on his own land in his own country, a nation where the government technically cannot possess land nor rent it to a third party without the permission of landowners. He spoke with confidence, in solidarity with other landowners who had campaigned for more compensation in the past and had succeeded. Knowing that Kwajalein Atoll had been celebrated as a "national asset" not only by the Marshall Islands but also the United States (Firth 1987, 66),[49] Kabua was also aware that his land was no ordinary military installation. As Wypijewski writes, "National Missile Defense could not exist as anything but an idea without America's occupation of Kwajalein" (2000, 6).

But American policymakers tend to perceive Kwajalein as part of a larger projection of power in the Pacific rather than on the specific terms that matter to landowners and other local people. "Ron," an American who grew up on Kwajalein and later worked there for more than a decade as a civilian consultant, surmised at the height of the stalemate in 2005 that the landowners did not understand how the United States really saw its relationship to Kwajalein and the Marshall Islands:

> A few of those landowners are really acting smug, but they're sorely mistaken if they think they'll get anything by sticking it out to 2016. They think their islands at Kwajalein provide the Marshalls' primary value to the US because of the missile and space exploration testing, but that's not true at all these days. More importantly, it's about the right of strategic denial that the US has with the whole of the RMI and other Micronesian states, and that means that we have the right, with this MUORA, to keep China, Taiwan,

or North Korea from doing any military activity in the Central Pacific. That's huge. In other words, no other country can base its military here, but the US would defend this area of the Pacific just as it would Iowa or any major American city. Some of the landowners think that if the US were to leave Kwajalein the military would leave and abandon all of its equipment and infrastructure, even shops and schools and other buildings. But first of all, the US has a commitment to the Marshall Islands anyway, so it would probably just reduce its presence here but not pull out entirely. And see, all the stuff out here is US government property, so if the US leaves, nothing is going to be given away. They'll take it *all* with them like they did at Johnston Atoll. And with strategic denial in place, even if the landowners think they can rent this place out to the Chinese to test missiles to make more money, they're not allowed to do that anyway, whether or not Kwajalein is a base.[50]

Indeed, the right of "strategic denial," forbidding any other nation to use the Marshall Islands for military purposes, is a large part of the Marshalls' value to the United States that extends far beyond the installation at Kwajalein.[51] As one former US congressman gleefully put it while addressing the House,

This [compact] is very much in the interest of the United States. Strategically, this agreement gives us the right of strategic denial, so that we are in a position for the *rest of time* to prevent any foreign power from establishing a military presence in Micronesia without our consent. That is an extraordinary concession made by the Micronesians and a very real achievement for the United States. (Aubuchon and Hezel 2003)

Nonetheless, such statements sidestep the reality that Kwajalein landowners never once unanimously *conceded* their land to *any* foreign power, including the United States, and certainly not "for the rest of time." Some felt that Kabua and other landowners were gambling with their chances and trying to "get" something out of the United States or the national government, yet such arguments do not take into consideration the histories of land being taken away in the first place. Majuro business owner Charles Dominick summed up the sentiments of many Marshallese who understood the larger story of the Kwajalein landowners' experience: "What is wrong with landowners ... [protecting] their own interest? I think what the US is paying them is very minimal compared to what the US is getting *out* of them" (Aubuchon and Hezel 2003).

2016

After pressure had been building for nearly a decade, in the spring of 2011 Kwajalein landowners finally sat down with RMI leaders in Majuro to engage in productive negotiations to draft a new land-use agreement.[52] After many closed-door meetings, on May 10 of that year the document was signed on Ebeye by Iroojlaplaps Imata Kabua and Anjua Loeak, and later by Iroojlaplaps Nelu Watak and Lukwor Litokwe, the four main stakeholders in Kwajalein Atoll (Chutaro 2011). The Land Use Agreement was also signed on behalf of the government by RMI president Jurelang Zedkaia, himself a paramount chief of Majuro and nephew of Imata, who was a catalyst in pushing for a breakthrough.

By resisting for eight years, Kabua and his fellow landowners had succeeded in protesting the injustice of inadequate compensation and unfair treatment, but by not signing they had effectively prolonged an undesirable situation, receiving land payments at pre-2003 rates and preventing Ebeye from receiving other infrastructure or humanitarian support. Meanwhile, the United States had been making land payments according to the new terms of the second compact, but with the difference going into an interest-earning escrow account that would only be accessible if the landowners signed. In the end, the signing was precipitated in part by accusations that landowners' efforts were all in vain and that they were holding the people of Kwajalein hostage with their own pride. Ongoing infrastructure problems on Ebeye and landowners' advancing age were also factors. But more than anything, the promise of a big payout was hard to decline. The escrow account had built to $32 million by that time, and many of the landowners had debts to repay.

Of course, there were also broader issues affecting the Marshall Islands as a whole: education, health, economy, and climate change. Since direct funding from the United States under the Compact of Free Association II is due to expire in 2023, after which the RMI will need to depend on the money it has invested in its trust fund, money from Kwajalein will be even more crucial to the Marshall Islands in the future. These kinds of pressures made it difficult for elderly landowner elites to continue their resistance, when the very survival of their grandchildren and great-grandchildren was so clearly at stake. Even so, Ri-Kuwajleen also worry that once the compact expires, perhaps the military use agreement for Kwajalein will become meaningless. Referring to the post-compact LUA, landowners wonder, "What good will the wheels [be] if the car that is obsolete cannot run?" (Philippo 2015, 219).

The year 2016—the fabled year when the previous lease was set to expire and true "homecoming" was anticipated—came and went in Kwajalein Atoll with little fanfare. The United States provided $21.2 million in that year, earmarked for Kwajalein landowners, out of the total $79 million from the Compact of Free Association. Separate from this, in 2016 two special funds for Kwajalein Atoll—Ebeye Special Needs and Kwajalein Development—totaled roughly $10 million.[53] But the United States never changed its position, despite the landowners' many years of protest. No literal homecoming took place, either.

Yet also in 2016, in what might be characterized as a true milestone *lejman jūri* moment in Marshallese history, Dr. Hilda Heine was elected the first woman president of the Republic of the Marshall Islands, promising to usher in a new era of change. The newly elected officials under her administration represented a new wave of Marshallese leadership in Kwajalein Atoll as well. David Paul, a young politician from Ebeye, and veteran statesman Alvin Jacklick (former Kwajalein Atoll mayor) defeated incumbents Tony deBrum and Jeban Riklon. With Carl Hacker in place as Tarlang Development Corporation (formerly Kwajalein Atoll Development Authority) director and Imata's son Hirata as mayor, the new alliance between chiefly and commoner power set about implementing several short-term improvements and supporting a $19 million water and sewer revamp funded by US and Australian grant money. They also moved forward on a new housing project for the displaced Mid-Atoll Corridor people and plans to rebuild Ebeye Elementary and Middle School.

The year 2016 also saw renewed dialogue with Kwajalein military leaders after communications had broken down during the stalemate over the Land Use Agreement, but much of this discussion was prompted by a list of grievances caused by new military regulations that had been plaguing the Ebeye community. The most shocking of these was a new rule by the United States National Security Administration (NSA) to begin taking fingerprints and iris scans for all non-Americans transiting to Ebeye through the Kwajalein installation, effectively treating Ebeye as if it were part of the base. As nearly all residents of Ebeye are not US citizens and the only way to take a domestic or international flight is to pass through Kwajalein, this meant that huge numbers of Marshallese Ebeye residents would be subject to this procedure. After the leadership of Kwajalein Atoll lodged their complaint, the US government reneged. Among other positive changes, the military also reviewed its policy of allowing Marshallese workers a mere twenty minutes to get from the airport or their workplace to the dock without facing disciplinary action for trespassing.

These kinds of changes, while generally positive, were minimal and anticlimactic—perhaps temporary—fixes as seen from the eyes of those who believed that 2016 would indeed be the year the United States would finally leave Kwajalein for good and they would be able to return to their land. Mayor Hirata Kabua argued that had the landowners stuck it out until the lease actually expired in 2016, at least they would have had more leverage to ask for what they wanted, like higher payments, health insurance, or a causeway between islands.[54] And meanwhile, walking around Kwajalein today, with its decreasing population of American workers, one cannot help noticing how much vast open space is now available, land where Marshallese people could live if they were allowed to do so. With the removal of the trailer housing that had once accommodated the population boom at the height of the Cold War, large sections of the residential area are now being left for nature to reclaim, with warnings about falling coconuts posted to protect the public. One spacious area has also been fenced off and made into a park where dog owners can let their pets run freely. That even dogs can run free on land that is off-limits to ordinary Marshall Islanders is yet another cruel joke for the Ri-Kuwajleen residents of Ebeye, some of whom feel so alienated from their land that they would rather not set foot on their island anymore. In the words of one young landowner, "That place just creeps me out."

So was all this resistance in vain? The mission of "homecoming" explored in this chapter is a potent narrative of agency and resistance. There are still landowners who vow to return to their land, dissatisfied with the lease or the ongoing relationship with the United States Army. And the success of "homecoming" may be more in the details of how it contributed to a stronger sense of local pride, for it constituted a Ri-Kuwajleen discourse of cultural nationalism created by the landowners to interface with both the RMI and the United States.

This may not have been a pan-Marshallese movement, but it

was rather a resistance movement founded largely upon the shared cultural heritage and identity of Kwajalein atoll genealogies, as well as the surrounding Rālik chain islands and atolls of the Kapin-Meto. While it came from a shared Marshallese experience of ambivalent and unequal relationships with outside forces, "homecoming" was a specific, essentialized version of the Ri-Kuwajleen experience, a "mapping" that concretized a particular representation of Kwajalein Atoll to advance the campaign for land rights and entitlements.

It represented landowners' ability to subvert colonial paradigms and flip the tables of power upside-down. By vowing to go home, the landowners pursued their own true liberation of the atoll by invading their homelands in a brazen reversal of Japanese and American military tactics. Drawing on American paradigms of democratic freedom of speech and civil disobedience, they made their voices heard. In their public narratives, the landowners also reappropriated the "country club versus slum" or "apartheid" binary between Kwajalein and Ebeye islets, so often used by foreign (particularly American) politicians, activists, and journalists to essentialize Kwajalein Atoll. And in reinscribing but transforming these narratives, the landowners simultaneously reasserted themselves as the heroes and survivors—not the victims—of military and nuclear colonialism.

Arguably this was not only an ongoing fight for fair compensation but also the continuation of a "Martial Islands" perpetuation of chiefly arbitrations over land and power, rooted firmly in the past. The context of the Kwajalein landowners' "homecoming" mission to be heard, to be treated fairly, and to gain adequate compensation for the military use of their land was indeed a heroic history on par with the struggles of the people of Bikini, Enewetak, Rongelap, and other nuclear-affected atolls. Practicing civil disobedience, hiring their own lawyers and public relations firms, broadcasting their messages through the media, and utilizing the very tools of democracy and freedom of speech that American "liberation" supposedly bestowed upon them, the Ri-Kuwajleen have been patiently waging their own battle ever since shortly after World War II.

Yet beyond this struggle for the justice bestowed by proper compensation, the thought of returning to the land represented a wish to restore wholeness to the atoll, a nostalgia for a time before any military set foot on the coral of Kwajalein. Utopian as it may seem, this was one of the things that landowners were deeply wishing during the stalemate, when they expected that their land-use agreement would expire and the United States military would leave Kwajalein Atoll in 2016. Fred Pedro encapsulated this sentiment in 2005 when he said:

> To the Kwajalein people, it's a time of calm and peace, because they've accepted the fact that in 2016 they may not have the money but their community will heal. I mean, look, there's a lot of laws and a lot of litigation going on among the Kwajalein landowners as to who's entitled to the money and this portion or that portion of the money. And one of the things they look forward to in 2016 is when they don't have that, and everyone in the community will finally be *real Marshallese* and there will be no more litigation, no more drama. They'll just go back to their land and they'll live on it. (conversation, Majuro, March 14, 2005)

Pedro's point that upon going home to their islands the Kwajalein people would "finally be *real Marshallese*" was quite telling. It suggested that so long as the landowners were compelled to squabble over land for the sake of a foreign power, they were not true Marshallese in a sense, that their lives were incomplete as long as their relationship to home was out of balance. Though there was much idealism in these words and visions, this underlying unbalance was caused by colonialism, war, and militarization, not by anything Marshall Islands had invited upon themselves. This was and is a desire for decolonization, demilitarization, and integrity, and it persists today, stronger than ever.

For many Kwajalein landowners, the resistant spirit of homecoming is alive and well, just as it was in 1982 and in 2003. In fact, no sooner had the new land-use agreement been signed in 2011, the landowners rejoiced about the release of their funds but made a toast to recommit to their campaign for justice: "*2016: History, 2086: Now,*" an outcry that was, not surprisingly, swiftly emblazoned as a slogan on T-shirts (Philippo 2015, 232). The Ri-Kuwajleen were not defeated; they simply shifted their attention forward to the next *jodik*. In another sense, today Marshall Islanders continue their *jodik* by "invading" America to claim their part of the bargain under the Compact of Free Association. As Irooj Michael Kabua described to me, ever since the first Marshallese invasions of Costa Mesa, California, in the 1960s, Marshallese have been colonizing the entirety of the United States.[55] Pursuing education and jobs, Islanders—especially those who cannot return to their own land—continue to migrate abroad at unprecedented rates, where they have set up communities so large that Marshallese politicians actively campaign there for their twenty thousand-plus absentee voters living in Hawai'i, Arkansas, California, Kansas, Missouri, Oregon, and elsewhere. A steady outpouring of residents from Ebeye and Majuro has led to a decrease in population density in the islands, but it has also established a stronger global Marshallese presence and network abroad.

The battles that Marshallese have peacefully and patiently been waging against nuclear abuse and military displacement in their home islands are now amplified by new campaigns abroad and on a global scale. For migrants who have gone to the United States as part of the immigration agreements under the Compact of Free Association, there is now an urgent fight for fair and affordable health care, a dire challenge that has been renewed by the formidable attacks upon national health care and immigration posed by the Trump administration. For Marshallese youth, such as those in the grassroots nonprofit organization Jo-Jikum, the fight is against global sea-level rise that threatens to submerge the Marshall Islands and imperil indigenous people all over the planet. Kathy Jetñil-Kijiner, poet and founder of this group, articulated the plea of young Marshallese activists when she poignantly addressed the United Nations Climate Change Summit in 2014 with a poem dedicated to her daughter. "We deserve to do more than just survive," she said of Marshall Islanders and all potential victims of climate change and environmental devastation. "We deserve to thrive" (Jetñil-Kijiner 2017, 73).

The renewal of the lease and the ensuing inability to return to ancestral homelands beyond 2016 has not been a barrier to Ri-Kuwajleen solidarity; the effect has been quite the opposite. Moreover, their struggles of resistance, like those of the nuclear-affected atolls, set a meaningful example for many Marshallese people everywhere, who were reminded of the value of standing up for what they believed in. And now that losing their islands to climate change is a tangible possibility, more and more people from all over the Marshalls are joining the battle for home. Guided by the deep-time legacies of their ancestors, embedded deep within the sturdy coral foundations of the reef, a new generation of environmental warriors and creative leaders from the Marshall Islands reimagines that home, too, as they navigate to new atollscapes all over the planet.

CHAPTER 9

Atollism

Reconnecting Kwajalein's Past into the Present

THE MANY ATOLLSCAPES OF KWAJALEIN exist all at once, layered one on top of another in an endless competition between the microhistories of coral and the macro-histories of concrete. The life journeys of myriad Islander canoe voyagers and castaways intersect with the agendas of clans and chiefly claims over Land; the spiritual inclinations of missionaries get caught up in the politics of the Church; the migrations of poor Japanese farmers and Okinawan fishermen collide with the expansionist fantasies of Empire; the military draft carries young men from Idaho and Shizuoka into the whirlwinds of War; the technological genius of engineers and scientists draws them to test the Bomb. The nationalistic demands of colonialism and war waging force Koreans to become Japanese, and Japanese to become Americans.[1] Marshallese deep-time histories collapse into the short but catastrophic histories of American nuclear testing. Japanese soldiers are forgotten; Americans are remembered. The childhoods of American and Marshallese youth are swept up into the sparring between Cold War superpowers. All of these travelers wander here, "harvest the flowers," and leave their mark behind.

As our paths cross and we all make sense of each other's lives, we inscribe our own meanings of place as we mediate the distance between past and future. Greg Dening calls these convergences and encounters of life "beach crossings." As he writes, "Let me represent all the crossings that are in even one beach crossing. They are all there—yours, mine—whether we know it or not, whether we like it or not" (Dening 2004, 19). We are all reef organisms, cross-pollinating and building our own meanings upon submerged volcanoes like Kwajalein, and it is through our memory and amnesia that we are both linked and separated.

The American layers of the atoll sit uncomfortably atop Marshallese and Japanese atollscapes, obscuring those layers of coral and concrete from view, allowing Americans to indulge their sense of home (for now) and denying that same experience to others. For those whose land and family are buried (quite literally) beneath that American atollscape, it is not only meaningful but necessary to re-member these histories as a process of healing trauma, not reconciling, but reintegrating the past into the now and here.

Re-membering this fragmented past is the work of children who, like me, grew up in the American community and continue to maintain their vision of the atoll as a hometown despite its transience and restriction as a military base. It is a project fraught with nostalgia shared by long-term American residents who long for the "good old days" before military budget cuts began to downsize the population and heightened security led to sometimes draconian measures. But it is also that commitment to Kwaj as home that calls at least some of us to action in solidarity with Marshall Islanders and others whose lives have been affected by militarism. For others, it is a commitment to Oceania that inspires them to fight against climate change.

Re-membering is the work of the bereaved families of Japanese war dead, who have negotiated for many decades with American officials to be allowed access to the base at Kwajalein so that they can pray for the souls of soldiers. Fighting against the strong currents of American victory and Japanese defeat, they journey back to the atoll in hopes of coming to terms with their loss and recuperating the heroic memories of a generation of men. Struggling against the double marginalization of their histories by both America and Japan, the families of Korean laborers have also been making their own pilgrimages back to the Marshall Islands in recent years in their quest for justice and reconciliation.

Most importantly, re-membering is also the resistance work of the Marshallese people who grew up in and around Kwajalein but whose homelands have been taken away. Enduring the "anxious anticipation"[2] of life on Ebeye and other islets that lie in the shadows of radars, the dislocated Ri-Kuwajleen try to maintain the memory of their genealogical roots as they fight to reinscribe their mappings of land and sea in opposition to relentless erasure. Other Marshall Islanders who migrated from other atolls to escape from the battles of the war or the "poison" of radiation[3] also keep their stories alive by passing them on to their children and grandchildren. And today, as people face the possibility that someday their homelands will be submerged by the sea, re-membering is an essential form of recalibration and retooling knowledge for future generations.

Here I present some re-memberings of Kwajalein's atollscapes. Watch how the coral grows back, reclaiming the concrete and breaking through into the sunlight, making the atoll whole again.

The Fragrance of Home: Re-membering Kwaj

Walking along Kwajalein lagoon one night on my way back from Ebeye, I see a group of people waving at me. They are seated in lounge chairs in someone's backyard, with tiki torches, a piñata strung between two palm trees, and pink flamingoes planted in the ground around them. Duran-Duran's "Ordinary World" plays in the background from an iPod. "Wanna join us?" my friend Lisa calls out.

I join this circle of single men and women in their thirties, most of whom are strangers to me, and it is as if I have just stepped into small-town America. It has been twenty-five years since I lived on Kwajalein and I have few friends I remember here. They are talking about the latest local basketball scores, what's on TV, an upcoming honeymoon to Portugal, how the daily boat up to the mission control room on Meck Island is way too early. One man in an ARMY T-shirt is boasting about how he's finally leaving "the rock" because of a disagreement with his boss. "Can't wait to get off this island!" The others in the group don't believe him: "You know you'll be back; no one stays away from this place for long!"

Lisa passes me a drink and asks, "What's it like on Ebeye this time of night? I've never been there after dark; hell I've almost never even been there during the day!"

A slightly older bachelor with a barbell mustache and a frayed red T-shirt interrupts her and gives me a firm handshake that hurts. "Hi, I'm Dan," he says as he seats himself down beside me. After I explain who I am, he winks and says in a heavy drawl, "No kiddin'—you're a Kwaj Kid just like me!"

Squinting at the moonlit lagoon, he takes a deep breath and says, "Bet you love this place, dontcha? I mean, that water, the sound of these palm fronds swishing around up above us. And you know that's not all of it, though." He turns away from the crowd and softens his voice.

"Kwaj is a smell, right? You know what I mean? It's a smell that gets under your skin and then you can never forget it. It's like this perfume that puts you to bed at night. It's this 'alone' kinda thing, just between you and the island. You feel it in your bones. And so many of these guys who come out here to Kwaj, they don't get it. They just come and go. Have little parties like this one, talk about the States all the time. . . . But if you grow up here and you live here for a long time, and you really love these islands, you feel connected to it and you know you belong here. It's something you can't describe in words. I feel like I have to protect this place, not for America but for the island itself. It's so hard to explain.

"I guess the smell here is like home. It's a peaceful fragrance of these flowers at night, of the lagoon, of the wind. It's the smell of the bakery down by the dry cleaners, the smell of the jet fuel when the planes take off. But it's also something else, something that doesn't have a name. Something only people who really grow up here know.

"Oh, if you could bottle up this smell somehow and you could tell all those people out there what it's about, they'd understand Kwaj once and for all. They'd get that it's not all about missile testing and the army and all that. It's about feeling connected to this place." He goes silent for a moment and squints again at the horizon, out at the flashing radar lights at the other end of the island.

"You know something, it'd be a really horrible thing if I couldn't ever come back here again and again like I do. With the war so many years ago, it's just strange how we came out here in the first place, about all those Japanese people who died out here. Every time I go down to one of those Japanese ships when I scuba dive, I think of what happened. And it's weird how when I was a kid, the kids of the chief from Ebeye would come over to my house and eat sandwiches with us for lunch. But that's Kwaj. For good or for bad, this place is my home, and I share it with these other people, and I don't know what it is, but it's that feeling I get like the island needs me here or something . . .

"A lot of Americans out here don't 'get' that. They just think about the money and do their jobs. The old-timers, like those Hawaiian guys who have been out here for ages, they understand. You know how it is—as a Kwaj Kid I gotta be out here, gotta do my part so no one else comes and messes it up. I love this place and so I wanna take care of it somehow. I feel like that's my real job."

Bereavement: Re-membering Family

Several months after Dan talked with me about the atollscape of home, I join the bereaved families of the Japanese war dead for the first time

Atollism: Reconnecting Kwajalein's Past into the Present 237

on a pilgrimage to Kwajalein to learn about the atollscapes they see. Flying with them from Tokyo back to Kwajalein, I participate in their memorial ceremonies in October 2005, a pilgrimage I will take with them for many years after that.

The bereaved families carry wreaths, flowers, bottles of *sake*, cartons of cigarettes, and photographs with them as we travel by catamaran across the lagoon to the Japanese Cemetery on Roi-Namur. As we cross the clear azure waters, three women throw flowers onto the water and call out to their fathers, whose ships lie on the bottom of the sea. One of them is Yukiko, a youthful woman in her late sixties. Dabbing at her grief-swollen eyes, she takes out a framed photo and shows it to me. It is of a man in a white navy uniform. His skin is darkly tanned, and his eyes stare into the camera with a faint expression of loneliness. His pants are spattered with specks of dark paint, his arms folded behind his back. In the background are vines, like the shrubbery along the reef of Kwajalein. "That's him," she says, tears brimming up. "Before he was drafted into the navy he worked for a paper mill. His name was Kametarō, but everyone called him Kame-chan for short. He was so popular in our town, always took care of people." She strokes her father's face in the photo lovingly and smiles.

"He used to ride me down to the beach on the handlebars of his bicycle when I was a little girl. When we went to drop him off at Yokosuka harbor in 1941, we went there with my mother, my sister, and our dog Meri. I was just six years old. The other people were shouting *Banzai! Banzai!* ("long life") to the emperor, but my family just stood there quietly and watched him sail away."

She points to the north. "They tell me his ship sank somewhere right over there."

"The first time I came here to this atoll, I felt something so warm and safe enveloping me," she says, whispering in a gentle voice. "I felt the warm breeze on my cheeks, the sunshine. The air smelled so sweet. I looked out to the open ocean and saw those waves, tasted the salt on my lips. It felt so familiar, so comforting, like I had been here before even though I hadn't. It felt like my hometown, my *furusato*. I mean, it *is* like home to me. I really feel that way, and I've never even lived here."

The next day we ride a bus to the end of the main islet of Kwajalein, passing the big missile-tracking radars and antennas, passing where I used to ride my bicycle with my father sometimes. We reach the memorial, which is labeled "Japanese Cemetery." For these families, however, the remains of the nearly seven thousand Japanese soldiers and sailors who died in Operation Flintlock are in various places on different islands, and in the sunken ships at the bottom of the lagoon. Only some of the remains have been repatriated to Japan. For the survivors of these men, the whole island is a cemetery.

The families begin their ceremony by singing the Japanese national anthem and a series of songs like "Umi Yukaba" (If I go away to sea) and "Sayonara, Yashi no Shima" (Goodbye, island of palms), both melancholic melodies with lyrics about leaving home and never returning. Many of the mourners cry as they sing together, facing the memorial as if they were looking into the faces of the lost soldiers.

This is followed by a long Buddhist chant led by Izumi-san, a Buddhist priest whose father died on the *Kōei Maru* when it was sunk near Kwajalein harbor. After she completes a small prayer and lights more incense, the other twenty bereaved individuals come up one by one, entering the small white picket fence, passing through the *torii* gate, and approaching the granite memorial as if it were a gravestone.

"I just can't keep myself from crying every time I come here and think about my brother Jōji," eighty-year-old Ayako explains to me after the ceremony is over. "Ah, my life has been so unlucky!" she chuckles dryly.

She tells me about her elder brother, how clever he was and how much she had looked up to him. From her purse, she produces a black-and-white photo of a young man wearing a three-piece suit, shot dramatically with a shadow behind him, like a portrait of Clark Gable, Cary Grant, or another movie star of the day.

"This was taken in Hollywood, can't you tell?" Ayako boasts. "Jōji went by 'George' in the States. He was born there because our parents were living in America at the time, and we had many relatives who had migrated to the States, but they decided to move back. When he was a teenager he moved to America by himself and he went to high school, Belmont High School in Los Angeles. Then he worked for awhile in the Olympic Hotel in Los Angeles, where a lot of important Japanese navy officers used to stay."

She tells me how when war seemed inevitable between the United States and Japan, Ayako's mother wanted George to return to Hiroshima so badly that she feigned illness and sent a telegram telling him to come back home urgently. He rushed back, bringing with him his golf clubs and other *accoutrements* of American luxury. He also came bearing presents for Ayako and his younger brother. But when he discovered that his mother was not ill he insisted on returning to America, where he felt his real home was.

"I remember we had a conversation that time. He was having some trouble with his girlfriend and didn't know how things were going to go with the war. I was just getting married to my husband. Our lives were changing and so much was so unpredictable, but he said to me, 'We're going to get through this together. *Ganbarō ne*—Let's be strong . . .'

"And those are the words that ring through my head each time I think about Kwajalein and the *gyokusai* that happened here," she says, wiping her eyes.

"After the war broke out, George had to leave America again on the last ship back to Japan, and then they drafted him immediately and shipped him out to Singapore. We barely had a chance to see him again. His English was fluent, so the navy needed him for communications. They sent him to Kwajalein in 1943. It was only supposed to be a half-year's assignment. He sent letters to us about how, wherever he was, he was so happy that he got to go fishing all day and then work at night. We had no idea where it was, because he couldn't tell us, but it sounded like a nice place.

"He was supposed to be transferred out of the atoll in March 1943, but the Americans invaded in January and February. And, well . . ." She pauses awhile and sighs.

"Our family didn't hear anything after that. But meanwhile in 1945 Hiroshima was bombed. Our town was far enough away that I was okay, but my husband was in the city that day working, and that is how I lost him . . .

"After my husband died I kept hoping that somehow we would hear something from Jōji, but in 1946 we got the bad news that he had been killed at Kwajalein. That's why I say my life is so unlucky, you see.

"Every time I come here to Kwajalein Atoll, I remember what Jōji said to me and I feel like he is right here with me. I feel like we're back together again."

Above the red *torii* shrine gate of the memorial, a white *kear* bird dances in the sunlight. "Maybe that's him there now," Ayako says.

Kapijukenen: Re-membering Marshallese Roots

Bubu has beautiful hands. I call her Bubu these days because she considers me to be one of her many grandchildren, and she is no doubt my Marshallese grandmother and always has been. Neitari is her actual name, and she used to be my family's housekeeper on Kwajalein in the 1970s, before the demonstrations, before the Marshall Islands became an independent nation, before we moved back to New Jersey and I left my childhood home. Her hands are wrinkled and her fingers are stiff with arthritis, but they are beautiful, young, and swift as she sits most of the day in her little house on Ebeye, weaving baskets and necklaces to sell. When my brother and I were little, she used to weave us an Easter basket every year.

Bubu sits cross-legged in the doorway of her small bungalow, deep within the maze of the brightly painted plywood buildings of Ebeye. Her house is a shed made out of spare wood, and the ceiling is made out of metal signs. One of them says WORK AREA: SPEED LIMIT 30. Surrounded by some of her teenage granddaughters, who practice their dance moves in step with hip-hop music, and her small grandsons, who kick up coral pebbles as they scurry around her small yard, Bubu patiently braids many fine strands of dried, pounded pandanus and palm fronds into an intricate pattern.[4]

"*Enana*—that's not good!" she giggles and scolds one of her grandsons as he tries to climb onto my head.

Bubu picks up one small cowry shell, pierces a small hole in it with an ice pick, and threads it into the weave of fibers. She repeats this with more cowries, again and again, making a long string of shiny white shells. She pulls the necklace tight, holding the weave together firmly with her callused thumb.

"Ah, now at school you're studying about old times here in the Marshalls, *emman, emman*—good, good," she says to me, nodding her head and flashing her toothless grin.

"I'll tell you a story of my island—about old times in the Marshall Islands," she says.

"Yes, a long, long time ago, there was a man named Kaibua from Arno Atoll who went to Mejit Island, and he fought and became the *irooj*. He met a woman named Lepat and they had two sons. One of those sons, the older one, got chosen to become the next *irooj*, without any fight, so the younger one got jealous and he shot himself."

She hesitates a moment and squints her eyes as she pulls the next shell into the necklace. "Ah, right, I forgot. See, the reason there was a gun there on Mejit was because some British people came on a ship and they gave a gun to Kaibua, and that's how the son shot himself. The son didn't die of the gunshot but he got a bad infection and later he died, but somehow we still ended up with two *irooj* on Mejit."

Bubu's story continues. She lists one name after another, one atoll and islet after another. Even her grandchildren cannot keep track of the vast and circuitous network of people and places she weaves together and re-members into the present.

"And then I was born," she says.

At this point I am humbled to realize that the long narrative of people and places Bubu is reciting is in fact the genealogy of her own lineage. I am surprised to learn for the first time that she is from an *irooj* family (indeed, a chiefly "daughter").

"I was one of twelve children, and I was born at the house of Kabua Kabua, at the place of the Kwajalein people at Jaluit Atoll. I wasn't born on Mejit, but my family came from there. Even before I married my husband, our families arranged our marriage, because we were both from the two different *irooj* families of Mejit.

"I remember before the war, back in those days there were plenty of Japanese then. I went to Japanese school. We learned to read and write *hiragana.* Every day we had to sing the Japanese national anthem. I still remember it."

"Sing it for us, Bubu," her granddaughter Laan says.

"Okay. I will now sing the song of the government of Japan, the song the Japanese out here used to sing." She looks up as some others gather around her small shack.

Bubu's face suddenly gets very solemn. She straightens her posture and puts down the necklace for a moment. She knits her eyebrows and squints her eyes and begins to sing:

> Oh say can you see
> by the dawn's early light
> what so proudly we hailed
> at the twilight's last gleaming.
> Whose broad stripes and bright stars . . .

"Hah?" She says, looking confused. "Am I singing the wrong song?"

She laughs hysterically with everyone as she realizes her mistake: "I always get them mixed up, you know!"

After the laughter has subsided, she looks off into the distance as she solemnly recites "Kimigayo," the Japanese national anthem, almost flawlessly. Her grandchildren watch in awe as this unfamiliar language comes from Bubu's mouth.

She continues her story: "All those times with Japanese before the war. I went to school at the Japanese school and I met many Japanese businessmen and teachers. In school, they taught us many things. We learned about *sakura.* Have you ever seen the cherry blossoms?

"When the soldiers came before the war things changed a lot. It got really strict and they beat some people sometimes if they didn't follow the rules. Those soldiers could be scary, but also there were plenty of young ones, many nice ones too. We went to other islands and we sang songs and did dances for the soldiers sometimes as a class, to help cheer them up because the teachers said they were homesick all the time.

"One day an American airplane came in really low over our schoolhouse all of a sudden and there was a machine gun sound, *ta-ta-ta-ta-ta-ta-ta!!*" Her eyes grow fierce.

"We went running for cover and our teacher told us to run home. And I remember I ran and ran to my mother because I was so scared. But there was this one girl, and she ran out in the other direction and a bullet hit her, and she died. That was so, so sad.

"My family has land rights in many places," she says. "So we went to Likiep Atoll to get away from the fighting. It was more peaceful there.

"Later, after the war I went back to my land at Jaluit and I lived there for awhile before I married my husband. He was a pastor, so we traveled together to many other islands for his church work, like Rong-Rong in Majuro Atoll, and other places—and then we came here to Kwajalein Atoll, to my mother's grandfather's land on Ero islet. It was such a nice place—good food, many coconut crabs, breadfruit . . . fish in the lagoon, good weather.

"One day the Americans came and they told us we had to move to Ebeye because they wanted to test the missiles and Ero and those other islands were not good to stay on anymore. They told us they would take care of us, and Ebeye was where my husband would work at the church, so we packed our things and we left from my family's land to this place here, to this land on Ebeye."

She sweeps some of the coral gravel out of her doorway and picks up one of her baby grandchildren and puts him on her lap. She tightens the small shells on the necklace she is making as the little boy grabs at her skirt.

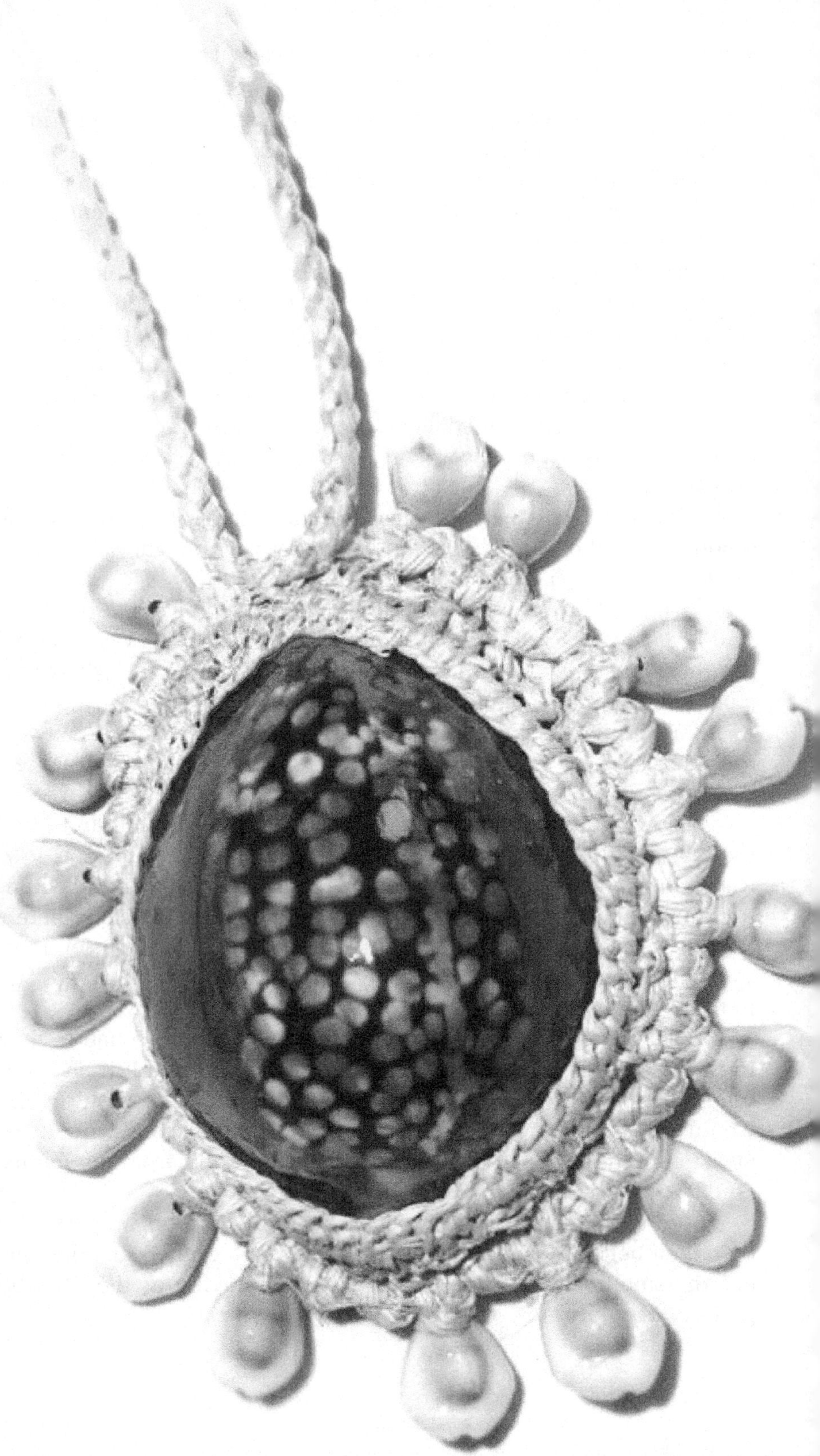

"The land where we live here on Ebeye is not really my place," she says. "Not like the land where I used to live—those places were where my family came from. In this place, I am so lucky because I have all my grandchildren with me, but it's so hot here on Ebeye. Too many people. Many flies. No good water. No fresh food. No trees.

"But Kwajalein is so close. I went there sometimes with my cousin back in the 1970s because she said maybe I could get some work to help my family back on Ebeye. And that's when I met your family and I met you," she laughs, covering her mouth. "I remember how small you used to be!"

Bubu's life between islands and atolls is a bit like the necklaces she makes: woven together intricately. Connecting and re-membering many atollscapes together, Bubu is aware of a Marshallese heritage of coral and concrete that is grounded in the past and alive in the present. Her genealogy stretches from deep time into the present, connecting one chief to another chief, one island to another island, one ancestor to another. But contradictory as it all is, and however painful, that genealogical story also involves Japanese and other "outsiders," including me.

"*Itok*—come here," she says, reaching out with both hands to place the necklace around my neck and give me a hug. "Now you know *our* story."[5]

Across the Waters

Despite nightmares that plague her of climate change and other crises that threaten to uproot the soul of her land and people, poet Kathy Jetñil-Kijiner is steadfast in her dreaming. Finding inspiration in Kwajalein's legendary sacred flowering *utilomar* tree, whose "magical white petals fell into the water and bloomed into flying fish," she writes:

> . . . I'd rather dream
> I'd rather imagine our
> next generation
> their voices turning the tides
> how our underground reservoir will drink in their chants
> how they will speak shark songs and fluent fish
> how they
> will leap

> petal-soft
> beautiful
> unafraid
> into the water
> before blossoming
> to fly
>
> —Kathy Jetñil-Kijiner[6]

Having journeyed through many re-memberings of the atollscapes of Kwajalein and told some of the multiple truths I discovered there, I stand for a moment, watching the turbulent white froth of the waters that pass between lagoon and ocean across the reef. The ocean is so rough that it looks impossible to cross to the next islet, even though at low tide it takes less than an hour to walk the shallow passage along the atoll. The light of the golden sunset hits the salt spray of the ocean, and I am reminded of how all these islands that seem so separate are all really connected.

The violent surf that roars between these islands is like the traumas of war, dislocation, and nuclear weaponry. In the same way these turbulent waters make it hard to see the links between islands, so does trauma create a rupture in the continuity of our lives. Trauma severs the links between our present and past, leaving us either to forget or to try and pick up the pieces. Our dismembered histories are like the islets of an atoll that seem separate but are really connected by reefs hidden in the shallow froth of the violent waves that crash between them. Making sense of our small and reef-like lives amidst this turbulence, we remember and bridge the disparate histories of the atoll together again into a coherent whole.

Our lives that converge upon this atoll are so much like the lives of coral. Like tiny coral polyps, each and every one of us is helpless against the powerful ocean currents that have swept us here, and yet we cling so tightly to the solidity of this atoll—this ancient mountain that once towered high—for one reason or another, and many call it home. Our tiny histories converge into the meta-histories of Oceania, Japan, and America as they play out at Kwajalein—the middle of Now-Here—part and parcel of what makes our world go around.

Those big histories look so permanent, hard as concrete. But they crack over time, and the coral breaks through again and grows on top in new directions. At least metaphorically. In the literal sense, the

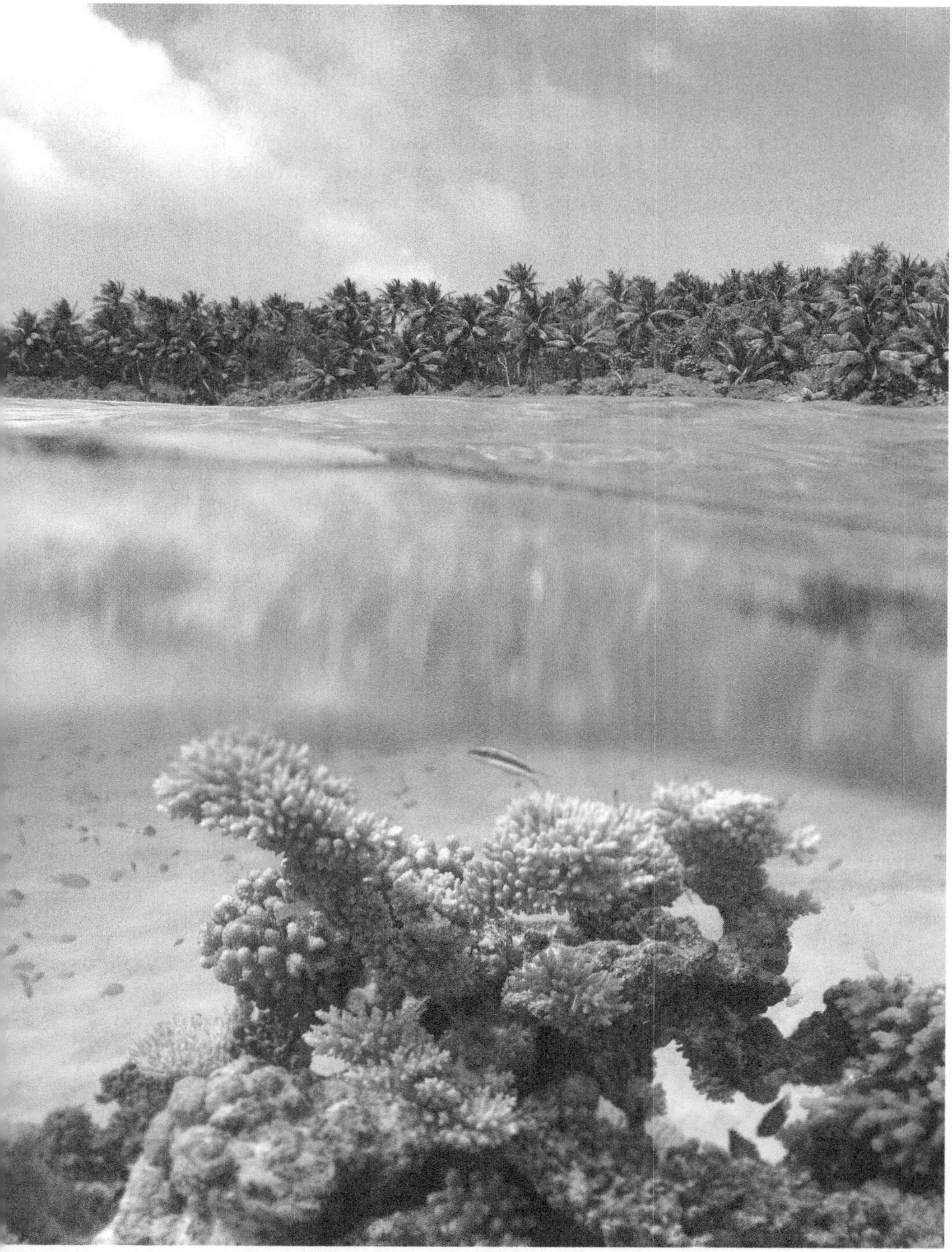

corals of our world are threatened as the oceans warm and acidify, and the turmoil of climate change challenges the very existence of low-lying places like the Marshall Islands. But like the trillions of coral microorganisms that bravely navigated the currents to create these reefs, coral's spirit of resilience continues to spread further and "blossom" with the Marshallese people, navigating onward to build new atolls of knowledge, culture, history, and hope wherever they settle.

Notes

Prelude

1   See D'Arcy (2006), who describes how the ocean is just as important as land for Pacific Islanders and how centrally these sea routes figured in the linkages between island societies.
2   See Katerina Teaiwa's work (2015) about multiple Pacific genealogies between islands across the sea, particularly in displaced Islander communities such as those of the Banaban people of Kiribati, who have lived for decades in exile on the island of Rabi in Fiji.
3   To ensure recognition and consistency throughout this book, I have chosen to refer to the atoll in most instances with its international and American spelling of "Kwajalein," as this has also been used widely by Marshall Islanders until relatively recently. Whenever I use the name "Kwaj," however, I am referring explicitly to the American settlement on the main islet of the atoll.
4   July 2016 population estimate from the CIA World Factbook, https://www.cia.gov, accessed December 1, 2016. This figure includes the population of more than twenty thousand Marshall Islands citizens residing in the United States.
5   Though most of the Marshallese population is located on Majuro or Ebeye, most of the Marshall Islands today are inhabited, except for places where lack of resources or residual radiation from American nuclear testing (such as at Bikini, Enewetak, and Rongelap Atolls) and military activity (several islands in Kwajalein Atoll) have made it impossible or unfavorable to live. Large communities of Marshall Islanders also live in the United States, where they have been able to freely settle and work under immigration agreements laid out in the Compact of Free Association between the US and the RMI.
6   Aside from Austronesian linguistic linkages, this cultural complex has been characterized by its "dentate-stamped" Lapita pottery; its domestication of

pigs, dogs, and chickens; its horticultural practices of carrying seedlings and cuttings on long canoe voyages; and the effective exploitation of marine environments in general.

7   Palau, the Mariana Islands, and other parts of western Micronesia were likely settled directly from Southeast Asia between 3,500 to 4,500 years ago (Rainbird 2004, 99), while the early settlers of the Marshall Islands continued to branch out across Micronesia from east to west, reaching into the Caroline Islands and eventually meeting with the other groups that had been expanding from the other direction.

8   German, Japanese, and American authorities all characteristically sought out alliances with chiefly authorities of different atolls as a way of obtaining influence over the local population. There was also much "mixing" between German/Portuguese and Marshallese, especially at Likiep Atoll, where traders Jose deBrum and Adolf Capelle started their own copra plantation in the late 1800s.

9   This is based on conversations with Hatfield Lemae in May 2005 and other elders who grew up in Jebwad.

10 As I describe elsewhere, the atoll has played a large role in weapons testing that began in the 1940s and the Cold War, but more recently in space surveillance and private space exploration ventures as well. Testing is commanded from Kwajalein islet and monitored throughout the atoll, but launch activity is centered around Meck (Meik) islet. See Wilkes (1991), who provides a dated but thorough overview of most of the Kwajalein testing facilities.

11 Though the American population of the Kwajalein installation was about two thousand when I began this research, it is in flux and rapidly declining at the time of this research as the army downsizes the installation to accommodate budget cuts and improvements in technology that reduce the number of people needed to support the testing operations.

12 The Kwajalein school system has changed since I was a child, and now it welcomes a small number of rigorously selected "Ri-Katak" Marshallese students in each grade, who commute to the American schools from Ebeye every day. Over the past several years the schools have also implemented a curriculum whereby students are required to study a semester's worth of history, geography, and "culture" of the Marshall Islands.

13 Named after the Marshallese expression eṃṃan (good), but usually pronounced "ee-mon" by Americans.

14 Former Kwaj Kid Robert Barclay writes about some of this mischief in his novel Meḷaḷ (2002), which he has mentioned is based on some of his own misadventures around the atoll.

15 See Dvorak 2004.

16 Camacho's book was also translated into Japanese by Nishimura Akira (Camacho 2016), and it is already generating interest in Japan by helping to nuance and complicate Japanese histories of empire and war in Saipan and

neighboring Guam, two territories that straddle the divide between Japanese and American empires and regimes of memory.

17 When speaking to Marshallese audiences, I found that they were most interested in learning about the Japanese past, as they were already familiar with most Marshallese and American viewpoints. In Japan, however, I noticed that there was such a widespread lack of *any* awareness of this wartime and prewar history that my primary emphasis was on Japanese encounters with Islanders.

Chapter 1: Coral and Concrete

1 In Jones (2007, 25).
2 This story is described in detail and analyzed thoroughly in Carucci's study of Ri-Kuwajleen places of cultural significance (1997a), but I asked a number of Ri-Kuwajleen elders and other Marshallese historians to elaborate further on this story. In this chapter I draw partly from conversations I had about coral and atolls with Irooj Michael Mañini Kabua, Ato Ḷañkio, Tarmwilliñ Rowadik, Kirong Sam, Pitoñ Jipile, and Manke Konol during the course of my research at Kwajalein.
3 A song about gathering *utilomar* has become the Kwajalein Atoll theme.
4 Carucci lists many variations of this story, and I heard other interpretations myself in my own research. Some interlocutors suggested that there were two "trees," one on land and another in the sea near Āne-bouj where the flying fish swirled around so abundantly in the sea that they looked like a fountain or a tree on the water. Indeed, this very place today is filled with flying fish. In 2004 the Marshallese Cultural Society ceremonially planted an *utilomar* tree at the southeastern edge of the Kwajalein golf course to honor this history.
5 Nakazawa Shinichi, "Sango, 'Yasei no Kagaku' to Deau" (Coral: Encountering *Les Sciences Sauvages*), Lecture at Keio University, Tokyo, November 29, 2015. Nakazawa, inspired by his mentor Claude Lévi-Strauss, heads the Institut pour la Science Sauvage at Meiji University.
6 Japanese personal narratives of war and the colonial era in the Marshall Islands are not easily obtained in the archives. I have obtained a number of self-published sources (such as Hayashi 1964, Kawazoe 1990, Kofukada 2000, Koshikawa 1992, or Suzuki et al. 1997) directly from survivors or bereaved families themselves. Aside from the material I did find in war archives, I also referred to a diary of a naval officer (Yui 1943) and the correspondence of three other Japanese soldiers and civilians who were killed at Kwajalein (Satō 1942, Masuda 1943, and Ueta 1943).
7 Miriam Kahn argues that these space/place arguments were not taken seriously in anthropology until relatively recently, and that in some respects the idea of politically produced discursive space has only served to widen the

age-old dualism in anthropology between "insiders" and "outsiders" (Kahn 2000, 8).

8   See, for example, editorials in *The Marshall Islands Journal* (February to September 2007), which promoted Marshallese out-migration to Guam to take advantage of the military buildup there.

9   Of course, there is also coral bleaching, and all that it implies. Steve Jones (2007) uses his own coral metaphor to tell the history of Oceania—except in his scientific version, coral is the canary in the coal mine that heralds looming environmental disasters awaiting the planet.

10   See, for instance, Halbwachs and Coser (1992), who look at the social aspects of collective memory in anthropology. Curthoys and Docker also address collective memory in historical context when they discuss "history wars" between different nations and groups, such as Americans and Japanese in relation to the Smithsonian Institution's planned exhibit on the Hiroshima bombing (2005, 221–224).

11   For more on the interpretation of "chiefs" in a Marshallese context—not only Marshallese *irooj* but Americans and Japanese as "chiefs"—see Walsh 2003.

12   *Rashōmon* is a murder mystery told in the form of a multilayered narrative, in which a number of people recollect their self-serving testimonies of what happened.

13   Nero writes that the Palauan idea of *elechar* (which roughly translates as "the present") is rather like a point that exists within a larger sphere of *cherechar* (the "past/future" or "forever") (Nero 1987, 33).

14   An offshoot of this project (Dvorak 2008) was published in a special issue of the *Contemporary Pacific* titled "Re-Membering Oceanic Masculinities." In that volume, "re-membering" took on an additional meaning of restoring agency to colonized people, given the colonial histories by which Pacific Islanders have been "emasculated" (Tengan 2008a) and imagined as helpless victims.

15   This became *Radikaru Ōraru Historī* (Radical oral history), Hokari's first book, in Japanese, which was published posthumously after his struggle with lymphoma (Hokari 2004).

Chapter 2: Mapping "the Martial Islands

1   Wood 1992, 7.

2   For instance, Jehovah's Witnesses, Mormons, Seventh-day Adventists, and Baha'i missionary groups have all attracted a large following throughout many of the atolls in the Marshall Islands.

3   For more on Christianity in Micronesia see, for example, Hezel's valuable histories of the region (1983, 1995). The book *Island of Angels* (2005), by Elden Buck, a former Kwajalein and Ebeye resident, is a rigorous study of the role and significance of the Protestant Church in Kosrae, with some mention

also of its history in the Marshall Islands. Written compassionately in both Kosraean and English, Buck's work is also a fine example of scholarship that engages multiply nuanced cultural and genealogical contexts.

4 See Dvorak 2004 and Dvorak 2016, where I look more closely at the "mission" being deployed in the present-day American context.

5 While ocean space and navigational knowledge has always been of tremendous importance to the Islanders who colonized Oceania, as D'Arcy (2006) points out, navigation is situated in a much broader context of identity and environment. It is not merely a cartographic methodology, but rather a means of linking space and time between islands and people, a literally fluid continuity.

6 Japan did run trading routes through these southern Micronesian islands, and eventually the Imperial Navy captured Tarawa and Nauru during the Pacific War, but its engagement was minimal compared to the assimilation and expansion policies undertaken in the Nanyō Guntō. Interestingly, however, Nanyō Bōeki Kaisha (NBK)—the main trading company that developed the region before the war—still operates throughout Oceania, and its Tokyo headquarters have served as the honorary embassy for the Republic of Kiribati to Japan.

7 See also Diaz 2002 and Hokuwhitu 2004 for perspectives on the centrality of sport in empire and the construction of colonized masculinities in the "militarized American Pacific Islands" and Aotearoa–New Zealand, respectively.

8 南洋, 東洋, and 西洋, respectively. *Hoppō,* the term used to denote "the North," had similar connotations in relation to Sakhalin, known in Japanese as Karafuto, as well as other northern territories in Asia.

9 Yūshūkan, the war memorial museum at the Yasukuni War Shrine in Tokyo, features this narrative prominently as justification for Japanese imperialism. It puts forth the view that Japan's actions throughout Asia and Oceania were defensive moves to secure the "East" (and eventually also the "South") against the threat of European and American colonization. This rhetoric, while true in some respects, belies the reality that Japan was also positioning itself at the political, cultural, racial, and economic pinnacle of its own imperial project, and that violence and aggression were often used to achieve this mission.

10 Nakajima Hiroshi, conversation with the author, Dunedin, December 12, 2006.

11 One of these books, for example, depicts "Marshallese" hunting birds by using boomerangs.

12 I viewed this original manuscript from 1885 archived at the Diplomatic Records Office of the Japanese Ministry of Foreign Affairs in Tokyo in 2005 and was able to reproduce some of these images from the collection *Nanyō Tanken Zukai* (Sketches from a South Seas expedition) with funding from the Marshallese Cultural Center on Kwajalein. According to Peattie (1988, 322),

it was presumed that these original materials were destroyed in the Great Earthquake of 1923 until they were unearthed in 1983.
13 Literally *ukiyo-e* were "pictures from the floating world," a genre of art started in the seventeenth century that included paintings and woodcuts depicting fanciful and caricatured landscapes and people.
14 There are some exceptions to this, such as the massive study conducted by the Nanyō Guntō Board of Education, *Nanyō Guntō Kyōiku-shi* (1938), which goes into detail about each of the schools in the Marshall Islands, atoll by atoll.
15 See the collected work of Hijikata (1993) and Nakajima (2001) in Japanese, and the translated work of Yanaihara (1939).
16 Yamaguchi Yōji suggested that the small Japanese and Okinawan settler population, along with Japan's essentializing view of Micronesia as a whole under the rubric of "Nanyō Guntō," were factors that contributed to the scarcity of sources about the Marshalls in particular (conversation on October 12, 2007, Tokyo).
17 Although American authorities accused Japan of violating its pledge to the League of Nations not to fortify its territories in Micronesia, Peattie (1988, 254) and many other scholars argue that naval authorities in both the US and Japan were certain that there would be a major military conflict between the two countries, even several years before the Pearl Harbor attack, and that Japan's desire to fortify its front lines in the late 1930s was understandable. Indeed, around 1939 there was a radical shift in Japan's approach toward Micronesia from a progressive civil administration and economic development showcase to one of concerted militarization and fortification. This traumatized and upset many Islanders who were forced into hard labor, and it is important to note that it also uprooted and shocked many Japanese and Okinawan settlers in the region, who were startled by the influx of military-minded officials (conversation with Yamaguchi Yōji, October 12, 2007, Tokyo).
18 The term "Nanyō" is rarely ever used nowadays in contemporary Japan except by conservative politicians or economists to refer to the Pacific Islands. This word no longer appears on contemporary maps, and it carries with it the baggage of prewar imperialism and militarism. Most people avoid using this word unless in historical context.
19 It is often these former campaigns with which many people in the southern Pacific and Australia are most familiar, but many amphibious US Marine units were deployed to the Central Pacific in 1943 to make a more direct assault through Micronesia. White and Lindstrom (White and Lindstrom 1989; Lindstrom and White 1990; and Lindstrom 2001) deal more closely with the broader "Pacific theater," especially in terms of how the war unfolded in different parts of Melanesia.
20 The previous Japanese civil administration and military command had (as

seen in the previous section) used *katakana* phonetics to represent the names of islets in the atoll, which also effectively Japanized indigenous namings. Some islands were also renamed with completely Japanese names. Like many islands in Kwajalein and throughout Micronesia that have such competing histories, these multiple names are still sometimes used interchangeably today.

21 See Wypijewski 2000.
22 The shape of Kwajalein islet itself has even been used as a logo that symbolizes the carefree and comfortable lifestyle Americans enjoy on Kwajalein. It is immediately recognizable to American residents of "Kwaj" and is emblazoned on postcards, stationery, golf visors, mugs, pendants, and T-shirts.
23 This is even more apparent in the highly detailed logistics maps of the island today, on which every single structure and device is numbered and inventoried.
24 Some Marshallese intellectuals and politicians have resurrected the term "Lolle Laplap" as a name for describing the precolonial Marshall Islands as a whole and promoting indigenous issues.
25 Given that this land is now gravely threatened by sea level rise, these questions of identity, power, and heritage are of extreme concern in unprecedented ways.
26 Neijon Edwards, conversation with the author, Honolulu, March 24, 2016.
27 Taking into account David M. Schneider's feminist critique of the ways Euro-American models of kinship have been taken for granted in canonical ethnography (1984), I should point out that Marshallese "traditional" culture has been engendered by much of the early exploration literature and postwar anthropological research in Micronesia. There is much debate about the naming and conceptualization of kin groups, not only among anthropologists, but within Marshallese "traditional rights" discourse as well (see Kabua 2005).
28 Sometimes this term is even used in a spiritual sense, by Marshallese (or even Americans and other non-Marshallese) who feel a strong affinity with Kwajalein Atoll or Kwajalein islet in general. For the purposes of this argument, however, I am focusing on this term as it is used politically to identify one's heritage in specific relation to Kwajalein Atoll.
29 Āne-Eḷḷap-Kan, often known as Carlos, is the only one of these islands where a Marshallese community was allowed to reside in the midst of antennas and testing facilities. A plant that powered radars and also provided electricity and running water to the community there was decommissioned in 2012, leaving residents who had enjoyed these conveniences to radically adjust to an outer island lifestyle.
30 Enewetak (Āne-wetak in Marshallese) in Kwajalein is a small islet, not to be confused with Enewetak Atoll, which is pronounced differently in Marshallese and located far to the northwest of Kwajalein. It was at this atoll,

not in Kwajalein, where nuclear weapons were tested in the 1940s and 1950s.
31 In Japanese, the equivalent term here, *jinushi*, has yet another connotation of literally being a "landlord."
32 See also Crocombe 1987 for more about land tenure in Oceania.
33 From conversation on October 9, 2005, Kwajalein.
34 Here we might compare Vilsoni Hereniko's likening of Waikiki's palms denuded of their coconuts to "eunuchs," suggesting a metaphor for how Islander men have been emasculated by colonialism and militarism (Hereniko 1999, 137).
35 This map was later revived by former Kwajalein Marshallese Cultural Center director Cris Lindborg, who also conducted her own research about how the main islet of Kwajalein may have looked during the prewar period. Ato Lañkio revised this map for me as he described the different land divisions and relations to the reef that surrounded the entire atoll.

Chapter 3: Chasing the Chieftain's Daughter

1 The word *shūchō* itself is now considered discriminatory language in Japanese, since the characters used to spell this word imply being a "savage" or "primitive person." To emphasize this, instead of the more contemporary word "chief," which could also be used here, I am opting to use "chieftain" to translate the word *shūchō* in the context of the early twentieth-century Japanese imperial imaginary, as some other researchers have. As "chieftain" was used so commonly in much of the European colonial adventure literature that inspired Japanese migrants, it evokes a similar sort of orientalist exoticism or "tropicalism."
2 These were *Chieftain's Daughter '79*, by the Captain Mojo Group led by Koyama Takahiro, and *Shūchō no Musume*, by the artist Umekichi.
3 Translated by the author from Kisō 1986, 260.
4 A counterpoint to this in American popular culture appears in the film *South Pacific* (Logan 1958), where Islander men are acted by "blacked up" white actors who portray various extraordinary representations of indigenous rituals (Jolly 1997, 112). See also White and Lindstrom 1989, and Lindstrom and White 1990 for more about the "cross-dressing" of race and blackness, as well as some of the ways African American soldiers were perceived by Islanders.
5 The word *dojin* (土人), which translates to "natives" but is made up of characters that literally mean "person of the soil," was replaced in official parlance in Nanyō Guntō by Commander Tōgō in 1915 to the more politically correct term *tōmin* (島民) or "islanders" (Higuchi 1987, 10). This did not stop anyone, especially in the Japanese "Naichi" home islands, from continuing to use the word *dojin* to refer casually to Micronesians, Ainu, or Taiwanese

indigenous people displaced by the Japanese empire. *Tōmin* is also remembered by Islander elders throughout the former colonies as a discriminatory label.

6 McClintock argues that the equation of the possession of land with the possession of the female body was a common trope in discovery literature of early European colonial expeditions, but that this "imperial megalomania" was contradicted by a troubling "fear of engulfment, with its fantasy of dismemberment and emasculation" (McClintock 1995, 26–27).

7 Translation by the author of Ishida's lyrics (Ishida 1930).

8 The connotation here in this version is that no chief would give his daughter as a bride to a man who cannot dance. Some later renditions of the song echo the earlier Yoden version of the lyrics that say that no woman by her own volition would "become the bride" of someone who cannot dance ("*dare ga oyome ni iku no ka*"). The symbolism of "dancing" in relation to masculine power (or sexual prowess) is also worth considering here.

9 While beyond the scope of this book, as Yaguchi Yujin elaborates (2011), the prewar "desire" for Hawai'i in Japanese popular culture should not be overlooked, either, especially in consideration of the tremendous out-migration of Japanese settlers and laborers for the sugar industry from the late 1800s onward.

10 In her award-winning tryptich, "In the Manner of a Woman" (2005), Samoan-Japanese artist Yuki Kihara critiqued the eroticized Pacific virgin archetype by emulating nude postcard images made of Islander women by Europeans, posing her own *fa'afāfine* body in sepia photographs as a way of calling attention to the violence of the heteronormative colonial gaze.

11 Yamaguchi Yōji, conversation with the author, October 10, 2007.

12 Many generic photographs were circulated widely through many Japanese publications, postcards, and promotional materials for the Nanyō Guntō, but I have rarely been able to identify the actual photographers. A number of images and archival references suggest that the main photographer in Jaluit was Naruse & Company, which was also credited with taking commemorative images or scenic photos in other parts of the mandated island territories as well.

13 Jolly makes the important point, too, that from a European perspective, clothed Pacific Islander women were also seen in the colonial gaze as being erotic; Beatrice Grimshaw, for instance, sexualized Tahitian women in her writing when she described the way their dresses were so loose-fitting and flowing (Jolly 1997, 107). It is important to remember, though, that Japanese attitudes toward nudity (and sexuality) in the nineteenth and twentieth centuries were of course quite different from those of Europeans or Americans, and they were not significantly influenced by the same sort of Christian values that shaped many "Western" perceptions.

14 Underscoring the currency of the racial category "kanaka" in Japanese,

there was another Nanyō-themed song from 1933 that played off the chieftain's daughter archetype, titled *Kanaka no Musume* (Kanaka girl), which romanticized Islander women in Pohnpei, Saipan, and all over Micronesia (Nakayama 1933).

15 *Chamoro-zoku yori mo bunka no teido ga hikui.*
16 The mention of pianos and other musical instruments as a mark of "high culture" throughout Micronesia by Japanese was a common motif I uncovered in many of the archival sources I consulted.
17 Interestingly, according to the exhibit "Kanak, L'Art est une Parole," held at the Tjibaou Cultural Center in Noumea in spring 2014, the term *Kanaka* is now used in Germany as a pejorative term to describe Turkish and Arab migrants, possibly echoing German colonial-era racism toward darker-skinned laborers.
18 This appeared at http://www.mofa.go.jp/mofaj/gaiko/oda/sanka/kyouiku/kaihatsu/chikyu/world_info/pacific/marshall/, accessed January 15, 2017.
19 Historically, country profiles produced by the Ministry of Foreign Affairs (Gaimushō) sometimes include another item of data titled "*kokuminsei*" or "national character." According to one such profile from August 2000, Marshallese traits included "*Ippan teki ni onwa de nonbiri shiteiru. Kono tame, chian wa yoi,*" which translates to "Generally warm and generous, laid-back and carefree. Due to this, the crime rate is very low."
20 The woodblock prints of French-born, Japanese-raised artist Paul Jacoulet offer a counterpoint here in that many of them romanticized the bodies of Micronesian men during the Japanese administration, providing a rare homoerotic colonial gaze (see Polak and Sawatari 2013).
21 Many of the European narratives of cannibalism in Oceania were consumed in translated form in Japan, but there were also Japanese narratives, such as in Suzuki Keikun's 1892 account of his travels to the Marshall Islands, *Nanyō Tanken Jikki* (Suzuki 1980), that hinted at fears of the "savagery" and the potential for "cannibalism" throughout. Suzuki was arguably also heavily influenced by the European exploration and ethnographic literature that predated his voyage.
22 Shimada Keizō himself denied claims by commentators that, like the "Daku-Daku Odori" that inspired the "Chieftain's Daughter" song, *Bōken Dankichi* was actually based on the life of Mori Koben, the Japanese "king" of Chuuk (Shimada 1976, 186–187). Even so, at the family grave of the Mori family in Kōchi Prefecture today, there is a memorial plaque to honor "The Man Who Became Bōken Dankichi."
23 The full title of the animation was *Omochabako Series Dai 3 Wa: Ehon 1936-nen* (Toybox Series 3: Picture Book 1936), produced by J. O. Studio, directed by Yoshitsugu Tanaka.
24 Originally written in 1941 as part of the manuscript that became *Nanyō Tsūshin*, Nakajima wrote a detailed travelogue of his impressions of the dif-

ferent islands he visited in a section titled "Kanshō: Mikuroneshiya Juntō-Kishō" (Atolls: Highlights of a journey through Micronesia).

25 Nakajima is fascinated here by the choice of *kanji* (八島嘉坊), a set of characters meant to phonetically spell out the name Yashima Kabō (Kabua), which I have confirmed was the Japanese name used by Iroojlaplap (paramount chief) Kabua Kabua during the Japanese administration. Yashima was undoubtedly a fitting name, chiefly if not emperor-like, as it references "Ōyashima," a term from Shintō divine cosmology that refers to the "eight august islands of Japan under heaven."

26 At the time, this would have been a significant income, even by Japanese standards.

27 Noda's three sons in Kosrae were Yamato, Michio, and Taitang. I had the privilege of visiting with Michio in Kosrae in 2006.

28 This history was related in part to me in conversations with Fumiko Kemem (Kwajalein, May 12, 2005), whose mother, Momoko, was the daughter of Kimie, and other descendants of Noda Tetsuzō, including Yamato's son Phillip (Tokyo, September 30, 2005), Noda's son Michio (Kosrae, November 22, 2006), and Dennis Momotaro (March 20, 2016). The Momotaro family has links to Noda through one of Noda's daughter's sons, who was nicknamed Momotaro (the Japanese Peach Boy hero) by Japanese soldiers and eventually used that name as his surname.

29 This phallic proverb is a sort of "boys will be boys" lament over male sexual appetite, likening men to sea worms that inevitably find their way into various "holes" on the reef.

30 As described by Stone, Kowata, and Joash (2000, 24), this expression reinforces matrilineal inheritance and the importance of following one's mother; it also implies the belief that men are likely to go away and father other children with other women.

31 Kaname Yamamura, conversation with the author, Majuro, May 12, 2005.

32 Kobayashi also draws the comparison with Yap, a patrilineal society, where there are no reported Islanders with Japanese heritage, even though Yap was one of the major colonial districts of the Nanyō Guntō (Kobayashi Izumi, conversation with the author, October 16, 2007).

33 See Nero (1987) for more about the significance of the *bai* meeting house, in regards to its form, façade, and role in Palauan society.

34 Junko Konishi (2005) surmised that Nanyō dances like these were innocently based on "traditional" Micronesian march-like dances, without contextualizing this in terms of the violent colonial and military histories that may have foregrounded local re-enactment of trauma. Jane Freeman Moulin, in contrast, characterized the Ogasawara group as stealing the spotlight from indigenous performers while engaging in fraught politics of transmission and cultural misrepresentation (Moulin 2005, 516).

35 I discovered other groups that perform renditions of Nanyō Odori today

in blackface in local festivals from Okinawa to northern Japan, as well as numerous archival images from the 1930s of Japanese and Okinawan settlers in Saipan posing for photos in their native minstrel attire.
36 Kurata Yōji, conversation with the author, Palau, February 26, 2010.
37 Humiko Kingzio, visit with the author, Palau, March 2, 2010.
38 Emlain Kabua, conversation with the author, Majuro, March 14, 2010.
39 See McLelland's study of postwar "queer Japan" for a discussion of the eroticization of Japanese men by American servicemen (2005, 59).

Chapter 4: Bones

1 My father, like many other engineers working for defense contracting companies in the 1970s, commuted by airplane across the atoll to Roi-Namur each day. Nowadays the workforce there is being downsized, with much of the equipment being controlled remotely in the United States through fiber-optics technology.
2 In my childhood naïveté, I assumed that the concrete Japanese buildings and battle emplacements from the war that remained were the only Japanese buildings that had existed. Probably like most children, I was not aware that these were only wartime fortifications or foundations and that on Kwajalein there were once Marshallese and Japanese dwellings, shops, churches, a Japanese shrine, a school, and other wooden buildings that had all been burned and obliterated during the invasion.
3 Crismon also explores this practice to some extent in her work, explaining that watching missile tests "has always been a form of entertainment on Kwaj, although it has always been officially discouraged" (2005, 254).
4 For more on this, see Dvorak 2008 (57–59), which was based on an earlier draft of this chapter.
5 According to Burris, total costs for a typical Kwaj Karnival in the 1960s through the 1980s, which were paid for from contractor donations and not government funds, amounted to more than US$120,000 (2004, 84).
6 Based on conversations with Ato Lañkio, March 2005, who taught me the *wāto* land-parcel divisions of Kwajalein islet.
7 Based on prewar and postwar aerial intelligence photos of Kwajalein, and JICPOA 1944a.
8 The Kwajalein Karnival, which apparently started at least as early as 1964 (Burris 2004, 84) featured prominently in many of the recollections shared with me during my research, not only for Americans but also for Marshallese and other Micronesians, who were given free access to the island during the festivities. Others have also described these combat photograph displays as a prominent part of the festivities.
9 The *Hourglass* is so named for the insignia of the US Army Seventh Infantry

Division, which, the newspaper's masthead boasts, "liberated the island from the forces of Imperial Japan on Feb 4, 1944."

10 I deliberately add imperial Japanese dates throughout this book to draw attention to the centrality of the imperial year system in Japanese imaginaries of time (even today) and their relevance in official public and state narratives. Here, for example, I am referring to the chronological year of the reign of the Shōwa emperor (Hirohito).

11 Translated by the author from lyrics of recording by Kingu Male Chorus 1939.

12 See also Denfield 1984, which provides more background on the mobilization of Korean laborers in Micronesia in general (but focuses almost exclusively on the context of Saipan and Tinian), as well as Weiner 1994, which looks at the overall problem of race relations and Korean laborers throughout the Japanese empire.

13 From the interrogation of Kang Ko Kae, prisoner of war captured at Enewetak aboard the USS *Electra*.

14 *Ninpu* (a Japanese word that elderly Marshallese still use to refer to wartime laborers, though they use the Marshallese version, "*niiṃbu*") carries with it the same derogatory connotation as "coolie" or "unskilled laborer," and it was likely the word used locally by Japanese superiors toward Korean and Marshallese laborers in particular. Marshallese elders say that often these laborers wore only *fundoshi* loincloths in the hot sun, which is consistent with images of hard laborers in other parts of the Japanese empire in the same period.

15 These concrete bathtubs remained after the destruction of wooden structures in the bombardment of Kwajalein.

16 Hatfield Lemae, conversation with the author, Jebwad, May 20, 2005.

17 In reverse, sometimes even Koreans in the employ of the Japanese military also made an effort to be more harsh on Islanders so they would be accepted by their Japanese superiors, like the Korean character of Kon in Oda Makoto's historical novel set in Peleliu, Palau, *The Breaking Jewel* (Oda 2003).

18 In some cases, Marshallese church leaders were publicly executed by Japanese military authorities, terrifying the local populations and creating bitter memories in the minds of many Islanders toward the Japanese military in general. For those families who were directly impacted, such executions spawned a deeper animosity toward all Japanese that persists into the present. Most elders, however, tend to differentiate between descriptions of wartime Japanese military atrocities and peaceful civilian prewar life.

19 This was the execution of the Makin Raiders, nine Marines who had been captured in Kiribati and were being held on Kwajalein. Several Marshall Islanders claim to have witnessed the executions, although Hayashi's personal account (Hayashi 1964) is the most authoritative and detailed written

history of the event that I have seen. Hayashi was found innocent during the postwar trials, although he had been present at the executions.
20 Yamaguchi Yōji, conversation with the author, October 12, 2007.
21 Satō family, conversations with the author, Kamakura, November 18–19, 2005.
22 This was, says Hayashi, the assessment of Combined Fleet commander Admiral Koga Mineichi upon appraisal of the losses suffered by Japanese forces in Rabaul.
23 The first character of this word, *gyoku*, means "precious jewel," but it also is a reference to the emperor and to royalty in general. Thus, the notion of *gyokusai* is that of a noble sacrifice made for the sake of the emperor.
24 In 2007, for instance, a major dispute between Okinawa Prefecture and the central Japanese government erupted when the government instructed textbook publishers to revise their fiscal year 2008 materials so that there was no mention of Japanese military officials ordering the mass suicides of Okinawan civilians (Ishiyama 2007).
25 These two islands were joined before the war by a causeway constructed mostly by Korean laborers, and they are now referred to as one island, Roi-Namur.
26 It should be noted that these dates correspond to US time zones on the eastern side of the international dateline, though Kwajalein actually lies on the west. Thus Japanese authorities announced the fall of Kwajalein ("Kuezerin *Gyokusai*") on February 6, 1944 (Shōwa 19), and it is officially observed at Yasukuni Shrine on that date.
27 Ijimura [Ishimura] Lautona, quoted in Poyer, Falgout, and Carucci 2001 (121) explains, "Nearly all of those of us who were with the *neinbu* (i.e. *ninpu* or "coolie" laborers) on Kwajalein sided with the Japanese and fought with them."
28 In counting *heiryoku,* or "military power," Japanese sources do not differentiate between Koreans and Japanese, as they were all deemed to be in the service of the empire. During and after the battle, American authorities were unable to differentiate between these groups and did not do so in their official recordings of deaths and casualties, but they did distinguish between Japanese and Koreans in the records of prisoners of war, from which one could reasonably estimate that between 1,000 and 1,100 Koreans died atoll-wide. There were about 260 Okinawans working as stevedores at Roi for the Sankyū Transport Company (JICPOA 1944f).
29 This information comes from records provided to me directly by the Marshall Islands War Bereaved Families Association.
30 The primary logistics contractor for the United States Army Kwajalein Atoll installation is required to hire an archaeologist to review planned construction and other activities for potential effects to cultural resources.
31 Leslie Mead, e-mail correspondence with the author, June 6, 2007.

32 The lyrics, based on a poem from the classic volume of poetry *Manyōshū*, translate to, "If I go away to the sea, I shall become a corpse floating in the water. If I go away to the mountain, I shall become a corpse from which grass grows. If it is for the emperor, I shall not regret my death." The song is sung every year by the bereaved families of the soldiers who died in Kwajalein Atoll.

33 Bonnie deBrum, conversation with the author, Ebeye, April 3, 2005; Kaname Yamamura, conversation with the author, Majuro, May 16, 2005.

34 In comparison, many islands in Oceania did not directly experience the war at all, such as many of the islands in southern Polynesia, where some preparatory defenses were arranged but no direct combat ensued.

35 I was able to meet with Lee Inshin at his home outside Seoul in June 2009 together with researchers from the Truth Commission on Forced Labor under Japanese Imperialism, an initiative of the South Korean government. Lee's job working as an assistant in the Japanese hospital on the main island of Mili spared him from death and enabled him to hear the stories of both Japanese and Korean survivors.

36 Though beyond the scope of this book, it is worth noting that Mr. Lee returned to Mili many decades later to seek the remains of his Korean compatriots, only to find that the mass grave had been dug up. In further research between 2010 and 2012, I learned that the bereaved families of the Japanese soldiers stationed at Mili made a concerted effort to repatriate remains from Mili to Japan on several occasions after the end of the war, which would mean that those remains (including Korean and Marshallese remains) were probably interred, knowingly or unknowingly, at Chidorigafuchi Cemetery in Tokyo. Japanese nationalist memorial groups deny the story of this massacre altogether (see Dvorak 2014).

37 Further studies have been done by Bill Remick, who observes that official numbers of Japanese war dead vary drastically between records and the numbers of estimated dead shown in photographs of postwar temporary graves (Remick 2015, 96). In March of 2014, the rising oceans caused by climate change flooded parts of Āne-bōn (Enniburr) islet in the north of Kwajalein Atoll during king tides, undercutting a landfill and revealing at least eight to twelve skeletons of Japanese soldiers, indicating yet another mass burial site.

38 It is important to point out that Kwajalein and Enewetak were the first atolls taken by the United States in the Marshalls, but that many atolls and islands were bypassed until much later, some not surrendering officially until 1945.

39 Kimie Hara explores this transition between Japanese and American rule in the "American Lake" in the broader context of Micronesia (Hara 2007).

40 Poyer, Falgout and Carucci's (2001) interlocutors in the Marshall Islands point out that prewar Japanese colonial times, while harsh and disciplined in many ways, were often more compatible with the Marshallese social

hierarchy than American "freedoms," which they felt degraded Marshallese customs.
41 In "Sanzen Gunpei no Haka" (Oda 1998), the author reflects on his complicated feelings upon visiting Kwajalein Atoll in the 1990s, adopting a Korean myth about the angry spirits of "Three Thousand Soldiers."
42 Here I echo Ruth Behar's call (1996) for self-reflexive, "vulnerable" anthropology.

Chapter 5: Capturing Liberation

1 Wenders 1992, 2.
2 Lutz and Collins 1993, 100.
3 See Lindstrom and White's multivalent readings of "black and white" in terms of race (1990, 27–29).
4 The theme of photography in the Pacific War has been dealt with brilliantly in Lindstrom and White's *Island Encounters: Black and White Memories of the Pacific War* (1990) and in Lindstrom's later chapter about similar themes (Lindstrom 2001). Here I emulate some of the same methodology used by these authors to frame the sorts of narratives that were encoded in war photography.
5 To my knowledge, after scouring Japanese archives and speaking with Japanese bereaved relatives of war dead, there are no surviving Japanese photographs or moving images of military confrontations in Kwajalein (if any were taken).
6 See also Sontag 1979; Pinney 1992; Barthes 1981, 2000.
7 I am indebted to former Kwajalein Range Services archaeologist Leslie Mead for collaborating in obtaining these valuable three thousand or more photographs from the National Archives and ephemera from other sources, as well as for discussing these images at length in the context of the archaeological record and the battle histories of Kwajalein Atoll.
8 By "women" here I am referring not only to the images of "native women" I discuss further on, but to a number of photographs of American nurses who also appear in the archives but are not named or identified, unlike most servicemen. Even in the same photograph, a soldier is typically labeled with rank, full name, and even hometown, while nurses' names are not indicated, no doubt a suggestion of their perceived marginality in the war project. I also identified no images whatsoever of nonwhite American personnel, despite many references to Japanese American interrogators/interpreters from Hawai'i or African American stevedores working in the dock areas of Kwajalein.
9 The racist term "gook" (which dates back to at least 1935, when it was used by Americans to refer to Filipinos and other Spanish speakers) was later revived during the Korean and Vietnam Wars. As with other pejorative terms

I quote in this book, I cite it here to expose and critique the intense racism that the US military used to justify its violence in the Pacific War.

10 In my use of the term "defender," I do not mean to minimize the experience of brutality and violence by Marshallese and other Micronesians or colonized people in relation to Japanese militarism. As Poyer, Falgout, and Carucci (2001) argue, however, and as I have gleaned from conversations with those who experienced the war, Kwajalein was one of the very few places, if not the only place, in Micronesia during the Pacific War where Islanders fought alongside Japanese in defense of their atoll (121).

11 In addition to the producers of these images, we should not overlook the tremendous power of the American public, who *consumed* this "liberation legend" through photography and text and were thus complicit in its perpetuation.

12 Here and elsewhere in this chapter, I write "Japanese" in quotes to indicate that both American documentation of the Kwajalein invasion tended to conflate Japanese with Koreans and sometimes even Islanders with Japanese heritage.

13 Leslie Mead explains (correspondence June 15, 2007) that whenever American veterans visiting Kwajalein observe this photograph in the war history exhibit, they comment that the marine must have been "cleaned up."

14 The photographs I mention in this paragraph would all be potentially offensive to bereaved families and survivors of the battle in the Marshall Islands and Japan, so I have chosen not to reproduce them here.

15 Here I borrow the methodology of choosing broad themes in images from the work of Rose (2001), Lutz and Collins (1993), Lindstrom and White (1990), and Lindstrom (2001).

16 The only pictures of dead bodies or "carnage" that I include in this chapter are some of the least graphic images and some used in popular media, to show how these photographs were disseminated in the press. I have opted to omit the more sensational images, but this should not be taken to mean that there are not scores of extremely graphic images of Japanese, Korean, and Okinawan male bodies piled up and strewn across the landscapes of Kwajalein Atoll.

17 Hinomaru literally means "sun disc" or "flag of the sun," commonly called "the rising sun" in American narratives.

18 Suzuki Yukiko, conversation with the author, Kwajalein, October 7, 2005.

19 There were of course instances during Operation Flintlock in which Americans also made sacrifices for their fellow soldiers, like Lt. Pfc. Richard K. Sorenson, who fell on a grenade to protect his unit on Roi and suffered severe injuries. Unlike Japanese maneuvers, which were portrayed as mere fanaticism in the media and in the English-language histories of the war that followed, such American gestures were celebrated as heroism. Sorenson was awarded a medal of honor for his bravery.

20 For more detail on this, see Kawano 2001, which explores the subject of sacrifice in comparative American and Japanese military discourses.
21 [祝]出征大木清君 "[*Shuku*]-*shussei: Ōki Kiyoshi-kun.*" Probably there is a character not visible in the image, *shuku* or *iwai*, which would normally be written to celebrate or commemorate an event.
22 The late 1930s government guidelines about *kokumin seishin* (national spirit) dictated the way the Japanese flag was to be displayed and treated; strictly speaking, any form of writing on the flag was not allowed.
23 "United States Code Title 4 Chapter 1—The Flag," §3 ("Use of Flag for Advertising Purposes; Mutilation of Flag") and §8 ("Respect for Flag"), respectively.
24 This is according to Ato Ḷañkio, who related that he had heard stories of Marshallese in Kwajalein Atoll at the time of the war who were deeply embarrassed and ashamed by having to disrobe and be photographed (conversation, November 10, 2006).
25 Excerpts from the Convention Relative to the Treatment of Prisoners of War, Geneva, July 27, 1929. Note that in later revisions of the Geneva Convention agreements, articles were added that unilaterally forbade the physical or mental torture of prisoners, including threatening and public humiliation.
26 Here are suggestive phallic overtones of "hard" and "soft" masculinity being played out between Japanese and Americans.
27 This arsenic derivative was used as an embalming agent on the battlefield.
28 A careful study of this photograph makes it abundantly clear that the men in the background are unloading, not loading, a body in the bomb crater: The two men hold the stretcher at the handles at its top, not on the bottom as they would if they were trying to retrieve the body for burial elsewhere (Leslie Mead, correspondence with the author, October 18, 2006).
29 Leslie Mead, personal communication with the author, October 18, 2006.
30 This American racial framing in many ways mirrored the Japanese discourse of the "Kanaka," in that Islanders were simply expected to be on hand to help out, regardless of what the task was.
31 Tengan (2008a) also discusses the media images that depicted the partial nudity and militarized masculinity of the Hawaiian men who were sent by the United States in the 1930s to colonize the Line Islands. Tengan points out, too, how the homoerotic gaze of these photographs attracted the interest of some American men (2008a, 38).
32 Many have argued that it is the sudden importation of American canned, sweetened, and processed foods to the Marshalls, together with the high consumption of hulled white rice introduced by Japan, that has contributed to the epidemic of diabetes that currently afflicts an estimated 50 percent of the adult population (*Marshall Islands Journal*, July 13, 2007, 8).
33 I learned this interesting fact from the sales representative of Kikkōman Shōyu, Inc. to the Marshall Islands on one of his routine inventory assessments, May 2005.
34 Cited in Carucci 1989, 85.

Notes to Pages 143–157

35 See chapter 8, where I elaborate on this argument about traditional leadership in Kwajalein Atoll.
36 I gave this image to present-day residents of Carlos, and others on Ebeye, who say that no such person of chiefly status, or *irooj*, would have existed aside from those who were already well-known, so he may have been a clan head or *a̧ḷap*, perhaps with a nickname of M̧ōkade, which means "expert" or "wizard."
37 Cigarettes are of course the source of another imported epidemic, lung cancer.
38 This photograph also reflects the military's perception of Marshall Islander women as "domestic help," given that prewar Japanese and postwar American soldiers hired Marshallese women to do their laundry on Kwajalein.
39 Granted, Hawaiians had been influenced by Christianity even longer than Marshall Islanders had, and hula—which was arguably used as a form of cultural resistance against American colonialism—had even been banned for sixty years by the *ali'i* (chiefs) due to the influence of missionaries in the 1800s (Desmond 1999; Silva 2004).
40 An example of these fine-woven mats can be seen in some of the images taken by Japanese photographers in the 1930s, such as the image of young women shown in chapter 3. Spennemann writes that according to most accounts, both men and women in the Marshall Islands had already stopped wearing much of their "traditional" clothing by the time missionaries arrived in the late 1850s, although women continued to wear mats as undergarments under their cotton dresses for some time (Spennemann 1998).
41 As Judith Butler writes about drag, "the parody is *of* the very notion of an original; just as the psychoanalytic notion of gender identification is constituted by a fantasy of a fantasy" (Butler 1990, 175).
42 Another parallel to this is how elderly Marshallese who experienced both Japanese and American periods tend to see each nation's imperialism as interchangeable or arbitrary sides of the same coin.
43 The Presidents' Day issue of the *Kwajalein Hourglass* in 2007 featured interviews with three Marshallese students of the Kwajalein base school system, who all reflected on the greatness of George Washington and Abraham Lincoln (February 17, 2007, 3).
44 The phenomenon of Marshallese workers saluting the American flag was commented on widely in the local media on Kwajalein as a rebuke to unpatriotic American residents.
45 Michael Kabua, conversation with the author, Ebeye, April 20, 2005.
46 Imata Kabua, conversation with the author, Majuro, March 14, 2005.
47 "Wesley," conversation with the author, Ebeye, March 2005.

Chapter 6: The Haunted Bathtub

1 For this chapter, I am indebted to advice from historian Peter Read, who explores the past through the spirits that inhabit the land, as in his book *Haunted*

Earth (Read 2003), which considers the intermingled histories of indigenous and settler communities in Australia through its haunted landscapes.
2. For more on Marshallese spirits and cosmology, see McArthur 1995 and Tobin 2002, which both explore these themes in depth, while Robert Barclay's novel *Meḷaḷ* (2002) uses this spirit world as a backdrop for the tensions between Marshallese and Americans in Kwajalein.
3. Wreck diving is a popular pastime for Americans on Kwajalein. Although at least twenty of the ships that sleep on the lagoon floor are Japanese, American divers usually only know them by the names of the buoy markers above them. Bereaved families of Japanese sailors expressed their concern to me about divers disturbing these underwater graves, although unfortunately many divers over the decades have looted various objects from the ships, including even human remains.
4. Peattie writes about how *gunka* were performed by military bands in Chuuk at the base there (1988, 260), and Hayashi (1964) describes how when he was in the command of a patrol ship in the Nanyō Guntō he used to blast cheerful march music through the loudspeakers to raise the morale of his soldiers.
5. Here I wish to acknowledge the generous hospitality of Meath and Emina John and their sons, the relatives of my Bubu Neitari Pound in Kwajalein Atoll.
6. Hatfield Lemae, conversation with the author, May 15, 2005.
7. An elderly Japanese fisherman, Sakamoto-san, explained this to me in the context of telling how his brother had died as a *tokkōtai* pilot (conversation, January 18, 2005).
8. Yasukuni is a shrine for all who died in battle for the Japanese empire, including conscripted Korean and Chinese laborers and—most controversially—Japanese officers who were convicted as war criminals. This has especially sparked angry criticism and protest from China and Korea when Japanese leaders pay their respects at the shrine, a gesture that is seen to condone Japan's military atrocities in those countries. "Enshrinement," however, was a bureaucratic practice, in which certification of the death of a soldier was forwarded by the Japanese military to Yasukuni, where it was stamped and filed away. No human remains are interred there. The shrine is also a magnet for right-wing conservatives and ultranationalists, and it features in revisionist historical texts such as the political comic books of Kobayashi Yoshinori (2001). This is discussed in more detail in Buruma 1994; Tanaka, Tanaka, and Hata 1995; and Safier 1997.
9. The Southern Cross (*minami jūjisei*) figures prominently in the symbolism of Nanyō and Nanyō Guntō, and Japanese colonists, soldiers, and writers mentioned it often in prewar literature.
10. Cherry blossoms were typically a symbol of fallen soldiers, particularly *tokkōtai* pilots, who, like *sakura,* fell in the prime of their youth.

Notes to Pages 165–170

11 This organization mainly represented soldiers who died throughout Kwajalein and Enewetak Atolls, but it also served to network the families of all soldiers who died in the Marshall Islands and Kiribati. In all, according to correspondence by President Ukita, 30,374 bereaved families were registered by the group as of 1965.
12 I have recovered this history mainly from the Host Nations Archives on US Army Kwajalein Atoll, for which I am grateful to former Host Nations liaison Maryanne Lane for access to these Japanese files from the 1960s. I am also indebted to Kurokawa Makoto, Takabayashi Yoshio, and Kusaba Hiroshi of the bereavement society for providing me with archival materials in Japan.
13 This practice of gathering coral stones, sand, or rocks, known as "spirit sand," or *reisha* (霊砂), became common practice throughout many of the war zones in the Pacific as a way of bringing back a piece of the land where soldiers died in lieu of the actual remains.
14 This memorial, which is covered in stones donated from all prefectures of Japan and Korea, is dedicated to all the soldiers (not only Japanese) who died in the battles of Kiribati and the Marshall Islands. A small replica of the monument is located inside Yasukuni Shrine.

Chapter 7: Dislocations

1 American intelligence reports (JICPOA 1944b) remark about the extreme thickness and impenetrability of these concrete structures, leading to a myth of "invincible Japanese concrete" that is retold again and again by local American historians (see, for instance, Burris 2004). But Mead argues that this thickness was in part to compensate for the poor quality of cement mixed with briny coral aggregate and iron reinforcing rods (rebar), which ultimately had the added benefit of making the concrete elastic enough to absorb the shock of gunfire and shrapnel (conversation on May 13, 2005).
2 There were a few scattered elders in Kwajalein Atoll who recalled that Japanese authorities had made payments of compensation or tribute to *irooj* in exchange for use of the land; former chief of staff Hayashi writes in his memoirs (1964) that Iroojlaplap Jeimata Kabua frequently paid visits to the Imperial Navy Admiralty on Kwajalein in the 1930s and 1940s.
3 Ramsey Reimers, conversation with the author, March 15, 2005.
4 See Mason 1948; Kiste 1974; Carucci 1997b; Niedenthal 2001; Barker 2004; Keever 2004; and Toyosaki 2005, all of which are outstanding histories and ethnographies of the plight of Bikinians and other nuclear-affected Marshall Islanders under the US Atomic Weapons Testing programs.
5 According to Jones (2007, 37), this amounted to the equivalent of more than one Hiroshima bomb being dropped on Bikini and Enewetak per day over the course of twelve years.
6 Greg Dening comments on the irony of these sexual metaphors in terms of

the way the United States "encompassed Oceania" (see Dening 2003, 18). Margaret Jolly also points out that the *Gilda* device was painted with an image of Rita Hayworth (Jolly 1997, 117).

7   This deadly nuclear weapon was innocently referred to as "the shrimp device," fastened into place in a concrete building on one of the islands of Bikini Atoll. See Sublette 2006.

8   The Bravo test was also directly responsible for raining fallout on the crew of the *Lucky Dragon V,* a Japanese tuna-fishing vessel from Yaizu, Shizuoka Prefecture. This horrified the postwar Japanese population and inspired Honda Ishirō's *Gojira,* a film about a massive reptilian creature that rises from the depths of the Pacific Ocean to haunt Tokyo (Honda 1954, 1956). Indeed, Godzilla was born in the Marshall Islands.

9   Numerous Japanese soldiers described the Kwajalein flies in their diaries and memoirs and attributed to them the dengue fever that many suffered during the late 1930s and early 1940s.

10 Various imported supplies had been more widely distributed during Japanese times, when Nanyō Bōeki Kaisha (NBK), Kaisan, and other trading companies operating out of Jaluit operated copra boats linking most atolls and islands and setting up shops at most sites.

11 In Kwajalein Atoll during Japanese times, there were power stations located centrally on Ebeye to service surrounding islands all the way north to Kōñejekāān-eṇ (Gugeegue) and all the way down to Kwajalein; in the north, a power station at Āne-bōn (Enniburr) serviced islands stretching over to Ruot (Roi) and Niṃur (Namur). This strategy was used in Jaluit Atoll and other sites from the late 1930s, where noisy power stations were sited remotely in the jungle of Aineman islet. Electricity was quietly provided to Iṃwej islet, where most soldiers resided in dormitories and barracks, or from Jaluit islet to the main population center of Jebwad islet, where the civilian community was. Many of the switches and controls, and even some light bulbs in the power station at Aineman, are still intact at the time of this writing.

12 Jimmy Matsunaga, conversation with the author, July 20, 2006.

13 This was explained in more detail to me by Ato Ḷañkio, from a conversation on May 10, 2005, Ebeye.

14 This was related to me by Harrington Dribo, the son of Handel Dribo, in a conversation on Ebeye, May 2005.

15 Ato Ḷañkio, conversation with the author, April 15, 2005.

16 In the case of Kwajalein land in the 1970s, these condemnation statutes were eventually challenged in cases such as *Dribo vs. Winkel* (KNC 2002b, 58).

17 The Mid-Atoll Corridor islet of Tar-wōj, explains Carucci, is central to Ri-Kuwajleen cosmology, as it forms part of a complex matrix between the coralhead Tarḷañ, several other islets, and the heavens, part of what holds the delicate balance of earth and sky together in a state of "anxious antici-

pation" (Carucci 1997a). Tar-wōj is also featured in Robert Barclay's novel *Meḷaḷ* (2002).

18 The term "opportunist" here was actually used by the Kwajalein military command at the time, a keyword that is used as a stereotype by many American military and civilian framings of Marshallese in the atoll.

19 By "landowners" here I am specifically referring to Ebeye landowners of the ten *wātos* on Ebeye, only some of whom also have land rights at Kwajalein and other places leased by the military. Ebeye landowners have historically had to operate without compensation for any of their land, for which they receive no rent money either from tenants or from the US military.

20 For more on the imagination of space as represented by the US Army telephone network at Kwajalein Atoll, see Dvorak 2004.

21 In December 2015, one such ferry was named after Staff Sergeant Solomon Sam, a Marshallese soldier from Majuro serving in the US Army, who died in Mosul, Iraq, in 2008. It was the only time that any American military vessel, let alone any military asset, had ever been named after a Marshall Islander hero.

22 Carucci points out that in Namo Atoll, there is an analogous *wāto* named Kuwajleen (Kwajalein), denoting the place where people from Kwajalein settled that land as well.

23 This was related to me by Floyd Corder, former site manager of Roi-Namur.

24 Conversation on Kwajalein, April 15, 2005.

25 Based on conversations on Ebeye with Charles deBrum (March 19, 2005), Neitari Pound (April 15, 2005), and Irene Paul (October 15, 2006).

26 For more about the environmentalist version of an imminent Marshallese demise, see the climate change documentary "Rising Waters" (Torrice 2000).

27 Bikinians, says Niedenthal, would still prefer nuclear islands over no islands at all (conversation, Majuro, March 17, 2016).

28 "Joan," former Kwajalein resident, e-mail correspondence with the author, July 2007.

29 Kauanui shows how this American racial discourse has been deployed by the US government in such a way that one's indigenous "purity" determines one's entitlement to land and compensation, with the likely result that after several generations, one's "Nativeness" becomes so diluted through intermarriage that the government will no longer need to provide any sort of compensation for land or damages (Kauanui 2002).

30 One explanation of the evolution of the spelling Ebeye suggests that the "j" sound in Epjā was read as a "y" sound by German administrators, and this was recorded by outside observers as a "y," which was further mispronounced by American invading forces, who pronounced "eye" as it would be pronounced in English. Japanese, on the other hand, had pronounced the island's name closer to its original Marshallese as "Ebije" or "Ebize."

Chapter 8: Homecoming, 2016

1. Quoted in dé Ishtar 1994, 28.
2. This motto, attributed to President Harry S. Truman, was used for several years by the Kwajalein landowners to mean that they have the ultimate responsibility and authority to determine the future of their atoll. Green, white, and orange are the official Kwajalein Atoll colors, and they are used by the local government (KALGOV). *Iroij* (now often spelled *irooj* as per the new orthography system) means "chief," although as Julie Walsh also observes, many of the Rālik chain *irooj* prefer to translate this title as "king" (or *lerooj*, female chief, as "queen"), after the monarchic titles bestowed on chiefs by European colonial regimes.
3. *jambo* = originally from the Japanese word *sanpo,* meaning to "walk or stroll about aimlessly." The Marshallese variation tends also to mean "excursion or trip," which could either be a short trip or a longer journey here and there.
4. The late senator Ishmael John from Enewetak was one of Imata Kabua's closest collaborators, together with Tom Kijiner Sr. (who eventually became ambassador to Japan).
5. Such jokes about nuclear radiation are common amongst Marshall Islanders, humor being a constructive way of dealing with the pain and frustration of American nuclear testing. In fact, Senator John had special-ordered frozen quail from Honolulu for dinner, but Runit Island in Enewetak Atoll is the site of a gigantic concrete-covered dome where US military cleanup crews dumped the contaminated radioactive topsoil from that atoll from the tests of the 1940s and 1950s. Many parts of Enewetak are still considered dangerous for habitation.
6. The Nitijela is the parliament of the Republic of the Marshall Islands, based partly on the United Kingdom and the United States, with elected representatives from different atoll districts.
7. *ripālle* = a white person, foreigner (often used to refer to Americans).
8. *Bwiro* is a fermented paste made out of breadfruit (*mā*) that can be preserved for many months without spoiling.
9. Local atoll governments in the Marshall Islands have offices in Majuro, the capital, and many government representatives and traditional leaders also live in this urban center in order to properly represent their widely dispersed constituencies to the national government.
10. This was a national convention organized by the Marshallese women's organization WUTMI (Women United Together in the Marshall Islands), a twenty-four-chapter group that demonstrates the political power of women in the Marshalls to make democratic initiatives for change. Later in this chapter I describe the way women's political action was central to Ri-Kuwajleen activism in the 1980s. WUTMI was also successful in lobbying for outside observers

to monitor the national elections of November 2007, and in 2011 they were instrumental in getting the government to pass the Domestic Violence Act.

11   This translation was provided in part by Maryia deBrum, Julius Lejjena, and Annette Note.

12   Actually, this song is also widely known and sung throughout the Marshall Islands as a popular song of celebration. Though its origins are unclear, it apparently dates back to at least the 1960s and was sung on Roi-Namur (Julius Lejjena, e-mail, September 12, 2007).

13   As LaBriola writes, celebration, sharing, and an overall sense of togetherness in the face of adversity are at the core of community life on Ebeye (LaBriola 2006). Carucci also shows how the displaced people of Enewetak commemorate the trauma of nuclear testing in the ways they celebrate Christmas in Ujelang Atoll (Carucci 1997b).

14   As can be understood from the legends recorded by Tobin (2002), Rālik hegemony has long been celebrated or critiqued through oral traditions and legends.

15   Landowners themselves have also harbored doubts and suspicions about the counsel of Marshallese leaders' American legal advisors, who they fear surreptitiously attempt to effect outcomes favorable to the United States (Philippo 2015, 217).

16   Nowadays, judges in the Republic of the Marshall Islands are mainly Americans, whose status as outsiders helps to maintain neutrality. Marshall Islanders also frequently wage legal battles over compensation in the United States courts system.

17   *Kajoor* (also spelled *kajur*) translates to "commoner," not having chiefly *irooj* status, but in Marshallese society, in fact *kajoor* also means "strength" and "power," because it only through the collective strength of the people that a chief can be empowered. Punning on this word, water, power, and other infrastructure has long been managed on Ebeye islet by a utility company called KAJUR, an acronym that stands for Kwajalein Atoll Joint Utilities Resources.

18   Tobin (2002) interprets *ao* as being close to the Polynesian concept of *mana*.

19   Alfred Capelle, Marshallese linguist, e-mail to the author, June 27, 2007.

20   This example is one of many in the dictionary that make subtle political commentary on the unique nature of the American occupation at Kwajalein. Another, *mọ*, the traditional word for "taboo" or restricted land for chiefs that is off-limits to commoners (such as the islet of Enṃaat), includes the example, *Emọ an jabdewōt armej etal ñan Kuwajleen*, "No one is permitted to go to Kwajalein" (Abo et al. 1976, 209).

21   It is important to note that many of the leaders of Operation Homecoming have been involved in the US Trust Territory of the Pacific government (including the Congress of Micronesia). They also had been educated in

American history and were well aware of the freedom of speech guaranteed by the US Constitution.

22   Handel Dribo, the tenacious elderly landowner who was featured in Adam Horowitz' film *Home on the Range* (1983), has been dubbed "The Marshallese Rambo" and celebrated as a Kwajalein hero by some young landowners for his bravery and tirelessness.

23   I gleaned details about the life of the late Handel Dribo from a conversation with his colleague Manke Konol and his son Harrington Dribo (May 2, 2005) on Ebeye. Handel, who was educated in Palau at a Japanese construction vocational school, had generally positive sentiments for the Japanese premilitary colonial period and was known for his fondness for Japanese popular music. He also started the first movie theater on Ebeye, where he showed John Wayne films (Horowitz 1983).

24   Another important consideration is that in the early stages of the formation of the Republic of the Marshall Islands, many government officials, including President Amata Kabua, were Kwajalein landowners and *irooj* in the first place; therefore they had opportunities to meet with high-ranking American officials.

25   Crismon also describes how the Community Relations Committee (CRC) meetings between the Host Nations Office on the military installation and Kwajalein leaders were started in 1983 after the protests to alleviate tension and resolve problems between Kwajalein Atoll local government, traditional leaders, and the military (Crismon 2005).

26   I heard Imata Kabua, Ataji Balos, and Alvin Jacklick all compared to Martin Luther King Jr. at different times.

27   Conversation on March 14, 2005.

28   Many participants indicated that they had been subjected to extensive surveillance, and hundreds of photographs of the protesters were apparently taken as evidence for US Army files, including many images of children. These images are still off-limits to the public.

29   The US Army eventually restored water and sanitation services to the protesters, but only after much pressure and a federal court order required it to do so (KNC 2002b, 62).

30   Horowitz's second film, *Nuclear Savage* (Horowitz 2011), returns to Kwajalein and other parts of the Marshall Islands to trace the plight of the Rongelap people displaced by nuclear testing, many of whom reside on Ebeye and Mejatto islets.

31   Granted, local "small" histories are rarely innocent or neutral. Different protesters that I interviewed tended to cast themselves as the heroes of the resistance, and there was, and still is, much shrewd political drama and positioning between different alliances and factions among all landowners.

32   Eminent domain is the supreme power of a sovereign nation over all the

property within its boundaries. It allows a nation to appropriate land for public use with compensation to landowners.

33 It was effectively because of this land-use agreement that no further "invasions" of Kwajalein took place since the compact was signed in 1986, as landowners begrudgingly acknowledged that they were bound to honor the terms of the LUA through 2016.

34 Some single American men have been known to frequent Ebeye at night to meet up with young Marshallese young women, although there is no extensive prostitution industry, and senior women leaders of Ebeye have spoken out strongly against such exploitive relationships.

35 Fred Pedro, conversation with the author, Majuro, March 14, 2005.

36 I met many women who were reluctant to talk about their involvement in the demonstrations as children, explaining that although they followed their mothers back to their homelands willingly at the time, they felt traumatized by the way they were branded as criminals by American authorities and worried that they might get into trouble for speaking out.

37 Fred Pedro, conversation, March 14, 2005.

38 From the film produced by Micronesian Seminar, *The US and the Marshall Islands: The Next Twenty Years* (Aubuchon and Hezel 2003).

39 This figure was also derived from an aggregate total of all the resources that had been used without compensation to date, including all the coral that had been dredged from the reef surrounding Kwajalein and other islets.

40 The distribution of land payments has always been a major controversy in Kwajalein Atoll, where a "1/3, 1/3, 1/3" system has supposedly been in place that theoretically divides these amounts for each land tract equally on a "traditional" basis between *irooj*, *aḷap*, and senior *rijerbal* groups. Since *irooj* are much smaller in number they receive the largest share of this amount and then distribute it to their families. Naturally *aḷap* and *rijerbal* classes are proportionally a much larger population, and the effect is that some lesser landowners receive very little money in the end, which they are then required to pass on to their relatives.

41 §212 of Compact II (US Department of State 2003, 20) titled "Kwajalein Impact and Use" provided for $15 million annually, adjusted for inflation, from fiscal year 2004 through 2013, after which the amount would be increased to $18 million or the $15 million plus the inflation adjustment, whichever was greater.

42 This figure of $19.1 million was the "lowest acceptable amount" when projected in terms of inflation and population growth over fifty years.

43 Literally "the House of Jeimata," Iroojlaplap Imata Kabua's grandfather.

44 The letter, dated October 4, 2005, was published in the *Marshall Islands Journal* on October 14 (page 6) in excerpted form and published online as an editorial in the East-West Center's *Pacific Islands Report*, archived at http://archives

rt.org/archive/2005/October/10-12-com.htm (accessed November 05).

Kabua's outrage about the "colonel on temporary duty" refers to an incident that had taken place on the Kwajalein military installation one month earlier, reported on the front page of the *Marshall Islands Journal* on September 16, 2005, in which Commander Beverly Stipe had forcefully evicted one of the American residents from the base. Regardless of the various political circumstances surrounding this expulsion, the fact that the commander was quoted as saying "Get off *my* island!" (emphasis added) became headline news and a major bone of contention for the already resentful Kwajalein landowners. Kabua's sexist use of the term "housekeeping" here is also an attempt to belittle the commander's gender.

46 Unlike in Japan or other countries where US bases are prevalent, one provision of the Compacts of Free Association allows citizens of those countries, including Marshallese, to join the US armed forces. As evidenced by the large numbers of Marshallese young men and women who enlist every year, many see this as a viable and worthwhile career option.

47 Kabua is also from the opposition party to Note's United Democratic Party.

48 It should also be mentioned that the Note administration was also credited with navigating an extremely difficult period of change while increasing government transparency and accountability, establishing better relations with new donor nations, and placing emphasis on education and health services.

49 Though many analysts suggested that Kwajalein's significance to the United States would fade with the ending of the Cold War, the global "War on Terror" and American anxieties about North Korea or China have reinforced Kwajalein's role as a premier testing installation. Recent comments by Pentagon officials and Strategic Missile Defense Command officials have made it clear that the United States desires to stay at Kwajalein Atoll for the long term.

50 "Ron," conversation with the author, May 7, 2005.

51 According to Rongelap senator Abacca Anjain (conversation on June 13, 2005, Honolulu), on September 11, 2001, in reaction to the terrorist attacks on the World Trade Center and the Pentagon, the right of strategic denial also allowed USAKA (currently USAG-KA) to impose a 200-mile (roughly 322 km) radius security zone around Kwajalein Atoll. This prohibited the Rongelap people living in exile on Mejatto islet in Kwajalein from getting much-needed food and medical care, because no boats or aircraft could move freely within and around the atoll for an extended period of time.

52 Landowner negotiators included chairman Christopher Loeak; senators Michael Kabua, Tony deBrum, and Jeban Riklon; a representative for Aḷap Fredley Mawilon, and a representative for Rijerbal Cad Subille. RMI government negotiators included RMI attorney general Frederick Canavor and foreign minister John Silk. Imata Kabua did not directly participate in the

negotiations but instead had his lawyer meet with the attorney general later (Philippo 2015, 173).
53 Giff Johnson, *Marshall Islands Journal* editor, personal communication, May 16, 2016.
54 Hirata Kabua, Kwajalein Atoll Local Government (KALGOV) mayor, and Scott Paul, manager, interview, March 14, 2016.
55 Michael Kabua, conversation with the author, Honolulu, March 23, 2016.

Chapter 9: Atollism

1 Fujitani (2007), writing about the commonalities between Koreans within the Japanese colonial project and Japanese who had migrated to the United States before the war, shows how the war forced both groups to deny their heritage and become exemplary citizens of each nation. He concludes that through a process of "modulated" state racism, Koreans became increasingly marginalized in Japan through the postwar, while Japanese Americans eventually became held up as the "model minority" in the United States (Fujitani 2007, 33–35).
2 Here I am echoing Carucci's encapsulation of Ri-Kuwajleen cosmology as a constant experience of fraught uncertainty amidst the turbulent changes and hardships brought by colonialism and the postwar American military presence, which he refers to as "anxious anticipation" (Carucci 1997a).
3 "Poison" (*baijin*) is the word often used in Marshallese for nuclear radiation.
4 An earlier version of this narrative was published in Dvorak 2014, 370–372.
5 Bubu, like many in her family, migrated to Sacramento, California, in her mid-seventies to receive better medical care, and she eventually passed away there. She was remembered back in the Marshall Islands with large memorial services on Ebeye.
6 This passage was excerpted, with permission from Kathy Jetñil-Kijiner, from the original longer version of her 2016 poem "Utilomar," published on kathyjetnilkijiner.com (accessed December 10, 2016).

Works Cited

Abo, Takaji, Byron Bender, Alfred Capelle, and Tony deBrum. 1976. *Marshallese-English Dictionary*. Honolulu: University of Hawai'i Press.

Akimichi Tomoya. 1997. "Nihon no Mita Oseania" (Japanese views on Oceania). In *Ibunka e no Manazashi* (Images of other cultures: Re-viewing ethnographic collections of the British Museum and the National Museum of Ethnology, Osaka), edited by Kenji Yoshida and John Mack, 236–249. Osaka: NHK Service Center.

Akutagawa Ryūnosuke. 1917. *Rashōmon, Meichō Fukkoku Zenshū; 66*. Tokyo: Aranda Shobō.

Appadurai, Arjun. 1991. "Global Ethnoscapes: Notes and Queries for a Transnational Anthropology." In *Recapturing Anthropology: Working in the Present*, edited by Richard Gabriel Fox, viii, 248. Santa Fe, NM: School of American Research Press.

Aubuchon, Jason, and Francis X. Hezel. 2003. *The US and the Marshall Islands: The Next Twenty Years*. Federated States of Micronesia: Micronesian Seminar. Video.

Balos, Ataji L. 1982. "Kwajalein Owners Vow to Fight On." *Honolulu Star Bulletin*, July 15, 1982, A-2.

Barclay, Robert. 2002. *Meḷaḷ*. Honolulu: University of Hawai'i Press.

Barker, Holly M. 2004. *Bravo for the Marshallese: Regaining Control in a Post-Nuclear, Post-Colonial World*. Case Studies on Contemporary Social Issues Series. Belmont, CA: Thomson/Wadsworth.

Barrie, J. M. 1928. *Peter Pan*. New York: C. Scribner's Sons.

Barthes, Roland. 1981. *Camera Lucida: Reflections on Photography*. New York: Hill & Wang.

———. 2000. *Mythologies*. Reprint of 1972 translation of 1957 original French edition. London: Vintage.

Bauer, F. H. 1960. *Kwajalein Atoll: Geography and Facilities, Technical Memorandum; No. Pmr-Tm-60-4*. Point Mugu, CA: Pacific Missile Range.

Beardsley, Felicia Rounds. 1994. *Archaeological Investigations on Kwajalein Atoll, Marshall Islands*. Honolulu: International Archaeological Research Institute.

Behar, Ruth. 1996. *The Vulnerable Observer: Anthropology That Breaks Your Heart*. Boston: Beacon Press.

Bell Telephone Laboratories. 1972. *A Guide to the Marshall Islands*. 3rd ed. Kwajalein: Bell Laboratories.

Blum, Betty. 2001. *Oral History of Ben Honda*. Chicago: Art Institute of Chicago.

Bragard, Véronique. 2005. "Transoceanic Echoes: Coolitude and the Work of the Mauritian Poet Khal Torabully." *International Journal of Francophone Studies* 8(2): 219–233.

Bryan, E. H. 1965. "The Marshalls and the Pacific." Special edition, *Kwajalein Hourglass*, October, 32–35.

Buck, Elden M. 2005. *Island of Angels: The Growth of the Church on Kosrae: Kapkapak Lun Church Fin Acn Kosrae, 1852–2002*. 1st ed. Honolulu: Watermark Pub.

Burris, Ted. 2004. *Kwajalein: From Stonehenge to Star Wars*. 1st ed. Binghamton, NY: Brundage Pub.

Buruma, Ian. 1994. *The Wages of Guilt: Memories of War in Germany and Japan*. New York: Meridian.

Butler, Judith. 1990. *Gender Trouble: Feminism and the Subversion of Identity*. New York: Routledge.

Camacho, Keith. 2011. *Cultures of Commemoration: The Politics of War, Memory, and History in the Mariana Islands*. Honolulu: University of Hawai'i Press.

———. 2016. *Senka o Kinen Suru: Guam, Saipan no Rekishi to Kioku*. Tokyo: Iwanami Shoten.

Carucci, Laurence Marshall. 1989. "The Source of the Force in Marshallese Cosmology." In *The Pacific Theater: Island Representations of World War II*, edited by Geoffrey M. White and Lamont Lindstrom, 73–96. Honolulu: University of Hawai'i Press.

———. 1997a. *In Anxious Anticipation of Kuwajleen's Uneven Fruits: A Cultural History of the Significant Locations and Important Resources of Kuwajleen Atoll*. Huntsville, AL: United States Army Space and Strategic Defense Command.

———. 1997b. *Nuclear Nativity: Rituals of Renewal and Empowerment in the Marshall Islands*. DeKalb: Northern Illinois University Press.

———. 2001. "Elision or Decision: Lived History and the Contextual Grounding of the Constructed Past." In *Cultural Memory: Reconfiguring History and Identity in the Postcolonial Pacific*, edited by Jeannette Marie Mageo and Amy K. Stillman, 81–101. Honolulu: University of Hawai'i Press.

Chapin, John C. 1994. *Breaking the Outer Ring: Marine Landings in the Marshall Islands, Marines in World War II Commemorative Series*. Washington, DC: History and Museums Division, Headquarters.

Chappell, David. 2013. *The Kanak Awakening: The Rise of Nationalism in New Caledonia.* Honolulu: University of Hawai'i Press.

Chutaro, Suzanne. 2011. "LUA Signed After 8 Years." *Marshall Islands Journal,* May 13, 2011.

Cowell, Andrew. 1992. "The Apocalypse of Paradise and the Salvation of the West: Nightmare Visions of the Future in the Pacific Eden." *Cultural Studies* 13(1) 138–160.

Crismon, Sandra. 2005. "Negotiating the Borders of Empire: An Ethnography of Access on Kwajalein Atoll, Marshall Islands." PhD dissertation, University of Georgia.

Crocombe, R. G. 1987. *Land Tenure in the Pacific.* 3rd ed. Suva, Fiji: University of the South Pacific.

Curthoys, Ann, and John Docker. 2005. *Is History Fiction?* Ann Arbor: University of Michigan Press.

D'Arcy, Paul. 2006. *The People of the Sea: Environment, Identity and History in Oceania.* Honolulu: University of Hawai'i Press.

Davis, Sasha. 2015. *The Empire's Edge: Militarization, Resistance, and Transcending Hegemony in the Pacific.* Athens: University of Georgia Press.

deBrum, Tony A. 2007. "An Overview of the Compact of Free Association between the United States and the Republic of the Marshall Islands: Are Changes Needed?" Statement of Senator Tony A. deBrum before the Committee on Foreign Affairs, US House of Representatives, Subcommittee on Asia, the Pacific, and the Global Environment, July 25, 2007.

———. 2010. "Final Attempt at Finding a Solution to the Impasse of Kwajalein." Statement of Senator Tony A. deBrum before the Committee on Foreign Affairs, US House of Representatives, Subcommittee on Asia, the Pacific, and the Global Environment, May 20, 2010.

deBrum, Leonard, Sue Rosoff, Cris Lindborg, and Eric Lindborg. 2005. *Joachim Debrum Photographs 1890–1930 Digital Archive Project.* Kwajalein, Marshall Islands: Marshallese Cultural Center. Photographic Archive and Database.

Dé Ishtar, Zohl. 1994. *Daughters of the Pacific.* North Melbourne, Vic., Australia: Spinifex Press.

de Laubenfels, M. W. 1950. "Ocean Currents in the Marshall Islands." *Geographical Review* 40(2): 254–259.

Deleuze, Gilles, and Félix Guattari. 1988. *A Thousand Plateaus: Capitalism and Schizophrenia.* London: Athlone Press.

Denfield, D. Colt. 1984. Korean Laborers in Micronesia During World War II. *Korea Observer* 15(1): 3–17.

Dening, Greg. 1988. *History's Anthropology: The Death of William Gooch,* A.S.A.O. Special Publications; No. 2. Lanham, MD: University Press of America.

———. 2003. "Deep Times, Deep Spaces: Civilizing the Sea." In *Sea Changes:*

Historicizing the Ocean, edited by Bernhard Klein and Gesa Mackenthun, 13–35. New York: Routledge.

———. 2004. *Beach Crossings: Voyaging across Times, Cultures, and Self.* Philadelphia: University of Pennsylvania Press.

Desmond, Jane. 1999. *Staging Tourism: Bodies on Display from Waikiki to Sea World.* Chicago: University of Chicago Press.

Diaz, Vicente Miguel. 2001. "Deliberating 'Liberation Day:' Identity, History, Memory, and War in Guam." In *Perilous Memories: The Asia-Pacific War(s),* edited by Takashi Fujitani, Geoffrey M. White, and Lisa Yoneyama, 155–180. Durham, NC: Duke University Press.

———. 2002. " 'Fight Boys, 'Til the Last . . .' Island Style Football and the Remasculinization of Indigeneity in the Militarized American Pacific Islands." In *Pacific Diaspora: Island Peoples in the United States and across the Pacific,* edited by P. R. Spickard, J. L. Rondilla, and D. Hippolite Wright. Honolulu: University of Hawai'i Press.

Diaz, Vicente Miguel, and J. Kehaulani Kauanui. 2001. *Native Pacific Cultural Studies on the Edge.* The Contemporary Pacific, vol. 13. Honolulu: Center for Pacific Islands Studies, University of Hawai'i Press.

Dirlik, Arif. 1993. *What Is in a Rim?: Critical Perspectives on the Pacific Region Idea.* Boulder, CO: Westview Press.

Dornelas, Maria, Sean R. Connolly, and Terence P. Hughes. 2006. "Coral Reef Diversity Refutes the Neutral Theory of Biodiversity." *Nature* 440(2): 80–82.

Dower, John W. 1986. *War without Mercy: Race and Power in the Pacific War.* 1st ed. New York: Pantheon Books.

———. 1999. *Embracing Defeat: Japan in the Wake of World War II.* 1st ed. New York: W. W. Norton & Co./New Press.

Duncan, James S., and Nancy G. Duncan. 1992. "Roland Barthes and the Secret Histories of Landscape." In *Writing Worlds: Discourse, Text, and Metaphor in the Representation of Landscape,* edited by Trevor J. Barnes and James S. Duncan, 18–37. London: Routledge.

Dvorak, Greg. 2004. "Remapping Home: Touring the Betweenness of Kwajalein." MA thesis, University of Hawai'i at Manoa.

———. 2008. " 'The Martial Islands': Making Marshallese Masculinities between American and Japanese Militarism." *The Contemporary Pacific* 20(1): 55–86.

———. 2014. "Who Closed the Sea?: Archipelagoes of Amnesia Between the United States and Japan." *Pacific Historical Review* 83(2): 350–372.

———. 2016. "Detouring Kwajalein: At Home Between Coral and Concrete in the Marshall Islands." In *Touring Pacific Cultures,* edited by Kalissa Alexeyeff and John Taylor, 97–140. Canberra: Australian National University Press.

Enloe, Cynthia H. 1990. *Bananas, Beaches & Bases: Making Feminist Sense of International Politics.* 1st US ed. Berkeley: University of California Press.

Feeser, Andrea, and Gaye Chan. 2006. *Waikiki: A History of Forgetting and Remembering*. Honolulu: University of Hawai'i Press.
Ferguson, Kathy E., and Phyllis Turnbull. 1999. *Oh, Say, Can You See?: The Semiotics of the Military in Hawai'i*. Minneapolis: University of Minnesota Press.
Finsch, Otto. 1893. *Marshall-Archipel*. English translation. [Wien].
Firth, Stewart. 1987. *Nuclear Playground*. Sydney: Allen & Unwin.
Foucault, Michel, and Colin Gordon. 1980. *Power/Knowledge: Selected Interviews and Other Writings, 1972–1977*. Brighton, Sussex: Harvester.
Frankael, Jon. 2002. "Strategic Registration from Metropolis to Periphery in the Republic of the Marshall Islands." *Journal of Pacific History* 37(3): 299–312.
Fujitani, Takashi. 2007. "Right to Kill, Right to Make Live: Koreans as Japanese and Japanese as Americans During WWII." *Representations* 99: 13–39.
Fukushige Hiroshi. 1987. "Girubāto-Māsharu Sakusen" (The Gilberts-Marshalls strategy). In *Gyokusai no Shimajima: Chūbu Taiheiyō Senki*, 35–45. Tokyo: Shiobosho.
Gotō Taketarō and Suzuki Tsunenori. 1885. *Nanyō Tanken Zukai: Māsharu Guntō Tanken Hōkoku* (Illustrations of an expedition to the South Seas: Report on the Marshall Islands expedition). Tokyo: Gaimushō Gaikōshiryōkan (Diplomatic Record Office).
Halbwachs, Maurice, and Lewis A. Coser. 1992. *On Collective Memory*. Chicago: University of Chicago Press.
Hanlon, David L. 1998. *Remaking Micronesia: Discourses over Development in a Pacific Territory, 1944–1982*. Honolulu: University of Hawai'i Press.
———. 2014. *Making Micronesia: A Political Biography of Tosiwo Nakayama*. Honolulu: University of Hawai'i Press.
Hara, Kimie. 2007. "Micronesia and the Postwar Remaking of the Asia Pacific: 'An American Lake.'" E-journal article. *Japan Focus*, August 10, 2007, http://www.japanfocus.org/products/details/2493. Accessed October 31, 2007.
Hatanaka, Sachiko. 1973. *Mandated Islands Censuses During the Japanese Period*. United States Trust Territory Government, Guam. Photocopy, University of Hawai'i Special Pacific Collection.
Hau'ofa, Epeli. 1994. "Our Sea of Islands." *The Contemporary Pacific* 6(1): 147–161.
———. 2000. "Epilogue: Pasts to Remember." In *Remembrance of Pacific Pasts: An Invitation to Remake History*, edited by Robert Borofsky, 453–471. Honolulu: University of Hawai'i Press.
Hayashi Kōichi. 1964. *Kuezerin-tō no Ima to Mukashi* (The present and past of Kwajalein islet). Tokyo: Kuezerin-tō Senbotsusha Izokukai (Kwajalein Bereaved Families Association).
Hayes, Peter, Lyuba Zarsky, and Walden F. Bello. 1986. *American Lake: Nuclear Peril in the Pacific*. Ringwood, Vic., Australia; New York: Penguin Books.

Heider, Karl G. 1988. "The Rashomon Effect: When Ethnographers Disagree." *American Anthropologist,* New Series 90(1): 73–81.

Hereniko, Vilsoni. 1999. "Representations of Cultural Identities." In *Inside Out: Literature, Cultural Politics, and Identity in the New Pacific,* edited by V. Hereniko and R. Wilson, 137–166. Lanham, MD: Rowman & Littlefield.

Hezel, Francis X. 1983. *The First Taint of Civilization: A History of the Caroline and Marshall Islands in Pre-Colonial Days, 1521–1885.* Pacific Islands Monograph Series, No. 1. Honolulu: Pacific Islands Studies Program, University of Hawai'i Press.

———. 1995. *Strangers in Their Own Land: A Century of Colonial Rule in the Caroline and Marshall Islands.* Honolulu: Center for Pacific Island Studies, School of Hawaiian, Asian and Pacific Studies, University of Hawai'i Press.

———. 2000. "Becoming a Professional Victim." Pohnpei, Federated States of Micronesia: Micronesian Seminar.

———. 2005. "The Call to Arms: Micronesians in the Military." *Micronesian Counselor* 58.

Hezel, Francis X., and M. L. Berg. 1985. *A Book of Readings on Micronesian History.* [Agana, Guam]: Trust Territory of the Pacific Islands.

Higuchi, Wakako. 1987. *Micronesia under the Japanese Administration: Interviews with Former South Sea Bureau and Military Officials.* Mangilao: Micronesian Area Studies Center (MARC), University of Guam.

Hijikata Hisakatsu. 1993. *Collective Works of Hijikata Hisakatsu.* 4 vols. Tokyo: Sasakawa Peace Foundation.

Hokari Minoru. 2001. "Cross-Culturalizing History: Journey to the Gurindji Way of Historical Practice." PhD dissertation, Australian National University.

———. 2004. *Radikaru Ōraru Hisutorī: Ōsutoraria Senjūmin Aborijini no Rekishi Jissen* (Radical oral history: Australian indigenous Aboriginal historical practice). Tokyo: Ochanomizu Shobō.

———. 2015. *Gurinji Journey: A Japanese Historian in the Outback.* Honolulu: University of Hawai'i Press.

Hokuwhitu, Brendan. 2004. "Tackling Māori Masculinity: A Colonial Genealogy of Savagery and Sport." *The Contemporary Pacific* 16(2): 259–284.

Honda Ishirō. 1954. *Gojira* (motion picture). Tōhō Pictures.

———. 1956. *Godzilla, King of the Monsters!* (motion picture). USA: Godzilla Releasing Corp. and Jewell Enterprises.

Hori Hidehiko. 1969. *Polydor Kayō Dai Zenshū 4: Natsukashi no Utagoe.* Record pamphlet. Tokyo: Polydor.

Horne, Gerald. 2007. *The White Pacific: US Imperialism and Black Slavery in the South Seas After the Civil War.* Honolulu: University of Hawai'i Press.

Horowitz, Adam. 1983. *Home on the Range* (motion picture). Oakland, CA: Primordial Soup Productions.

———. 2011. *Nuclear Savage* (motion picture). Oakland, CA: Primordial Soup Productions.
Hosokawa Shūhei. 1992. "Nanyō Seiyō Ongaku no Nihonka/Taishūka 43" (The Japanization/popularization of South Seas and western music). *Music Magazine* 10: 144–149.
Ishida Hitomatsu. 1930. "Shūchō no Musume" (song). Tokyo: Polydor Records.
Ishiyama, Hisao. 2007. "There's No Escaping Reality of Battle of Okinawa." Asahi Shimbun Online English Edition (October 27, 2007), http://www.asahi.com. Accessed November 15, 2007.
Jetñil-Kijiner, Kathy. 2017. *Iep Jāltok: Poems from a Marshallese Daughter.* Tucson: University of Arizona Press.
JICPOA (Joint Intelligence Center Pacific Ocean Areas). 1944a. *Japanese Defenses of Kwajalein Atoll (JICPOA Bulletin No. 48-44).* Honolulu: United States Government. Circulated to Australian Royal Navy and archived in National Archives of Australia, Melbourne.
———. 1944b. *Base Installations, Roi, Namur, and Enniburr Is., Kwajalein Atoll (JICPOA Bulletin No. 46-44).* Honolulu: United States Government. Circulated to Australian Royal Navy and archived in National Archives of Australia, Melbourne.
———. 1944c. *Item #7496, Translation of Captured Japanese Document.* Honolulu: United States Government. Circulated to Australian Royal Navy and archived in AWM 54, National Archives of Australia.
———. 1944d. *Item #8312, Translation of Captured Japanese Document.* Honolulu: United States Government. Circulated to Australian Royal Navy and archived in AWM 54, National Archives of Australia.
———. 1944e. *Item #6437, Translation of Captured Japanese Document.* Honolulu: United States Government. Circulated to Australian Royal Navy and archived in AWM 54, National Archives of Australia.
———. 1944f. *Item #7354, Translation of Captured Japanese Document.* Honolulu: United States Government. Circulated to Australian Royal Navy and archived in AWM 54, National Archives of Australia.
Johnson, Giff. 1979. "Ebeye and Kwajalein, a Tale of Two Islands." *The Progressive* 43(1): 47.
———. 1980. *Ebeye, Apartheid U.S. Style.* Photocopy ed. Honolulu: Hawaiian and Pacific Special Collection, Hamilton Library, University of Hawai'i at Manoa.
———. 1984. *Collision Course at Kwajalein: Marshall Islanders in the Shadow of the Bomb.* Honolulu: Pacific Concerns Resource Center.
———. 2005. "Iroij Imata: US Money Move Illegal." *Marshall Islands Journal,* October 14, 2005, 6.
———. n.d. *Marshall Islands Journal,* issues from 2004–2007.
Jolly, Margaret. 1997. "From Point Venus to Bali Ha'i: Eroticism and Exoticism in Representations of the Pacific." In *Sites of Desire, Economies of*

Pleasure: Sexualities in Asia and the Pacific, edited by Lenore Manderson and Margaret Jolly, 99–122. Chicago: University of Chicago Press.

———. 2007. "Imagining Oceania: Indigenous and Foreign Representations of a Sea of Islands." *The Contemporary Pacific* 19(2): 507–545.

Jones, Steve. 2007. *Coral: A Pessimist in Paradise.* London: Little Brown.

Juda, Tomaki. 2004. "Statement by Senator Tomaki Juda on the 50th Anniversary of the H-Bomb Test on Bikini." Yokwe Online, February 29, 2004, www.yokwe.net. Accessed June 7, 2007.

Kabua, Michael Mañini. 2005. "Ralik Iroij Michael Kabua Shocked by T.R.C. Ruling." *Marshall Islands Journal,* May 13, 2005.

Kahn, E. J. 1966. *A Reporter in Micronesia.* 1st ed. New York: W. W. Norton.

Kahn, Miriam. 2000. "Tahiti Intertwined: Ancestral Land, Tourist Postcard, and Nuclear Test Site." *American Anthropologist* 102(1): 7–26.

Kauanui, J. Kehaulani. 2002. "The Politics of Blood and Sovereignty in Rice v. Cayetano, *Political and Legal Anthropology Review* 25(1).

Kawamura Minato. 1994. *Nanyō, Karafuto no Nihon Bungaku* (Japanese literature of the South Seas and Sakhalin). Tokyo: Chikuma Shobō.

Kawano Hitoshi. 1996. "A Comparative Study of Combat Organizations: Japan and the United States During World War II." PhD dissertation, Northwestern University.

———. 2001. *"Gyokusai" no Guntai, "Seikan" no Guntai* (Army of "sacrifice," army of "survival"). Tokyo: Kōdansha.

Kawazoe Katsuki. 1990. *"Dai 50-Gō Kusentei" no Senseki* (The wake of the No. 50 submarine chaser). Nagasaki: Kawaguchi Insatsu.

Keever, Beverly Deepe. 2004. *News Zero: The New York Times and the Bomb.* Monroe, ME: Common Courage Press.

Kelly, John. 1997. "Gaze and Grasp: Plantations, Desires, Indentured Indians, and Colonial Law in Fiji." In *Sites of Desire, Economies of Pleasure: Sexualities in Asia and the Pacific,* edited by Lenore Manderson and Margaret Jolly, 72–98. Chicago: University of Chicago Press.

Kihara, Shigeyuki. 2005. "Fa'afafine: In the Manner of a Woman" (photography exhibition). Sydney.

Kingu Male Chorus. 1939. *Taiheiyō Kōshin Kyoku* (phonograph record) Tokyo: Kingu Records.

Kirch, Patrick Vinton. 2000. *On the Road of the Winds: An Archaeological History of the Pacific Islands before European Contact.* Berkeley: University of California Press.

Kisō Tetsu. 1986. *Uta no Furusato to Kikō* (The birthplace and environment of songs) Tokyo: Tokyo Hōsō Shuppan Kyōkai.

Kiste, Robert C. 1974. *The Bikinians: A Study in Forced Migration, Kiste and Ogan Social Change Series in Anthropology.* Menlo Park, CA: Cummings Publishing Company.

———. 1993. "New Political Statuses in American Micronesia." In *Contemporary Pacific Societies: Studies in Development and Change,* edited by Victo-

ria S. Lockwood, Thomas G. Harding, and Ben J. Wallace, 67–80. Englewood Cliffs, NJ: Prentice Hall.
KNC (Kwajalein Negotiation Commission). 2002a. *Compact Negotiations 2002: Statement on Behalf of Kwajalein Landowners*. Majuro: Kwajalein Negotiation Commission.
———. 2002b. *Socio-Economic Conditions of Kwajalein/Mid-Corridor Landowners and Ebeye Community 1950–2002*. Majuro: Kwajalein Negotiation Commission.
Kobayashi Izumi. 2007. *Mikuroneshia no Nikkeijin* (Micronesians of Japanese descent). Tokyo: JIPAS (Taiheiyō Shotō Chīki Kenkyūjo).
Kobayashi Yoshinori. 2001. *Gōmanizumu Sengen Supesharu: Sensōron 2* (Declaration of arrogance special: On the war 2). Tokyo: Gentōsha.
Kofukada Sadao. 2000. *Nankai Kaiko Nanajū-Nen* (70 Years' reflection on the southern seas). Tokyo: Poppī Shuppan.
Konishi, Junko. 2005. *Ogasawaran Dancers' Encounters with Pacific Dances*. 1st International Small Island Cultures Conference. Kagoshima University Centre for the Pacific Islands, Kagoshima.
Koppel, Tom. 1995. *Kanaka: The Untold Story of Hawaiian Pioneers in British Columbia and the Pacific Northwest*. Vancouver: Whitecap Books.
Koshikawa Taeko. 1992. *Nankai Ni Chitta Chichi no Sensō Nikki* (War diary of my father who fell in the South Seas). Tokyo: Asahi Shinbun.
Kurosawa Akira. 1950. *Rashōmon* (motion picture). Tokyo: Daiei Films.
LaBriola, Monica. 2006. "Iien Ippān Doon (This Time Together): Celebrating Survival in an 'Atypical Marshallese Community.'" MA thesis, University of Hawai'i.
Lal, Brij V., and Kate Fortune. 2000. *The Pacific Islands: An Encyclopedia*. Honolulu: University of Hawai'i Press.
Lang, Sharon. 2017. "SMDC History: USACS Albert J. Myer to Connect Kwajalein Test Facilities in February 1961." www.army.mil. Accessed February 7, 2017.
Lee, In-Shin. 2006. "Japanese Massacre Survivor Remembers." *Dong-A Ilbo* Online Edition, October 26, 2006, http://english.donga.com. Accessed July 27, 2006.
Lefebvre, Henri. 1991. *The Production of Space*. Oxford: Blackwell.
Lindstrom, Lamont. 2001. "Images of Islanders in Pacific War Photographs." In *Perilous Memories: The Asia-Pacific War(s)*, edited by Takashi Fujitani, Geoffrey M. White, and Lisa Yoneyama, 107–127. Durham, NC: Duke University Press.
Lindstrom, Lamont, and Geoffrey M. White. 1990. *Island Encounters: Black and White Memories of the Pacific War*. Washington, DC: Smithsonian Institution Press.
Linka, James. 1977. *Report of Fact-Finding Team on Kwajalein-Ebeye*. Arlington, VA: Department of the Army.
Loeak, Anono Lieom, Veronica C. Kiluwe, and Linda Crowl. 2004. *Life in the*

Republic of the Marshall Islands (*Mour Ilo Republic Eo an Majōl*). Majuro [Suva]: University of the South Pacific Centre, Institute of Pacific Studies, University of the South Pacific.

Logan, Joshua. 1958. *South Pacific* (motion picture). Magna Corporation.

Low, Morris. 2003. "The Japanese Colonial Eye: Science, Exploration, and Empire." In *Photography's Other Histories*, edited by Christopher Pinney and Nicolas Peterson, 100–118. Durham, NC: Duke University Press.

Lutz, Catherine. 2006. "Empire Is in the Details." *American Ethnologist* 33(4): 593–611.

Lutz, Catherine, and Jane Lou Collins. 1993. *Reading National Geographic*. Chicago: University of Chicago Press.

Maga, Timothy P. 1988. *Defending Paradise: The United States and Guam, 1898–1950*. Modern American History. New York: Garland Publishing.

Mansfield, Nick. 2000. *Subjectivity: Theories of the Self from Freud to Haraway*. New York: New York University Press.

Marshall, S. L. A., and Joseph G. Dawson. 2001. *Island Victory: The Battle of Kwajalein Atoll*. Lincoln: University of Nebraska Press.

Mason, Leonard. 1948. *Micronesia: Isolation or Assimilation?* Honolulu: Hawai'i IPR Notes 3, 1–7.

———. 1987. "Tenures from Subsistence to Star Wars." In *Land Tenure in the Marshall Islands*, edited by Ron Crocombe, 1–27. Suva: Institute of Pacific Studies.

Masuda Kō. 1974. *Kenkyūsha's New Japanese-English Dictionary*. 4th ed. Tokyo: Kenkyūsha.

Masuda Ryūichi. 1943. "Correspondence of Masuda Ryūichi." Unpublished correspondence donated by Masuda family.

Matsuda, Matt K. 2006. "A.H.R. Forum: The Pacific." *The American Historical Review*, June 2006, http://www.historycooperative.org/journals/ahr/111.3/matsuda.html. Accessed November 15, 2006.

McArthur, Phillip Henry. 1995. "The Social Life of Narrative in the Marshall Islands." PhD dissertation, Indiana University.

———. 2004. "Narrative, Cosmos, and Nation: Intertextuality and Power in the Marshall Islands." *Journal of American Folklore* 117(463): 55–80.

McClintock, Anne. 1995. *Imperial Leather: Race, Gender, and Sexuality in the Colonial Contest*. New York: Routledge.

McLelland, Mark J. 2005. *Queer Japan from the Pacific War to the Internet Age*. Lanham, MD: Rowman & Littlefield.

Metz, Christian. 1985. "Instant Self-Contradiction." In *On Signs*, edited by Marshall Blonsky, 259–266. Baltimore, MD: Johns Hopkins University Press.

Miller, Merle. 1944. "After the Battle of Kwajalein." *Yank: The Army Weekly*, March 10, 1944, 3–5.

Moorehead, Alan. 1966. *The Fatal Impact; an Account of the Invasion of the South Pacific, 1767–1840*. 1st ed. New York: Harper & Row.

Moulin, Jane Freeman. 2005. "Review of *Oltobed a Malt* (Nurture, Regenerate, Celebrate) the Ninth Festival of Pacific Arts in Koror, Palau, 22–31 July 2004." *The Contemporary Pacific* 17(2): 512–516.

Morris-Suzuki, Tessa. 2001. "Photographic Memory: Image, Reality, and War." Paper read at Imagining the Past, Remembering the Future: War, Violence, and Memory in Asia conference. March 8–10, 2001, Cebu, Philippines.

———. 2005. *The Past within Us: Media, Memory, History.* New York: Verso.

———. 2007. *Exodus to North Korea: Shadows from Japan's Cold War.* Lanham, MD: Rowman & Littlefield.

Muench, Bruce. 2002. *Spam Cans, Rice Balls and Pearls: Snippets of Memory from World War II.* Austin, TX: Turnkey Press.

Myerhoff, Barbara. 1982. "Life History among the Elderly: Performance, Visibility, and Re-Membering." In *A Crack in the Mirror: Reflexive Perspectives in Anthropology,* edited by J. Ruby, 99–117. Philadelphia: University of Pennsylvania Press.

Nakajima Atsushi. 2001. *Nanyō Tsūshin* (Nanyō communiqué). Tokyo: Chūō Kōron Shinsha.

Nakayama Shinpei. 1933. "Kanaka no Musume" (song). Tokyo: Victor Records.

Nanyō Chiri Gakkai (South Seas Geographical Society). 1932. *Dai Nippon Teikoku Inin Tōchi Nanyō Guntō Chiri Fūzoku Daikan* (A pictorial, geographic, and cultural survey of Japan's Imperial South Seas Islands). Tokyo: Bunshinsha.

Nanyō Guntō Kyōiku-kai. 1938. *Nanyō Guntō Kyōiku-Shi* (History of education in the South Seas Islands). Tokyo: Nanyō Guntō Kyōiku-kai.

Nanyō-chō. 1936. *Waga Nanyō* (film). Japan: Yokohama Cinema Shōkai. Archived at the Japan National Film Center, Tokyo. 35mm, six reels, 47 min.

Nero, Karen L. 1987. "A Cherechar a Lokelii: Beads of History of Koror, Palau, 1783–1983." PhD dissertation, University of California, Berkeley.

Niedenthal, Jack. 2001. *For the Good of Mankind: A History of the People of Bikini and Their Islands.* Majuro, Marshall Islands: Micronitor Publishing.

Nishino Ryōta. 2016. "The Self-Promotion of a Maverick Travel-Writer: Suzuki Tsunenori and His Southern Pacific Islands Travelogue, *Nanyō Tanken Jikki.*" *Studies in Travel Writing* 20(4): 1–14.

Oda Makoto. 1998. *Aboji o Fumu* (Stepping on Father). Tokyo: Kōdansha.

———. 2003. *The Breaking Jewel (Translation of Gyokusai).* Translated by Donald Keene. New York: Columbia University Press.

Ogiu Haruo. 1966. *Senji Gyōkei Jitsuroku* (A true account of wartime prisoner mobilization). Urawa, Saitama: Kyōsei Kyōkai (Association for Criminal Justice and Corrections).

Ōno Shun. 2001. *Kankō Kōsu De Nai Guamu Saipan* (Guam and Saipan off the sightseeing course). Tokyo: Kōbunken.

Peattie, Mark R. 1988. *Nan'yō: The Rise and Fall of the Japanese in Micronesia, 1885–1945*. Pacific Islands Monograph Series, No. 4. Honolulu: Center for Pacific Islands Studies School of Hawaiian Asian and Pacific Studies, University of Hawai'i Press.

Perez-Hattori, Anne. 2007. "They Were Treated Like Animals in a Parade." Paper for Australian National University, Canberra.

Philippo, Jim. 2015. *Kwajalein Atoll: The Legacy of Faith and Hope, as Told by Iroijlaplap Imata "Jabro" Kabua, Paramount King and Former President of the Republic of the Marshall Islands*. Bloomington, IN: Xlibris Printing.

Pinney, Christopher. 1992. "The Parallel Histories of Anthropology and Photography." In *Anthropology and Photography 1860–1920*, edited by Elizabeth Edwards. New Haven, CT: Yale University Press, 74–95.

Polak, Christian, and Kiyoko Sawatari. 2013. *Un Artiste Voyageur en Micronésie: L'Univers Flottant de Paul Jacoulet.* (A traveling artist in Micronesia: The floating universe of Paul Jacoulet). Exhibition Catalog. Paris: Musée du Quai Branly.

Pollock, Nancy J. 1970. *Breadfruit and Breadwinning on Namu Atoll, Marshall Islands*. Ann Arbor, MI: University Microfilms International.

Poyer, Lin, Suzanne Falgout, and Laurence Marshall Carucci. 2001. *The Typhoon of War: Micronesian Experiences of the Pacific War*. Honolulu: University of Hawai'i Press.

Pratt, Mary Louise. 1992. *Imperial Eyes: Travel Writing and Transculturation*. London: Routledge.

Rainbird, Paul. 2004. *The Archaeology of Micronesia, Cambridge World Archaeology*. Cambridge: Cambridge University Press.

Read, Peter. 2003. *Haunted Earth*. Sydney: University of New South Wales Press.

Remick, Bill. 2015. *Just Another Day in Paradise: A History of Kwajalein*. Sun City, AZ: Bill Remick Publishing.

Richard, Dorothy Elizabeth. 1957. *United States Naval Administration of the Trust Territory of the Pacific Islands*. Washington, DC: Office of the Chief of Naval Operations.

Robertson, Jennifer. 1995. "Mon Japon: The Revue Theater as a Technology of Japanese Imperialism." *American Ethnologist* 22(4): 970–996.

Rose, Gillian. 2001. *Visual Methodologies: An Introduction to the Interpretation of Visual Materials*. Thousand Oaks, CA: Sage.

Rottman, Gordon L. 2004. *The Marshall Islands 1944: Operation Flintlock, the Capture of Kwajalein and Eniwetok*. Oxford: Osprey.

Rowa, Aenet. 2005. "Yokwe Blog." Yokwe Net, April 17, 2005, http://yokwe-blog.net. Accessed May 28, 2007.

Rudiak-Gould, Peter. 2004. *Practical Marshallese*. Albany, CA. Self-published volume.

Russell, John. 1991. "Race and Reflexivity: The Black Other in Contemporary Japanese Mass Culture." *Cultural Anthropology* 6(1): 3–25.

Sacks, Oliver W. 1996. *The Island of the Colour-Blind.* Sydney: Picador.
Saeki Eisuke. 1932. *Umi no Seimeisen: Waga Nanyō Shotō* (film). Yokohama: Yokohama Cinema Shōkai. 35 mm, 16mm; 72 min. film, "talkie" version. Archived by Mainichi Films Company, Tokyo and Japan National Film Center, Tokyo.
Safier, Joshua. 1997. "Yasukuni Shrine and the Constraints on the Discourses of Nationalism in Twentieth-Century Japan." MA thesis, University of Kansas.
Sahlins, Marshall David. 1985. *Islands of History.* Chicago: University of Chicago Press.
———. 2003. "Anthropologies: From Levianathology to Subjectology—and Vice Versa" (Part I). *The Central States Anthropological Society Bulletin* 38(2): 9–13.
Said, Edward W. 1993. *Culture and Imperialism.* London: Chatto & Windus.
Satō Shigeru. 1942. "Correspondence of Satō Shigeru." Unpublished letters, from Satō Ryūichi.
Schneider, David Murray. 1984. *A Critique of the Study of Kinship.* Ann Arbor: University of Michigan Press.
Sebald, Winfried Georg. 2000. *Vertigo.* New York: New Directions Publishing.
Seitz, Ali. 2007. "Toledo Physician Has Mission to Repatriate World War II Relics: Survivors in Japan Value Artifacts Deeply" (online article). *Toledo Blade,* July 2, 2007, http://toledoblade.com. Accessed July 19, 2007.
Shapiro, Michael J. 1997. *Violent Cartographies: Mapping Cultures of War.* Minneapolis: University of Minnesota Press.
Shigematsu Hitoyoshi. 2002. *Hakubutsukan Abashiri Kangoku* (Abashiri Prison Museum). Abashiri: Taimuzu-sha.
Shimada Keizō. 1976. *Bōken Dankichi Manga Zenshū, Shōnen Kurabu Bunkō.* Tokyo: Kōdansha.
Silva, Noenoe K. 2004. *Aloha Betrayed: Native Hawaiian Resistance to American Colonialism.* American Encounters/Global Interactions. Durham, NC: Duke University Press.
Sims, Eugene C. 1996. *Kwajalein Remembered: Stories from The "Realm of the Killer Clam."* 1st ed. Eugene, OR: Eugene Print.
Soja, Edward W. 1989. *Postmodern Geographies: The Reassertion of Space in Critical Social Theory.* London: Verso.
Sontag, Susan. 1979. *On Photography.* Harmondsworth: Penguin Books.
Sontheimer, Michael. 2005. "How the Camera Became a Weapon." *Spiegel Online,* February 1, 2005, http://www.spiegel.de/international. Accessed June 25, 2007.
Spennemann, Dirk H. R. 1998. Essays on the Marshallese Past. http://micronesia.csu.edu.au/Marshalls/html/essays/es-ed-1.html. Accessed July 12, 2007.
———. 2004. *The First Descriptions of the Southern Marshalls: The 1788 Accounts of Thomas Gilbert, Edward Home, and John Marshall.* Majuro: Micronitor Publishing.

Stevenson, Robert Louis. 1930. *Treasure Island.* London: Standard Book Co.
Stone, Donna, Kinuko Kowata, and Bernice Joash. 2000. *Jabōnkōnnaan in Majeḷ: Wisdom from the Past.* Majuro: Alele Museum.
Storey, John. 1996. *What Is Cultural Studies?: A Reader.* London: Arnold.
Sublette, Carey. 2006. "The Nuclear Weapon Archive: A Guide to Nuclear Weapons." www.nuclearweaponarchive.org. Accessed November 23, 2006.
Sudō Naoto. 2010. *Nanyō Orientalism: Japanese Representations of the Pacific.* Amherst, NY: Cambria Press.
Suzuki Fujita and family. 1997. *Nanmei no Chichi* (Our father of the southern ocean). Kita-Ibaragi-shi: Ibaragi Suzuki-ke Ijikai.
Suzuki, Tsunenori (Keikun). 1980. *Nanyō Tanken Jikki* (Account of an expedition to the South Seas). Republication and transliteration into modern Japanese of 1892 original. Tokyo: Tōyō Bunkō.
Takayama Jun. 1995. *Nankai no Daitankenka Suzuki Tsunenori* (Suzuki Tsunenori, the great adventurer of the southern seas). Tokyo: Sanichi Shobō.
Tanaka Nobumasa, Tanaka Hiroshi, and Hata Nagami. 1995. *Izoku to Sengo* (Bereaved families and the postwar). Tokyo: Iwanami Shinsho.
Tarte, Sandra. 1995. *Japan and the Pacific Islands: The Politics of Fisheries, Access, Aid and Regionalism.* Uppsala: Life and Peace Institute.
Teaiwa, Katerina Martina. 2015. *Consuming Ocean Island: Stories of People and Phosphate from Banaba.* Bloomington: Indiana University Press.
Teaiwa, Teresia. 1994. "Bikinis and Other S/pacific N/oceans." *The Contemporary Pacific* 6(1): 87–109.
———. 1999. "Reading Gauguin's *Noa Noa* with Epeli Hauʻofa's *Kisses in the Nederens:* Militourism, Feminism, and the Polynesian Body." In *Inside Out: Literature, Cultural Politics, and Identity in the New Pacific,* edited by Vilsoni Hereniko and Rob Wilson, 249–263. Lanham, MD: Rowman & Littlefield.
Tengan, Ty P. Kāwika. 2003. "Hale Mua: (En)Gendering Hawaiian Men." PhD dissertation, University of Hawaiʻi at Mānoa.
———. 2008a. "Re-Membering Panalaʻau: Masculinities, Nation, and Empire in Hawaiʻi and the Pacific." *The Contemporary Pacific* 20(1): 27–54.
———. 2008b. *Native Men Remade: Gender and Nation in Contemporary Hawaiʻi.* Durham, NC: Duke University Press.
Tobin, Jack. 1954. *Ebeye Village: An Atypical Marshallese Community.* Majuro, Marshall Islands. Photocopied report in University of Hawaiʻi Library Pacific Collection.
———. 2002. *Stories from the Marshall Islands: Bwebwenato Jān Aelōñ Kein, Pali Language Texts.* Honolulu: University of Hawaiʻi Press.
Tomita Masao. 2005. *Nanyō Odori* (the South Seas dance). Edited by Nanyō Odori Hozon Kyōkai. Ogasawara: Ogasawara-son Sangyō Kankō-ka.
Tomiyama, Ichirō. 2002. "The 'Japanese' of Micronesia: Okinawans in the Nan'yō Islands." In *Okinawan Diaspora,* edited by Ronald Y. Nakasone, 57–70. Honolulu: University of Hawaiʻi Press.

Torrice, Andrea. 2000. *Rising Waters: Global Warming and the Fate of the Pacific Islands* (documentary). Torrice Productions.
Townsend, Susan. 2000. *Yanaihara Tadao and Japanese Colonial Policy: Redeeming Empire*. Richmond and Surrey: Curzon Press.
Toyosaki Hiromitsu. 2005. *Māsharu Shotō Kaku no Seiki: 1914–2004* (The Marshall Islands' atomic century, 1914–2004). 2 vols. Tokyo: Nihon Tosho Sentā.
TTPI (US Trust Territory of the Pacific Islands) Office of the District Administration. 1965. *Marshalls District Handbook of Information*. Majuro: US Trust Territory of the Pacific Islands.
Turnbull, David. 2000. *Masons, Tricksters and Cartographers: Comparative Studies in the Sociology of Scientific and Indigenous Knowledge*. Amsterdam: Harwood Academic.
Ueta Jōji. 1943. "Correspondence of Ueta Jōji." Unpublished letters, donated by Okui Ayako.
United States Army Materiel Command. 1964. *Kwajalein Test Site*. Kwajalein, Marshall Islands: U.S. Army Materiel Command.
United States Department of State. 2003. "Compact of Free Association: Agreement between the United States and the Republic of the Marshall Islands Amending the Agreement of June 25, 1983, concerning the Compact of Free Association, as Amended." Majuro, April 30, 2003.
US Army Kwajalein Atoll (USAKA). *Kwajalein Hourglass* (newspaper), various issues, 1980–2007.
US Army Pictorial Service. 1944. *What Makes a Battle* (propaganda short film). Astoria, NY.
US Marine Corps (USMC). 1944a. *Report of Interrogation of Japanese Prisoners of War as of 1–8 March 1944, Aboard U.S.S. Electra, Eniwetok (File 1929)*. March 14, 1944. San Francisco: US National Archives.
———. 1944b. "Kwajalein Operations: 4th Marine Division and 7th Infantry Division Supported by Battleships Wipe Out the Japanese at Roi-Namur and Kwajalein in February 1944" (newsreel).
Vonnegut, Kurt. 1973. *Breakfast of Champions; or, Goodbye Blue Monday!* New York: Delacorte Press.
Walker, James A., Lewis Bernstein, and Sharon Lang. 2004. *The Eastern Mandates Campaign: A Staff Ride Guide for Operation Flintlock, the Seizure of Kwajalein*. Huntsville, AL: US Army Space and Missile Defense Command History Office.
Walsh, Julianne M. 2001. "Exposure and Disclosure: Public A(nthro)pologies." *Public Anthropology,* www.publicanthropology.org/journals/grad-j/(2)Hawaii/Walsh.htm. Accessed August 12, 2007.
———. 2003. "Imagining the Marshalls: Chiefs, Tradition, and the State on the Fringes of U.S. Empire." PhD dissertation, University of Hawai'i at Manoa.

Weiner, Michael. 1994. The Mobilisation of Koreans During the Second World War. In *Race and Migration in Imperial Japan,* edited by Michael Weiner, 187–208. London: Routledge.
Weisgall, Jonathan. 1994. *Operation Crossroads: The Atomic Tests at Bikini Atoll.* Annapolis, MD: Naval Institute Press.
Wenders, Wim. 1992. *The Logic of Images: Essays and Conversations.* London: Faber and Faber.
White, Geoffrey M., and Lamont Lindstrom. 1989. *The Pacific Theater: Island Representations of World War II.* Pacific Islands Monograph Series, No. 8. Honolulu: University of Hawai'i Press.
Wilkes, Owen. 1991. *Chasing Gravity's Rainbow: Kwajalein and US Ballistic Missile Testing.* Canberra Papers on Strategy and Defence, No. 81. Canberra: Strategic and Defence Studies Centre Research School of Pacific Studies, Australian National University.
Wood, Denis 1992. *The Power of Maps.* New York: Guilford Press.
Wypijewski, JoAnn. 2000. "Imperial Geographic: A Walk Amid the Earthly Work of Star Wars." Unpublished manuscript, received from author.
Yaguchi Yujin. 2011. *Akogare no Hawai: Nihonjin no Hawai-kan* (Hawaiian yearning: Japanese perspectives on Hawai'i). Tokyo: Chūo Kōron Shinsha.
Yamashita, Shinji. 2000. "The Japanese Encounter with the South: Japanese Tourists in Palau." *The Contemporary Pacific* 12(2): 437–463.
Yanaihara, Tadao. 1939. *Pacific Islands under Japanese Mandate.* Shanghai: Kelly and Walsh, Ltd.
Yoneyama, Lisa. 1999. *Hiroshima Traces: Time, Space, and the Dialectics of Memory.* Berkeley: University of California Press.
Yoshida Kiyoshi. 1931. *Nanyō Guntō Kaisetsu Shashinchō* (A photographic commentary of the South Seas islands). Garapan, Saipan: Kenbunsha.
Young, James E. 1988. *Writing and Rewriting the Holocaust.* Bloomington: Indiana University Press.
Yui Tsunejiro. 1943. "Diary of Yui Tsunejirō." Unpublished diary.
Yun, Seol-Young. 2007. "Kyōsei chōyōsha 4,000-nin ga gisei ni natta shima ni dōshite kagaisha Nihon no irei-hi dake nanoka . . ." (Why is there only a memorial for Japanese assailants on islands where 4,000 forced draftees were victimized? [Japanese translation of article in Korean])." Daum Online Korea, August 26, 2007, http://news.daum.net/foreign/others/200708/24/seoul/v1788804.html. Accessed August 30, 2007.
Zackios, Gerald. 2007. "Statement of the Hon. Gerald M. Zackios, Minister of Foreign Affairs, RMI Before the US House of Representatives Committee on Natural Resources, Subcommittee on Insular Affairs." Yokwe Online 2007, www.yokwe.net. Accessed July 24, 2007.

Image Notes

Page No.	Description
8	Aerial photo of Kwajalein islet by landsat-7 satellite, from US Army Kwajalein Atoll.
11	Photo of me at age four on Kwajalein riding my first bicycle, taken by Christine Dvorak, 1977.
20	This small piece of coral (photograph by the author) was found on the islet of Enṃaat, one of the most sacred places in Kwajalein Atoll. Irooj Michael Kabua granted me permission to access this islet in 2005.
41	Map reproduced from Yoshida 1931.
42	Map by Gotō and Suzuki 1885, courtesy of the Japan Ministry of Foreign Affairs Diplomatic Record Office.
43	"Kwajalein Port," from Gotō and Suzuki 1885, courtesy of the Japan Ministry of Foreign Affairs Diplomatic Records Office.
49	US Marine Corps, 1944 (reprinted in Kwajalein orientation materials, circa 1975).
50	United States Navy, "Operation Crossroads Orientation Manual," 1950.
51	Map from US Army pamphlet produced for Kwajalein orientation materials, 1972 (for more on this map, see Dvorak 2004).
52	Map reproduced from a technical briefing document for Kwajalein Test Site (US Army Materiel Command 1964).
59	Video still of Ato Lañkio describing his land on Kwajalein islet, by Greg Dvorak, 2006.
59	Map by Ato Lañkio, 2005. Ato later collaborated with former Kwajalein Marshallese Cultural Center curator Cris Lindborg in 2005 to add

more detail about the location of homes and buildings during the Japanese period.

71 Postage cancellation stamp from Jaluit District in Nanyō Guntō, circa 1930s (from Yamaguchi Yōji collection).

73 This image, reproduced from Yoshida (1931, 110), is peculiar for its time because after the heavy mission influence of American missionaries and Spanish/German colonization, Marshall Islanders had widely adopted European dress by the end of the 1900s (Spenneman 1998). Marshallese young women would ordinarily not have dressed in these hand-woven mats or gone bare-breasted during the 1930s. The girls also hold leaves and flowers in their hands from the *utilomar* plant, the "Kwajalein flower" that I discuss in chapter 1.

74 The girl depicted in this image from a geographical almanac of the South Seas (Nanyō Chiri Gakkai 1932, plate 68) may have been of German or Portuguese descent, perhaps the relative of copra trader Adolf Capelle or his business partner Jose deBrum, who built a successful trading enterprise at Likiep Atoll during the German administration of the islands.

85 The family of Kaname Yamamura's father, gathered in Nagasaki in late 1930s, on one of the trips Kaname took to Japan to help his father do work for the Nanyō Bōeki Kaisha trading company. Kaname is second from left in the back row; his father is fourth from the left (photo courtesy of Kaname Yamamura).

87 Parao Kaitaku Shiryōkan's *bai*, taken by Greg Dvorak, August 23, 2005, Kobayashi, Japan.

93 With my mother, on a Japanese pillbox bunker on Roi-Namur, age three (taken by Walter Dvorak, 1976).

101 This photograph of Japanese Imperial Navy sailors was presumably taken on Kwajalein in 1942 or 1943. It was provided to me by the Marshallese Cultural Center on Kwajalein, but its origins are unknown.

119 Photo by Corporal John Fabian, originally from the Public Affairs Office of the Department of Defense (NA-70267, US Marine Corps).

121 Image #NA-70675, National Archives.

124 Layout from US Army publication *Yank* magazine coverage of Operation Flintlock, 1944 (Miller 1944, 4). The offensive slur here is reproduced deliberately to critique American racist ideologies that were used to justify extreme dehumanization and violence toward Japanese, Koreans, and Pacific Islanders during the Pacific War.

125 Map from the film, "What Makes a Battle" (US Army Pictorial Service 1944).

Image Notes

127 Image #A-41735 United States Air Force Collection, National Archives.
129 Closeup of Image #A-41735 United States Air Force Collection, National Archives.
132 Image #NA-72003, National Archives.
134 Image #NA-70296, National Archives (photo by Corporal John Fabian).
136 Image #NA-74285, National Archives (photo by Sergeant A. Zurick).
138 Air Force Collection, Image #A-41767, National Archives.
140 Image # NA-72209, National Archives (photo by Sergeant Dick Tennelly).
141 Image #NA-78811, National Archives (photo by Staff Sergeant K. G. Jones).
143 Air Force Collection Image #A-41732, National Archives.
145 Image #NA-78807, National Archives (photo by Staff Sergeant K. G. Jones).
146 Image #NA-78806, National Archives (photo by Staff Sergeant K. G. Jones).
148 Air Force Collection, Image #A-41733, National Archives.
150 Image #NA-86693, National Archives (photo by Staff Sergeant Donald E. Brooks).
152 Image #NA-93273, National Archives (photo by Corporal A. B. Mannell, US Marine Corps).
159 Jaluit Nanyō-chō Weather Bureau, May 2005 (photo by Greg Dvorak).
159 Jaluit Nanyō-chō Weather Bureau, circa 1938 (photo from Nanyō Kyōkai Archives).
169 With the radar balls and antennas of Kwajalein islet faintly visible in the distance, one can see just how close Kwajalein is to Ebeye; one can easily walk between the islands at low tide (photo by Greg Dvorak, 2006).
176 Kabua Kabua, pictured here, is the same person referred to as "Kabua-seinen" (Young Chief Kabua) by Nakajima Atsushi in his famous book *Nanyō Tsūshin* published during the 1930s, mentioned in chapter 3 (US Army photo courtesy of Marshallese Cultural Center, Kwajalein).
178 Mid-Atoll Corridor evacuees carrying an elderly woman as they disembark from a military ship during their relocation to Ebeye, 1964 (US Army photo courtesy of Marshallese Cultural Center, Kwajalein).
184 Street scene on lagoonside Ebeye, photograph by Greg Dvorak, August 2015. Note the man wearing the "Mid-Corridor" shirt in foreground and how collective displacement serves as a marker of identity for those affected.

198 Cemetery and church, with Cold War–era US missile-tracking radar balls in the background, on recently decommissioned Āneeḷḷap-kaṇ (Carlos) islet, March 2016 (photograph by Greg Dvorak).

206 Photo by Joachim deBrum c. 1890, plate 63 in collection, as described by Leonard deBrum on November 12, 2004. This photograph would have been taken during the time of the German administration of the Marshall Islands (image courtesy of the Alele Museum, Majuro).

213 Police surveillance of "young protesters" at Kwajalein, 1982 (photo courtesy of Giff Johnson).

237 Portrait of Suzuki Kametarō, April 20, 1943, possibly taken on Kwajalein (photo courtesy of Suzuki family).

239 Portrait of Ueta Jōji ("George"), circa 1939, taken in Los Angeles (photo courtesy of Ueta family).

241 Neitari "Bubu" Pound poses with four of her granddaughters on Ebeye, July 2006 (photo by Greg Dvorak).

244 One of Bubu's shell necklaces, made in 2006 out of coconut sennit and shells that her grandchildren found for her on the reef (photo by Greg Dvorak).

247 Coral at Pikeej, west reef, Kwajalein Atoll, March 2016 (photo Greg Dvorak).

Index

Page numbers in **boldface** type refer to illustrations

Able detonation, Operation Crossroads, xxix
access, Ebeye/Kwajalein divide, 169, 172, 173, 178, 182
aelōñ [M], 21, xxiii
Ailuk Atoll, 171
Akiyama Monzō, 103, 106, 165
aḷap [M] clan head, xxiii, xxx
ALTAIR radar, 173
American World War II military operations: Hiroshima & Nagasaki bombings, 117, 170, 171, 240; Operation Flintlock, xxix, 48, 95–97, 104–109, 110, 112–113, 170, 238; pre-invasions, 168; Roi-Namur (Ruotto and Nimuru), xxix. See also photographic images; World War II
Americans: hegemony of, 26–27; influence of, 20–21; post-liberation relations, 153–156
Āne-Bōn (Enniburr/Santo) (KA) (Third Island), 173
Āne-Buoj (Enubuj/Carlson), 176
Āne-Eḷḷap-Kan (Ennylabagen/Carlos), xv, 56, 108, **143**, 144, 148, **148**, 198
Arno Atoll, 241
atollscapes: overview, 27–30, 233–234; climate change and, 244, 246–248; coral metaphor, 246–248; history and, 2; Kwajalein Japanese war dead, 160–166; re-membering and, 31
Australia, 3, 31, 41, 75, 168, 203, 228, 254n19, 268n1
Austronesian linguistics, xiv, 3

bai [Palau], xxiii, **87**
baijin [M] (poison), xxiii, 234, 277n3. See also poison; radiation
Baker detonation, xxix
Balos, Ataji, 209, 212, 214
Banaba, 20, 168–169, 249n2
banzai [J], xxiii
baptism, 139–140
Barclay, Robert, 184
Barthes, Roland, 36
bathing, baths (ofuro) [J], xxix, 100, 139-141, 160-163, 166, 261n15. See also ofuro
battle emplacements, xxix, 92–93, 96, 98, 104, 105, 134
benign neglect, 152–153
bereavement: izoku [J], xxvi, 163–166; of Korean relatives, 31, 234; Marshall Islands War Bereaved Families Association (MIBFA) (Māsharu Hōmen Izokukai) [J], 163–166, 236–240; Yasukuni Shrine memorial prayer, 165. See also ireisai [J]

299

bikini (swimsuit), 170
Bikinians, 24, 170
Bikini Atoll: Bravo, xxiv, 171; nuclear testing, 20, 26, 50, 170; Operation Crossroads, xxix, 49, **50**, 170; relocations from, 170; settled, 4; tourist industry, 184
BK. *See* NBK (Nanyō Bōeki Kaisha; South Seas Islands Trading Company)
blackbirding, 75
Bōken Dankichi (Dankichi the Adventurous) (manga) (Shimada), 77–81, 89, 98
borders/boundaries: American power and, 34, 182; coral use in, 21; Ebeye/Kwajalein divide, 183, 188; Marshallese concepts of, 57; racial borders, 84
Bravo, xxiv, 171, 270n7
breadfruit (mā) [M], xxiv, xxviii, 58, 197
bwebwenato [M] traditions, xxiv, 4, 29. *See also* oral traditions
bwij [M] (matrilineage), xxiv, 55–56, 191. *See also* matrilineality

Camacho, Keith, 16, 153, 250n16
Capelle, Adolf, 14
Carlos, 49, **143**, **148**. *See* Āne-Eḷḷap-Kan (Ennylabagen/Carlos)
Carucci, Laurence M., 19, 29, 58, 107, 142, 180, 262n27, 263n40, 265n10, 277n2
Castle Series, xxiv, 171, 270n7
cemeteries: Chidorigafuchi Cemetery, 46, 47, 263n36; Japanese Cemetery in Kwajalein Atoll, 13, 50, 93, 237, 238; Yasukuni Shrine, 163–166
censorship, 102, 116, 130
Chamoro [J], xxiv, 74
Chamorro (Chamoru) Mariana Islanders, xxiv, 74, 89, 117–118
Chidorigafuchi Cemetery, 46, 47, 263n36
chiefs (*irooj*). *See irooj* [M] (chiefs)

chieftain's daughter narrative: colonial gaze and, 71–72, 76–77; dusky maiden narrative, 68–77, 147; images of, 72–74, 76–77; racialization of, 74–76
China: colonization of, 76; international relations, 226; laborers from, 268n8. *See also* Manchuria
Christianity: ABCFM Protestant mission, 5, 35; baptismal imagery, 140–141; Catholic Church, 35; influence of, 147, 201; Japanese soldiers and, 100; missionaries, 35, 140
Chuuk (Truk): Federated States of Micronesia, 76; Japanese use of, 98–99; Korean conscripted laborers at, 99; Mori Koben and, 66, 83
climate change: atollscapes and, 246–248; effects on Marshall Islands, 227; fight against, 232, 234; flooding, 27, 188; historical narratives and, 187–188; Jetñil-Kijiner, Kathy, 232, 244–246
Cold War: missile testing, 175, 178; nuclear testing, 27, 33
colonialism: American, 6–9, 48–53, 154, 223–224; chieftain's daughter narrative, 72; children and, 24; concrete metaphor and, 25–27; education; European, 4–6, 22, 33, 35, 55; forced migration, 24–25; Kwajalein Japanese schools, 44, 58, 61, 88, 98, 100, 242–243, 274n23; overview, 25–27; resistance to, 97; unbalance caused by, 231. *See also* Japanese colonialism
COM (Congress of Micronesia), xxiv, 209, 273n21
commanders: Akiyama Monzō, 103, 106, 165; coercion of naval commanders, 202; Commander Tōgō, 256n5; Japanese commander ghost, 157; Koga Mineichi, 262n22, 276n45; of Kwajalein

base, 13, 154, 165, 210, 212, 218, 223, 224, 276n45
Compact (of Free Association), xxiv, 210, 211, 214, 218, 219, 221, 224, 226, 227–228, 231; RMI and, 219, 249n5
compensations: 1964 lease agreement dispute, 209–210; Americans and, 169, 177; British Phosphate Mining Company, 168; demonstrations for, 174, 208; homecoming narrative, 13, 54, 183, 190, 199, 202, 230; Imata Kabua on, 222–223, 225, 227; Japanese and, 168; *jodik* [M] (invasion, protest), 208; lack of, 57, 179; land rights and, 202–203; *lejman jūri* and, 218; mid-corridor children, 177; for nuclear testing, 27; relocation and, 177; Ri-Kuwajleen landowners and, 179; RMI and, 215, 220, 222; US avoidance of, 175
concrete metaphor, 25–27, 34–35, 37
Congress of Micronesia (COM), xxiv, 209
copra trade: Ebeye (Epjā, Ebize) and, 172; foreign navies and, 202; Germany, 5, 20, 24; Japan, 20, 46, 58, 159
coral: boundaries and, 21; coral colonization, 21–22; coral metaphor, 2, 21–25, 27, 28, 37, 246–248; Darwin on, 18, 21–25, 171; defined, 18; as history, 19–20; Marshallese identity and, 21; Marshallese terms for, xxiv, xxix, xxxi; as metaphor, 2; as sacred object, 265n20; use in sacred spaces, 21, 165–166
coralhead: defined, xxiv; dredging and, 26, 173–174; Tarḷañ, xxx, 19; U.S. destruction of, 26
cosmology, 4, 60, 180, 277n2
Council of Irooj, xxix
creolization, 24
cross-dressing, 67, 149

Crossroads, Operation, xxix, 49, **50**, 170
cultural nationalism, 190–191

Daigo Fukuryū Maru (*Lucky Dragon V.* fishing vessel), 278n8
Dai Tōa Kyōei Ken [J] (Greater East Asia Co-Prosperity Sphere), xxiv, 40, 81
Daku-daku Odori: Ishida version, 68–69; "Nanyo Odori" comparison, 89; narrative of, 86; original version, 63–68, 78
dance, dancing (Nanyō Odori, dojin odori, odori). *See* Nanyō Odori
Darwin, Charles, 18, 21, 170–171
deBrum, Joachim, 73, 207
deBrum, Jose, 207
deBrum, Tony, xiv, xv, 191, 215, 228
deep time: coral metaphors of, 17, 22–23; genealogy and, 244; land battles and, 200–206
Deleuze, Gilles, 28
Dening, Greg, xiii, 15–16, 21, 32, 34, 37, 233
development: agricultural, 88; aid for, 91; American discourses of, 34; discourse on Ebeye, 172, 179, 183–190, 203; funding for, 203, 228; KNC proposal for, 220–221; mapping and, 38
Diaz, Vicente, 27
dislocations: overview, 167; Castle Bravo, 171; Ebeye/Kwajalein separation, 179–180; homecoming narrative, 54; land changes, 168; Mid-Atoll Corridor, 175–179; Operation Crossroads, 170; relocations, 168–173, 175–178; travel issues, 178–179, 180. *See also* historical narratives
dojin [J], xxiv, 76
dojin matsuri [J] ("native" festivals), 67
dojin odori [J]. *See* Nanyō Odori
Domeny de Rienzi, Grégoire Louis, 1
drag, 67, 149

dredging, 9, 26, 173–174, 181
Dribo, Handel, 68, 100, 174, 209–210, 213, 214–215, 274n23
Dumont D'Urville, Jules, 1, 38
dusky maiden narrative, 68–77, 147

Ebadon *See* Epatōn (Ebadon)
Ebeye (Epjā, Ebize): conditions on, 19, 171–172, 173, 177–179; copra trade and, 172; decreased population density, 232; description, xxiv–xxv, 3; development discourse, 172, 179, 183–190, 203; development funding, 228; Ebeye/Kwajalein divide, 12, 173, 176, 179–180, 182, 183, 188, 230; historical narratives, 183–192; homecoming narrative, 209–216; Japanese occupation of, 61–62, 105; KNC and, 220–222; land rights, 179; Land Use Agreement of 2011, 227; *lejman jūri* and, 216–218; maps, 43; Marshallese residents, 36, 177, 195, 234; NSA and, 228–229; post-liberation, 153; protests, 208–209, 213, 216; relocations to, 25, 53, 171–172, 175–177, 176–177; resource scarcity on, 19
Ebon Atoll (Epoon), xxv, 5, 35
education: carpentry school (Mokkō), 274n23; Ebeye and, 191, 228, 250n12; *gakkō* [J] public schools, xxv, 61; *gunka* [J] (patriotic military songs), 98; Japanese vocational school (Palau), 274n23; Kochi Imperial Secondary School, 63–68; Kwajalein (American) school system, 173, 175, 181, 189, 250n12, 267n43; Kwajalein Japanese schools, 9, 44, 58, 61, 88, 98, 100, 242–243, 274n23; mission schools, 6, 100; Nanyō Guntō study on, 254n14; Nanyō Guntō textbooks, 44; national anthems, 242; segregation in, 100

eminent domain, 215–216, 274n32
Enewetak Atoll (Āne-Wetak): amphibious landing on, 107; Bikini Resurvey Project, 171; conscripted laborers, 98–99; homecoming narrative, 230; land evictions, 206; land leases, 56; nuclear testing, 20, 26, 97, 167, 170; Operation Flintlock, xxix, 106–107, 110, 170; relocations, 170; in Yasukuni Shrine memorial prayer, 165
Enṃaat, 175
Enniburr. *See* Āne-bōn (Enniburr/ Santō/Third Island)
Ennylabagen (Āne-Eḷḷap-Kan/Carlos). *See* Āne-Eḷḷap-Kan (Ennylabagen/ Carlos)
Epatōn (Ebadon), 3, 178
Epjā. *See* Ebeye (Epjā, Ebize)
Ero, 175, 243
eroguro nansensu, 65, 69–70
Exodus, Operation, 191

fa'afāfine [Samoa] (third-gender), xxv, 257n10
fallout, 171; Bravo test, 270n7
Finsch, Otto, 204
fisheries, 91
flags: *hinomaru* [J] rising sun emblem, xxv, 120, 126, 129, 131; images of, **119**, 120–121, **121**, 125, **125**; looting of, 118, 119–120, **119**, 126–127, **127**, 129–131, **129**; victory and, 96, 120–121, **121**
Flintlock, Operation, xxix, 48, 95–97, 104–109, 110, 112–113, 170, 238
flooding, 27, 188
flying fish, 20, 244
forced migration, xxviii, 24, 46, 53, 54, 88, 168, 170, 177
Foucault, Michel, 25, 35, 181
Fujitani, 277n1
fundoshi [J], xxv, 64, 140, 261n14
furusato [J], xxv, 238

gakkō [J] public schools, xxv, 61
Gauguin, Paul, 71
Gea. *See* Kā (Gehh) (Gea)
geisha, 146
gender: androcentric narrative, 96; assumed roles of, 91; cultural representations of, 79–80; divisions of, 58; gendered subordination, 74; land rights and, 49; martial masculinities, 72, 94–95, 119, 141; third-gender persons, xxv, 257n10
genealogy (*bwij/jowi*): of chiefs (*irooj*), 20, 72, 200–201, 242–244; co-opting of, 26; of coral, 22, 25, 34; cultural nationalism and, 190–191, 229–230; deep time, 17; historical narratives and, 180–181; Japanese-Micronesian genealogies, 81–87, 90; Marshallese mapping of, 54–60, 234; narratives of, 180–181; notions of region and, 38–39; origin stories and, 2; "outsiders" and, 244; reconnecting Marshallese genealogies, 53–60; re-membering Marshallese roots, 154, 240–244; research methodology and, 15–17; written on land, 180
Geneva Convention, 133, 266n25
German colonialism: copra trade, 5–6, 20, 24; *irooj* and, 225; Jaluit (Yarūto, Jālooj, Jālwōj), xxvi, 5–6; *kanaka* [J] term use, 75; Lebon (Kabua the Great), 200, 204, 205; marching exercises of, 89; Micronesia and, xxvi, xxviii; Nauru, 38; WWI territory loss, xxviii, 6, 33, 66
Gilbert Islands. *See* Kiribati
global warming. *See* climate change
Godzilla. See *Gojira* (Honda 1954, 1956)
Gojira (Honda 1954, 1956), 270n7
Gotō Taketarō, 41–43, **42–43**
grass skirts, 64, 67, 78, 81, 88–89,
148–149, **148**. See also *dojin matsuri* [J] ("native" festivals)
Gramsci, Antonio, 23
Greater East Asia Co-Prosperity Sphere (Dai Tōa Kyōei Ken), xxiv, 40, 81
Guam (Guåhan), 4, 22, 27, 35, 39, 41, 47, 118, 172, 175, 224
Guattari, Félix, 28
gunka [J] (patriotic military songs), xxv, 98, 158–159
gyokusai [J] (crushed jewel) mission, xxv, 103–109; Japanese commemoration, 164; post-battle imagery, 117, 122–126; re-membering, 239

handicrafts, 148–149, 160, 194, 240, 244
Hanlon, David, 34, 185–187, 189, 208
Hau'ofa, Epeli, 21, 28, 32, 180
Hawai'i/Hawaiians: ABCFM, 35; *ali'i* (ruling chiefs) representations, 201; American militarism and, 201; blood quantum and, 191; Hawaiian workers, 173; interisland warfare, 34; Japanese imperialism and, 46, 47; Japanese tropicalism and, 77; *kānaka*, 75; *mo'olelo* study, 180; music of, 67; Nanyō Odori and, 90; Operation Homecoming and, 212, 214, 220; oral traditions, 28–29; tropicalism and, 67, 148–149; undersea communications lines, 41; workers, 173
Hayashi Kōichi, 81, 100, 103, 261n19, 262n22, 268n4, 269n2
hegemony: development discourse and, 185–186; reinforcement of, 9, 16, 96, 153, 189, 223–224; rewriting history, 25–27; space and, 25, 27
Heider, Karl G., 29
Hezel, Francis X., 4, 186, 202, 205
Hijikata Hisakatsu, 77, 254n15
hinomaru [J] ceremonial flag, xxv, 120, 126–131, **127**, **129**

Hiroshima & Nagasaki bombings, 117, 170, 171, 240
historical narratives: Americans and, 181, 182, 183–185, 188–189, 191; ancient genealogies and, 180–181; boundaries of land, 182; climate change and, 187–188; coral metaphor, 34–35; cultural nationalism, 190–191; Ebeye/Kwajalein separation, 183–192; Japanese and, 181, 182; migrants, 189–190; missile testing, 182; postwar development, 183–184
history: atollscapes and, 2; big/little narratives of, 33–34, 246–248; coral as, 19–20; historical revisionism, 25; Japanese military narrative, 36
Hokari Minoru, 31, 252n15
Homecoming, Operation, 194, 196–197, 211–214, 220, 273n21, 274nn28–29
homecoming narrative, 54; 2016 negotiations, 227–232; climate change and, 232; cultural nationalism and, 229–230; deep time, 200–206; Ebeye/Kwajalein divide, 187–189; eminent domain laws, 215, 274n32; Imata Kabua and, 222–227; land rights battles, 200–206; Land Use Agreement of 2011, 227–228; *lejman jūri*, 216–218, 228; migration and, 231–232; as mission, 39, 53–54, 190, 199–200; nostalgia and, 230–231; NSA and, 228–229; nuclear heritage, 197–200; Operation Homecoming, xxix, 194, 196–197, 211–214; overview, 193–197; postwar battle, 207–210; protests, xxiv, 207–210, 213, 231–232; renegotiations, 219–222; RMI government and, 214–216; RMI/US renegotiations, 219–222. *See also* Compact (of Free Association)

homoeroticism, 141, 258n20, 266n31
homosociality, 64, 98, 119, 140–141, 144–145, 162–163, 266n26
Horowitz, Adam, 213, 274n30

Imiej (Iṃwej). *See* Iṃwej (Imiej)
Imperial Japan: *Bōken Dankichi* (Dankichi the Adventurous) (manga) (Shimada), 77–81, 89, 98; Dai Tōa Kyōei Ken (Greater East Asia Co-Prosperity Sphere), xxiv; defensive narrative, 253n9; Nanyō Guntō/Trust Territory fo the Pacific, xxiv, 47, 62, 125, **125**; Operation Flintlock, xxix. *See also* Imperial Japanese Army (IJA); Imperial Japanese Navy (IJN); Japan; Japanese Expansionism
Imperial Japanese Army (IJA): conscripted workers and, xxvii, 98–100; defensive fortification, 97–102; invasion by, 95–97; Kwajalein Japanese war dead, 128, 160–163, 163–166, 236–240, 263nn36–37; military rule by, 100–102; POWs, 106, 117–118, 132–135, **132**, 262n28
Imperial Japanese Navy (IJN): *Akibasan Maru* (IJN), 158; *Amatsukaze-Maru* (IJN), 166; *Asakaze Maru* (IJN), 23, 162; *Dai-Roku Kyō-Maru* (IJN), 162; draftees, 102; Fourth Fleet, 98, 103; *gunka* [J] (patriotic military songs), 98; *gyokusai* [J] (crushed jewel) mission, 103–107; *Hakosaki Maru* (IJN), 99; *jōriku* term use, 208; *Kōei Maru* (IJN), 238; *Kokushima Maru* (IJN), 99; Kwajalein command center, 6, 100; Pacific military presence, 45–47; POWs, 106, 117–118; *Shōei Maru* (IJN), 23; Tarawa & Nauru capture, 253n6; *Tateyama Maru* (IJN), 158; war dead burials, 108, 156, 263n37

Iṃwej (Imiej), xxvi, 160–163, 270n11
indigenous/nonindigenous binary, 25, 53–60
indigenous people. *See* Ri-Kuwajleen [M]; benign neglect of, 152; Chamorro (Chamoru) Mariana Islanders, xxiv, 74; climate change and, 232; displacement of, 92; images of, 74; indigenous/nonindigenous binary, 25, 53–60; Lolle Laplap, 255n24; missionaries and, 5; racial classifications, xvii, 74–75; stereotyped imagery of, 78; viewpoint of, 29, 38, 39
Inshin, Lee, 107, 263n35
iǫkwe [M] (*yokwe*), xxvi, 185, 197–199
ireisai [J], xxvi, 163–166. *See also* bereavement
irooj [M] (chiefs): Council of Irooj, xxix; defined, xxiii, xxvi; disputes and, 28; land rights and, xxx; *mǫ* (taboo), 179; Namo Wāto, 180; *rijerbal* and, xxx; *shūchō* [J], xxx, 90, 256n1. *See also iroojlaplap* [M] (paramount chiefs)
iroojlaplap [M] (paramount chiefs), xxvi, 82–83, 87, 177, 203–205; Kaibuke, 5; Loeak, Anjua, 227; Lomade, 203. *See also* Kabua, Amata; Kabua, Imata; Kabua, Jeimata; Kabua, Kabua; Kabua, Lebon (Kabua the Great); Kabua, Lejolan; Litokwa, Lukwor; Watak, Nelu
izoku [J], xxvi, 163–166. *See also* Marshall Islands War Bereaved Families Association (MIBFA) (*Māsharu Homen Izokukai*) [J]

Jabor (Jebwad), xxvi, 6, 66, 159, 270n11
Jaluit Atoll (Yarūto, Jālooj, Jālwōj): copra trade, 5–6, 270n10; defined, xxvi; as district capital, 45; genealogy (*bwij/jowi*), 242–243; Japanese food trading at, 142; Japanese-Micronesian genealogies, 82–84, 91; Japanese migration and, 66; Japanese structures at, 103, 111, 125, 159–160; "native" representations of, 70–71, **71**, 73–75, **73**
Japan: colonies, xxviii; copra trading, 20, 46, 58, 159; expansionism (*nanshin*), xxviii, 39–48; Hiroshima & Nagasaki bombings, 117, 170, 171, 240; influence of, 20–21; Kōchi Prefecture, 63–68, 258n22; Kumamoto Prefecture, 66; mainland (Naichi), xxviii; Miyazaki Prefecture, 13–14, 87–88; NBK and, xxviii, 60, 253n6, 270n10; occupied territories, xxviii; overseas development assistance, 27; postwar returnees, 87–91; racial hierarchies, 69–70; territory ceded to, xxviii, 33; tropicalism, 63–68. *See also* Daku-daku Odori; Imperial Japan; Okinawa/Okinawans; Okinawa Prefecture
Japanese colonialism: awareness of, 91; forced laborers, 46; Jaluit (Yarūto, Jālooj, Jālwōj), xxvi, 6; Jebwad (Jabor), xxvi. Korean conscripted laborers, 24; legacies of, 16; mapping of, 39–48; Nanyō Guntō, 5–6, 44, 47; photography and, 76–77; prewar narrative, 87; prisoner workers, 46, 99; WWI territory gain, 33. *See also* Nanyō Guntō/Trust Territory of the PacificKorean
Japanese expansionism (*nanshin*): mapping of, 39–48; Nanyō Odori memories and, 87–91; overview, 61–63; racial imaging and, 68–77; tropicalism, 63–68, 70
Japanese language, xvi; hiragana [J], xxv; Marshallese language and, xiv; orientalist prewar word meanings, xxx
jebwa [M] stick dance, xxvi, 149

Jebwad (Jabor), xxvi, 6, 66, 159, 270n11
Jetñil-Kijiner, Kathy, 232, 244–246
JICPOA (Joint Intelligence Center Pacific Ocean Areas), xxvi, 99
jodik [M] (invasion, protest), xxvi, 207–210, 208, 213, 231–232
Joint Intelligence Center Pacific Ocean Areas (JICPOA), xxvi, 99
jowi [M] (the matriclan), xxvi, 55–56, 191

Kā (Gehh) (Gea), 175
Kabua, Amata, 91, 201, 213, 214, 225, 274n24
Kabua, Emlain, 91, 151
Kabua, Hirata, 228, 229
Kabua, Imata, 155, 193–197, 212, 221–225, 227, 228, 272n4, 276n52
Kabua, Jeimata, 42, 269n2
Kabua, Kabua, 83, **176**, 177, 242, 259n25
Kabua, Lebon (Kabua the Great), 42–43, 200–201, 203–205
Kabua, Lejolan, 177, 201
Kabua, meaning (governor), 200–201
Kabua, Michael Mañini, 192, 231, 251n2, 276n52
Kabua, Seagull, 196
kaitaku [J] (settlement, pioneering), xxvi, 87–91
kajoor [M] (commoners, power), xxvi, 206, 273n17
kamikaze [J] missions. See *tokkōtai* (special attack forces)
kanaka [J], xxviii, 75–76, 257n14
kanaka dojin [J], 75–76
kanji [J] use, xv, xxvii, 259n25
katakana [J] use, xv, xxvii, 130, 254n20
Kenpeitai, 99, 130
Kezerin [J]. See Kwajalein Atoll
Kijiner, Tom, Jr., 203
Kijiner, Tom, Sr., 272n4
Kiribati (Gilbert Islands), 5, 19, 38–39, 46, 48, 76, 103, 105, 164, 168, 187, 249n2, 253n6, 261n19, 269nn11,14
KMR (Kwajalein Missile Range), xxvii, 9
Koga Mineichi, 262n22, 276n45
Konol, Manke, 100, 251n2, 274n23
Korean language, xvi, 182
Koreans: abuses against, 102, 107; bereaved relatives of, 31, 234; burial of, 9, 110, 128, 156; construction workers, 98–99, 168, 181–182; forced laborers, 46; during Kwajalein invasion, 106; Kwajalein invasion deaths, 6, 9, 14, 97, 106, 184, 262n28; migrants, 277n1; as *ninpu* [J] (conscripted laborers), xxviii, 24, 181–182; perspectives of, 15, 27; POWs, 106, 117–118, 132–133, 262n28; revolt, 107; as *setsueibutai* [J] workers, 26; silent crossings of, 24; small histories of, 34; *tanki kōin* [J] (short-term) laborers at, 99; Yasukuni Shrine, 268n8, 269n14
Korean War, 50, 97, 167, 173, 264n9
Kosrae, 22, 39, 40, 45, 76, 83, 147, 259n27
KRS (Kwajalein Range Services), xxvii, 167, 264n7
Kuezerin [J], xxvii, 2, 165, 262n26. See also Kwajalein
Kurosawa Akira, 29
Kwaj, 8–9, 11–15, 36, 50–51, 53, 93–96, 110–111, 157, 173, 175, 181, 183, 188, 211–213, 217, 225–226, 234–236, 249n3, 250n14. See also USAG-KA (United States Army Garrison Kwajalein Atoll); USAG-KA (United States Army Garrison Kwajalein Atoll) ("Kwaj")
Kwajalein Atoll, xiv–xv, xxvii; American housing in, 172–173; American residents, 36; atollscape spirits, 157–159; Ebeye/Kwajalein separation, 179–180; history

of, 20; importance of, 1–2; Japanese military rule, 97–102; land payments on Kwajalein islet, 19; mapping of, 1; name origins, 20; Operation Flintlock, xxix; Operation Homecoming, xxix; reef destruction around, 26; re-membering, 235–236; setting and background, 2–9

Kwajalein, Battle of. *See* liberation narrative

Kwajalein Missile Range (KMR), xxvii

Kwajalein Negotiation Committee (KNC), 219–222

Kwajalein Range Services (KRS), xxvii

Kwajalein tree. See *utilomar* tree story

Kwaj Karnival, 95–97

Kwaj Kid, 9–14, 157, 235–236, 250n14

labor camps: establishment of, 169–170, 173; relocations of, 171–172, 173

laborers: abuses against, 102; black-birding, 75; forced laborers, xxviii, 24; Japanese prisoner workers, 46, 99; *kanaka*, xxvii, 75; Marshallese, 100; *ninpu* [J] (conscripted laborer), xxviii, 24, 100. *See also* Koreans

lagoon: Bikini lagoon, 170; coralheads in, 19, 60; dredging and, 174; ferry across, 180; images of, 43, **43**, 49, **50**; Jaluit lagoon, 160, 162; Japanese shipwrecks in, 13, 14, 111, 158, 238; Mid-Atoll Corridor, 175–178; missile testing and, 94, 175; narratives of, 56; nuclear testing and, 26; rebirth site, 140; significance of, 2

Lalibjet (god of the sea), 21

landfill, 9, 56, 174

land rights: dredging and, 174, 181; Ebeye land repossession, 179; land measurement, 174; Marshallese understanding of, 56–60; Mid-Atoll Agreement, 175, 177; *rijerbal* and, xxx; *wāto* [M], xxxi

Land Use Agreement (LUA), 194, 218, 220–228

Ḷañkio, Ato, 58–60, **59**, 61, 174, 251n2, 256n35, 266n24

Lee Inshin, 107, 263n35

Lefebvre, Henri, 25

lejman jūri [M], xxvii, 216–218, 228

lerooj [M] (female chief), xxvii, 86, 91, 200, 272n2

Liberation Day. *See* Memorial Day

liberation imagery: bathing imagery, 139–141; disparaging imagery, 145–149; flag imagery, 120–122, 126–131; mapping of, 48–53; post-battle imagery, 122–126; re-imaging/re-imagining, 113–118; war dead burial, 135–138

liberation narrative: American view of, 155; anti-Japanese imagery, 150–151; bathing imagery, 139–141; Battle of Kwajalein, 112–113; cleanup metaphor, 138–139; dehumanization, 131–135; disparaging imagery, 145–149; eradication of Japaneseness, 150–153; flag imagery, 120–122, 126–131; gratitude imagery, 141–145; Kwaj Karnival, 95–97; overview, 118–120; post-battle imagery, 122–126; post-liberation relations, 26–27, 153–156; re-imaging/re-imagining, 113–118; steppingstone campaign as, 48–53; war dead burial, 135–138

Lindstrom, Lamont, 137, 144, 146, 149

Litokwa, Lukwor, 205, 227

Loeak, Albert, 177, 203–205

Loeak, Anjua, 227

Loeak, Christopher, 219, 276n52

Lucky Dragon V (*Daigo Fukuryū Maru*), 270n8

Majuro Atoll, xxviii, 3, 39, 47, **152**, 153, 172, 195, 202, 211, 218, 219, 227, 232, 249n5, 271n21, 272n9

Makin Raiders, 100–101, 261n19
Manchuria, 14, 40, 44, 76-77, 100, *See also* China
maps/mapping: Japanese expansionism (*nanshin*), 39–48; Marshallese genealogies, 53–60; missions encoded in, 35–36; mythologies and, 35–37; overview, 33–35; political intent of, 37–39; of U.S. "liberation" invasion, 48–53
Marshall, John, 33
Marshall, Samuel, 127
Marshallese, **136**; abuses against, 107; burial details of, 136–137; during Kwajalein invasion, 106; as laborers, 100; land rights, 56–60; liberation imagery, 135–138; maps/mapping and, 53–60; Marshallese language (*-kajin m̧ajel*), xiv–xv, xxvi, 24; revolt, 107
Marshallese-Japanese children (*otoshidane*), xxiv, 24, 82–86, 151, 259n30
Marshall Islands, Republic of the (RMI). *See* RMI (Republic of the Marshall Islands)
Marshall Islands War Bereaved Families Association (MIBFA) (*Māsharu Hōmen Izokukai*) [J], 163–166, 236–240
masculinities: bathing imagery, 139–141; cultural representations of, 79–80; masculinization of land, 49; militarized masculinity, 72; representations, 77–78
matrilineality, 49, 54, 55, 86, 216–217, 259n30
Matsuda, Matt, 19
McArthur, Phillip H., 29
Mead, Leslie, 106–107, 136, 264n7, 265n13
Meck (Meik), 53, 56, 174, 250n10
Mejatto, 178, 274n30, 276n51
Mejit, 83, 241–242
Melanesia, xxviii, 3, 38, 47, 75, 254n19
Memorial Day, 95, 96, 155, 197
memorials/memorial services (*ireisai*) [J], xxvi, 46, 96, 165–166, 236–238, 240, 253n9, 263n36, 269n14, 277n5
Micronesia, Federated States of: civil government in, xxviii; German Period, xxvi; Japanese Colonial Period, xxvi; land seizures by U.S., 175; NBK and, xxviii, 60, 253n6, 270n10; translation of, 1; U.S administration of, xxxi; U.S. agreements with, xxiv
Mid-Atoll Corridor, 175–177
Mili Atoll (Mile): defined, xxviii; Korean/Marshallese revolt, 107; repatriate remains from, 263n36; *tanki kōin* [J] (short-term) laborers at, 99
Military Use and Operations Rights Agreement (MUORA), 219, 225–226, 228
minzoku [J], xxviii, 76
missile testing: historical narratives of, 182; homecoming narrative and, 189, 199, 208–209; land payments for, 19; location secrecy for, 182; Mid-Atoll Corridor, 175–178; mission of, 36; MX missile, 213; Nike X missile, 52, 167, 173; relocations from, 25, 175–178, **176**, **178**; restrictions on movement from, 178–179; Star Wars, 33; Vandenberg Air Force Base, California, 53, 175, 219; watching, 94, 111, 260n3; Zeus missile, 52, 167, 173
missions, 5, 35–37
MK-21 nuclear bomb, 171
mo̧ (taboo), 179
Momotaro, 80, 259n28
moʻolelo, 29, 180
Mori Koben, 66, 79, 82, 83, 258n22
Morris-Suzuki, Tessa, 28, 34, 116
Muench, Bruce, 1, 114, 128, 151–152
MUORA (Military Use and Operations Rights Agreement), 219, 225–226, 228
Myerhoff, Barbara, 31

Index

Nakajima Atsushi, 45, 77, 82–84, 259n25
Nakazawa, Shinichi, 21
Namo Atoll, 58, 100, 180, 181, 271n22
Namo Wāto, 174–175, 180, 181
nanshin [J] expansion, xxviii, 39–48
Nanyō-chō [J], xxviii, 14, 44–45, 159
Nanyō Guntō/Trust Territory of the Pacific, xxiv, 47, 62; defined, xxviii; as umi no seimeisen, xxxi. See also Chuuk (Truk); Kosrae; Micronesia, Federated States of; Palau; Pohnpei; RMI (Republic of the Marshall Islands); Saipan
National Geographic, 74, 147, 170
national memory, 26, 33
National Security Administration (NSA), 228–229, 276n51
«native» festivals (dojin matsuri [J]), 67
Nauru, 38, 39, 46, 76, 99, 253n6
navigation, xxvi, 2–4, 13, 38, 54–55, 191, 253n5
NBK (Nanyō Bōeki Kaisha) (South Seas Trading Company), xxviii, 60, 253n6, 270n10
neiṃbu [M] conscripted laborer). See ninpu [J] (conscripted laborer)
Nero, Karen, 29–30, 252n13
ninpu [J] (conscripted laborer), xxviii, 24, 261n14, 262n27
nisshōki [J]. See hinomaru [J] ceremonial flag
Nitijelā (Marshallese parliament), xxix, 194, 222, 272n6
Noda Tetsuzō, 83, 83–87, 194, 259nn27–28
North Korea, 34, 226, 276n49
nostalgia, 11, 63, 81, 87–91, 151, 213, 230, 234
Note, Kessai, 221, 224–225
nuclear testing: Bikini Atoll, 20, 170; Castle Bravo, xxiv, 171, 270n7; compensations for, 27; dislocations of land, 170–171; effects of, 26; Enewetak Atoll, 20; Gilda,

309

270n6; Operation Crossroads, xxix, 49, **50**, 170

Oceania: atolls in, 19; historical narratives of, 33–34; Kwajalein and, 2
Oda Makoto, 109–110, 184, 261n17
odori [J]. See dance
ofuro [J] (Japanese bath), xxix, 100, 160-163, 166, 261n15
Okinawans: construction workers, 99, 102; during Kwajalein invasion, 106; Kwajalein invasion deaths, 106; Nanyō Odori, 90–91; POWs, 133; war dead burials, 156
Okinawa/Okinawans, xxviii, 21–22, 24, 34, 41, 90–91, 97, 99, 102–104, 106, 108, 114, 133, 135, 137, 156, 158, 168, 224, 233, 254nn16–17, 260n35, 262nn24,28, 265n16
Okinawa Prefecture, 262n24
Operation Crossroads, xxix, 49, **50**, 170
Operation Exodus, 191
Operation Flintlock, xxix, 48, 95–97, 104–109, 110, 112–113, 170, 238
Operation Homecoming, 194, 196–197, 211–214, 220, 273n21, 274nn28–29
oral traditions: atoll creation story, 19; bwebwenato [M] traditions, 29; Hawaiian, 28–29; re-membering and, 31–32; utilomar tree story, xxxi, 20, 244, 246–248
orientalism, xxx, 66–71, 78, 90, 148–149, 185–186, 187–188, 256n1. See also shūchō no musume [J] archetype; tropicalism
otoshidane (Marshallese-Japanese children), 24, 82–86, 151, 259n30
out-migration (kaitaku) settlement, 87–91

Palau: bai [Palau] meeting house, 87–88, **87**; carpentry school (Mokkō), 274n23; civil govern-

ment in, xxviii; Compact (of Free Association), xxiv; Daku-daku Odori, 88; Japanese migration to, 66, 88; Japanese profile of, 76; Japanese settlers in, 86, 88; military photography from, 147; model of history, 29–30; Nanyō Guntō and, 40, 44–45, 47; Nanyō Odori, 88–91; postal seal of, 70; reefs of, 22; settlement of, 250n6; U.S. agreements with, xxiv
Palauan model of history, 29–30, 252n13
paternalism, 79, 83, 94, 145
patriarchy, 86, 216, 260n32
Pedro, Fred, 211, 218, 231
Pentagon, 210, 212, 214, 224, 276nn49,51
Philippines, 3, 35, 40, 47, 48, 100, 131, 224
phosphate-mining operations, xxv, 20, 168
photographic images: *gyokusai* [J] (crushed jewel) mission, 117, 122–126; Japanese colonialism and, 76–77; Kwajalein, Battle of, 113–153; Operation Flintlock images, 95–97; Palau, 147; US Army and, 122–123, **124**; US Marine Corps (USMC) and, 116, 119–121, **119, 121**, 139–141, **140, 152**; war remains/remnants, 109–111
Pikeej (Bigej), 175, **247**
Pohnpei, 22, 39, 40, 45, 66, 76, 172, 258n14
poison (*baijin*) [M], 173, 234, 277n3. *See also* radiation
Pound, Neitari "Bubu," 240–244, 241, **241, 245**
POWs (prisoners of war). *See* prisoners of war (POWs)
Poyer, Lin, 107, 142, 262n27, 263n40, 265n10
prisoners of war (POWs): Japanese, 106, 117–118, 132–135, **132,** 262n28; Korean, 106, 117–118, 132–133, 262n28; Okinawan, 133; US Marine Corps (USMC) and, 132–135, **132, 134**
propaganda films, 44–45, 77, 133
prostitution, 147, 217, 275n34
Protestant missions, xxv, 5, 35

racial classifications: *Chamoro* [J], xxiv; dusky maiden narrative, 68–77, 147; *kanaka* [J], xxviii, 75–76, 257n14; Marshallese-Japanese children (*otoshidane*), xxiv, 24, 82–86, 151, 259n30; *minzoku* [J], xxviii, 76; *ninpu* [J] (conscripted laborer), 261n14
radars: ALTAIR radar, 10, 173; "Iọkwe Radar Song," 196–198; radiation hazard, 173, 234; Roi-Namur (Ruotto and Nimuru), xxix, 92, 173, 197; Space Fence, 53; space-surveillance, 53, 197; as symbols, 198, **198**; tracking, xxix, 53, 173, 238; TRADEX radar, 10
radiation: ALTAIR radar, 173, 234; *baijin* [M] (poison), xxiii, 234, 277n3; displacement from, 12, 234; effects of, 167; humorous references to, 155, 272n5; residual radiation, 249n5
Rālik Chain, xxvi, xxix, 4, 12, 41, 55, 107, 180, 200, 203–207, 216, 230, 272n2, 273n14
Rashōmon effect, 29, 252n12
Ratak Chain, xxviii, xxix, 4, 55, 107, 200, 203
Reagan Test Site (RTS), xxvii, xxx, 7, 53, 167
reisha [J], xxx, 165–166, 269n13
relocations: to Āne-Bōn (Eniburr/Santo) (KA) (Third Island), 173; Bikinians, 24, 170; to Ebeye, 25, 171–172, 175–177; Enewetak Atoll, 170; to Kili Island, 170; labor camps, 169–170, 171–172; Mid-Atoll Agreement and, 175–177; missile testing and, 25;

Rongelapese, 24, 170, 274n30; to Rongerik Atoll, 170. *See also* Mejatto

re-membering: defined, 31; family, 234, 236–240; Kwajalein, 234, 235–236; Marshallese roots, 240–244; overview, 30–32

research methodology: genealogy (cf. *bwij* and *jowi*), 15–17; language issues, xiii–xvi; multiplicity of truths, 28–29; personal background, 9–15; personal narratives, xvi–xvii, 92–95, 109–111; *Rashōmon* effect, 29; violent language use, xvii

rhizome model, 28

rijerbal [M] (worker, commoner class), xxiii, xxx, 205, 275n40

Ri-Kuwajleen [M] (Kwajaleinese/ indigenous Kwajalein person): defined, xxx; oral traditions, 19–20; reconnecting Marshallese genealogies, 53–60; relocations of, 169–170, 171–172, 177–178. *See also* homecoming narrative

ripālle [M] (Westerner), xxx, 272n7

RMI (Republic of the Marshall Islands), 55, 199, 200; Compact (of Free Association), 219, 249n5; defined, xxx, 2–3; eminent domain, 214–215, 274n32; Land Use Agreement, 220–227, 227; name origins, 33; National Telecommunications Authority of, 179; negotiators, 276n52

Roi-Namur (Ruotto and Nimuru): ALTAIR radar, 173; defined, xxix, 261n14; Japanese emplacements, xxix; missile-tracking radar site, 173; reef destruction around, 26; relocations from, 173; space-surveillance, xxix; *tanki kōin* [J] (short-term) laborers at, 99; TRADEX radar, 10

Rongelap Atoll, 171, 230, 249n5

Rongelapese, 24, 170, 274n30, 276n51. *See also* Mejatto

Rowa, Aenet, 141–142

Rowa, Anjain, 175–176

RTS (Reagan Test Site), xxvii, xxx, 7, 53, 167

sacred space: coral use in, 20–21; U.S. destruction of, 26, 175

Sahlins, Marshall, 23, 57

Said, Edward, 23

Saipan, 22, 35; Japanese community in, 86, 90, 101; Japanese expansion and, 40, 45, 47; Japanese migration to, 66; Japanese/Okinawan settlers in, 260n35; Japan histories and, 250n16

Santō. *See* Āne-Bōn (Enniburr/Santō) (KA) (Third Island)

sea-level rise. *See* climate change

sekiseitai (patriotic corps), 99

semiology, 36–37

setsueibutai [J], xxx, 26

shūchō [J], xxx, 90, 256n1. *See also irooj* [M] (chiefs)

shūchō no musume [J] (chieftain's daughter): defined, xxx, 62; "Shucho no Musume" song, 62–63, 68–72, 86. *See also* Dakudaku Odori

Soja, Edward, 25

South Seas Islands. *See* Nanyō Guntō/ Trust Territory of the Pacific

space-surveillance, xxix, 7, 20, 53, 197, 250n10

SpaceX corporation, 36, 53

Spanish colonialism, 20–21, 35

steppingstone campaign: islands use as, 26, 33, 167; Japanese shaping of, 26; Operation Flintlock, xxix, 48, 95–97, 104–109, 112–113, 238; U.S. "liberation" invasion as, 48–53

Stevenson, Robert Louis, 22, 79, 82

strategic denial, 225–226

suicidal self-sacrifice: *gyokusai* [J] (crushed jewel) mission, xxv, 103–109, 117, 122–126, 164, 239; *tokkōtai/tokubetsu kōgekitai*

(special attack forces), xxx, 125, 163
Suzuki Tsunenori (Keikun), 41–44, 42–43, 46, 200, 258n21

Taiwan, xxviii, 3, 22, 40, 194, 225, 256n5
Tarḷañ [M], xxx, 19
Tarlang (ferry), 180
Tar-wōj, 175–176, 270n17
Teaiwa, Katerina, 20, 168, 249n2
Teaiwa, Teresia, 71, 141
Tengan, Ty Kāwika, 28–29, 180, 266n31
third-gender persons, xxv, 257n10
Third Island. *See* Āne-Bōn (Enniburr/ Santō) (KA) (Third Island)
thirdspace, 25
time: deep time, 22–23, 200–206; Marshallese sense of, 27–28; in Palauan model of history, 30
Tōjo, Hideki, 98
tokkōtai/tokubetsu kōgekitai (special attack forces), xxx, 125, 163
Torabully, Khal, 24
TRADEX radar, 10
tropicalism, 47, 63–68, 67, 70, 148–149, 256n1. *See also* orientalism
TTPI (US Trust Territory of the Pacific Islands). *See also* US Trust Territory of the Pacific Islands (TTPI)

umi no seimeisen [J] ("The Lifeline of the Sea"), xxxi, 44–45, 98
United States: aggression of, xxxi; agreements with, xxiv. *See also* Compact (of Free Association)
land seizures, 175
USAG-KA (United States Army Garrison Kwajalein Atoll) ("Kwaj"), xxxi, 7–9, 13, 35–36, 56, 167, 218, 250n11, 262n30, 276n51. *See also* KMR; USAKA (United States Army Kwajalein Atoll)
USAKA (United States Army Kwajalein Atoll), xxxi. *See also* KMR; USAG-KA (United States Army Garrison Kwajalein Atoll)
US Army, xxvii; evacuations by, 176–177, **176**; KRS and, xxvii; Kwajalein invasion, 105; missile testing, 167; Operation Homecoming, 212–213, 274nn28–29; photographic images, 122–123, **124**; Reagan Test Site (RTS), xxx, 167; Sam, Solomon, 271n21; Seventh Infantry Division, 105, 123, 261n9; USAG-KA (United States Army Garrison Kwajalein Atoll) ("Kwaj"), xxxi, 7–9, 13, 154, 167, 218, 250n11, 276n51; USAKA (United States Army Kwajalein Atoll), xxxi, 35–36, 56, 262n30, 276n51; USASMDC (United States Army Space and Missile Defense Command), xxxi, 7; war dead burials by, 136, **136**; *What Makes a Battle?* (1944 short) (US Army Pictorial Services), 123, 125
USASMDC (United States Army Space and Missile Defense Command), xxxi, 7
US Department of Defense, 120, 179, 210, 219
US Department of Energy, 6, 26
US Marine Corps (USMC): Fourth Marine Division, 105, 116, 141, 145; Kwajalein invasion, xxxi, 6, 48, 105, 118–119; Makin Raiders, 100–101, 261n19; Operation Homecoming, 214; Pacific military presence, 254n19; photographic images, 95, 116, 119–121, **119**, **121**, 125, 139–141, **140**, **152**; POWs, 132–135, **132**, **134**; racial stereotypes and, 114; war dead burials by, 135–137, **136**
US Trust Territory of the Pacific Islands (TTPI): administration of, 169, 172, 175, 179; androcentric

narrative of, 96; comparisons to, 39; COM resolutions and, 209; critique of, 185; defined, xxxi; eminent domain concept, 215, 274n32; establishment of, xxiv, 6–7, 144; images from, 147; *irooj* and, 225; *lejman jūri* and, 218; Operation Homecoming leaders and, 273n21

utilomar tree story, xxxi, 20, 244, 246–248, 251nn3–4, 296n73

Vandenberg Air Force Base, California, 53, 175, 219
venereal diseases, 217
volcanoes, 3, 18, 21, 30, 170–171, 219

war dead: American burials, 108; Kwajalein Japanese war dead, 108, 160–163, 163–166, 236–240; liberation narrative and, 135–138; mass burials, 108; re-membering and, 31
War on Terror, 33, 97, 276n49

wāto [M] (land parcel), xxxi, 58–60, **59**, 174, 180–181, 271n19
Wood, Denis, 33, 37, 38
World War I, 6, 33, 38
World War II: American narratives of, 33, 94, 96; battlefields, 20; Geneva Convention, 133, 266n25; Japanese command center, 6; Japanese war dead numbers, 46–47; photographic images, 112–113; steppingstone campaign, 33; toll on islets, 19
Wotje Atoll, 84, 92, 99

yakyū [J] (baseball), xxxi, 39
Yamamura, Kaname, 84, 85, **85**
Yap, Micronesia, 22, 41, 45, 66, 70, 76, 147, 259n32
Yasukuni Shrine, 164, 262n26, 268n8, 269n14
yosegaki writing, 129–131

Zedkaia, Jurelang, 227

About the Author

Greg Dvorak is professor at Waseda University in Tokyo, specializing in Pacific/Asian cultural studies, gender studies, and history. Having spent his childhood on the US military installation in Kwajalein Atoll in the Marshall Islands and much of his adult life in Japan, his work deals with intersections between Oceania, Japan, and the United States. After pursuing his MA at the University of Hawai'i Center for Pacific Islands Studies as an East-West Center Fellow, he went on to complete a PhD at the Australian National University before returning to Japan, where he lectured at the University of Tokyo and Hitotsubashi University for many years. Aside from teaching/publishing in English and Japanese on themes of popular culture, art, gender, and nationalism, he is an experienced photographer and filmmaker. He is also founding director of ProjectSANGO, a grassroots project and consultancy linking communities across the archipelagos of Oceania and Japan through contemporary art.

Made in United States
North Haven, CT
10 September 2023